"With her unique blend of intellectual curiosity, spiritual insight, and compassionate sensitivity, Avril Pyman has created a fascinating portrait of one of the most complex and elusive figures of Russia's Silver Age. She succeeds in uncovering the underlying unity of experience and vision that informed the myriad strands of Florensky's journey of discovery, and skilfully relates her subject to the broader historical and cultural context of those tragic times."
*Pamela Davidson, Professor of Russian Literature, The School of Slavonic and East European Studies, University College London, UK*

"In this wonderful biography, Avril Pyman brings to life the tragic genius of Pavel Florensky: theologian, philosopher, mathematician, art critic. With a profound knowledge of his cultural and religious world, Pyman enables us to hear the authentic voice of the martyred priest who is now gaining an audience in Orthodoxy and beyond."
*Andrew Louth, Professor of Patristic and Byzantine Studies, University of Durham, UK*

"Avril Pyman has produced a beautifully written and well-researched biography of the enigmatic Pavel Florensky. Eschewing hagiography, Pyman examines Florensky's remarkable life as scientist and priest, mathematician and mystic, Renaissance man and Russian patriot of the early decades of the 20th century. Her book tells the story of an extraordinarily gifted individual whose intellect, empathy, and understanding even the Stalinist purges could not eclipse. The first major biography of Florensky in English, Pyman's work brings his extraordinary life to the attention of the wider readership it deserves."
*Maria Carlson, Professor and Associate Chair, Department of Slavic Languages and Literatures, University of Kansas, USA*

# PAVEL FLORENSKY:
## A Quiet Genius

*The Tragic and Extraordinary Life*
*of Russia's Unknown Da Vinci*

## Avril Pyman

**Foreword by Geoffrey Hosking**

continuum

NEW YORK • LONDON

2010

The Continuum International Publishing Group Inc
80 Maiden Lane, New York, NY 10038

The Continuum International Publishing Group Ltd
The Tower Building, 11 York Road, London SE1 7NX

www.continuumbooks.com

Library of Congress Cataloging-in-Publication Data
A catalog record for this book is available from the Library of Congress.

ISBN: 978-1-4411-8700-0 (hardcover)

Typeset by Fakenham Photosetting Ltd
Printed in the United States of America

# Contents

To the memory of Kirill Konstantinovich Sokolov
Who laid it on me to finish this book
And helped me so much with the early chapters.

# Acknowledgements

This is one of those books that have been in the writing an unconsciably long time and I would have to go through a long list of people, most of whom are now dead, to make adequate acknowledgements. So I shall confine myself to the living, and to those who actually helped with the text.

First my thanks are due to Father Andrew Louth, theologian and mathematician, who spent valuable time vetting every chapter, correcting my appalling spelling and making acute comments, criticisms and structural suggestions. Second, I have to thank Christine Cumming for typing and endless retypings to incorporate these suggestions and my own self-editing. Third, I am lastingly grateful to Natalia Rumiantseva for help with the final editing of the book, finding missing facts and dates on computer and conjuring further materials from the internet; also, for letting me see her own video-record of relevant recent lectures and discussions at the St Petersburg Christian Humanitarian Institute where she works. I should also thank Dina Magomedova for telling me about her time as secretary to A. Losev and as editor of Simeonovich-Efimova's recollections of Florensky, as well as for downloading recently published articles and publications. Vladimir Petrovich Enisherlov presented me with the numbers of *Nashe nasledie* containing a most revealing publication of letters between Ol'ga Aleksandrovna Florensky, her brother, his friend and her husband Sergei Troitsky, Z. N. Hippius and D. S. Merezhkovsky. From further back I am grateful to Evgenia Ivanova for alerting me to new publications of Florensky's works, for sharing the results of her research in Lambeth Library on Florensky's publication in *Pilgrim* and for introducing me to some members of the family at a *panikhida* for Father Pavel held in the flat which is now a Florensky Museum. I have also to thank Svetlana Andreevna Dolgopolova for arranging a most instructive visit to that museum and Igumen Andronik, who was kind enough on this occasion to present me with his then newly published book on Florensky's 'Anthropodicea' and who generously gave permission to reproduce photographs from the family archive as illustrations to this book. I am also grateful to his sister Maria Sergeevna Trubacheva for help in compiling the index of proper names. In 2006 the Mother Superior of the Convent of the Dormition in Perm most generously presented me with her copy of an important republication of Florensky's letters from the camps with new information on his last days 'Vse moi dumy o vas'; a dear friend of mine and my late husband's, Rima Bylinskaia, gave me Deacon Sergei Trubachev's invaluable memoirs. A standing invitation from the Moscow Humanities State University has enabled me to obtain multiple-entry visas to Russia over the last few years, which has greatly facilitated research. Dr Andrei Batsanov did sterling work on the translation of the titles of Florensky's technical articles and Valerii Zarovniannykh shared with me his professional photographs of Solovki, one of which serves as background to the picture on the dust jacket. Sophie Snegir helped me to coordinate my response to editorial queries on computer from Sue Cope, the excellent publisher's editor, and Haaris Naqvi, the editor-in-chief of this volume has taken great care for its presentation and given constant encouragement throughout. Professor Pamela Davidson kindly read through the typescript and made invaluable corrections and suggestions. Aleksandr Ershov and my daughter Irina Sokolova-Snegir have helped me to obtain rare publications. Irina also helped me search out details of the dramatis personae on computer for the index, as did Dr Krastu Banev and Professor Dina Magomedova. Irina has made my working life easier in more ways than I can say.

My heartfelt thanks go out to them all. This book could not have been written without them.

# List of Illustrations

1 Head of Pavel Florensky by N. Vysheslavets, 1922. Reproduced, as are almost all the illustrations to this book, by courtesy of the Florensky family collection who retain the copyright, in this case from Ne pechal'tes' obo mne by Igumen Andronnik (Trubachev), Soviet izdatel'stva russkoi pravoslavnoi tserkvi, Moscow, 2007.

2 Florensky's mother, Ol'ga Pavlovna Saparova (Saparian) (1859–1951) in the 1870s. He was said to resemble her greatly except, on his own wry admission, that 'whereas she was very beautiful, I was very ugly'. By courtesy of the Florensky family archive, reproduced from P. A. *Florenskij e la cultura della sua epokha*, Atti del Convegno di Michael Hagemeister e Nina Kauchtschischwili, Blaue Horner Verlag, Marburg, 1995, from the section compiled by Michael Hagemeister and Pavel Florenskij: 'Sein Lebensweg in Photogaphien und Dokumenten.'

3 Ol'ga Pavlovna, Aleksandr and Iulia Florensky with the two eldest children, Iulia (nicknamed Liusia), on her father's knee, and Pavel, on small chair. By courtesy of the Florensky family archive, reproduced from P. A. *Florenskij* (Marburg, 1995), from the section compiled by Michael Hagemeister and Pavel Florenskij: 'Sein Lebensweg in Photographien und Dokumenten.'

4 Pavel Florensky as a school-boy, 1887–1889. By courtesy of the Florensky family archive, reproduced from P. A. *Florenskij* (Marburg, 1995), from the section compiled by Michael Hagemeister and Pavel Florenskij: 'Sein Lebensweg in Photographien und Dokumenten.'

5 Pavel Florensky in the uniform of a student of Moscow University (1900–1904). By courtesy of the Florensky family archive, reproduced from P. A. *Florenskij* (Marburg, 1995), from the section compiled by Michael Hagemeister and Pavel Florenskij: 'Sein Lebensweg in Photographien und Dokumenten.'

6 Andrei Bely (B. N. Bugaev, 1880–1934), pastel drawing by Ol'ga Florenskaia, 1912. 'Involuntarily, once again I clasp white flowers to my heart.' Reproduced

from Pavel V. Florenskii and Tatiana Shutova, 'Tri tysiachi verst I chetvert' veka prolegli mezhdu nami', *Nashe nasledie*, No. 79–80, 2006, p. 131.

7 The Monastery of St Sergius, wood-engraving by Vladimir Favorsky, 1919. Courtesy of K. Sokolov and A. Pyman, 'Florensky and Favorsky, Mutual Insights in the Perception of Space', *Leonardo*, Vol. 22, No. 2, 1989, p. 240.

8 Pavel Florensky and Sergei Troitsky with Florensky's family in Tiflis, 1907. From left to right, standing, back row: Sergei, Pavel, Pavel's brother Aleksandr; seated: Elizaveta Pavlovna Melik-Begliarova, Liusia (christened Iulia), Aleksandr Ivanovich, Ol'ga Pavlovna, Repsimia Pavlovna Tavridova; seated on floor: Andrei, Raisa (nicknamed Gosia), Ol'ga (nicknamed Valia), and Elizaveta. By courtesy of the Florensky family archive, reproduced from Pavel V. Florenskii and Tatiana Shutova, 'Tri tysiachi verst i chetvert' veka prolegli mezhdu nami', *Nashe nasledie*, No. 79–80, 2006, p. 127.

9 Pavel Florensky, 1909. By courtesy of the Florensky family archive, reproduced from *P. A. Florenskij* (Marburg, 1995), from the section compiled by Michael Hagemeister and Pavel Florenskij: 'Sein Lebensweg in Photographien und Dokumenten'.

10 Vasilii Mikhailovich Giatsintov, Anna Mikhailovna Giatsintova (Florenskaia) and Pavel Florensky, 1911. By courtesy of the Florensky family archive, reproduced from *P. A. Florenskij* (Marburg, 1995), from the section compiled by Michael Hagemeister and Pavel Florenskij: 'Sein Lebensweg in Photographien und Dokumenten'.

11 The Florenskys' new home in Sergiev Posad as from 1915. 1996, reproduced from *Pavel Florensky, Beyond Vision: Essays on the Perception of Art*, ed. Nicoletta Misler, tr. Wendy Salmond, Reaktion Books, London, 2002, p. 22.

12 Mikhail Nesterov, 'The Philosophers', Pavel Florensky and Mikhail Bulgakov in the Florenskys' garden, Sergiev Posad, Spring, 1917. From *Vozvrashchenie zabytykh imen, Katalog vystavki, Sovetskii fond kul'tury*, Moscow, 1989, plate 7. Original picture in the Tretiakov Gallery, Moscow (further Vozvrashchenie zabytykh imen as in 34).

13 Florensky in his office at the State Experimental Electrotechnical Institute (GEEI), Moscow, 1925. Reproduced from *Pavel Florensky, Beyond Vision: Essays on the Perception of Art*, ed. Nicoletta Misler, tr. Wendy Salmond, Reaktion Books, London, 2002, p. 25.

14  Vladamir Favorsky, cover for 'Number as Form', wood engraving. Courtesy of K. Sokolov and A. Pyman, 'Florensky and Favorsky, mutual insights in the perception of space,' *Leonardo*, Vol. 22, No. 2, 1989, p. 242.

15  Florensky picnicking with his family near Zagorsk towards the end of the twenties. Seated from the left to right: Father Pavel, Mik, Ol'ga, unknown woman in white headdress, Maria, Anna Mikhailovna; kneeling behind them: Vasilii and Kirill. By courtesy of the Florensky family archive, reproduced from *P. A. Florenskij* (Marburg, 1995), from the section compiled by Michael Hagemeister and Pavel Florenskij: 'Sein Lebensweg in Photographien und Dokumenten'.

16  Pavel Florensky and some of his dependants in 1932. Florensky seated on steps in centre with Maria. Standing from left to right: Ol'ga Pavlovna, Nadezhda Giatsintova, Mika, Iulia Aleksandrovna, Anna Mikhailovna. Strictly speaking, it was the other sister, Gosia (Raisa), who was dependent, at least in part, on her brother until her death from the family scourge of tuberculosis. Iulia worked as a psychiatrist. By courtesy of the Florensky family archive, reproduced from *P. A. Florenskij* (Marburg, 1995), from the section compiled by Michael Hagemeister and Pavel Florenskij: 'Sein Lebensweg in Photographien und Dokumenten'.

17  A shared joke with Anna and Mika, 1932. By courtesy of the Florensky family archive, reproduced from *P. A. Florenskij* (Marburg, 1995), from the section compiled by Michael Hagemeister and Pavel Florenskij: 'Sein Lebensweg in Photographien und Dokumenten'.

18  Florensky at the piano, 1932. By courtesy of the Florensky family archive, reproduced from *P. A. Florenskij* (Marburg, 1995), from the section compiled by Michael Hagemeister and Pavel Florenskij: 'Sein Lebensweg in Photographien und Dokumenten'.

19  Police photograph of Florensky after his arrest, 27 February 1933. By courtesy of the Florensky family archive, reproduced from *P. A. Florenskij* (Marburg, 1995), from the section compiled by Michael Hagemeister and Pavel Florenskij: 'Sein Lebensweg in Photographien und Dokumenten'.

20  Florensky with P. N. Kapterev in Skovorodino at the Permafrost laboratory, 1934. By courtesy of the Florensky family archive, reproduced from *P. A. Florenskij* (Marburg, 1995), from the section compiled by Michael Hagemeister and Pavel Florenskij: 'Sein Lebensweg in Photographien und Dokumenten'.

21 'When you look out of the window you can imagine yourself in Italy', view from the window of the old forge by the Holy Lake, photograph of 2002. Reproduced from the archive of P. A. Florensky, 1889. From Sviashchennik Pavel Florenskii, *Vse dumy o vas. Pis'ma semi iz lagerei i tiurem 1932–1938*, compiled by P. V. Florenskii and N. A. Zhivulin, choice and preparation of photographs by P. V. Florenskii, V. P. Stoliarov and A. I. Oleksenko, Satis' Derzhava, St Petersburg, 2000.

# Dates and Transliteration

*Dates:* In 1918 the Russian calendar was brought into line with European and American usage, i.e. the New Year was no longer celebrated on January 13 but on January 1 (still an excuse, nearly a century later, for one more party to celebrate the Old New Year on the thirteenth at the end of an exhausting winter break involving two Christmases, a feast which the Russian Orthodox Church still celebrates on January 7). In this book all the pre-1918 dates are given in the old style (OS), so subtract 13 days if you need to know how this compares with our accepted usage. After 1918, the reader will find some double-dating because Florensky and his friends continued to think and date their letters according to the old calendar, which the Russian Church uses to this day. Single dates after 1918, however, correspond to contemporary usage worldwide and are in the new style (NS).

*Transliteration:* In an attempt to make this book more user-friendly to non-Russian speakers, I have kept the use of patronymics in the text to a minimum and retained familiar spellings: Florensky, Tolstoy, Popova, Akhmatova, Iudina. With the exception of famous female surnames such as the last three, I have not modified the endings of proper names according to number and gender in the Russian way, so the Florensky women-folk are also called Florensky and, in the plural, the Florenskys. In the Glossary, for ease of recognition, I have kept to the convention adopted in the text, but added in the patronymics.

In the notes, however, I have used the Library of Congress transliteration system and the bibliographical conventions familiar to Slavists. Florenskii here appears with two 'i's as author or subject of articles, letters, etc. published in Russian. Occasionally, in Continental publications, he morphs into Florenskij. The criterion is to use the spelling adopted in this or that publication or an accepted convention for transliteration from the Cyrillic script. The majority of sources for this book are in Cyrillic. Florenskii's four-volume *Works* (*Sochineniia*) are referred to as *S*; for *Sobranie Sochinenii* (*Collected Works*) by some other authors we have used *SS*. Frequently quoted sources are given with full publication details at first mention, where an abbreviated form is signalled and used thereafter.

# Foreword

The first quarter of the twentieth century in Russia was one of the great turning points of European intellectual, cultural and political life. For much of the latter part of the nineteenth century the arts had been mostly realist in spirit, while much political thinking had a positivist and socialist colouring, either Populist or Marxist. But around 1900 the dominant aesthetic attitudes began to give way to trends which were in one form or another anti-realist, beginning with Symbolism, which posited a deeper reality underlying the appearances of everyday life. In politics and intellectual life the centre of gravity began to move away from socialism to a deeper concern with property, the rule of law, religion, the State and the nation – the traditional watchwords of conservatism. One publication of 1903 summed it up in the title 'From Marxism to Idealism': its author, Sergei Bulgakov, explained why he had made this transition. Marxism claimed to be 'scientific socialism', but in fact this dual term concealed a rift between science and prophecy. The scientific analysis of bourgeois society might be correct, but it did not lead logically to the creation of socialism. The analysis was determinist, but building socialism was a moral choice, an act of freedom. No science, however successful, could tell human beings how they should act, or according to what moral principles they should live their lives; that was the business of philosophy and religion.

Bulgakov was not alone. In fact in 1902 a collection of essays had appeared, *Problems of Idealism*, all of the contributors to which had begun adult life as socialists, but then moved away from it. The failure of the socialist-inspired revolution of 1905–1906 intensified these changes of heart, especially since it was followed by the rapid dissolution in 1906–1907 of the First and Second Dumas, the first serious prototypes in Russia of a modern elected parliament. While all socialists and most liberals blamed the repressive policies of the regime for this failure, a few, notably Sergei Bulgakov and Petr Struve, also blamed the rigid and intransigent attitudes of the left-wing parties.

In the essay collection *Vekhi* (*Landmarks*) many of the authors of *Problems of Idealism* reassessed their thinking, now in political as well as philosophical terms. It reproached the left-wing intelligentsia for having no positive ideals. They had renounced truth, beauty, goodness, even God Himself in the name of progress and sympathy for the oppressed people. Changing society, its authors agreed, entailed changing human beings, which was a task for religion, not politics.

This was the intellectual milieu in which Pavel Florensky grew up. In his youth, though never a socialist, he accepted the dominant view that natural and social life were predetermined according to laws that scientists had either discovered or would certainly one day discover. The notion that free will and moral choice were an illusion made him feel both helpless and worthless, and drove him into a deep depression. He recovered from it, paradoxically, thanks to an insight derived from mathematics, which one might have thought of as the guarantor of rigid scientific determinism. Inspired by his Moscow University maths teacher, Nikolai Bugaev, Florensky discovered the potentiality of the study of discontinuous functions, as exemplified in quantum physics, which was beginning to replace Newtonian physics and mathematics as a way of understanding atoms and electrons. He came to believe that deterministic science was based on the assumption of a smooth progression along a continuum, while the newly developing theory of discontinuity left openings for the paradoxical, intuitive and irrational; in a word, for creativity, not only in mathematics but in other fields of human endeavour. A recent study places him, along with Dmitrii Egorov and Nikolai Luzin, as one of a 'Russian trio', which, inspired by such semi-mystical illuminations, built on the insights of the more sober French mathematicians, and formulated the hypotheses which launched the Moscow School of Mathematics.[1]

This mathematical insight was the turning point in Florensky's life. In searching for another, non-determinist foundation for elucidating truth, he looked back to old Russian traditions, especially that of the Orthodox Church. Offered the chance of doing graduate work in mathematics at Moscow University, he turned it down and instead embarked on a course of study at the Moscow Theological Academy in Sergiev Posad, with the aim of becoming a priest, as indeed he eventually did. He had become convinced that truth – the truth one needs for living – was to be discovered not through sense impressions, through rational and empirical science (even though he was to become a very productive scientist) or through individual mystical insight, but only through the centuries-old collective experience, the discipline, the collegiality and the liturgy of the Orthodox Church. This was the viewpoint he expounded in *The Pillar and Ground of Truth* (1914), which was couched in the form of 12 letters to a close friend. Florensky believed that intimate, mutually honest friendship was essential to a fruitful spiritual life. In this way medium and message complemented each other.

Florensky thought real knowledge was ensured only by the love of knowledge, self-discipline, openness to beauty and to other people, and that these qualities were best upheld within the Church. Reason had its place in the scheme of things, but on its own could lead only to permanent doubt; it needed to be shaped and channelled by the qualities of human beings best nurtured in the Church. Already, as a student at Moscow University, he wrote to his parents: 'At the moment the most urgent task – not mine, of course, but that of our epoch – is to create a religious science and a scientific religion.' He wanted to 'produce a synthesis of ecclesiality and secular culture.'[2]

At the end of the third letter, 'Triunity (or Three in One)', Florensky, in the spirit of Pascal's wager, urges the non-believer to abandon forms of cognition that can only lead to eternal scepticism and to take what Kierkegaard called the 'leap of faith', towards a faith which promises both certainty and eternal life. In Florensky's own words, 'It pays to exchange certain nothing for uncertain infinity.'[3] He then conducts a brief etymological enquiry into the word 'faith' in various Indo-European languages, coming to the conclusion that their root is to be found in the concept of trust. For Florensky, it seems, trust and its associate, faith, are the indispensable pre-requisite of knowledge – whether trust in God, the Church, other persons or the reliability of truth.

Interestingly enough, modern secular social scientists, coming from a structural-functional tradition which would have been thoroughly alien to Florensky, have been reaching similar conclusions. The German sociologist Niklas Luhmann, for example, asserts that trust is a form of epistemological parsimony necessary as a pre-requisite for decisions and actions. In normal life one is simply not able to assemble all relevant information and assess all the risks involved in a particular course of action. 'The complexity of the future world is reduced by the act of trust. In trusting, one engages in action as though there were only certain possibilities in the future.'[4] In a similar spirit, the American political scientist Russell Hardin sees trust as a superior tool in getting to know about the world and other people: 'If I generally distrust people, I will discover little about their actual trustworthiness because I will choose not to interact with them. It follows that I will have to make choices with less information to go on than other, more optimistic people have.'[5] Guido Möllinger even evokes Kierkegaard's 'leap of faith', urging the rationality of acting on 'as-if faith', as if doubts had been favourably resolved, since this increases the likelihood of a favourable outcome.[6] In all these secular thinkers trust, the close cousin of faith, is seen as an indispensable lubricant of knowledge, decision-taking and action in the real world.

Florensky's concept, though, has an extra dimension. In his thought trust and the search for truth have their natural grounding in the Church, for that is where community and mutual self-help come together with the beauty and discipline of the liturgy to generate their own insights, which are fuller than any individual could produce on his/her own. Florensky believed this potentiality of the Church was most completely realised in Orthodoxy. He took this belief seriously enough to become a priest and for several years to take on himself the burden of running of a parish and the care of the souls within it, even as he was conducting research and writing numerous articles and reviews.

This is where his Russian patriotism comes in. For some reason, most Western observers deny Russians the right to a national pride or patriotism of their own – and it must be said that many Russian intellectuals feel the same way: to the present day they often pronounce the world 'patriot' with disdain, as a term of abuse. This attitude is in striking contradiction to the widespread appreciation of Russian culture, both in the West and among Russian intellectuals. Florensky was both a religious and a cultural patriot. Like the Slavophiles and Vladimir Solov'ev, he believed that Western Christianity had succumbed to an obsession with power (Roman Catholics) or with the Word (Protestants). Only Orthodoxy had preserved the original purity of patristic Christian teachings in its icons (he was a leading theorist of iconology), its architecture, its liturgy, its monastic life and in the devotional practices and teachings of its *startsy*, its 'elders' or holy men who acted as spiritual counsellors for all who needed their help. He considered though that Orthodoxy was endangered by those same Western influences, a tendency which he strove to contest.

The living symbol of historical Orthodoxy he saw in the Trinity St Sergius Monastery, centre of Russian Orthodoxy since the fourteenth century, one of whose leading defenders he became after the Bolsheviks came to power. In it, he declared, 'We feel ourselves more at home than when we are at home.' He maintained that St Sergius had dedicated it to the Holy Trinity 'as an appeal for the unity of Russia, in the name of a higher reality'. 'Here', he wrote, 'is not only aesthetics, but a feeling of history and of the people's soul, and a conception of the Russian state (*gosudarstvennost*) … Here, more tangibly than anywhere else, one feels the pulse of Russian history … here Russia can be perceived as a whole.'[7]

Florensky has been called the twentieth-century Russian Leonardo da Vinci, so great was his erudition in very diverse scientific fields: he published serious studies in mathematics, physics, electrodynamics, folkloristics, philology, art history and theory, philosophy and theology. In the 1920s he was editor of a new *Technical Encyclopedia*, to which he himself contributed more than a hundred articles. He worked in the State Commission for the Electrification of Russia, a project which he believed in and was glad to contribute to, though he astounded and alarmed his colleagues by attending meetings dressed in a priest's cassock. Even after his arrest he continued his researches. Exiled to the Far East, he investigated the properties of permafrost, while in the bleak and unpromising surroundings of the Solovki prison-monastery in the far north, he worked on how to extract iodine and agar from seaweed.

At the same time, he was working on what was to be his second major philosophical work, his 'anthropodicy', 'On the Watersheds of Thought', which is known to us only in fragments, since the turbulent circumstances of his life prevented him from completing it. Devoted scholars in the Soviet Union began to publish excerpts from it in the 1960s in various journals, so that the increasing number of readers interested in Florensky could begin to form a picture of his later thought. These fragments were gathered together for publication only in the 1990s, after the collapse of the Soviet Union.

His letters from captivity display the full strength of his devotion to his wife and children, his knowledge of them and concern for their spiritual well-being and personal development. He was by no means a cloistered thinker, but a rounded and complex personality, one moreover who bore more than his fair share of the burdens of this world. His final years were blighted by the Stalinist penitentiary system, which separated him from his family, and ended his life prematurely. It gave him no chance to bring his insights to the full maturation which they needed and from which we would all have learnt.

Avril Pyman's fine biography, the fruit of many years of detailed research, gives a very full picture of the man and an introduction to his thought. It will bring a figure of cardinal importance, hitherto scarcely known in the West, to the attention of a wide reading public.

Geoffrey Hosking
Emeritus Professor of Russian History, University College London

# *Preface*

This book is not a definitive biography. Florensky's archive, preserved by his family in Moscow or painstakingly located in the collections of his contemporaries, the Moscow Theological Academy and various learned institutions with whose members he corresponded, contains much material to which I have not had access, nor attempted to do so. His diaries remain unpublished. There is said to be a whole volume of reminiscences about him in preparation. Invaluable personalia are still coming out in periodicals such as *Novyi zhurnal* and *Nashe nasledie*, which have necessitated constant updatings of my manuscript as it was being revised for publication. Quite apart from all this, I am not qualified to assess Father Pavel's work in physics, mathematics and applied science, though I have made the best use I can of the special studies and bibliographical data provided by scholars competent in these fields.

Why, then, did I choose to spend the culminating years of my working life puzzling out the biography of a man so far beyond my intellectual scope? Basically, because I needed to do it and, I believe, it needed to be done. Florensky's life covers the period of Russian cultural history which has, since I began to read for a PhD in Cambridge in 1952, only 15 years after his death, been my primary field of study. Since completing my *Life of Aleksandr Blok* (OUP, 1979, 1980), I have always longed to return to biography and, of all the outstanding figures of Russia's Silver Age, Florensky is a supremely interesting, archetypal subject – who lived his ideas. The fashionable portrait painter James Gunn, long ago commissioned by Iron Trades to paint my father for their boardroom, told him: 'I enjoyed that. You've got a face.' Florensky had 'a life', a life which touched on the Russian Religious Renaissance, on art and literature, on Nature and the study of the physical world, on the tragedy of the Russian Revolution and on the key mid-twentieth-century subject of the concentration camp. It was a life of scholarship and service, of intensely experienced identity problems, of dramatic familial interest, of joy, suffering and endurance, a very private life full of unanswered questions. Those I have raised but mostly left unanswered, for lack of evidence, seeking rather to evoke the personality of the man and his ideas as far as the climate of these could be established from published sources, set as vividly as possible in time and space.

There is enough material already available in print to have enabled me to do this without becoming intimately involved in the world of largely family-engendered archival scholarship which has gradually disinterred Florensky's memory through publications of his post-revolutionary writings, very few of which came out in his lifetime. The survival of this family and their devotion to this task seems to me a remarkable testament to the power of prayer, which brings me to the other, objective reason why it is important to set Florensky's work firmly within the chronological framework of his biography now without further delay ... simply because any such undertaking may soon be complicated by the demands of hagiography. Father Pavel was perceived as a martyr by his friend Sergei Bulgakov, who wrote a moving obituary for him in the Paris-based émigré journal *Vestnik* (*Le Messager*) and, in the same journal, the editor Nikita Struve boldly concluded a memorial piece with the words: 'Father Pavel, pray to God for us.' The Swiss Benedictine, Father Gabriel Bunge, in his treatise on Andrei Rublev's incomparable icon of the Holy Trinity, ascribes the dictum that 'There exists the icon of the Trinity by St Andrei Rublev, therefore, God exists' to *Saint* Pavel Florensky. Nevertheless, Florensky's name was not on the list of 'new martyrs' recently canonised by the Russian Orthodox Church. The year 2007 was the seventieth anniversary of his execution and again rumour was rife that the extensive commemoration of this event might lead to consideration of his canonisation. It saw the publication of a new life by Igumen Andronik, *Obo mne ne pechal'tes'*, clearly intended to state the case for this. The complexity of Florensky's intellectual heritage and, indeed, of his personality, as well as prolonged, only recently resolved uncertainty about the manner of his death and the whereabouts of his grave have, in the past, presented formidable stumbling blocks to any such initiative. Florensky did not, for instance, perish like the early martyrs for a refusal to bow down before idols or, indeed, to renounce his priestly calling. He was condemned to be shot, together with many others of various race and faith, on a trumped-up charge of 'anti-Soviet, Trotskyite propaganda'.

The factual account of Florensky's life stops here. He himself, however, was always one to think in terms of aims rather than causes. In a letter to his 'brother in Christ' Sergei Troitsky, the addressee of the 'letters' of *The Pillar and Ground of Truth*, written just after his release from his first 'political' imprisonment at the hands of the Tsarist police, the youthful, as yet untried Florensky gave stumbling expression to the intention of his whole life:

There is only one thing that would suffice for me and that is ceaseless ascetic endeavour, requiring strenuous concentration of all the forces of one's soul, not allowing for one moment of second thought and ending, in the near future, with the cross. Yet I know very well that I am absolutely unworthy of this and agonise over this unworthiness in the awareness that I cannot become better otherwise than through this endeavour and this cross. Here I get all muddled up and torment myself.

(Letter of 29 April 1906, quoted by Florensky's eldest grandson Pavel Vasilevich
Florensky in an article entitled by words quoted from it: 'Cherez podvig zhe i krest',
*Novyi zhurnal*, No. 243, 2006)

Before he came face to face with the firing squad, Florensky was granted 31
years of 'strenuous concentration' in which to 'become better', though he never
claimed to have become worthy of the cross. At his ordination as a priest, it
would have been the part of the congregation to cry 'Axios'. The part of this
biographer is simply to tell the story.

# *Childhood*

> The early manifestations of God's world began with the realm of plants, as a kind of direct communication from it. It was as though one were peering over the shoulder of the Creator, who, thinking himself unobserved, was making toys and decorations.
>
> Carl Jung[1]

The eldest child in a family of eight, Pavel Florensky's earliest impressions were those of a nomad. His mother and father lived in railway carriages and under canvas by the River Kura in Azerbaijan. Snakes and scorpions made the world a perilous place for an infant, but the river, flowing clean from a great reservoir, was a source of joy. Once the baby managed to roll off the edge of its steep bank, only to be caught by laughing, dark-eyed Aunt Sonya, his mother's sister, bathing in the water below. There was always someone to care and to catch during that brief time of freedom from the constraints of nineteenth-century civilisation when he was still an only child. Perhaps it was only remembering the memory, but the shock of the drop between earth and water remained with him, the first arbitrary break in the continuum of experience.

There was a flat in the Georgian capital of Tiflis, where Pavel was christened in the Church of David Mtatsminsky, but his first two winters and the summer between were spent at Evlach, a dusty, little settlement in process of development round a junction of the Transcaucasian railway in a broad, hot basin, part steppe, part malarial swamp, enclosed on three sides by mountains with the fourth, the south-east, opening onto the coastal plain between Astama and Baku on the Caspian Sea.

Pavel's father, Aleksandr Ivanovich Florensky, the son of a doctor and grandson of a priest from a long line of priests and deacons, was a Russian railway engineer, engaged by the government to extend the empire of the Tsar along the line of rail: southward from Tiflis to Baku, then from Batumi to Arkhatsykhsk. He eventually became assistant to the Director-in-Chief of the Caucasian railway network. Aleksandr's attitude to life was much influenced by the fact that his father, Ivan Andreevich Florensky, had been one of the fabled generations of priests' sons *(popovichi)*, who rebelled against the ideological forcing house of the seminary, renounced theology for science and channelled

hereditary zeal and early training in self-denial into the propagation of a secular
utopia in which men and women would be equal partners in labour 'on the
field of Russian enlightenment'. Like Turgenev's Bazarov, many became doctors
as Ivan did; others became teachers or journalists, always radical, often forced
by a repressive regime into illegal activities, exile, prison or revolution – and
correspondingly ineffective. Ivan Florensky even died like Bazarov, infected
by cholera in the course of his medical duties. Aleksandr Ivanovich was of
a gentler, more constructive generation, concerned to better the lot of their
fellow-countrymen through practical 'small deeds', not hardened by rebellion
against their fathers but, on the contrary, full of pious admiration for their
fathers' ethos, tested as it so often was by lives of heroic dedication. They were,
on the whole, less exigent towards their fellows, less iconoclastic because more
aware of the threat of social and cultural chaos, more inclined to value beauty,
even moderate and judiciously enjoyed pleasure, agnostic rather than aggressively atheistic. Aleksandr Ivanovich permitted himself a certain reverence
for such concepts as nature, the family, motherhood and for the free human
spirit which must be allowed to find its own way along the paths of reason and
experiment, neither forced – especially when young and malleable – into any
religious mould, nor encouraged to proselytise (even for free thought) or hector
others into renouncing traditional beliefs. His 'holy scriptures' were Goethe's
*Faust* and Shakespeare's plays. Surrounded by wild peoples and wild nature, he
was concerned to preserve the 'cosmos' of the family home and would, says his
son, have offered Dostoevsky, that explorer of chaos within, a soothing drink
of sugared water and kept him away from the children. These latter he carefully
preserved from the irrational, enchanting Pavel from an exceptionally early
age by teaching him to set up ever more complex technical experiments and
patiently assuaging his fathomless scientific curiosity, but forbidding fairytales
as overstimulating to the imagination and the Gospels as beyond the critical
grasp of a young child. When something in the vibrant solemnity of his eldest
son inspired a passing priest to present the boy with a *prosfyrka* (a round of
unleavened bread specially baked and blessed for distribution after the liturgy),
Pavel, aged six at the time, was told to accept it with all courtesy but, after some
debate at home, it was given to the nanny.

Salome Saparova or Saparian, Pavel's mother, known after her marriage as
Ol'ga Florenskaia, was from an old Armenian family who believed themselves
descended from pre-Romanic Greeks – Lydians and Phrygians – though
Florensky himself, who, particularly after his marriage, developed a keen interest
in genealogy which he never had time or opportunity to follow up, was to
disinter many other theories about their ethnic origin. Originally from Giulistan
in Karabakh, the Melik-Begliarovs (as the principal line of the family was called),
paid feudal allegiance to Persians and Turks (from whom came the title *melik*)

but eventually[2] sought refuge from the plague with all their kin and dependants in neighbouring Georgia. When the main branch of the family returned, some of the younger members, according to one version the fairytale 'three brothers', chose to stay in Georgia and founded their own families under different surnames (Saparov is derived from the Georgian for 'shield' and suggests some soldierly service to their new home). However, they retained their Armenian identity and, in spite of the odd Georgian match, tended to intermarry among themselves or back into the original Armenian branch of the family.

Salome's father was as unlike Pavel's paternal grandfather as it was possible to be: the decadent, effeminate scion of an inbred clan in whose home Oriental luxury and Western European refinement reflected the trade in fine woods and silks he carried on between Persia and France, exporting priceless raw materials and importing exquisite manufactured goods. Camel caravans with luxury goods from the East would make a point of turning into Saparov's courtyard on Veliaminovskaia ulitsa in Tiflis, knowing they would find a ready and discriminating patron, but the languages spoken at home were Russian and French and wholehearted support was given to the Russian State which kept the area stable and so made possible the epicurean, cosmopolitan Saparov lifestyle. Family wealth, it is true, in spite of a sideline in oil and asphalt, was ebbing rapidly – but not family pride. Pavel Saparian was not a particularly national-istic, still less an ardently religious man, but the Armenian-Gregorian Church had for over 1,500 years been the one institution his divided and subjected race had preserved in all purity, the one constant symbol of their identity, and the Saparov family history was steeped in its traditions. Although clever and culti-vated guests of all nationalities visited his house and shared his board, there was amongst Saparov's extended family of doubly and trebly related cousins and uncles and aunts a certain enclosed and static quality. A hereditary predis-position to tuberculosis and a tendency to acquiesce in the cultured indolence of the *status quo* suggest a degree of somewhat effete clannishness, against which several of Pavel Saparov's children rebelled, insisting on their right to marry 'foreigners' – Georgians or Russians – and disassociating themselves utterly from the tradition of exclusive wealth and privilege – though unable to shake off a certain disdain for the rough and tumble of everyday life which led some to accuse them – and their children – of spiritual pride. Florensky's mother, Ol'ga Pavlovna, fired by a visiting professor's opinion[3] that she should be improving her education rather than living in idleness, ran away from home with the help of her 'socialist' brother Arzhak (Arkadii Pavlovich, as he was called in Russian) to study in St Petersburg, where she met and fell in love with the student engineer Aleksandr Florensky. When she returned home her father did not approve the engagement, but the couple continued to correspond with the help of Arzhak (himself temporarily disinherited for his intention to marry

a Georgian girl he had been in love with since his schooldays). They were wed
after Aleksandr Florensky completed his studies in 1880, by which time Pavel
Saparov had died, shattered by a catastrophic fire in his Tiflis home: 'in such a
family as the Saparovs', wrote Ol'ga Pavlovna's son, 'the marriage of a daughter,
and a favourite daughter at that, to a Russian without wealth or position was a
crying scandal'.[4]

Florensky's parents preserved a friendly, even close relationship with Ol'ga
Pavlovna's sisters and their husbands who grew to like and accept her Russian
husband, but cut themselves off from their ethnic origins in other ways. Except
for the virtually obligatory christening of children into the Russian Orthodox
Church at which Pavel, suffering agonies of embarrassment, stood godfather
to his own younger siblings, they abjured all religious practice, partially, or so
Florensky supposed, in order to avoid any possible rupture due to their different
confessional allegiances. Ol'ga Pavlovna went further, rejecting her cultural
heritage altogether, refusing to speak Armenian or to satisfy her children's
natural curiosity about the lives and personalities of their exotic forebears.
Only among her possessions did they come across tantalising clues: a walnut
snuffbox bearing the profile of Louis XIII, an antique medal in memory of
Shakespeare, the odd piece of precious jewellery. Ol'ga Pavlovna, who did her
best to keep them away from 'such trifles', was too gentle to ward them off
when they actually found these things in her open jewel box, but told them
nothing. She and Aleksandr Florensky took a tragic view of Armenia as a
country condemned to fade from history through sheer cultural inertia and to
be absorbed by more vigorous, younger nation-states.

Aleksandr Ivanovich, in his turn, cut off by *his* father's rebellion from his
grandparents and their traditions, had grown away from his native Russian
element. Indeed, it was almost as if he thought it necessary to compensate his
wife for abandoning her cultural heritage by ignoring his own, though the
family did observe some cultural customs common to both: the Easter Table,
laden with delicious cold foods that could be eaten in any order as and when you
felt like it for a whole week while the servants took time off to enjoy the holiday;
the exchange of Easter gifts (home-made by the children); the Christmas tree;
the decoration of the house with green branches on Trinity Sunday; a tendency
to serve traditional Caucasian vegetarian dishes during Lent, though chicken,
for some reason, 'did not count' as meat! In springtime there would be all-day
expeditions to gather wild flowers in the mountains. It was by no means a
colourless life but it lacked the cultural well-spring of a shared faith – a lack that
was perhaps all the more to be felt in the climate of mutual affection and respect
and the expectation that the children would, in their own strength, grow up like
their parents – decent men and women with a strong feeling of obligation to
their less fortunate fellows.

To Pavel the well-ordered micro-world of family residences in Tiflis and Batumi, where his father was stationed for several years, was somewhat arid. As a grown man he recalled with delight his mother's clear voice singing Schubert's Lieder but he and she were shy, reserved beings and there seems to have been little warmth in their relationship – less than the little boy would have liked. Besides, she was invariably busy with the next baby. His father, even when at home, was more mentor than friend. Pavel's only tender love was for his Aunt Julia, his father's spinster sister, who took care of him when the family returned from Evlach to live in Tiflis where he and she slept across the courtyard from Aleksandr Ivanovich, Ol'ga Pavlovna and the younger children. To cross the yard 'all on his own' was a terrifying experience, because Pavlik had once seen there a huge, stygian figure looming over a turning wheel from which showered gold fountains of flying sparks ... As everyone explained, it was only the knife-grinder, but the little boy felt he had seen what he ought not, some eruption of primal chaos from beneath the smooth surface of his ordered life. However, he learned to overcome his terror of the courtyard, secure in the knowledge that the dark passage led from light to light and that in this too, but now in an infinitely reassuring sense, the world was not as it seemed: for the two flats were one home.

Aunt Julia shared his passion for all things frail and ephemeral, the bird on the wing, the nodding violet hiding modestly from view when the rhododendrons and azaleas were crying out to be gathered and admired, his favourite snowdrops, cyclamens and Christmas roses, the scents he ground from various flowers to present to his female relatives – and longed to try out in his own bath. She shared his sense of wonder, his feeling for nature and, though she maintained the family united front of enlightened rationalism, Pavel sensed in her a hidden 'yes' to the magical life-force he perceived as seeping through every pore of the natural world and later called God. The Saparov sisters thought Julia Ivanovna rather sentimental, but Pavel Florensky claims in his memoirs that he was 'in love' with her. Perhaps he needed the 'in love' to distinguish his feeling for her from the non-love he felt for most of the rest of the family, whom he tended not so much to dislike as to take for granted. Julia was his sweetheart, his soulmate – but as for the rest of humankind:

> I did not love people ... Even animals, mammals, left me sufficiently indifferent – I felt them too close akin to humans. What I did love was air, wind, clouds, my brothers were cliffs, my spiritual kindred minerals, especially crystals, I loved birds, and most of all growing things and the sea ... People may consider this monstrous or see in it a lack of moral feeling, but that is how it was; without the least illwill on my part I did not love the human being as such but, with all the power of my being, I was in love with nature ...[5]

Again he uses the word 'in love' which, in a more grown-up context, he would replace by 'Eros': 'Either complete indifference, failure to notice, total coldness – or all-consuming passion, pumping through me, enveloping me with fire. I hardly experienced emotions, because in my soul Eros would suddenly flare up; Paul-Saul, that is Eros, always was an erotic.'[6]

Pavel, moreover, as he grew from babyhood to boyhood, had discovered a fundamental grudge against human life. He was not a girl … and all the pretty things he coveted, the floating silks and chiffons, the complex pleats and delicate, pastel colours, the flowery scents and opalescent jewellery, and the dazzling prospect, when grown up, of a hat with a humming-bird – were to fall to the lot of his younger sister Liusia (short for Julia), who had no fine feeling for such things. Boys were not supposed to be interested in 'glad rags' which, Florensky explained to his grandchildren, was why he had never made the least effort to look smart in his uninteresting, masculine attire.

However much they might discourage this incipient, and most probably inherited, taste for feminine finery, his parents could not resist the little boy's consuming desire for a humming-bird and one unforgettable day he and Aunt Julia were permitted to set off downhill to the harbour of Batumi to buy her a new hat – and he himself was to choose the humming-bird to trim it. Pavel was ecstatic and it took him till darkness had fallen and the shop was closing to make up his and Julia Ivanovna's mind to purchase the very smallest, most exquisite and most expensive bird. But the tiny creature, specially wrapped to avoid crushing it and proudly carried by Pavel himself, slipped out of the bag on the long uphill trudge in the dusk and, though the understanding Aunt Julia retraced every step of the way with him, was never found. Later, his father presented him with a beautifully illustrated book about humming-birds, but pictures could not replace the wonder of the three-dimensional reality, the soft, delicate feathers of *his* bird.

Gradually, the child hardened towards the feminine side of his own nature, not towards his inborn aestheticism, for his interest in costume soon extended to art and music and he realised that the beautiful as such was not necessarily the monopoly of women, but towards the sentimental and subjective, what he called 'psychologism in intellectual opinions'. He conceived an 'almost physical revulsion to the imprecise, the cosmetic'.[7] He himself felt this as intolerance and, perhaps, lack of charity, and was inclined to blame his mother who, on being presented with what Pavlik considered to be a particularly touching picture he had painted in the spirit of the illustrated journals of the time of a princess weeping for the death of her fiancé, had confirmed by the tone of her voice his own suspicion that he had been guilty of a positively indecent lapse of taste: 'not only I myself but all the brides within me, the princesses, the crowns, the deaths and other related circumstances were instantly shrivelled, consumed by burning shame …'[8]

Balked of fairytales and romance, the little boy turned his attention to the natural world and found it, especially in the environs of Batumi, a source of wonder. 'My later religious-philosophical convictions', he wrote at the age of 41, 'came not from philosophical books, which with rare exceptions I tended to read little and very reluctantly, but from childhood observations and perhaps most of all from the character of the landscape to which I was accustomed.'[9]

Batumi, the southernmost port of Georgia, and its environs, where Pavel spent his fifth and sixth years, provided this landscape. Literate and well instructed by his father in the elements of the natural sciences and proper scientific method, armed with knowledge and an investigative turn of mind, the child was still free from the dulling routine of school, his imagination untrammelled, his time his own. An indelible impression was left by the all-day family expeditions his father organised through the mountain gorges to Adzhiz-Tskhali, along his own putative line of rail where the first newly constructed bridge, to the minds of his children, was their own property because it was their father's bridge – however much Pavel might privately regret the rope ferry it replaced.

On the way out from Batumi they would pass a freak settlement of black Africans, leisured, colourful and living to all appearances in complete harmony with nature, who, Pavel dreamed, might some day adopt him as one of their own. Then came slagheaps from a copper refinery and he thrilled to the thought of the getting of ore from the underworld and to the strange smell of sulphur which, for all his subsequent experiments with sulphuric acid, he could never reproduce to the same effect at home. The first gorge, that of the once gold-bearing River Chorokh, was full of mists and waterfalls and walled with black basalt columns. As the horses pulled them slowly up the Adzhalsk road, Pavel learned to look at 'the earth not only as a surface but in cross-section, and to look at time itself "with a side-long glance",[10] taking in a succession of geological eras simultaneously and seeing the grasping roots together with the trunks and branching foliage of the lush vegetation:

> The fourth coordinate – time – came to life for me in such a way that it lost its frightening character of eternal return, became cosy and enclosed, something like eternity. I grew accustomed to seeing the roots of things. That habit of vision later grew through all my thought and defined its basic character – the will to move along verticals and a certain indifference to horizontals.[11]

Further up the gorge the tributary river Adzhais-Tskhali poured itself into the Chorokh and they had the choice of following the course of this second stream beside their father's railroad through another steep-sided ravine towards Arkhaltsyk or continuing alongside his friend Passek's line to follow the Chorokh itself to Artwin. A halt would be made for lunch in one of the railway huts along the way, where the chief engineer's family could be sure of a royal welcome. The journey was supposed to be dangerous because of the Adzhary, Mohammedan Georgian tribesmen much given to banditry, but the local bandits had conceived a liking for the Russian engineer who had brought his magical form of transport to their mountain fastness and the Florenskys, jogging along in their flower or berry-laden diligence, were never molested. Pavel and Liusia each had their 'very own' mountain torrent and vigorously disputed the place of honour next to the coachman.

An unfailing and more familiar source of wonder was the sea. The children were taken down to the pebbly beach every day, sometimes three times a day, and Pavel and his sister collected sea-smooth stones, layered by time, which allowed them to hold the centuries in small, hot hands. The lapping, briny water with its wavering seaweed and abundant fish and molluscs seemed to him the very source of life, and stranded starfish and transparent jellyfish bore witness to life's amazing variety. Tasting, grinding, smelling, making drawings, listing and comparing, the child brought to the study of this rich source all the systematic technique he had already absorbed from his father, but constantly discovered miracle, inexplicable breaks in the chain of cause and effect, elusive glimpses of perfection juxtaposed with the monstrous and extraordinary. It seemed to him that nature was playing a game with him, that she *wanted* him to discover her secrets and welcomed his enquiring disposition. He did not need or wish to know the unknowable (how could one?), but only to be assured of its existence. To justify intuitive certainty he needed to weigh, measure and dissect, yet this necessary activity would not reveal the essence of things, only how they worked, interacted, could be *used*, and transformed – as, for instance, in his father's domestic experiments with substances that would burst into flame on contact with water or with home-made sparklers. 'What I wanted was to get to know that world which is by definition unknowable, not by breaking its mysteries, but by observing it on the quiet.'[12] In the experiments, the seemingly miraculous was entirely explicable (he himself helped to set them up), but the truly miraculous was inherent in nature itself, in the elements of the experiments, their potential for regeneration, and in the physical reality of his marine treasures with their iodised smell which always, thereafter, when he lived and worked far from the sea, filled him with a sense of absolute recall. The lowered eyes and the sideways glance is a stock ingredient of almost all physical descriptions of the adult Florensky. On early photographs, the boy Pavel stares into the camera with a certain childish *hauteur*, but the sidelong glance was already habitual in his search for mysteries denied him by the dogmatic authority of 'grown-up' science.

Later, in a chapter of *For My Children* entitled 'Osobennoe' (The Extraordinary), begun in mid-October 1916 and completed on 25 July 1920 (it was written in snatches when he was free from more pressing tasks), Florensky explained his childhood absorption in nature as a search for the particular in the general, for the *Urphänomen* in the phenomenon, 'for the unusual yet sweetly known and familiar revelation from native deeps ...'[13] Through such Socratic moments of recall all later experiences would fall into place and the often turgid, impassioned rush of his pragmatic thought would clarify and crystallise. Florensky himself explains:

> In precisely such a way from very earliest youth the categories of knowledge and first philosophical concepts took shape in my mind. My later thinking neither reinforced them nor brought a more profound understanding but, on the contrary, when I began to study philosophy it destabilised and eclipsed them, giving nothing in their stead but a bitter aftertaste. Yet gradually, delving into the fundamental concepts of an integral understanding of the world and making my way through them logically and historically, I began to feel firm ground under my feet and, when I looked back, that firm ground turned out to be the very same ground on which I had taken my stand since earliest childhood: after all these mental excursions I had come back full circle to the point from which I set out. Indeed, I had discovered nothing new but had simply 'remembered' – yes, remembered that foundation of my personality which had been laid in childhood or, to put it more exactly, was the fundamental seed of all intellectual growth from the first moments of consciousness.
>
> All my life I have thought, basically, about one thing: about the relationship of the phenomenon to the noumen, of its manifestation, its incarnation. It is the question of the symbol. And all my life I have pondered one single question, the question of THE SYMBOL.[14]

Of course, that was not how the pensive five-to-six-year-old would have put it at the time and the grown-up Florensky, struggling to set things out for his children in simple language, was acutely conscious that science, philosophy and theology, no less than poetry, is one long search for the right words. The indwelling spirit which shone through the objects of his study was never, either to the small boy or to the man, something outside or independent of the objects themselves. Although it exceeded and was not to be identified with them, it could not be perceived by the observing subject otherwise than through them. 'The Kantian separation of noumena and phenomena (even when I had no suspicion of the existence of any one of these terms: "Kantian", "separation", "noumena" and "phenomena") I rejected with all my being.'[15]

In other words, at no stage did Pavel the boy or Florensky the man wish to disassociate the transcendental notion of the noumen, the thing which exists in and for itself independent of our sensual perception, with its manifestation in the real physical world. Then and later it was these 'manifestations' he sought, studied and treasured – and he felt that to strip the 'soul' of the world of its symbolic or fleshly veil would be an act of indecency, rape, even murder. As a child, Pavel learned to reason and express himself in a language adequate to the world of phenomena, but all that was within his power to express remained somehow peripheral to his inmost experience, for which at the time he had no words and which he kept to himself.

He certainly did not associate this inmost experience with conventional religion. The nextdoor children, the Lileevs whose parents were artistes of light opera and thus in his view altogether inferior to his own serious parents in matters of education, regularly attended church, and the Florenskys received a complaint that their eldest son had tried, in his no doubt exasperatingly superior little way, to talk them out of the absurdity of their belief in a good God who was the all-powerful creator of a world full of evil and sorrow. It was explained to him that some people needed to cling to their faith and, though his parents would prefer him strong and independent and able to work things out for himself, he was not of an age to be sure, and anyway, it was discourteous and unkind to denigrate ideas which other people held dear.

'Other people' were contingent upon his cocooned family life. In Batumi, the Florenskys' flat looked out upon an inner courtyard over a long balcony loaded with flowers and little trees in tubs with oranges and lemons, blossom and fruit. Here he would work away at his collections and his potions or sit with the Lileev children and watch the other denizens of the yard.

Opposite lived a Jewish family, two brothers and two sisters. Pavel had an irrational dread of the last letter in the Russian alphabet 'Я': of the very sound 'Ya-a-a' and the fact that it was contained in the magical but perilous words *yad* (poison) and *mishyak* (arsenic). It so happened that one of the men of the flat was called 'Yankel' and the name, shrilled out many times a day by one or other of his womenfolk, conjured up frightening associations. From the Lileev children, Pavel had heard that there was a nasty word for Jewish people – 'Yids' – which one must never say in their hearing as it would make them very angry. So, no doubt wishing to impress and also to try out the truth of this information, he remarked loud and clear from the safety of the balcony as Yankel's sister hurried across the yard with her shopping bag: "There goes that Yid-woman again." She berated him for being a wicked, ill-brought-up little boy – which possibly gave him status in the eyes of the Lileevs and certainly proved their parents' point. In *For My Children*, Florensky admits to a later sense of transgression, but records in a different context that his own father, who would not have dreamed of using the word *Yid* and who, determinedly tolerant in his agnosticism, treated priests, mullahs and rabbis with equal respect, would occasionally mutter in a worried voice that the Jews would 'eat us up' and that something would have to be done about 'that people'.[16] Something was 'done' about Yankel and his siblings: they disappeared overnight, leaving their flat open and empty, and the children found pieces of a printing press, assumed to have been used for criminal, but equally possibly, though this does not seem to have occurred to either family, for revolutionary purposes.

The Turkish quarter down by the harbour undoubtedly housed a criminal element, but it fascinated more than it repelled. It was said to be a warren of smugglers, but coral and Venetian beads brought by the tarred boats bobbing at their moorings along the quayside were sold there in dark shops, and the purveyors of these treasures were eager to please a potential buyer, or even a wonderstruck little boy dragging sister, nanny or aunt behind him just to look at their wares.

Books and stories played a part in Pavel's life even then but a secondary one to his immediate impressions of the world around him. His father told him tales of adventure, discovery and invention, of stars, planets and – best of all, because unpredictable – comets, and he was grateful for them and interested, as he was for the information contained in the Russian and French nature magazines[17] and in Meier's 'Conversational lexicon', though all this touched no deep chords. The Pavlenkov edition of Pushkin and the works of his father's beloved Goethe were available to him as soon as he could read. Once he found Aunt Julia's New Testament but began at the beginning and painstakingly ploughed his way through Matthew's chapter on the genealogy of Christ which, oddly, though in full accordance with his later passion for genealogical tables, he did not find dull. However, his comments and questions led to Aunt Julia confiscating the book, saying rather regretfully that he was not ready for it.

In their anxiety to avoid the irrationality of fairytale and the premature influence of religious reading his parents had, however, made one mistake. The Greek myths were considered to have long since lost their religious force and could be classed as education rather than superstition – and the boy assimilated the world of myth as a natural and inalienable part of the real world of his childhood. He knew he was living hard by the river where Jason had come to find the Golden Fleece and he had seen the very rock on which Prometheus was crucified. The Eden of his spirit was ancient Colchis, 'a country of Asia', as Lemprière tells us,

> at the south of Asiatic Sarmatia, east of the Euxine sea, north of Armenia, and west of Iberia, now called Mingrelia. It is famous for the expeditions of the Argonauts, and as the birthplace of Medea. It was fruitful in poisonous herbs and produced excellent flax. The inhabitants were originally Egyptians ...[18]

Nymphs and satyres, centaurs, titans and serpent-haired Gorgons were present to Pavel's childish imagination before the river-maidens and wood-demons of Russian folklore, the elves and fairies of Perrault, Grimm and Andersen (with

whom he had only the slightest 'contraband' acquaintance through Goethe and
Pushkin), and long before the mirrors and shadows of his later beloved E. T.
A. Hoffmann. They were stored in his subconscious memory together with the
drop into the River Kura, the knifegrinder, the lost humming-bird, the jellyfish
and the basalt pillars of the Chorokh Gorge.

## 2

# *School*

*Natural philosophy*, the study of nature or of the spatiotemporal world. This
was regarded as a task for philosophy before the emergence of modern science,
especially physics and astronomy, and the term is now used only with reference to
pre-modern times.

*The Cambridge Dictionary of Philosophy*

Like Winston Churchill, Florensky always maintained that everything worth
learning he had learned in spite of school, notwithstanding the fact that he
completed the eight-year course at the Second Tiflis Classical Gymnasium
(1892–1900) with a gold medal and the accolade 'first pupil'. The years
spent in Tiflis from the time his childhood idyll began to fade after leaving
Batumi until the summer of 1899, when he passed through the spiritual
crisis that was to give impetus to all his future life and thought, he regarded
as uneventful and undifferentiated, like the span of a bridge from one
pier to the next: 'I learned a lot directly from my father. But mainly, I learned
from nature … I drew, took photographs, studied. Made observations of
geological, meteorological and such-like character, and always on the basis of
physics.'[1]

Michael Hagemeister, the most distinguished expert on Florensky's life and
work outside Russia, writes of his schooldays:

> he independently undertook geological, meteorological, zoological and physical
> research, made a collection of plants and minerals, wrote articles on themes from
> natural science, one of which on the luminosity of the glow-worm (*Lampyrus nocti
> luca*) is said to have appeared in a German journal towards the end of the 1890s.[2]

Such was Florensky's alienation from the state educational process that, on
his school timetable, he encircled not only religious instruction and church
parade, which he regarded as impositions altogether foreign to his upbringing,[3]
but most other lessons as well with a mourning band to denote hours lost to
the pursuit of knowledge. Homework was tossed off during breaks so that he
could devote his free time to self-directed studies and wider reading. He was,
however, subsequently grateful for instruction in Ancient Greek and Latin

and benefited, in the senior classes, from association with an inspired teacher, Georgii Gekhtmann, who particularly favoured him and his friends.

Florensky was not alone in his alienation. Indeed, Tiflis' schools at that time were a positive nursery of disaffection and, shortly after Pavel went on to Moscow University, the grumbling and resentment all about him began to breed isolated acts of violence in classroom and playground. In a world of crumbling beliefs, people sought new certainties as different as possible from those imposed upon them by the system. Iosif Dzugashvili, for instance, the future Stalin, Florensky's senior by three years, studying at the Tiflis Theological Seminary from which he was expelled in 1898, was heading from the stifling conformity of government-sponsored religion to materialism and the new orthodoxy of Marxism-Leninism, whereas Florensky, moving in the opposite direction, was gradually coming to the conclusion that the language of science was unable to express the fullness of being and eventually, thanks to an emotional and intellectual crisis and mystical experience, was to leave school with his feet firmly set on the way which was to lead him to unreserved acceptance of the Orthodox Christian Church.

Meanwhile, among Florensky's own classmates at the Second Classical Gymnasium, there were rebels aplenty – political and cultural: the future Menshevik Iraklii Tseretelli; the future Bolshevik Lev Kamenev, then known as Lev Rozenfeld, whose father, like Pavel's, was an engineer engaged on the construction of the Transcaucasian railway; and David Burliuk who was to attain notoriety as the scandalous futurist artist who 'discovered' the poetic talent of Vladimir Mayakovsky and, in 1912, was one of the authors of 'A slap in the face to public taste' in the form of a Futurist manifesto.

Florensky, who says of himself that his parents' inability to protect him from the horror of state-imposed vaccination as a very small boy had imbued him with a lifelong attitude of stoic non-resistance to authority, was by nature disdainful rather than disruptive. Sustained by the continuity of a supportive home background, he got on well with the quieter, more thoughtful boys such as Vladimir (Volodia) Ern and Aleksandr (Sasha) El'chaninov with whom, together with Tseretelli, he organised a literary-philosophical circle in class VII. Indeed, Florensky's year at school was considered a vintage one and five of his classmates, including Ern and El'chaninov, were, like him, to finish the course with the distinction of a gold medal, not to mention almost twice their number who achieved silver. However wearisome the curriculum, the teaching must in fact have been of an acceptable standard. At 15, Pavel was on good enough terms with the physics teacher Mikhail Gorodensky to exchange letters with him during the holidays, as was Ern with the history teacher Gekhtmann a year or two later. The boys, moreover, undoubtedly found stimulation in one another's company.

Volodia Ern, who was fair-haired, blue-eyed and earnest, though not devoid of humour, is often described as of Germanic or Swedish origin, but had in fact taken his surname and patronymic from his chemist stepfather, born in Revel (now Tallin, Estonia) and educated at Derpt University, his mother's second husband who had legally adopted her son by one Gavril Andreevich Aref'ev, a Russian citizen.[4] Of himself, Ern says that he was always more subject than object in a loving relationship, but his serenity and the luminous innocence of those blue eyes endeared him deeply to his friends, as did what he called his 'Christian Eros' for men and women. 'Eros' was a very fashionable word in early twentieth-century Russia and, following Plato, was considered by Viacheslav Ivanov and other disciples of Vladimir Solov'ev to be an essential ingredient in teacher–pupil relationships, same-sex friendships and creative work. Eros was the 'pontifex', the bridgebuilder between the real and the ideal (or the 'more real' if we are to use Ivanov's terminology), and when Ern wrote to his young wife of his 'Christian Eros', he was trying to explain that if people loved him it was because they saw themselves ideally reflected in his love towards them.[5] Whether the boys used such terms among themselves, at least before Plato came up in the school curriculum, is doubtful. It was, however, precisely in their shared passion for the Ancient World, especially Greece, and in their philosophical and later religious interests that Florensky and Ern found a true affinity. Ern was a stranger to the natural sciences, the study of which he identified with materialism. After his friend's untimely death at the age of 35, Florensky wrote warmly:

> you and I studied together from the second class of the gymnasium, were in and out of one another's homes, shared a room during our years at university, afterwards frequently met and stayed with one another; together we went through many crazes for things that mattered most deeply to us, caught fire from those dreams which later crystallised into the convictions which shaped our lives. Probably there are few ideas which we did not talk over together. Our common thought was permeated by philosophical interests and ardent feelings of closeness, we lived out our friendship not languidly but enthusiastically, sometimes quarrelling because of the hypertension of youthful thought. Together we wandered through forests and over rocks, mostly over rocks, together read Plato on mountain alps and sun-warmed rocky ledges.[6]

Ern's published letters bear witness to these quarrels, over purely abstract matters but no less painful for that, and to his abiding affection for 'Pavlusha', as he and El'chaninov tenderly called Florensky. Exclaiming over his first sight of sister Liusia's baby, Ern gives us a rare glimpse of how Pavlusha's friends must have seen him as a boy: 'A true Florensky! ... Fine, quirky lips and a timid, sweet smile. Dark-dark eyes, with an oily gleam.'[7] The word-picture can just be reconciled with the rather formal group photographs of a neatly cropped, adolescent

Florensky, but comes to life most convincingly in a later, 1907 portrait of him, luxuriantly coifed with embryo beard and moustache, by his sister Ol'ga.[8]

Pavel's feelings for Sasha El'chaninov were more extreme. The son of an officer, Sasha was possessed of sensitive good looks, a fine bearing and great charm. Pavel was 'almost in love' with him, a state he describes in relation to Aunt Julia as 'a mutual defusion of personality'.[9] Unlike Ern, El'chaninov was 'receptive' to Florensky's overriding interest in physics and his resurrecting of the old English term 'natural philosophy' to cover not only his ardent desire to master the laws of natural science, known and as yet unknown, but, through them, to discover the meaning of life, his own, the world's, the universe's. Later, Florensky claimed that he would not have admitted to such a desire in his early teens, because he wished to be a pure scientist, not a dilettante given over to cross-disciplinary speculation, but in his memoirs he states that this, albeit subconsciously, is precisely what he *was* looking for: a way of reconciling science with the mythical feeling for the world he had as a child. El'chaninov caught fire from Florensky's ideas, reflecting them back to him, as it seemed, in a more profound and subtle form, and for several years Pavel believed that they were of one mind, companions in an all-absorbing quest. The two became inseparable at work and at play. Florensky needed to become 'as one' with all his loves, sharing the minutiae of daily life, caring for them in illness, experiencing together nature or music (another, almost painful passion), the labour of experiment and excitement of thought – and he lived at a frightening pitch of concentration: 'I was never hysterical that I can remember and was psychologically stable', he explains in *For My Children*,

> But there was in me a heightened impressionability, a constant inner vibration of all my being to the impressions I was receiving and keeping to myself. It was an almost physical feeling of myself as a string thrumming to Nature's bow or a disc receiving an impression.[10]

This was not inspiration in the artistic sense: what took form in response to the promptings of Nature were mathematical patterns, symbols, schemae, as tantalising as half-formed lines of verse in the mind of a poet. As the years passed and the boy absorbed all that school and available books could teach him in physics, he became increasingly aware that he had no words to describe these shifting, elusive patterns which threatened to invalidate all he had been taught. It was a torment to him that he could not always interpret the symbols, even to himself, because there was no interlocutor with whom he could discuss them.

The relationship with El'chaninov broke on this frustration and on the older boy's inability to respond to the all-embracing tenderness of Florensky's feeling, which, he was later to admit, was the epitome of what true friendship should

be but – for him – unendurable.[11] Florensky, less charitably, but then he was
the more hurt, wrote in his account of the breaking of their friendship that
El'chaninov was a 'Don Juan (not to be understood in a coarse sense)' and that
he was generally considered even by his friends as something of a butterfly that
flits from flower to flower.[12] He claims that it was he who initiated the break but
that, had he not done so, El'chaninov would surely have left him:

> He was the only one to whom at that time I could get inwardly close. With my
> schoolmates and other acquaintances my contacts were superficial and – deliberately
> superficial. We could chat on and I was not unpopular, but what really interested me,
> my thoughts about physics, I kept to myself …

He and El'chaninov had tried, but eventually failed to establish real communication at this level and failure had led to evasions, a kind of flawed intimacy:

> This was the only aspect of life in which I did not move unless I was jolted into it, but
> these jolts led – without any outward cause – to a bust-up, not to a cooling-off but
> precisely to a bust-up, which took on all the formal trappings of a quarrel, but a quarrel
> without a cause. One fine day we suddenly began to say 'you' [instead of the intimate
> 'thou'] to one another, then stopped talking to one another, seeing one another, cut
> one another dead in the street, didn't even say good morning … Thinking about all
> this, many years after El'chaninov and I had completely made it up, though without
> renewing what had been between us before, I see clearly that a far more hurtful and
> fundamental break would have occurred anyway, even if I had been more sensible in
> my assessment of the importance of physics and the degree of El'chaninov's capacity for
> deep thought …[13]

Florensky did not know, when he dictated this account of their friendship in
December 1923, that El'chaninov would eventually also commit himself to the
priesthood.[14] Both these sons of the Russian intelligentsia had a hard way to
travel, but each had to tread his own path – alone. The loneliness was not of
Pavel's choosing, nor was he aware, when he broke with Sasha El'chaninov as a
schoolboy, that the kind of intense spiritual kinship of which he had dreamed is
a grace given briefly to light the way – seldom a permanent and firm foundation
on which to build a life. Being faithful and true,[15] and normally too absorbed in
whatever he was doing for either philandering or introspection, such awareness
would not have come naturally.

It was before the break with El'chaninov, in June and July 1897, that Pavel
was packed off to Germany, in the company of his Saparov aunts Liza (Elizaveta
Pavlovna) and Remso (Repsimia or Raisa Pavlovna) and Liza's daughter Margot,
to the 'White Hart' sanitorium near Dresden where, it was hoped, Dr Heinrich
Lahmann would prescribe treatment for what turned out to be a psychosomatic

eye condition and, in general, a regime which would strengthen the boy's resistance against the ever present threat of tuberculosis. It seems likely that Pavel was suffering from overwork and already beginning to experience moments of discouragement in his single-minded pursuit of knowledge. He was diagnosed as being only slightly short-sighted but run down and in need of a nourishing diet, rest and regular exercise. From Dresden Pavel and his relatives journeyed on to Cologne and Bonn, where they joined 22-year-old Datiko (David) Melik-Begliarov, Aunt Liza's son, who was studying estate management at the Academy in Bonn-Poppelsdorf. A photograph taken on 19 July 1897 shows a half-smiling Pavlusha looking very young and, for once, more fair than dark and more Russian than Caucasian in contrast to the exquisite, black-haired and black-eyed, unmistakably Armenian Aunt Elizaveta and Uncle Sergei Melik-Begliarov. Repsimia's chatty letters to Ol'ga Pavlovna and Florensky's own rather stiff and dutiful epistles to his family at home afford us a literary snapshot of him at the age of 15.

For a boy brought up on Goethe and Schubert, it must be said the letters show him as singularly unresponsive to his surroundings. Aunt Remso wrote to her sister in her first letter from Dresden on 7 June 1897.

> In my opinion Pavlia[16] still needs to rest – he seems quite unable to throw off that yellow look. About Pavlia I really can't say whether he is bored or enjoying himself; he goes for walks with the rest of us. We have made several excursions on a steamer towards Pilnitz and the day before yesterday got as far as Pilnitz itself. The banks of the Elbe are really very pretty: so much soft greenery and such peace … We saw the new opera *The Return of Odysseus*. I don't know what Pavlia thought of it … Pavlia won't undertake anything on his own, can't even buy a stamp … In general his face and mood are very calm – I think he may find things more interesting in Bonn and with Datiko's help will be able to do what really interests him … Do you know what Pavlia is up to at this moment? Blowing soap bubbles for want of anything better to do.

The high point of Florensky's own letter to his father, written four days later on 13 June, is a visit to a shop selling apparatus for his physical experiments. He retails the price of 'coils' (presumably induction coils) and 'an electric machine of special construction which produces photographs of x-rays in five minutes.'[17] This letter crossed with one written by Aleksandr Ivanovich on the same day urging his son to wait before making any purchases (for which he promises to reimburse Repsimia) and see what was on offer in Bonn with the help of Datiko. The brief but warmly affectionate parental letter also gives his Pavlusha news of El'chaninov 'who called in for Xenophon' and exhorts him to have a good time, eat plenty, forget his books till the winter and buy something pretty for his sisters.

No doubt it was in accordance with the consensus that her nephew had been overdoing his book-learning that Aunt Remso decided against employing a German tutor for him and opted for lessons in bicycle riding! Aleksandr

Ivanovich, for his part, advises his son simply to make good use of the opportunity to talk to Germans, get used to the sound of the language and maybe read simple children's stories. In the physics shop in Dresden Aunt Remso had to find an assistant with whom Pavlia could speak French, so it is to be assumed that he did not at the time have a working knowledge of spoken German. Knowing, presumably, that science was not to be put aside for health reasons like school work, Pavel's father urged him to visit the optics shop in Cologne, the chemical laboratory in Bonn and to take out a subscription to J. C. D'Almeida's *Journal de physique théorique et appliquée.* As to the wonderful machine seen in Dresden, he himself had no experience of such a thing and he advised noting the address of the shop and details of delivery to Tiflis so that they could order what was needed together on Pavel's return home – advice that was cheerfully ignored.

To Ol'ga Pavlovna, who was spending the summer with the younger children at the spa-town of Borzhomi, Florensky wrote a true schoolboy's letter on 15 July: he hadn't got round to writing for a long time but was now *making* himself write although she had not written to him for a long time either. He then embarks on an animated description of Cologne: the cathedral, the eau-de-cologne, the wonders of the automatic slot machines in the amusement arcade and the still greater wonder of the pianola that plays itself. A brief duty letter to Liusia on the following day is perhaps more honest: 'I, with Aunt Remso and Datiko are now living in Bonn, but we are not enjoying ourselves very much.' Indeed, the party was not a happy one. When the three of them arrived back in Dresden, Aunt Lisa was diagnosed as requiring further treatment at the 'White Hart'. She was, however, undecided because of the expense. Her grown-up children Margot and Datiko were not prepared to dance attendance on her and Datiko was seriously at odds with his father and trying to negotiate a free hand in running the family estate, or at least a part of it, before returning home. As to Pavel, having purchased the electric machine 'about which he has been dreaming like a man in love', as his Aunt Remso, quite distracted at having to cope with all these warring egos, informed his mother, he was only too delighted when the day eventually came to head for home. He does not even mention the trip to Germany in his *For My Children* and recounts Datiko's troubles with belated interest in notes on the Saparov family as though they had not impinged upon his consciousness at the time.[18] Pavel's father's last letter to him in Germany had contained a rather harassed warning not to get too excited about moving from their flat to a 'home of our own'. He feared his family might be disappointed with it and wish themselves back in the rented flat: 'I hope you too will be able to restrict your requirements, as the others also will have to live without any special conveniences.'[19] This rather killjoy attitude was typical of Aleksandr Ivanovich, who even tended to deplore his son's invariably coming home with top marks from school for fear he should grow too pleased with himself. Florensky recalls with some irritation that his father always insisted on sobriety and modesty in all things – even down to the use of punctuation: an exclamation mark, for instance, was considered the height of impropriety!

Despite his father's warnings, it was presumably either in 1897 on his return from abroad or shortly thereafter[20] that Pavel was installed in his own wing of the new family home, once more across the courtyard from the main building, in a room he was allowed to arrange according to his own taste and needs. This room looked out through large windows over the usual railed gangway onto a courtyard with enormous acacia trees and, on hot summer nights, he obtained a through draft by sleeping with door and windows wide open. The walls were bare and plain white with roomy fitted cupboards of unstained ash for his books, papers and apparatus; two large tables, also of ash, took up most of the floor space. On these tables he worked, set up experiments and made new instruments. To one of them, as to a workbench, were screwed an English vice and an anvil and their drawers were full of mechanic's and carpenter's tools. The only other furniture was a wooden divan bed, a chair and a writing table with an inkstand. Pavel could not stand anything else on that smaller table, not even a book.

This was his sanctum, the place where he pursued his single-minded, extra-curricular effort to extend the bounds of his knowledge of the natural world. Aleksandr Ivanovich, attentive and more sympathetic than he allowed himself to appear, told his son at about this time that his special strength lay neither in the study of the particular nor in generalisation, but along the borderlines of the general and the particular, the abstract and the concrete. Pavel did not at the time welcome this percipient assessment, because all his energy was concentrated on particular problems and, though he read widely, for preference English and French scientists on and around his subject, he read always with relation to real problems he happened to be involved with at the time. He felt that there was no other linguistic clothing for his thought than the familiar scientific language of cause and effect and that, without it, he would simply lose the capacity for thought altogether. Experience and intuition, for which there was no place in this linguistic framework, simply belonged to another department of things which could not be proved and only related to his scientific studies through his passion for 'exceptions'. His philosophical reading and discussions were not helping, or so it seemed at the time, to close the gap between intuition and proof.

So, throughout the next two years, from summer 1897 to summer 1899, he laboured at the cyclopean task of constructing, piece by piece, a holistic yet scientific world view. General mathematical and physical principles he grasped easily, seldom experiencing them as new, 'remembering' rather than discovering them as though memory were programmed into the Florensky genes or, as he was to put it in the language of the 1920s, as though he were imbued with 'a hereditary tendency to scientific thought ... not so much a matter of individual characteristics as family traits, a mental hyperactivity passed on with native plasma'.[21] On the other hand, he neither fully understood nor remembered things learned by rote; he had to repeat for himself the processes by which scientists of the past had reached their conclusions, testing them with the help of his own largely home-made instruments. This arduous process of digesting and internalising acquired knowledge slowed him down and he considered himself in some ways ill-educated. In *For My Children* he explains:

> you see, the plus-side of my uneducatedness was a significant degree of independence from prevailing concepts, an attitude like a blacksmith's to a nail or a horseshoe that if needs be he can forge for himself, but not at all like that of a histologist (a fine point engraver), for example, to his microscope, which he is not only incapable of making or mending but the physical theory of which he does not even clearly understand.[22]

He felt at home in this pragmatic, experimental world of his, a primitive Titan forging his own understanding of physical science, undaunted and indeed unimpressed by received knowledge. Whether this approach, at once homespun and mythical, would have helped or hindered him had he fulfilled his ambition to pursue the study of pure physics, Florensky never found out. All he knew was that the days, weeks, months and years of tenacious concentration had taken him to the edge of physics as it was taught in Tiflis at the end of the nineteenth century. By the age of 16 he had outstripped his teachers and could go no further – and he had not even the right of entry to those libraries which were available in the city. The skills he had acquired in making his own apparatus were no longer technically sufficient to supply his immediate requirements and his father, struggling to feed, clothe and educate a large family, could not give much financial help, even had his precocious offspring known precisely what he needed. Moreover, Florensky had begun to share a feeling quite widespread towards the end of the nineteenth century that the edifice of theoretical physics was virtually complete:[23]

> In physics itself at the end of the 19th century, in spite of its successes, there was to be felt an absence of directing principles and a lack of correspondence between the system of physical knowledge, canonically structured to represent an almost complete edifice, and physical experiment.[24]

Only quantitative additions to knowledge and the odd decorative flourish, perhaps, now appeared possible.

Florensky was not interested in papering over the cracks in the walls of the edifice which he had always experienced, albeit subconsciously, as welling with mystery and promise. He felt with his whole being the imminence of catastrophic change: in physics, in 'natural philosophy', in philosophy itself, in the entire post-Renaissance concept of life in the universe ... When, a few years after he left school, Florensky learned of Kauffman's discovery of additional, speed dependent, electrodynamic mass in cathodes: 'it gleamed at me like something long familiar, precisely what I had expected. The further development of similar concepts led to the principle of relativity ...'[25]

But by that time he had given up and was content to see others make the great discoveries, for he had become fully aware, more consciously than in childhood, that Truth is there for the discovering, but that to comprehend the Whole Truth is a task beyond the mind of the individual. For a few brief years in adolescence he had forgotten this in his Eros for physics and he was to remember the period as one of utterly disinterested creative work. His contributions to applied science in the Soviet period, undertaken to earn money for his family, were – so he told his children – just a bit of fun compared with the laborious pursuit of knowledge he had engaged in as a young lad.

When exactly the pursuit became a self-imposed duty rather than a labour of love Florensky himself could not say with certainty. At first there would be dark days when, alone in the high, white room with the uncluttered tables, he was struck by an inexplicable melancholy he had never known and no new task presented itself, nothing seemed worthwhile. Then, after the break with El'chaninov, who had served as his link with other boys in his class, with the philosophical society and indeed with the whole world outside his obsessive preoccupation with science, Florensky fell into a true depression: 'I felt as if I had descended into a dark cellar ... The light had gone out and the trap door closed with a bang behind me.'[26]

The feeling, overwhelming enough in waking hours, inundated his dreams with black desolation and one night he awoke from the depths of nightmare to hear himself saying aloud: 'It's impossible without God.' In May 1894, Pavel's beloved Aunt Julia had died and now, in this pathless waste, he began to feel her presence, perhaps to remember something from her pre-school religious instruction, when his parents had allowed her to prepare him for obligatory confession and Holy Communion, prompting him to the very conclusion he had heard himself proclaiming. Then came the call: he was lying unable to sleep in the hot Georgian night when he suddenly felt himself propelled by some irresistible will out of his bed, through the window and over the railings into the brilliantly moonlit courtyard. A clear voice that could have been either man or woman (he later thought perhaps an angel, a messenger of God, though quite possibly using a real human voice) called him by name: 'Pavel'. He had no doubt that the voice was physically real and that it was a summons. It came once more: Pavel – and he knew beyond doubt that there was a way before his feet and he was being called to tread it. Before, he had been half unconsciously searching for God. Now God, through his real physical hearing, had answered, summoning him to His service. True to the characteristic zeal he later came to believe was inherent in his given name,[27] Pavel was to follow the call doggedly step by step until the end of his life, though he recorded no feeling at the time that the way he embarked upon then would be the way of the Cross.

Not surprisingly, given his agnostic upbringing and hostility to religious studies and practice at school, Florensky did not immediately see his direction clearly. Lev Tolstoy exercised incomparably greater influence over the religiously inclined intelligentsia in the years leading up to his excommunication in 1901 than did the Russian Orthodox Church and Pavel had been tremendously impressed by his *Confession*. Grown sceptical of the future of science and culture, he felt that perhaps he was intended to renounce them and seek wisdom of another kind in the simple life, an idea which echoed his Rousseauesque childhood dream of joining the negro community near Batumi and which was to resurface throughout his life in the form of frequently reiterated admiration for the natural wisdom and spontaneity of the unlettered. Now he actually went so far as to write a letter to Count Tolstoy seeking his advice:

18 22 / X 99 Tiflis. To L. N. Tolstoy.
Lev Nikolaevich! I have read your works and come to the conclusion, that one has no right to live as I am living at present. I am finishing school and am faced with having to go on living at someone else's expense; I think the only way to avoid this is by following your advice; but to put it into practice I need the answers to a few questions: is it permissible to use money? How does one obtain land? Can it be got from the government or in some other way? How does one satisfy one's intellectual needs? Where can one obtain books, journals – if one is not permitted to use money and physical labour only brings in enough to eat? Should one allow time for intellectual work (self-education)?
P. A. Florensky[28]

One wonders whether poor Lev Nikolaevich received many such letters. To this one, at least, he made no reply. Possibly, Florensky never actually posted it. During the last school holidays of 1899 spent with his father and younger brother at Kutaisi, he read a good deal about spiritism, just as another young student, Carl Jung, who had only recently made his choice between medicine and philosophy, was doing a year or so earlier in Basel.[29] Having been brought up to tell the truth (he had been inexpressibly shocked as a small boy when one of his aunts had told an outright lie to get him into an entertainment for which he was considered under age), Florensky was credulous. It did not occur to him to doubt the claims of the spiritists, but the mystic in him disliked the laboratory atmosphere of the séances described and the scientist found the experiments insufficiently rigorous. That same summer, he was able to browse through the new 'decadent' periodical *The World of Art* (*Mir iskusstva*) which opened up hitherto quite unexpected horizons in its approach to language, painting and fine printing. In the literary part of the journal he also came upon a host of ideas which touched chords in the depths of his being with which he had lost contact during his sustained scientific marathon. The young editors of *The World of Art* considered themselves Nietzscheans to a man and had persuaded Vladimir Solov'ev to write an article for them on the Superman in an unsuccessful attempt to inveigle him into an ongoing dialogue with their journal. Florensky, together with Ern and El'chaninov, with whom he was again on speaking terms, embarked upon an enthusiastic study of Solov'ev's works, which sought to make Christianity acceptable and relevant to the modern mind. On leaving school, the three friends actually set out for Moscow together in the hopes of meeting Solov'ev, but arrived too late, for on 31 July (13 August) 1900, in an aura of prophecy and poetic vision, their new-found mentor died, aged 47. *The World of Art* published an obituary by Vasilii Rozanov which, seeking to express the relationship of philosophy to poetry in Solov'ev's works, indicated a way out of the terrible dumbness which had so far, for Florensky, blighted all possibility of communication. Rozanov wrote:

> Tiutchev was right a thousand times that everything expressible is untrue and that everything true is inexpressible. It is the same in philosophy; sometimes one wants to say that philosophers in prose are carpenters because of the imperfection of their medium, whereas poets are also philosophers, but already jewel-smiths, thanks to the refinement and iridescence of their material.[30]

By the time of his triumphant graduation at the end of the school year 1899–1900, Florensky had recovered from his depression and was directing his questing enthusiasm into new channels, once again borne along by his friends. It was not too difficult, therefore, for his parents to dissuade him from the idea of renouncing the modern world and 'going to the people', whither he had briefly inclined under the influence of Tolstoy. He himself now needed and wanted to explore a whole new world of thought and, as father and mother made clear, it was his duty as the eldest son to obtain a proper qualification which would enable him to earn a living in some congenial field of work. But which?

Florensky was now resigned to the thought he had reached an impasse in pure physics. In the natural sciences he had long had nothing to learn from his teachers. He was still only nominally a member of the Russian Orthodox Church and, although he was considerably shaken by the spiritual experience which had released him from depression and determined to advance on the religious way, he had as yet no thought of taking up theology as an academic discipline. So, without particular enthusiasm, Florensky opted for the Department of Higher Mathematics in the Physico-Mathematical Faculty of Moscow University, a choice which would have an unexpected and decisive influence on his future development.

# 3

# From the Physico-Mathematical Faculty at Moscow University to the New Religious Consciousness

> The objects of the physical sciences have ceased to be physical objects. Galileo foretold the change, saying that science does not worry about the essence, but just about the measurement of things: what is scientific in any science is its mathematical frame. But mathematical relations do not exhaust reality. They leave one other dimension, a more or less deep one of the real world. Let us call it 'the dimension of existing'. ('Essence' or *ousia* was the traditional term, connected with the verb 'to be'.)
>
> Professor Vittorio Mathieu[1]

In an attempt to describe his state of mind towards the end of his schooldays, Florensky wrote that it was as though a film had formed over his mental processes: 'the concept of the continuum which, by its very existence, excluded the miraculous'.[2]

From this mathematical expression of that generally accepted determinism which seemed to stifle all speculation, whether in the realm of physical research or in the search for insights into ultimate reality, Florensky was emancipated by mathematics and by the support he found for his own intuitions in the research and mathematical philosophy of the Dean of the Physico-Mathematical Faculty and founder of the Moscow Mathematical-Philosophical Society Professor Nikolai Bugaev,[3] whose introductory course on mathematical analysis he attended during his first year at university.

'For me mathematics is the key to a world view', Florensky wrote to his mother on 5 October 1900, 'such a world view for which there would be nothing so unimportant as not to be worth studying and nothing that was not linked to something else.'[4] Ten days later, in a letter to his father, it is apparent that the idea of opening up the mysteries of other disciplines through mathematics is finding strong confirmation in Bugaev's lectures:

One really good lecturer we have is Bugaev, who is quite famous for his published works. He scatters his lectures with jokes, aphorisms, comparisons, makes excursions into psychology, into philosophy and ethics, but does it all in an appropriate manner which only serves to give clarity to his explanations. His course is an introduction to analysis and differential equations and it is my great good luck that I shall acquire a really decent grasp of this subject which interests me more than others we are studying at the moment.[5]

In the next letter he is more specific:

> It is so agreeable to me that my thoughts coincide with the thoughts of our Bugaev; in his lectures he constantly emphasises (not, of course, in such an obvious way that everyone should notice), and in a specialist article (in *Voprosy filosofii i psikhologii* (*Questions of Philosophy and Psychology*) No. 9, 1899), he makes the point that mathematics may be compared to two children with equal rights – analysis and arythmology, that these are not exhaustively expressed by the idea of continuity, that only the analogy itself is merely a more particular example of continuity and that, when all's said and done, the all-too-brilliant successes of analysis have turned the mathematicians' heads and they've got carried away …[6]

The interesting thing about this letter is the writer's scholarly humility. Florensky cannot yet answer his father's query as to the importance of discontinuous functions in physics because, he says, 'I don't know mathematics and haven't made a study of the question for that reason.'[7] Yet he recognises the principle of discontinuity: on the one hand, from his understanding of Mendeleev's periodical system and, on the other, from observation of Rowland's spectrum, parts of which hung in the university auditorium. His mind leaps to respond to his teacher's ideas even before he has fully formulated them for himself in mathematical terms.

S. M. Polovinkin, the author of a special study on the students' mathematical circle founded by Florensky in his third year at university,[8] takes up Bugaev's term 'arythmology' which Florensky, in his letter to his father, sees as complementary to 'analysis', to make the sweeping assertion:

> Arythmology is P. A. Florensky's philosophical method and pervades his entire *oeuvre*. In the narrow sense of the word, arythmology is the theory of discontinuous functions. In the wider sense – it is the idea of discontinuity, an integral factor, according to his [Florensky's] judgment, of a whole new way of looking at the world which was then in process of formation, which was just coming into being to replace various types of analytical ways of thinking based on the concept of the continuum.[9]

The discovery of a scientifically viable way to demolish the 'film' of determinism liberated Florensky's creative imagination and rekindled his 'Eros' for further study. At last he could discuss in a proper analytical manner of which there was no need to be ashamed the kind of theorem which he had been unable to formulate, much less demonstrate, during his lonely struggle with school physics. Bugaev's 'arythmology' did not emancipate the scholar from the 'chain of reasoning' essential to the mathematical process of thought, but it did establish the possibility of breaks in the chain, the legitimacy of the 'arbitrary jump' which left room for intuition as well as speculative calculation. Above all, it created space within the framework of the scientific methodology essential to Florensky's intellectual probity to explore intuitions about the physical make-up of the universe in the light of his childhood anamnesis[10] and the mystic, intensely personal experience of his adolescence in order to build a new, holistic world view.

Once launched upon his studies at the university, Florensky, for all his enthusiasm for his professor's ideas, was not one to confine himself to the official curriculum. Attendance at lectures was supplemented by intensive reading in the Moscow libraries. He pursued the implications of his mathematical findings back to Solomon and Pythagoras and outwards through various disciplines including philosophy, psychology and aesthetics to draw tentative conclusions about an impending upheaval in the way his contemporaries would perceive the world, which would involve not only the discovery of new truths but the exhumation of truths long buried in the substrata of the past. The ideas of Georg Cantor may have originally attracted Florensky thanks to their metaphysical implications, which were better known and more widely discussed in Moscow intellectual circles than were the mathematical implications of the German scholar's set theory and work on transfinite numbers.[11] Be that as it may, the railway engineer's son set out to puzzle his way step by step through the mathematical findings on which Cantor based his metaphysics and Bugaev his 'monadological' philosophy:

> I want to proceed exclusively from the fact, and in so doing to put the more real phenomenon not behind, but before the less real. When I say 'I want' it is in the sense that, in general, I consider this absolutely essential for anyone trying to found a world view at this time.[12]

To this end, Florensky devoted many hours to a close study of Cantor and Dedekind, at the time available only in German, a language in which he still lacked facility, and elected to write his candidate's dissertation, for which he received the highest grade, 'On the characteristics of flat curves as loci for breaks in the continuum'. His work as an undergraduate was not – as has since been pointed out – entirely free from error, but it was carried out on the cutting edge of contemporary research in Moscow and earned him the wholehearted commendation of teachers and peers.

In spite of his extraordinary industry and love of independent study, Florensky did not become a recluse working exclusively to his own agenda. On the contrary, he always understood the pursuit of knowledge – as later the pursuit of salvation – as something which loses all savour unless undertaken 'together'. As a student, he initially welcomed and later sought intellectual community and he was active in founding an undergraduate sub-section of the Moscow School of Mathematical Philosophy to which he acted as secretary. The circle, chaired by the lecturer Nikolai Zhukovsky, was attended by teaching staff as well as students and, through the lecturer Dmitrii Egorov and Florensky's lifelong friend and junior by one year Nikolai Luzin,[13] played a seminal role in the further development of research in Higher Mathematics at Moscow University.

Florensky's fruitful association with the Moscow School of Mathematical Philosophy may have been providential; it was certainly not planned. The three friends from Tiflis originally set out for St Petersburg University, where the prevailing philosophy in the Mathematics Department was positivist and Florensky's inter-disciplinary ambitions would have met with little or no encouragement. It was Pavel's good fortune that only Sasha El'chaninov was accepted in St Petersburg (by the Historico-Philological Faculty) and that he and Volodia Ern had to make their way back somewhat ignominiously to Moscow, where they succeeded in registering for the Physico-Mathematical and the Historico-Philological Faculties respectively and, somewhat chastened, sought digs near a friend of the family who had exercised her influence on their behalf, Varvara Semennikova. Florensky even stayed for a while with Aleksandra Vladimirovna and Gotlieb Pekok, the parents of his father's stepmother. In spite of their warmth and kindness and the exciting circumstance of their having a daughter who had made a career for herself as a singer in Italy, the conservatism and strict monarchism of these honorary grandparents was not to be borne by a young man in search of vocation, salvation and an independent world view. Pavel at first missed his own family. The change from the Florensky home where he was loved, fed, kept clean and tidy and surrounded by an admiring gaggle of younger brothers and sisters for whom, as his letters and whole later life go to show, he felt an almost fatherly responsibility, however much he may have taken them for granted, was a severe shock to the system. In provincial yet cosmopolitan Georgia Pavel had been just another boy of mixed parentage, one of many exotic petals in a rich pot-pourri. Here, in the old Russian capital, he stood out: an almond-eyed, soft-spoken visitor from some older civilisation with a huge nose, no small talk and rather ungainly manners, a misfit and a conundrum. He wrote to his mother from the Pekoks' with a genuine twinge of homesickness:

> I keep on imagining that I'm sitting in my own room and only have to go out to find myself in our dining room, but when I do go out it is into a sort of twilit corridor. It's not actually being able to make one's wishes come true, you see, only to know it's possible

that they might. I can sit any length of time all by myself, if only I know that I can get to you if I want to, and the mere possibility of that is enough for me, for the most part; but without that possibility I'm sad and miserable.[14]

Things began to look up when he and Ern decided, for economy and convenience, to give up their respective digs and take a room together in the Nicholas the Second Students Hostel, 42 Bol'shaia Gruzinskaia ulitsa, not far from the Moscow Zoo and, according to Florensky's letters home, at that time within walking distance of open fields, though it is now considered the 'quiet centre' of Moscow. At the hostel, it was rumoured, the two friends dutifully practised the ascetic discipline of sleeping on bare boards after a frugal supper of black bread and boiled water. In winter, Florensky reinvented the time-honoured way of keeping buns and sausages fresh by deep-freezing them between the double windows and then warming them up on his reading lamp. A notice on the wall of the book-strewn room requested visitors not to distract the inhabitants from their studies by unnecessary talk, a notice generally understood to apply to Pavel's calculations rather than to Vladimir's philosophising, which blossomed in the convivial corridors and on the staircases of the hostel and only died away reluctantly at the door of their 'cell'. In the evenings, though, the studious Pavlusha was sufficiently human to make for the empty dining room where he would sit long at the piano, playing Mozart, Beethoven and his mother's beloved Schubert, or simply improvising.[15]

Once the semester got under way, Florensky did indeed find himself far too busy for idle chatter or for nostalgia. From the beginning, he subscribed, over and above his mathematical studies, to a course of lectures on psychology by Lev Lopatin and to Sergei Trubetskoi's seminar on ancient philosophy, which he attended with Ern at the Historico-Philosophical Faculty. He also engaged in serious independent study of the history of art and, with intense satisfaction, read and reread Plato. From 6 October 1902, he began to take part in the philosophical section of the new Students' Historico-Philosophical Society and undertook to contribute to a collection of translations of philosophical texts an annotated translation of Kant's doctoral dissertation, the short title of which he rendered as 'Physical monadology', with an introduction by the translator. The latter was eventually published in a theological journal in 1905 after Florensky had completed his course of studies at Moscow University,[16] but the collection for which the translation was intended never materialised.

These excursions into the humanities were, however, merely a well-planned supplement to the attempt to found a world view on mathematics, the close study of which Florensky now undertook under the tutorship of Bugaev, Boleslav Mlodzeevsky, whom he found brilliant but irritatingly mannered, Leonid Lakhtin and Nikolai Zhukovsky. In his own time, he explored the

cross-disciplinary relevance of Cantor's set theory and work on transfinite
numbers and 'actual infinity' which could, he felt, only be understood through
the new 'logic of discontinuity' and through readiness to make jumps and cross
boundaries.[17] For all that Florensky saw mathematics as the key science which
must be fully mastered during his time at university, he also needed to test out 'the
logic of discontinuity' in other disciplines with which he was at that time more
familiar: with relation, for instance, to the findings of the Dutch biologist Hugo
de Friz, the Russian botanist-geographer Ivan Kozbinsky, the German physio-
chemist Gustave Taumann and English, French and German psychologists.

Fundamental to Florensky's attempt to establish an all-embracing world
view were Professor Bugaev's essays in philosophy which impressed him by
their sanguine advocacy of 'measure in the areas of thought, will and feeling',
the accomplishment of which is perceived as 'the task of the modern philosopher, politician and artist'.[18] Bugaev's philosophy was a creative extension of
Leibnitz's monadology to include the possibility that the monads or primary
particles, which, Leibnitz posits, compose our universe, are not necessarily
'windowless', unchanging parts of the continuum set in harmonious motion by
the First Monad or God, but can merge, change and enter into mutual, loving
relations with one another. According to Bugaev, monads develop arythmically,
teleologically rather than causally, having as their final aim the enlargement
of the psychic content of each monad not only in fusion with one another (in
becoming complex diads, triads, etc.) but in order to reflect and embrace the
whole universe. As created parts, however, these monads, which both compose
and partake in the Creation, cannot encompass the Creator Which or Who is
conceived, as in Leibnitz, as the Primal Monad that will eventually unite all
others in itself.[19] Where Leibnitz, convinced that without the concept of the
continuum our scientific understanding of the world would simply fall apart,
allowed for intrasubstantial causality (or divine intervention in the order of an
otherwise unbroken chain of cause and effect), Bugaev perceived the possibility
of breaks in the chain as a natural phenomenon, observable and calculable in
mathematical terms. Cantor's set theory, which posits that a 'set' or 'group' or
'multiplicity' can be perceived as a unit, struck Florensky as confirmation of
Bugaev's concept of 'complex monads' which reflect but do not contain the
One Monad just as Cantor's sets of transfinite finite numbers reflect but do not
contain the set of absolute infinity. With mounting excitement, he was now
discovering a new language of mathematical symbols, a new, *logical* method
and a dynamic, integral world view on which he was to build all his life in later
studies of theology, art and linguistics.

Possibly it was the implications of these mathematical ideas for the human
person that the young Florensky found most empowering in his search for a
'world view'. Nineteenth-century determinism did not, according to his mentor

Bugaev, allow for any satisfactory explanation of the actions of the individual human being endowed with free will and the ability to set aims. Florensky extended the concept of 'free will' to cover faith, creativity, beauty and *podvig*, a peculiarly Russian word meaning an act of courage, endurance or ascetic endeavour which comprises sustained self-discipline and self-denial in some higher cause. Human potential for choice, faith and creativity could only be 'measured' within the framework of arythmology which allows for acceptance of effects without cause – not only in the realm of mathematics but in observed irregularities in the evolution of certain species and in the development of the individual and society.

Florensky saw clearly and – because of the catastrophic fascination for 'the abyss' he had felt since childhood – *welcomed* the fact that such acceptance opened up the ancient terror of chaos, infinity, formlessness. To admit real breaks in continuity (as opposed to the occasional, extremely rare, interference of Divine Providence posited by Leibnitz) was to deny the German philosopher's majestic concept of pre-established harmony, to admit the possibility of total breakdown. Bugaev and the Moscow School of Mathematical Philosophy tended to think that this perceived threat to the cosmic order could be averted or at least 'managed' by the study of the laws of probability and by energetic organised human response in the fields of social engineering and technico-scientific ingenuity. Humanity, it was hoped, would be strong enough to keep chaos at bay. Florensky, from the beginning, was less sanguine. He felt impelled to look chaos in the face. Rather than seek for ways of controlling reality and papering over the cracks in the old analytical system, Florensky advocated the acceptance of antinomies, of seemingly contradictory, mutually exclusive truths, and, in his new-found language of mathematical symbols, of various spatial planes permitting of various true solutions to apparently intractable problems. On 27 September 1900 he wrote to his father:

> What I want is a position equally satisfactory to the intellectual, aesthetic and ethical requirements of the human being, which means that its foundation cannot be comprehensible to fictive pure reason. For this, such a position would take account of countless spatial surfaces, the geometrical location[20] of possibilities. Only the intersection of geometric locations with aesthetic and ethico-religious surfaces can yield a single point, the point of the absolute, if not the absolute in its wholeness, then a qualitative likeness of the whole. That will be the sector penetrating to the very centre of the absolute, possibly an infinitessimally curved arc.[21]

If this sounds confusing, it must be remembered that the writer was only just beginning his course at the university and was dealing with concepts not yet fully formulated even by those authorities on which he relied. He was at this stage just beginning to 'feel' rather than to see his way towards his lifework of constructing – by leaps of intuition and painstaking trial and error – an all-embracing philosophy, and bombarded his father, whom he used as a touchstone for new ideas, with mathematical formulae and equations which no doubt conveyed a meaning beyond that which he was as yet capable of formulating in everyday language. He was determined to base his world view on the 'measurement of things', even if this meant, or rather precisely *because* this meant, doing without the comforting certainties of identity, contradiction and 'tertium non datur' and embracing paradox. 'Paul-Saul' – in Florensky's speculations on the significance of his given name – tended always to accept or reject ideas wholeheartedly, but was quite capable of believing passionately in two apparently mutually exclusive ideas at one and the same time.

It was not long before Florensky, through his contacts with the Historico-Philosophical Faculty and his reading of the 'decadent' press, became joyously aware that, though he was approaching his world view by his own road, he was not alone in the struggle against previous certainties. On the contrary, there were people of his own age, or almost a generation older, university students, burgeoning scientists, artists, poets and thinkers, especially among the so-called representatives of 'the new religious consciousness', whose thoughts were turning in a very similar direction, away from materialism and the old dualistic idealism which perceived the ideal and the real as forever separate and the former as beyond the grasp of the mind, towards a new, existential, non-deterministic understanding of a universe where matter is imbued with an ideal reality which it is possible to express, or at least to suggest, through symbols – whether mathematical or artistic. 'The need for an inclusive, many-faceted world-view is spreading through society like a tidal wave', Florensky began his first article for the new Symbolist journal *The Balance* (*Vesy*). 'It is not just a requirement of the mind, it is a deep thirst.'[22]

In fact, though their ideas were indeed gathering momentum 'like a tidal-wave' at the turn of the century, Florensky's like-minded contemporaries were still a minority, an embattled avant-garde, to whom this obscure student's talent for working on the borderline of various disciplines appeared not dilettante, as he had once feared at school, but of intense interest and very much in the spirit of the times. He owed his awareness of the unique confluence between art, thought, religious renewal in lay society and the established Church not only to the university philosophical societies, but to events in St Petersburg, particularly the convocation of the Religious Philosophical Meetings (1901–1903), which were much discussed in the Symbolist press, especially in *The World of Art,* and which were eventually reported verbatim in the journal *The New Way* (1903–1904). The 'returning' intelligentisa wanted, without renouncing science and culture, to re-establish communion with the faith of the Russian peasantry and it was precisely the ultra-refined avant-garde who thought to approach the problem through what they termed 'historical Christianity' as represented by the Russian Orthodox Church, an institution of which the intelligentsia as a whole and the religiously inclined student of mathematics and philosophy Pavel Florensky in particular knew remarkably little.

The Meetings were set up by the poet, novelist and critic Dmitrii Merezhkovsky, his wife, also a fine poet and short story writer, the sharp-tongued essayist and later memorist Zinaida Hippius, their close friend Dmitrii Filosofov, first cousin to Sergei Diagilev, and with him co-founder of *The World of Art* of which he was the literary editor, the writer Vasilii Rozanov, the artist Aleksandr Benois and a few other interested laymen, a key figure among whom was Valentin Ternavtsev, a minor official of the Holy Synod who served the refined aesthetes as a link with the secular authority that governed the Russian Orthodox Church. Ternavtsev was an eirenic figure capable, on the one hand, of explaining the ethos of the intelligentsia to a Church accustomed to look upon them as deviant apostates and, on the other, of eliciting respect for the shackled dignity of a state-run Church which yet remained the servant and guardian of doctrine and sacrament. Ternavtsev, as a practising Orthodox, and Rozanov, whose ambivalent attitude to the Russian Orthodox Church was at least 50 per cent love and who felt at home in the company of priests and believers (another world and a different culture from that of the secular, Europeanised Merezhkovskys and the majority of their friends), enjoyed the trust of Vasilii Skvortsov, editor of *The Missionary Review* (*Missionerskoe obozrenie*), and a high-ranking official who had the ear of the Procurator of the Holy Synod Konstantin Pobedonostsev. Pobedonostsev permitted the 'god-seekers', as they came to be called, to ask the blessing of the Metropolitan of St Petersburg, Antonii (Vadkovsky), for a series of meetings for discussion with the Church to be chaired by the Rector of the St Petersburg Theological Academy. To Skvortsov, the Procurator expressed the hope that these would be private meetings and kept out of the papers because he did not trust the clergy to keep the line when faced with wily dialecticians from the intelligentsia.[23]

Admittance to the meetings was nominally by invitation only and they could therefore proceed without the police presence normally obligatory to control discussion at public gatherings. Nevertheless, they were, almost from the outset, very much in the public domain, and soon became known as the sole refuge of free speech in Russia. Pobedonostsev's patience finally snapped in the spring of 1903 when polemics arising from the debates caused an open scandal in the popular press which was brought to the attention of the Tsar: further meetings were forbidden, though the themes discussed continued to reverberate in *The New Way*, in its successor *Questions of Life* (*Voprosy zhizni*, 1905) under the editorship of Nikolai Berdiaev and Sergei Bulgakov, and in the theological journals up until and throughout the 1905 Revolution. The proceedings were printed in full in the year 1906, when Russian publishing was freed from preliminary censorship.

The Meetings were unique in that they were precisely what their name implies: not just discussion groups, as were the various religious philosophical societies which sprang up in Petersburg, Moscow and Kiev after 1906, but actual 'meetings' between people of secular culture and men of the Church whose ways would not otherwise have crossed.

Florensky, Ern and Ern's new friend, the first-year Moscow student Valentin Sventsitsky, a fiery, prophet-like figure who had introduced an unprecedented note of political radicalism into the debates of their Historico-Philosophical Society, naturally followed these events with intense interest. In the autumn of 1903, Florensky, with Ern and Sventsitsky in tow, sought out Boris Bugaev (Andrei Bely), the son of the mathematics professor Nikolai Bugaev who died that same year, and a leading light in 'decadent' literary circles, a friend of the Merezhkovskys and a close friend of Vladimir Solov'ev's nephew Sergei. In spite of his youth, Bely had just graduated from university with a first-class degree in the natural sciences and was a highly innovative poet much admired by Symbolists in both capitals. Bely introduced Florensky to Valerii Briusov and the Merezhkovskys who, at the time, were cooperating closely on the journal *The New Way* which Dmitrii Sergeevich hoped to persuade Briusov to edit. The link with St Petersburg was cemented by El'chaninov who, being closer to the centre of events, was in a position to recommend Ern and Sventsitsky to the Merezhkovskys as possible contributors to their journal,[24] but it was Florensky who began to write for *The New Way* and, from 1904, for Briusov's *The Balance* on a quasi-regular basis.[25] It has since become a matter of some debate whether or not Florensky was influenced by the new religious consciousness,[26] but the fact is that he was part of it at a time when Merezhkovsky's impact on society and on the teaching Church was at its height and the publication of the debates at the Religious Philosophical Meetings were ever more starkly illuminating the choice facing the 'returning intelligentsia': whether or not to rejoin the Church.[27] When Florensky began to publish in the 'decadent' press it was not as an Orthodox seduced by exciting new ideas nor yet as an agnostic intrigued by the rediscovery of religion, but as a fellow-'god-seeker', not yet reconciled with his native church and with his own intellectual contribution to the great ongoing debate, his own nascent 'mathematical world-view', which he was eager to communicate to others who were seeking, as he was, a symbolic language capable of conveying the reality behind the symbols:

> My studies of mathematics and physics led me to acknowledge the formal possibility of theoretical foundations for a religious world view for all humanity (the idea of discon-

tinuity, the theory of functions, numbers). Philosophically and historically I became convinced that it is possible to speak not of religions, but of religion, and that this is the inalienable possession of all humankind, although it takes many different forms.[28]

Such were the ideas Florensky expounded in his articles and propounded to Bely at their first meeting, of which the poet left a vivid, profoundly perceptive, albeit ideologically skewed and, as always, fantastically grotesque account:

The whole essence was in Florensky.

With his greenish-brown, very ugly and old-fashioned face with its jutting nose he sat in the armchair as though his sharp eyes were glued to his socks; murmuring scarcely audibly through his nose, he began to speak of my father's ideas which meant much to him, in a most interesting and acute manner. Most probably it was he who initiated the visit of the three friends to me; he was the only one who was interested in the new art; and understood it. Ern at that time was slow in the uptake on aesthetics; Sventsitsky had vulgar tastes; and, anyway, Florensky could not but be interested in me as the son of my father: he valued father's ideas.

The longer I listened to him, the more he won me over; in a dying voice he murmured of models for 'N' dimensions sculpted by Carl Weierstrass and that there is Hegel's evil infinity and finite infinity according to the mathematician George Cantor. It reminded me of something long familiar from children's books; the dying voice, the little smile, sad and scared; the refined, somehow fragile intellect, not robust, not soaring in flight but crawling slowly, with a tail stretching out beyond the confines of history; Florensky should be drawn in Egyptian outline; at his feet I would put a crocodile!

. . .

Later I came upon him with Briusov at *The Balance* ... And Briusov listened respectfully, but more to the arythmologist, to the ultrarefined decadent than to the mystic or religious philosopher: again it seemed to me that he was a bas-relief from Memphis, splashed with brownish-yellow and greenish colouring, emerging from the sulphur-yellow stone and slowly making his way through the millennia, thousands of versts,[29] in order to materialise from Memphis in the 'Metropole house',[30] where *The Balance* had merrily installed itself, or maybe it was from Atlantis he had materialised: to talk about the growing significance of Egypt for the XX century.

After that he would materialise at my place, avoiding my Sunday receptions, – as though stalking; in secret fear, not meeting my eyes, murmuring amazing things: his original thoughts lived on in me.[31]

It was the beginning of a close but short-lived friendship. Bely attended meetings of the History of Religion branch of the University Student Society founded under the wing of Professor Sergei Trubetskoi, chaired by the historian Sergei Kotliarevsky and attended by long-haired radicals, a handful of Bely's own acquaintances from Gryph, the rival decadent publishing house to Skorpion, including the 'revolting' brothers Koiriansky, and a scattering of women students. The 'apocalyptic troika', as he called Ern, Sventsitsky and Florensky, formed the heart of this society and the first meeting which Bely attended with his friend, Aleksei Petrovsky, was dominated by Sventsitsky, who spoke, according to Bely, as if in tongues and had to be logically interpreted to those present by the rather schoolmasterly, deliberately simplicistic Ern. The effect on the girl students was electrifying and Bely suspected the red-eyed, red-bearded Sventsitsky of a deliberate attempt to hypnotise his public, an attempt to which Florensky remained immune.

Indeed, while preserving the ideological alliance with his friends and even dreaming of an Order dedicated to finding the way forward for serious Christian thinkers and to producing a journal more consistent in its aims and tone than *The New Way*, Florensky had already distanced himself from Ern and his new ally and moved out of the hostel to settle in his own room on the Ostozhenka, Egorov's house, No. 40. Ern and Sventsitsky had set up together in a flat on Obydennyi pereulok near the Church of Christ the Saviour which, in the fraught atmosphere of the first Russian Revolution, was to serve as a meeting place for their society at a time when student gatherings were regarded as, and indeed most often were, potentially subversive.

It was to a meeting at this flat that Bely introduced the Petersburg poet Aleksandr Blok and his wife on 15 January 1904, when he read (from *The World of Art* proofs) his piece on 'Symbolism as a world view'. Florensky wrote to his mother of this occasion:

> Professor Bugaev's son read an article of his which is soon to be published. The better I get to know him the more I understand what a remarkable person he is, deep-thinking and completely devoid of the vulgarity of 'practical life' which is to be found to a greater or lesser degree in everyone, or at least in very many people. This last time he produced an enchanting impression even on those who were prejudiced against him [presumably Ern and Sventsitsky who, Bely said, 'distrusted' him and who may well have been aware of his antipathy towards them]. I saw him once at an evening reception among a lot of famous, talented, and any rate more or less original people. And all of them in comparison to Bugaev seemed so pathetic, such nonentities, although he hardly said anything.[32]

Over the summer vacation of 1904, Florensky attempted, by post from Tiflis, to enlist Bely's support for his Order and his forthcoming journal. Bely, however, had his own group of friends, the Argonauts and, though sympathetic to the idea of a journal and ready and eager to promise them his religious poetry, was understandably reluctant to be drawn into an esoteric Order with people of whom he knew little and whom, with the exception of Florensky, he found personally repellent. Neither was he really sympathetic to the Order's declared aim of effecting a rapprochement with the Russian Orthodox Church, albeit in order to reform that institution from within,[33] still less to Florensky's own increasing commitment 'to bring about a synthesis of ecclesiastical and lay culture, to join the Church wholeheartedly, without any compromises whatsoever, to honestly accept all the positive teaching of the Church, the scholarly-philosophic world-view together with the art etc.' That, as Pavel Aleksandrovich had written to his mother on 3 March 1904, was what seemed to him the most important aim of his Order which, although in some circles it earned them a reputation for 'obscurantism', was nevertheless attracting to them an ever greater following, including some dissidents from among the clergy. The friends might differ on matter of detail but, in the turmoil leading up to the 1905 revolution, it seemed important to Florensky that they continue to present a common front and to work towards the same aims: 'I personally, and many others, am convinced of the necessity of becoming part of the Church more than of anything else...'[34]

To Bely, who never shook off the contempt for institutional Orthodoxy into which he was born and bred and whose free artist's spirit, while yearning for community and support, shuddered away from the constrictions of 'the narrow way', such a commitment was unacceptable. It is doubtful, however, if Florensky thought it necessary to be quite so definite in communication with his mystic friend – a process which he described as a kind of aerial badminton, a patting back and forth of winged thoughts and inexpressible intuitions – as he was with his positivist mother. As for Bely, in the academic 'gap' year 1903–1904 between the award of his degree in natural sciences, the sudden death of his father on the following day and his re-entering the University attached to the Historico-Philological Faculty, he came so close to equating art with religion that, to Florensky, it seemed that his poetry could almost be used for liturgical purposes. Bely was deeply affected at this time by a private and personal cult of St Seraphim of Sarov, which involved dreams of the 'simple life' in communion with the people and their Church, and by a rather unlikely friendship dating from October 1903 with Bishop Antonii (Florentsov), a charismatic spiritual director who was living retired in the Donskoi monastery.

It was Bely or his friend Petrovsky who introduced Florensky to Bishop Antonii in March 1904. Typically, Bely was to distance himself from the 'mountain heights' of discipleship within the next year, pleading his need of 'open space' as 'a man of the steppes',[35] whereas Florensky, having discovered a spiritual director capable of controlling and cultivating the boundless steppe he felt to be part of his own make-up, remained devoted to the man and responsive to his counsels to the day of his death in 1918.[36] In the spring of 1904, however, uncertain of their direction and carried away by euphoric ideas of community and friendship, the two young men together sought Antonii's blessing to become monks. It was refused and the Bishop advised Pavel to find out more about the Orthodox Church and test his own resolve by embarking on a course of study at the Moscow Theological Academy at Sergiev Posad. Postulants, he said, should be more eager to learn than to teach. Plans to reform an institution to which one had not yet fully committed oneself were clearly incompatible with monastic vows.

To the distress of his parents, particularly of Aleksandr Ivanovich who began to fear nothing would come of his brilliant son because of his constant changes of direction and unpredictable crazes for new ideas, Florensky rejected Professor Zhukovsky's offer of a research post attached to the Chair of Mathematics at Moscow University, bequeathed the secretaryship of the Student Mathematico-Philosophical Society to his friend Luzin – and accepted Bishop Antonii's advice.

# 4

# The Melting Pot: Autumn 1904 – Autumn 1908

To obtain a general understanding of something from every angle we must first
subject it to one-sided examination from each point of view in turn; synthesis is
undesirable until each and every method of perception has been exigently tried
out as a separate exercise: otherwise, instead of achieving a holistic fusion we will
obtain a confusion of elements which have not had time to take definite shape, not
harmony but din ... Yet to maintain the one is not in the least to deny the other: if
*science* can and should develop with optimal methodological rigour according to
*its own* methods, it still does not follow that scientists may not, at the same time,
see things from many different points of view ...

P. A. Florensky[1]

Florensky, unlike his one-time hero Vladimir Solov'ev, was not a natural
synthesist. On the contrary, his thought follows apparently parallel lines which
meet only in 'non-Euclidian space'. Essentially antonymical, it conceives of
fusion as dependent upon demonstrable breaks in the continuum, as capable of
taking place only in the space where geometrical points can be imagined beyond
or beneath the flat surface of what is sensually perceived.[2] Florensky's decision
to pass his own life through the differential point of commitment to the Russian
Orthodox Christian Church was, therefore, a venture into another 'space' where
other rules apply, a step from what he called 'the empirical' or empirically
perceived 'real-world' into 'the empyrean' or the heavenly, 'more real', noumenal
world symbolised by but by no means equivalent to the empirical. He did not
seek to impose synthesis by reason nor yet to retreat from the harsh light of
science into the womb of traditional faith. On the contrary, the rekindling –
through study and experience – of primal childhood wonder at the miraculous,
glimpsed through what he called the psychophysical, material world, gave the
impetus necessary for him to perceive the reintegration of self into the world as
the Body of Christ as the crossing of a real, existential threshold.

This threshold Florensky beheld 'from a different point of view'. He did
not seek to cross it 'as a separate exercise' as he had negotiated the various
approaches which had brought him face to face with it: the ways of scientific
enquiry, of mathematical calculation, of pantheistic ecstasy, of the study of
symbols, the power of words and the emblematic resonance of names and

numbers. He was not seeking shelter from the apocalyptic forebodings nor yet justification of the Chiliastic dreams which pervaded Russian society on the eve of the 1905 Revolution. Neither was his plunge into religion an atavistic attempt to immerse the troubled, contradiction-torn modern self in the primaeval chaos of an as yet dimly illumined familial and anthropological past, the 'subliminal' mother-sea he had heard about in Lopatin's lectures.[3] Though he had attempted or would attempt all these paths as separate exercises, Florensky approached the threshold of commitment to the Church quite differently: along the narrow way and through the straight gate of Jesus Christ.

If many of Pavel Aleksandrovich's contemporaries and, indeed, later readers, have failed to perceive this, as they did and have,[4] it is most probably because he did not, at the time, publish the formulation of his credo which he hammered out in the Caucasian mountains in 1904 under intense pressure from family and friends to justify his change of course.

The dialogue 'On the empirical and the empyrean' was not published until almost 50 years after Florensky's death[5] and, although he declared the intention of returning to the theme of Christ the Saviour after the publication of his major theological opus *The Pillar and Ground of Truth*, he never, in the course of a busy and varied professional life, rediscovered the impulse to reiterate the ABC of faith so passionately affirmed in this early work.

'How do you hope to be saved?' the abbot of the Trinity St Sergius Monastery had once asked three young postulants. Only the simpleton among them, Florensky's beloved *starets*[6] Isidor, had given the perfect answer: 'By the sufferings of my God Jesus Christ crucified.' Recording this after Isidor's death in February 1908 Florensky found it superfluous to comment.[7]

At the time he wrote the dialogue, however, Pavel Aleksandrovich was making his first crucial apologia in a hostile, or at best unsympathetic, environment and was impelled to spell out the reasons for his new-found allegiance to the Body of Christ which is the One Catholic and Apostolic Church (provocatively, he used the word *kafolicheskaia* as in the Latin Creed rather than the usual Church Slavonic *sobornaia*[8]).

He was, of course, also spelling out these reasons for his own benefit. The dialogue takes the form of a discussion between *A* and *B*, is dedicated to Florensky's old schoolfriend Aleksandr El'chaninov and originates from an invitation from the Merezhkovskys to publish their correspondence in *Novyi put'*. El'chaninov, having graduated from the University of St Petersburg, was soon to follow Florensky to the Moscow Theological Academy but did not – at the time – stay the course.[9] The positivist *A*, however, does not speak only for El'chaninov but advances opinions close to those held by the other all-important Aleksandr in Florensky's life, his father. Both the playful references to Faust's discussion of religion with Gretchen and the initially gentle but condescending tone of *A*'s effort to enter into the position of the new-fledged Christian *B* confirm the paternal contribution to this 'character'. Yet *A* is also, undoubtedly, Pavel Florensky's own *alter ego*, the Saul who wrote the schoolboy diaries, who fiercely desired to become a 'pure' scientist and who regarded scripture lessons and compulsory religious observance as a sad waste of time.

The discussion opens with *A*'s somewhat patronising delineation of a positivist interpretation of Jesus Christ as the hero of the improbable but, at the present state of our knowledge not altogether impossible, mythical concept of a fallen world which stands in need of redemption. Jesus Christ, according to *A*, might be said to have believed that, by sacrificing His imperfect mortal body, He would rise again in a glorious body free of sin, having shaken off the congenital sickness of fallen nature and so set an heroic example for others to follow.

'Wait', interrupts *B*. 'That is factually incorrect. Not set an example but changed everything by His death and His resurrection and so enabled nature and mankind to restore the order once lost.'

*A* agrees to admit, as a working hypothesis, even this, to him, still more improbable 'psychophysical' possibility, but suggests that, in such case, the Resurrection would serve as the reason why Jesus should be awarded or even, like certain heroes of the Ancient World, be considered to have 'earned' divine status.

'Of course not', claims the hitherto taciturn, painfully deferential *B*. 'Jesus Christ did not become a god but was and is God … Jesus Christ is not a God because He rose from the dead but rose from the dead because He is God … The Divine does not follow from the empirical but, on the contrary, the empirical manifests the Divine.' He goes on to explain more fully that, in as much as the Fall was the result of an upset in the heavenly order of things (the 'Empyrean') and was ensuant upon an act of human free will which 'damaged' the relationship between God and man:

> God, as such, could not alter the damaged state of humanity because humanity, being at once a *member* of the mystically damaged relationship and an independent entity, could not be made clean from without by any exterior agent and, at the same time, did not have the power to purge itself from within. The only solution was the incarnation of God. Because the action could not of necessity be imposed from without, God *became* man, thanks to which it became possible to act from within. Man, for his part, had not the power to act from within, so God took it upon Himself to act for him. The restoration could only be affected by a Being who, comprising in Himself the two natures, Divine and Human, would be possessed of two wills able together to produce a single moral solution. *The Godman* resolved the dilemma, either horn of which was, in itself, insoluble, by substituting for the divisive 'either' 'or' the unifying 'and' 'and', thus achieving the reinstatement of humanity. The whole crux of the matter, though, is

in the fact that Jesus Christ did not become a god but was True God while, at the same time, remaining man. It was not some kind of social mission ...

B–Paul goes on to invoke against A–Saul's benevolent but uncomprehending scepticism the Epistles of their namesake, the Apostle. It is with the help of Pauline texts fundamental to the establishment of the Christian Church that he explains the impossibility of the imitation of Christ outside a full and loving acceptance of the mystery of His dual nature which, alone, opens up the possibility of Salvation (through the Sacraments which touch upon both worlds), the final restoration of Paradise, of the Empyrean.[10] It is the Incarnation which has once and for all made this possible, but the work is continuous and requires human cooperation within the Church in the work of building the Kingdom of God on Earth. Ethics and morality are totally inadequate to this task unless the motivation be love, and he quotes the famous passage from 1 Corinthians 13.1–3 as an expression of 'the basic condition of the ethical life'. To become a member of the Body of Christ as it comes into being within the historical process it is necessary to make membership of the Church, not one's own caprices or desires, the axis around which one's being revolves. Any manifestation of the ethical life outside the love of Christ is necessarily suspect, because from the empirical point of view it is, as often as not, impossible to distinguish whether or not apparently virtuous behaviour is motivated by pride, fear, conformism, calculation or plain indolence. Only within the incomparably wider and deeper framework of the 'Empyrean' can we free ourselves of evil, from the selfish thirst for gratification which leads us to rob and slay (or at least to wish we dared to do so), or from the voluptuous impulse to inflict pain – physical or mental:

> Only the spiritual man, by inwardly acknowledging God and opening himself to His influence, can become a conscious conduit of divine forces or living member of the Body of Christ, fulfilling *his own particular* function with joy. Such a one does not live for himself and does not die for himself; whether he lives or dies, – it is for the Lord that he dies (see Romans 14.7–8). That is why such a one can say 'But we have the mind of Christ' (1 Cor. 2.16). That is why such a one can say with justice: 'Yet not I, but Christ liveth in me' (Gal. 2.20).

Having found his tongue in this categorical assertion of fundamental doctrine, B–Paul goes on eagerly for the next 14 or so pages to outline all the mathematical discoveries which, over the last four years, have confirmed for him the existence of that other dimension, that 'Empyrean' which is inherent in yet infinitely exceeds the 'empirical' and which, he says, relates to the separate elements, the distinct disciplines of the empirical world as a full chord relates to single notes.

The 'Empyrean' – B–Paul maintains – belongs 'to the invisible things of Him', which 'from the creation of the world are clearly seen, being understood by the things that are made, even His eternal power and Godhead (Romans 1.20)'.[11] A–Saul, dominant in the first part of the dialogue, can scarcely get a word in. The future Father Paul Florensky has won the argument with himself and with the enemies of his own household. The rest of his life was to be devoted to the existential implementation of this victory, which included the constant broadening and deepening of knowledge and the sharing of the many and various links perceived between the 'Empyrean' and the 'real' psychomaterial word, but not a reiteration *in extenso* of first principles. He would surely – then and later – have subscribed to the opening invocation of Derzhavin's majestic ode: 'Christ'.

> Oh You Who cannot be described
> By pen or mortal eye or ear
> Nor yet by ornate language
> But only adored in the Spirit
> And in ardent faith.[12]

The unambiguous declaration of faith in the redemptive power of the Incarnation, Death and Resurrection of Jesus Christ marked not a step on the way but a turning point in Florensky's development, no less fundamental than the 'call' which had first summoned the schoolboy Pavel to shake off his depression and set out on his search for God. 'End of university: crisis: *discovery of religion*', he writes in one of the plans for his unfinished memoirs.[13]

The sphere of biography is, by its nature, of the 'empirical', not the 'Empyrean', for it was in the 'empirical' that Pavel Florensky was called upon to live out the religious commitment which altered the course of his life and remoulded his personality. Even for the mystically inclined literati and philosophers with whom he had begun to associate in Moscow, to have entered a monastery in company with the notorious decadent Andrei Bely, or to have 'gone to the people' like the poet Aleksandr Dobroliubov, who founded his own sect, or Leonid T'an-Shansky, an aristocratic friend of Blok's and Bely's, who after January 1905 dedicated himself to the 'illegal' revolutionary underground, would have met with much greater sympathy and understanding than the decision to seek enlightenment of an institution widely regarded as retrograde, government-dominated and intellectually provincial.[14] Florensky was not the only one of his contemporaries among the intelligentsia to embark on four years' further education at the Moscow Theological Academy, but it was nevertheless an act of considerable moral courage which, for a time at least, alienated even his closest friends.

It was Florensky's great grace that, having overcome the trammels of contemporary prejudice,[15] he committed himself to this strange new world with all his heart, mind and strength and accepted all the help he could get from two very different spiritual directors. A growing enthusiasm for and admiration of the Russian people, whom he felt as the living embodiment of elemental popular culture, creative in a way the disunited, analytically minded intelligentsia could no longer hope to be, led him to seek spiritual guidance from a second, very different *starets*, Father Isidor, a simple Elder of the Gethsemane Skete, a filial of the Trinity–St Sergius Monastery. Father Isidor's spiritual nurture was, for the next four years, to complement the advice of the austerely handsome, intellectually radical and energetic Bishop Antonii. The latter clearly perceived Florensky's potential value as an 'Apostle to the Gentiles', uniquely qualified to explain Orthodox Christianity to the estranged intelligentsia. He enlisted the younger man's help in various projects of a missionary or conservationary nature,[16] discouraged him from overenthusiastic mortification of the flesh such as wearing chains under his clothes, and encouraged him to follow advice given in September 1905 by a third *starets*, Anatolii (Potapov) of Optyno-Pustyn,[17] to invoke the blessing of the Doctors of the Church on that creative, scholarly vigour which, had it not been for him, Florensky might have tried to surpress as a source of unbecoming pride. Antonii was a man who had known the world and, before his wife died and he took monastic vows and was consecrated bishop, a happily married life. He was interested in human relationships, heredity, racial types and inborn traits of character which he regarded – non-judgementally – as ineradicable, like physical characteristics, but which, carefully controlled in youth, become less troublesome as, with the years, the blood begins to flow more calmly. At the same time, he had that charisma which Florensky saw as a gift to those 'under the special protection of Sophia', shared 'sometimes' by Andrei Bely, and always by the great friend of his years of study at the Academy Sergei Troitsky. For this reason, Florensky followed Antonii's advice even when it went against his own will, against his very nature.

From Father Isidor, for whom 'events of Sacred and Church History were far more vivid than the bustle of the world', the future Father Pavel learned not so much the 'active way' as a joyous acceptance of suffering, not self-imposed but gladly borne as experience sent by a loving God, which was to stand him in good stead in the bleak years to come. He also took immense pleasure in the warm welcome accorded him in Isidor's fairytale cell with its extraordinarily fresh air, flowers, home-made, knobbly furniture, photographs, decorative sweet-papers, kitch popular prints, scraps of verse pinned like texts to the walls and 'ascetic jam' (made by Isidor himself from a mixture of berries and horse-radish – or, on occasion, salted cucumber). He appreciated the benevolent irony with which – by some miracle without pretence or offence – the gentle monk would deflate self-satisfaction, and the categorical firmness with which he would check ill-natured gossip. Above all, Florensky was attracted by the active love Father Isidor manifested in his unreserved approval of loving relationships and encouragement of harmony between friends, his passion for giving presents (the monastery no longer issued him with new robes or boots as they knew he would give them away), his ability to talk to animals and plants, his gift of bringing comfort and joy to the just and the unjust, Christian and Pagan, even, on occasion, to the confusion of the authorities in time of war and revolution, to such undesirables as a convicted agitator or suspected Japanese spy. At the same time, this most unworldly elder shared Vladimir Solov'ev's feeling of living in the last times and concern for the need to reconcile the Churches: 'The times of Antichrist are upon us. Soon there will be such a persecution of Christians that we shall have to hide', he would say. At confession, he 'sorrowed with you, but never got angry. His attitude to everything was calm, simple, even-tempered, and he would just say with love: "You need to pray more ..." The way the Starets took confession was outwardly simple, but was quite special thanks to a kind of indescribable breath of Eternity ... It was as though you were making your confession before the Universe'.[18]

For all Florensky's new and growing absorption in the Moscow Theological Academy and the Russian Orthodox Church in both the eternal and ethno-graphical sense of the word, embodied for him by the simple sanctity of Father Isidor and the sheltered austerity of the Trinity St Sergius Monastery, he did not at once disassociate himself from the troubled life of the capital. Sergiev Posad, in Soviet times Zagorsk, was on the line of rail, situated only 60 kilometres north of Moscow and one stop on from that centre of modernist art and music, the merchant Mamontov's estate at Abramtsevo.[19] The unpretentious beauty of the surrounding countryside – mixed forest, flowering meadow and clear waters – found a contemporary interpreter in the 'Russian pre-Raphaelite' Mikhail Nesterov,[20] and the wonder of the ancient monastery with its unique icons and splendid architecture played a major part in the wider modernist rediscovery of Ancient Rus'. It was as a reader of the *World of Art* and modernist literature and as a semi-foreigner, fresh from the mountain peaks, turgid seas and precipitous gorges of his southern home, that Pavel Florensky discovered and fell in love with the younger, more rustic tradition of Sergiev Posad. True, his paternal roots were deeply embedded in the ensouled, ideal, central Russia which was now revealing itself to him and, like the secrets of Nature in his childhood, inviting exploration, but these roots he had still to disinter and the process of naturalisation was only just beginning.

Meanwhile, Florensky was drawn back to Moscow, both literary and political, by his friendship with Andrei Bely, at its closest during his first semester at the

Academy, and by the intellectual ferment stirred up by Ern's and Sventsitsky's ever more revolutionary skirmishes around the borders of the Established Church. In his relations with these last a powerful factor was the schoolboy ethos, common to all Russian intellectuals whether of left- or right-wing persuasion, that to fail in solidarity in the face of government oppression is quite simply something a gentleman – or, in the parlance of the time, a 'decent human being' – does not do.[21]

With Bely, on the other hand, Florensky at this stage appeared to have had an affinity which both understood as shared revelation, or at least as shared, if fleeting, perceptions of objective noumenal truth, glimpses of the 'Empyrean'. As Florensky had written from Tiflis in the summer of 1904:

> We who have never agreed a system of symbols, can speak to one another in symbols, we understand one another. Surely that does not mean *nothing*. We are unscientific, splendid. But such spiritual unity is a fact, it requires an explanation. The surge of energies requires an explanation. The joy requires an explanation ... We cannot invent symbols, they come of themselves, when one is filled with some *other* content ... I sometimes think: later, *then* it would be good to organise anonymity. A brotherhood would publish a journal; there would be neither 'mine' nor 'yours'. That's just a dream of mine: it would all depend on how much we are to be filled with Christ. You can't do things like that to order'.[22]

To this letter Bely, who was, at the time, cooling towards organised religion, replied: 'but of course we are thinking along the same lines ... Evidently, the thought of our time is hovering on the breeze ... It is a delight and a joy to work, when you feel that "it" is itself demanding expression.' In a more down-to-earth postscript, he added: 'I've applied to the University. And how about your Academy? *I hope you'll come often to Moscow, and to see me, of course. I hope we'll see each other all the time'.*[23]

So they did – at least during the first year of their renewed studies. A contributory factor was the circumstance that Bely's close friend Aleksei Petrovsky had entered the Academy the year before Florensky. All three continued to participate in debates organised by Ern and Sventsitsky, despite the fact that all three, together with El'chaninov, who was trying to reintegrate with his old friends after his separation from them at the University of St Petersburg, were, for different reasons, reluctant to associate themselves too closely with the overtly political Christian Brotherhood for Struggle. This Brotherhood was far from being the 'Order' of Florensky's early letters to Bely. Founded by Ern and Sventsitsky together with the ex-Marxist co-editor of *Voprosy zhizni (Questions of Life)*, Sergei Bulgakov, Bulgakov's friend Aleksandr Glinka (pen-name A. Volzhsky) who had followed him 'From Marxism to Idealism'[24] and by yet another firebrand from Tiflis, the priest Iona Brikhnichev, the Brotherhood soon attracted disaffected members of the white clergy from the Circle of 32, later the Union of Church Renewal: Ioann Egorov, Grigorii Petrov, Konstantin Ageev and others.[25]

The participation of these members of the married priesthood was in line with Florensky's and his friends' original idea of working for reform within the Church, but it lent the 'Brotherhood' a pragmatic complexion quite different from the Christian mission to the intelligentsia they had originally envisaged. It involved its members directly in reform of the Church, an institution whose internal squabbles interested Bely very little or not at all. He felt the Revolution was now taking place not in the cloistered minds of a few seers but on the streets, and was inclined to agree with the Merezhkovskys and their friends that there was nothing to be hoped for from the 'historical Church'.[26]

Florensky, on the other hand, who had placed all his hope in the Church, must by now have been aware of the diversity of opinion within it. He must also have been aware that the Brotherhood's confrontational policies were undermining the efforts of the more liberal among the higher-ranking black clergy to exploit the historical moment to press for reform from above. The bishops and many educated Christians, including some of Florensky's teachers at the Academy, were exploiting the revolutionary movement to deploy intense diplomacy to incline Tsar, Synod and Government towards a policy that would ensure the continued loyalty of the Russian Orthodox Church. Their aim was to persuade the Tsar to convoke a Local Council (*Sobor*), a foregathering of bishops such as had not been permitted in Russia since 1666–1667. An all Russian *Sobor*, which, it was understood, could only be canonically convoked by the anointed emperor, was considered the essential preliminary to reform from within. The demand emanating from the likes of Ageev and Petrov that lower-ranking white clergy and even lay parishioners should participate in any such gathering was unhelpful. It was anathema to the Holy Synod and to influential forces around the throne opposed to the convocation of a Council, and enabled these to use the threat of turbulence in the Church itself to keep the always indecisive Nicholas II in a state of vacillation. Although the Tsar and his prime minister Sergei Witte understood the need to reconcile the throne and the hierarchs, Konstantin Pobedonostsev, long-serving Procurator of the Holy Synod, and many other mandarins of the autocracy, including Witte's eventual successor Petr Stolypin, still thought only in terms of control: that is, of maintaining quasi-military discipline in seminaries and theological academies, of a specially appointed ecclesiastical censorship with the right to pre-censor religious publications and even sermons, and of requiring priests to report on sedition, including information obtained under the seal of confession – this at a time when many pastors were beginning to identify with and even to lead socialist movements among their own flocks, many lecturers at the theological academies actually encouraging students to strike in favour of reform.

A Council, even one comprising only members of the black clergy, would certainly have tackled such abuses, which were widely debated in the press. As a first step, they would have sought to abolish the Synod and restore self-governance to the Church under a patriarch. A more general gathering of Christian Orthodox priests and laymen, on the other hand, would, it was felt by the moderates, have had no such clear-cut agenda and might well have degenerated into a tribune for the airing of long pent-up grievances.

Florensky adhered to neither faction. He was not, even as a first-year student at the liberally inclined Moscow Theological Seminary, particularly involved with all these political tensions. Indeed, sensitive to the prophetic forebodings of Vladimir Solov'ev, he was inclined to share Blok and Bely's conviction that the restoration of institutions from the past, such as the patriarchate, would in no way avert the oncoming storm which threatened to engulf all their lives but might, on the contrary, lead to politicking within the Church. Nevertheless, he had joined the Church in search of reconciliation, not polarisation, and he felt strongly that all arguments for reform should be addressed *ad hominem*, rather than be bandied about between party and party, and should proceed from within the Church itself. Before committing himself, he had seen, from the outside, a myriad faults and recoiled from what he perceived as the encrustation of Christian belief in a hard shell of dead metaphor, abstract doctrine and government regulation. Having penetrated this shell, he had discovered: life … scarcely flickering, as it sometimes seemed to him, yet uniquely venerable and holy. He wrote to Bely at the end of his first year at the Academy and after the two had agreed to differ:

> And it was then I realised that I would never again emerge from whence I had perceived all this … that I would not emerge, because I do not believe in spiritual spontaneous generation, I do not believe in the possibility of 'settling' the Church. 'Our' Church, I told myself, is either a complete nonsense, or it must grow from its own sacred seed. This I have discovered, and now I will cultivate it, will nurture it up to the point of mystery, but I will not throw it out to be devoured by socialists of all shades and colours. If I am at fault, Boris Nikolaevich, in so far as I do see life and holiness behind the thick encrustation of filth (thicker-seeming for me, perhaps, than for others because it is *hurting* me), if it is a sin to love that which is holy, then I am at fault indeed before all those who disagree with me. All I can say to them is: I can dissemble, but I cannot help feeling as I feel …[27]

The ideological estrangement between Bely and Florensky, which resulted in the latter abandoning his project for an extended review of the former's verse, 'until all the Symphonies should be completed',[28] was in fact precipitated not so much by politics, which were peripheral to both their world views, as by anti-climax in their personal relationship, or at least in that life-drama (*zhiznetvorchestvo*), which was a *sine qua non* of all Symbolist relationships at the time.

Florensky, Petrovsky and Sergei Solov'ev played the part of closest confidants in Bely's battle with his fellow-poet Valerii Briusov for the soul of a lady – in which Bely had assumed the role of guardian angel and Briusov the mask of demonic tempter. The lady was Nina Petrovskaia, the prototype of the unbalanced Renata, the heroine of Briusov's novel *The Fiery Angel* and Prokofiev's opera of the same name. In the novel, set in seventeenth-century Germany, the authorial persona, the *Landsknecht* Ruprecht, Renata's willing partner in the black arts and would-be rescuer, fails to win her heart from the noble Count Heinrich, who has rejected her all too human passion in pursuit of a disembodied, chivalrous ideal. The rudiments of the plot were present in their lives. Nina Petrovna, a member of Bely's Argonaut circle, unhappily married, intelligent and above all attractively sympathetic to men of genius, had formed an intense friendship with Bely, who, bent on delivering her from the dark visions induced not so much by black magic as by drugs, had shied away from physical consummation of their romance. Briusov, jealous of Bely's brilliance, moved in to seduce the despairing Nina, acquiring a fatal taste for morphia in the process, and coolly played the situation for all it was worth for the plot and characterisation of his book. On 23 November 1904, Bely received a challenge to a duel written in verse on a piece of paper folded like an arrow and entitled: 'From Loki to Baldur'. (This was the age of Wagner and Briusov invariably cast himself as the bass-baritone, the jealous, base-born or menial villain.) Help from the Theological Academy was dramatically enlisted: 'Briusov has shed his mask. Take measures. Bugaev. Solov'ev. P.S. Tell Sventsitsky.' Hot-foot from Sergiev Posad, Florensky and Petrovsky rallied round their half-demented principle. On 1 December 1904 they tried to deliver a letter to Briusov in the office of *The Balance*. He was 'not at home' and Florensky was so upset by Bely's condition and the thought of the impending duel that, for him, the whole story took on the colouring of his own 'cathartic' Solov'ean poem 'St Vladimir', written the previous winter in the style of his friend's Symphonies. Like the Symphonies, 'St Vladimir' contains coded references to contemporaries and Briusov, as 'the Panther', is already represented as a force for the powers of Antichrist, who intend to impose a type of spiritism as State Religion and seduce the population by all kinds of apparently attractive social reform. In the poem, the band of brothers who oppose the naissant Antichrist defend women and Jews from his misled soldiers, who only have to be reminded of the saving name of Christ to repent and desist from their evil-doing. Aware of their youth and vulnerability, half-amused at their own presumption, the brotherhood leads a band of pilgrims 'to flee to the mountains' where, surrounded by the gold, azure and white of Bely's poetry, the colours of Sophia, they struggle through clouds of chaos to attain flower-strewn summits. In the spirit of this self-deprecating optimism, Florensky now essayed to call Briusov to repentance:

> I understand magic and because of this I can see into corners of your soul you would rather not have exposed; and at that point your personality becomes dear to me but, at the same time (don't be angry, don't get too annoyed), it is also pitiable, at times even pathetic ...'

As Florensky saw it, Briusov had become the instrument and victim of the dark forces he himself had conjured. If only he could shake off the demons, albeit for a moment – Florensky wrote – he would understand that Bely and his allies are not his enemies but his brothers in Christ.[29] Aware that his attempts at expression were inadequate to what he was trying to say, Florensky neither published the poem[30] nor sent the letter. It was left to Bely's more practised pen to compose a poetic riposte to Briusov's challenge, 'To the ancient enemy' – and to Florensky to deliver it on 18/19 December, again to the office of *The Balance*.

To everyone's amazement and relief, Briusov, under pressure from Viacheslav Ivanov from abroad as well as from Bely's youthful friends, surrendered gracefully, acknowledging Bely-Baldur, 'Son of the sun', as victor in the poetic duel. It was not until his novel began to come out in serial form in *The Balance* in 1906 that Bely and his erstwhile 'seconds' fully realised that the older poet had been setting them up to pose for his literary experiments. By that time, however, all those involved were feeling somewhat sheepish about the whole saga.

By the spring of 1905, Florensky was – not surprisingly – becoming increasingly reluctant to abandon Sergiev Posad for the frenetic atmosphere of Moscow. Bely, in a letter of 18 April 1905, urged him to attend Merezhkovsky's lecture on Church reform at Margerita Morozova's, and, on 2 May 1905, what he described as the opening session of the Society in Memory of Vladimir Solov'ev, which would, he wrote, comprise only thoroughly committed people.[31] Obviously aware of the sobering influence of his friend's Orthodox environment, Bely added a reluctant rider to this invitation: Pavel Aleksandrovich might, if he wished to do so, bring his new friend Sergei Troitsky, a priest's son and graduate of the Theological Seminary, who was, like Petrovsky, in his second year at the Academy. Florensky's increasing rapprochement with the Church in daily life and Merezhkovsky's and his circle's increasing estrangement from it may well have been at the bottom of 'our differences this winter' which Florensky mentions at the beginning of his next letter to Bely of 15 July 1905 from the neutral distance of a Tiflis engulfed in revolutionary and racial disorders. Indeed, the troublous times were reflected in a general disruption of relationships. Bely continued to respond to Florensky on a personal level but not to his friends. Ern and Sventsitsky's Christian Brotherhood for Struggle had, he wrote back to Florensky, knocked all the religion out of him; talk of Church reform now made him 'sicker than castor oil'. He was, he explained, giving careful thought to sociology and the ethics of terrorism, but he had been glad of Pavel Aleksandrovich's letter explaining his personal adherence to the Church and thought that somewhere deep down he himself was 'probably' still a Christian. Florensky did not reply to this letter until more than a year later when, on 31 January 1906 he wrote: 'I remember you often, dear Boris Nikolaevich, but the closer I feel you, the less I want to come and see you, as I know that Moscow and everything about Moscow – will put me in a bad mood ...'[32] The letter is in a minor key; Florensky confides the difficulty of achieving perfect friendship, naked soul to soul, and complains he has nowhere to publish his work: for some it's too modernist, for others too mathematical, for yet others too mystical and theological. On the one hand, he cannot renege on the method he has adopted, on the other, he feels that, by lapsing into unproductive study and meditation, he is not fulfilling his appointed task. 'The freedom God grants is such that it forces one to take life seriously ...' This was the last surviving letter until 1910.[33]

Nevertheless, Florensky continued to keep in touch with Ern and Sventsitsky, however much he may have deplored their combative approach to Church reform, and with the Vladimir Solov'ev Society, which did not open officially until the autumn of 1906,[34] and in which, together with Bulgakov and Nikolai Berdiaev, his old friends were extremely active. He also valued the opportunity to publish afforded by Put' (The Way), financed by Morozova and closely associated with the Vladimir Solov'ev Society and many of his former friends and mentors from Moscow University days.

It was not necessary for Pavel Aleksandrovich to make the journey to Moscow, however, to experience the seismic shocks which were convulsing Russian society. The Church itself was in ferment. Pobedonostsev had retired as Procurator of the Holy Synod after the publication of the Tsar's October Manifesto and was replaced by a liberal friend of Count Witte's, Prince Aleksei Obolensky, who presided over the institution of a pre-Council Commission, membership of which was drawn from black and white clergy and from lay professors from the theological academies, to discuss the make-up and agenda of the Sobor, which everyone, it had seemed, from the Tsar downwards now agreed should be called. The Commission opened on 6 March 1906, at the Aleksandr Nevsky Monastery in St Petersburg, and embarked on an ambitious programme of preliminary work – ignored by the rumbustious and vituperative First Duma and shaken by the after-shocks of revolution which continued to undermine the society of which the Church had once been the very heart, but which now appeared all too ready to marginalise Christianity altogether. Within less than two months reaction set in. On 17 April Witte was dismissed, Stolypin appointed in his stead and Obolensky replaced by Prince Aleksei Shirinsky-Shikhmatov, whom Witte, aptly enough, had once nicknamed 'Check-mate', and who at once suspended the work of the Commission. In July 1906, the dissolution of the First Duma provided an opportunity for a reshuffle and Petr Izvolsky became Procurator of the Holy Synod for the next three years. Although he reconvened the pre-Council Commission on 25 October 1906, he gave the delegates only until 15 December, when the Commission was summarily disbanded by the Tsar himself. To Stolypin it was clear that to summon a full Local Church Council, especially if laymen and white clergy were permitted to take part, was to risk disruption. His policies, successful in the medium term but harsh at the time and disastrous in the long run, envisaged economic reform, control of socially combustible ideas and ruthless repression of revolutionary activity. Throughout 1906 and thereafter even the most moderate and enlightened ecclesiastical reformers, the loyal opposition such as Metropolitan Antonii (Vadkovsky), who had not long ago given his blessing to the institution of the Religious Philosophical Meetings in St Petersburg but had refused it to the League of Russian People, were subjected to calumny and abuse in publications sponsored by the League, a reactionary organisation linked to the Black Hundreds who had the ear of the Tsar.

Nevertheless, until the dismissal of Witte and for some time thereafter, the freedoms of speech, assembly and publication granted by the October Manifesto held. It was clear to everybody that this period of relaxation would be brief and that the authorities were now preparing to use force to quench dissent. Society seized the moment to vent its indignation loud and clear – or, at the very least, to warn and plead with the powers that be to enter a process of reconciliation rather than retraction. The Theological Academy itself was in ferment, the teachers as radicalised as the students.

Florensky was carried away with the rest. On 18 March 1906 he sent a postcard to Bulgakov in Kiev offering to distribute a proclamation from the Christian Brotherhood for Struggle together with an 'Open letter to the Bishops', which he himself had been instrumental in preparing, and indicating he had already put Ern in touch with sympathetic priests[35] – taking care, in proper conspiratorial fashion, to post it from Moscow rather than from Sergiev Posad. Four days previously, on the Sunday of the Veneration of the Holy Cross, he himself had pronounced a moving penitential sermon, 'The cry of blood', prompted by the death sentence carried out on Lieutenant Shmidt, declaring that 'every shot of the firing squads was aimed at the body of Christ'. It was, as befitted a Lenten sermon, a call to repentance without respect of persons. We are oppressing those that feed us, Florensky said, and our prayers cannot rise to God unless we repent.[36] The sermon was enthusiastically welcomed by fellow-students at the Academy who clubbed together to print it in the form of a brochure which the Brotherhood, in Moscow, was quick to circulate, and which, through Ern, soon reached as far as Brikhnichev in Tiflis. It was not intentionally inflammatory. Shmidt, who had conducted himself bravely and given a moving speech at his trial, describing himself as no ringleader but an ordinary man caught up on the elemental tidal wave of life yet refusing to renege on his support for the mutinous sailors under his command in the 1905 Sevastopol Insurrection, was a sympathetic victim figure, later immortalised by Pasternak. Florensky was not so much playing politics as following the example of Vladimir Solov'ev, whose warning that blood begets blood in an open letter calling for mercy for the assassins of Alexander II had cost him his university post in 1881.[37] 'The cry of blood' likewise anticipated Lev Tolstoy's 'I cannot keep silent' of 1908. In the turbulent spring of 1906, however, the consequences for its youthful and obscure author were more extreme. The Academy authorities, many of whom were sympathetic to the emotional thrust of their most brilliant student's sermon, looked on aghast as the willowy young bookworm Florensky, together with another student who had played a conspicuous part in the student meeting and composition of the open letter to the Bishops, Mikhail Pivovarchuk, were hauled off to gaol by the Secular Arm and sentenced to three months in the rough and tough Taganka Prison. Florensky served only ten days of his sentence and both he and Pivovarchuk were released in time for Easter thanks to the energetic intervention of the Rector of the University, Bishop Evdokim and of Grigorii Rachinsky, founder and chairman of the Vladimir Solov'ev Society, guardian of Sergei Solov'ev and friend of Andrei Bely. Naturally, Florensky's former schoolfriends, who were themselves in constant trouble with the law, though none as yet had been actually arrested, were profoundly concerned for 'poor Pavlusha'[38] – although, to judge by the slightly amused tone of their letters, they felt that he was a most unlikely revolutionary hero. Briefly, Florenky's fame spread throughout Russia and even the Merezhkovskys momentarily forgave him his adherence to the 'historical Church' because they felt his sermon was from their own 'future Church'. They suggested he be persuaded to write his 'thoughts in prison'[39] as a contribution to a collection of revolutionary articles they were planning to publish in Paris, a suggestion deplored by Bulgakov as totally lacking in tact and understanding. Florensky himself never sought to make capital out of the incident and, at the time, was welcomed back into the academic fold. Undoubtedly, though, it restored his credibility and enhanced his reputation amongst his old friends from the intelligentsia.

In 1907, Florensky paid a last *homage* to Andrei Bely with the publication of his own poems under the derivative title *In the Eternal Azure* (*V vechnoi lazure*).[40] He also became a member of the Circle of Seekers after Christian Enlightenment (Kruzhok ishchushchikh khristianskogo prosveshcheniia), founded by the now firmly Orthodox ex-disciple of Lev Tolstoy, Mikhail Novoselov and the *zemstvo* deputy Fedor Samarin. The Circle included some members of the Vladimir Solov'ev Society such as Bulgakov and Trubetskoi and, for a time, Berdiaev and Marietta Shaginian, but was more conservative and neo-Slavophile in orientation. The membership extended to Pavel Mansurov, director of the Foreign Ministry archive, Valentin Kozhevnikov, disciple of Nikolai Fedorov, the new Rector of the Moscow Theological Academy Bishop Fedor (Aleksandr Vasil'evich Pozdeevsky) and the priest Iosif Fudel. As the years went by, it was this circle rather than the Vladimir Solov'ev Society that Florensky was to find compatible and, though he never totally disassociated himself from Ern and El'chaninov, he was, in the years between the revolutions, to collaborate more closely and amicably with Novoselov, Bulgakov and later, of course, from 1909, with his own Rector, Bishop Fedor – altogether more sober if less colourful associates. The convergence of his worlds, the world of the Church and the world of the radical artistic and scientific intelligentsia, the one represented for him by the serenity of Sergiev Posad, the other by smoke-filled rooms in Moscow, the one encrusted in tradition, the other tattered and centrifugal in the aftermath of one revolution and in expectation of the next, was the natural outcome of Florensky's steady will to achieve an all-encompassing world view implemented through experience. From April 1906 he was secure enough in his vocation to resume a correspondence with his mathematician friend Luzin, recovering at the time from a nervous breakdown in Paris. The world of the Church, however, was gradually gaining ascendance over heart and mind.

From the beginning of Florensky's four-year course at the Moscow Theological Academy, the day-to-day experience of community life in proximity to the most holy and historic of Russian monasteries, the excellent resources of the Academy Library, the new friends and new fields of study were complemented by a stimulating exchange of ideas with the teaching staff. The director of studies for Florensky's thesis, Professor Sergei Glagolev, thought so highly of his pupil that, from the beginning of Florensky's third year at the Academy in the autumn of 1907, he encouraged him to assume the teaching of an in-house course on the history of philosophy. Professor Aleksei Vvedensky was an acknowledged authority on Kant whose opinions had influenced Florensky's thinking on the German philosopher's monadology in his paper for the student's philosophical circle at Moscow University. He saw the introduction to Florensky's translation into print in the Academy's journal.[41] Vvedensky was the founder of the Ontological School, a school inspired by the tradition of St Sergius, the ethos of which accorded well with Florensky's own inclinations and practice and was predominant at that time in the Moscow Theological Academy and its organ *Bogoslovskii vestnik*.[42]

It was Vvedensky who, in December 1904, had initiated the correspondence between Florensky and Vladimir Mashkin (Archimandrite Serapion) an ex-pupil of Vladimir Solov'ev's with a degree in mathematics, who had spent four years on Mount Athos before taking vows. Mashkin had elaborated a system of Christian philosophy based on mathematics and was pleased to invite the exceptional student who appeared to share so many of his interests to visit him at Optyno-Pustyn, where he was living in retirement. However, he died in February 1905 before a meeting could be arranged. Florensky spent part of the summer vacation (August–September 1905) working on Mashkin's archive among the fabled *Startsy* of Optyno-Pustyn and, with the blessing of the Father Superior, took the manuscript of a 2,250-page philosophical treatise and other papers back with him to the Academy to prepare them for publication. Although unable to complete this vast editorial task, Florensky gained much from the posthumous contact with a like-minded spiritual explorer in search of a mathematics-based world view illumined by religious experience. At the same time, Mashkin represented a welcome continuity of the tradition of Vladimir Solov'ev. Florensky freely acknowledged the influence of Mashkin's ideas on his thesis,[43] and took to heart the monk's teaching that, above and beyond all ideas, 'the art of arts is life itself as lived in God'.[44]

For all Florensky's complaints to Bely of the difficulty he experienced in finding publishers during these transitory years, adherence to the teaching Church opened up not only new subjects and new fields of interest but also new outlets for publications, particularly for translations.[45] True, the semester essay on 'The concept of the Church in Holy Writ' was not published in Florensky's lifetime,[46] but an attempt to stimulate a Rozanov-style[47] correspondence about 'Questions of religious self-knowledge', calling upon practising Christians to share experience of the Sacraments with the readership, was serialised in the modest but comparatively widely read journal *Khristianin*, then republished in pamphlet form.[48] The Academy's own journal *Bogoslovskii vestnik* printed Florensky's introduction to El'chaninov's essay on Speransky, in which he advocated the need for a systematic study of mystic literature (as with his early interest in Spiritism, very much along lines later elaborated by Carl Jung) and his own article on Flaubert's *The Temptations of St Anthony*, highlighting the absence of joy in the French novelist's account of the Saint's resistance to temptation and the consequent emasculation of the temptations themselves.[49] *Bogoslovskii vestnik* also, albeit with some misgiving, published the somewhat chaotic but profoundly interesting and revealing article 'On types of growth' which Florensky wrote back in his native Caucasus, in his home city of Tiflis, over the summer vacation of 1905, 'in a conflagration of bombs and strikes', a piece the editor found 'not without interest but difficult and very mathematical',[50] but which concludes, in an unexpected lurch towards intensely personal experience, with the first spiritual love letter to Sergei Troitsky, the 'quiet and tender friend' to whom are addressed all the subsequent 'letters' of

*The Pillar and Ground of Truth*, the dissertation in epistolary form which was
to constitute – at least until the recent exhumation of unpublished later work –
Florensky's chief claim to fame as a theologian.[51]

The thrust of all Florensky wrote as a student of the Theological Academy,
whether the approach were through philosophy, literature, mathematics or
theology, was the quest for 'living religious experience' as the 'only legitimate
way to understand the dogmata'[52] but, to begin with at least, he was throwing
his net wide and with an unpractised hand. 'Holistic fusion' continued to elude
him.

Of all the works prepared at this time, it is the most spontaneous and least
ideological, the collection of *chastushki* from the district of Kostroma,[53] which
stands as a *unicum* amongst Florensky's publications yet as an integral part
of his experience of life. The study was a product of the author's deepening
interest in what Viacheslav Ivanov would have called the 'synthetic' folk culture
of Russia[54] and of his friendship with Troitsky, who invited him for part of the
1905 summer vacation and several times thereafter to stay with his family at
his home village of Tolpygino in the district of Kostroma. Here the two young
academicians combined such praiseworthy activities as preaching to the local
peasants and organising lending libraries with collecting *chastushki*, the impro-
vised quatrains which were generally held to be characteristic of the transition
from folk song to factory jingles but which Florensky presented as an ancient,
quite independent genre, having much in common with Martial's epigrams
and various oriental forms such as the Japanese *tanku*. Together with Troitsky
and his family, a student friend Vladimir Il'insky and one of the local peasants,
they amassed a great deal of material that shed valuable light on a fast-fading
oral tradition and took pains to provide exact phonetic transcriptions of the
dialect. In his introduction to the collection, Florensky pointed out not only
the similarities between the *chastushka* and ancient forms but its affinities with
contemporary poetry: parallelism; sudden, often purely associative, shifts of
theme and register; sound-painting (onomatopeia, assonance, alliteration);
individualism; subjectivism; ahistorical concentration on the present moment
to the exclusion of past and future. The book became very popular with
Modernist poets. Hippius and Briusov had already attempted imitations of the
*chastushka*, Bely exploited its rhythms extensively in his post-1905 poetry and
Blok, who put the genre to such brilliant use in the high poetry of *The Twelve*,
kept his copy of Florensky's book throughout the period of War Communism,
when cold forced him to sell or feed to the stove a good part of his library,
including the more celebrated *Pillar and Ground of Truth*.

As he worked on the collection, Florensky eagerly imbibed the rhythms of
daily life in the Russian countryside, especially in Sergei's home. The harmony

he perceived between the priest's family and peasant parishioners, the strong supporting fabric of custom, fast and feast interwoven with everyday observance and the interpenetration of seasonal work, marriage, birth, death, eating and drinking with ancient religious insights combined to implant and firm in a slowly growing conviction that his own priestly forebears, some of whom had hailed from this very Kostroma region, had gone fatally astray when they abandoned their calling. The poem 'Kostromskaia storona', dedicated to Sergei 'with whom I experienced all this', is a wistful attempt to conjure the elusive spirits and ritual celebrations of these ancestors from the whispering leaves, wreathing mists and green-bearded branches of the Kostroma countryside.[55]

Always acutely sensitive to nature, Florensky responded with open heart to this sparsely inhabited northern land with its huge, clean-floored forests, mighty River Volga and sturdy, wooden buildings. Sergei was for him the embodiment of its freshness, serenity and simplicity. True to his upbringing and early training, the priest's son was a straightforward advocate of traditional Christian virtue, intellectual humility and moderate asceticism. The Promethean Florensky, child of luxuriant Colchis with its smoking, sulphurous abysses, perfumes, poisons and sunscorched summits, had always detested moralising of any sort and was not naturally humble. In Sergei, though, the beauty of simpler certainties struck him as a revelation of luminous goodness, an incarnation of the Sophianic principle granted to him personally and comparable to the various manifestations of Sophia through lyrical, chivalrous love so ardently preached at the time by Bely and Sergei Solov'ev in their thoroughly confused cult of Liubov' Mendeleeva and 'certain others who enjoy special grace'[56] as perceived through the prism of Vladimir Solov'ev's and Blok's poetry.

> Once he and I had to wait with the railway guard all the cold night long in his shelter at the station. Drained by two sleepless nights and chilled to the bone, I involuntarily let my head fall on my friend's knees and drifted off to sleep. In my sleep he appeared to me as an Archangel and I knew he was shielding me from all evil powers. Perhaps, in that cold night, hungry and exhausted, I was completely at peace for the first time in my life …[57]

The young men made a pact of friendship in Christ, celibacy and mutual fidelity, which Florensky regarded as binding as a marriage or monastic vow:

> Always, whether serious or sparkling *divina levitate* (with divine frivolity), he was true to himself: always trusting and chaste as the dove; always wise as the serpent … Pure and translucent in the exact meaning of the words, untarnished and spotless. Perhaps the most suitable word is virginal – virginal not in the sense of παρθενεία or ἀγαμία (celibate) but in the sense of ἁγνεία (immaculate).[58]

At the same time, there was nothing pale and wan about Sergei. A vegetarian who neither smoked nor drank, he was yet open and even-tempered, with an earthy sense of fun and ardent sympathy for reform in Church and countryside rooted in unaffected fellow-feeling for the peasants amongst whom he had spent his childhood. Even when playing the fool, laughing and talking nonsense, his friend noted, Sergei radiated serenity. Pavel had actually checked this out, never taking his eyes off him for a whole day in their shared quarters. In spite of the 'poetic' language which had a pernicious effect on his prose and betrayed him into embarrassing rhapsodies about morning dew and lilies of the valley, Florensky was not a sentimentalist at heart: rather a titanic, passionate, unquiet spirit. His devotion to the priest's son, lovingly approved by Father Isidor, who warned only against possible quarrels, whatever perturbation it may have touched off in the more sophisticated mind of Bishop Antonii, was, at the time, life-enhancing and youthfully high-spirited.

One joint endeavour was the founding of the MDA[59] Philosophical Society in the autumn of 1905. Troitsky, following in El'chaninov's footsteps, acted as go-between between the reclusive Florensky and his peers in his capacity as secretary to the nascent society and as official opponent to Florensky's paper for the society on 'Dogmatism and the dogmata',[60] the first attempt to formulate an approach to problems which he was to examine in detail in his dissertation. At the opening session, attended by the editor of *Bogoslovskii vestnik* and by the Rector Archbishop Evdokim (Meshcherskii, Rector from 1903–1909) as well as by fellow-students, Troitsky spoke to his friend's paper using the familiar 'thou' and in robust terms which made it clear that the text had been argued over in the process of composition in the privacy of their shared study. Florensky had elected – provocatively enough – to put the case, made by the god-seekers at the Religious Philosophical Meetings in St Petersburg (1901–1903) and published in their journals in prose and poetry, for the revitalisation of existing dogmata and the possibility of a new, creative approach – not arrogantly and dismissively as they had done 'from outside', but in terms acceptable to the Church, from within, as from one of their own. Quoting Merezhkovsky, Minsky, Viacheslav Ivanov and others who sought direct religious experience, relevance to contemporary life and, in particular, a clarification of the Church's teaching on the Third Person of the Holy Trinity and the imminence of the Last Days, he pointed out with gentle humour that dogmatic theology – even, if not *particularly*, amongst the truly Orthodox – produced 'politely-smothered yawns' instead of that 'burning within' felt by the disciples who walked with the Risen Christ towards Emmaus. To the ex-seminarian Troitsky, it seemed as though his clever friend were undermining the very certainties around which their 'lesser brethren' constructed the edifice of faith: 'I've already listened to your paper and wasn't satisfied with it then and still feel the same way', he burst out at the beginning of the debate and insisted throughout that the requirement that dogma should formulate personal religious experience was too subjective and confusing for weaker minds and objectively unreliable in so far as it valorised 'soul' or 'heart' at the expense of 'spirit' and 'truth'.

The editor of *Bogoslovskii vestnik* Ivan Popov was much less combative: 'Your pain is quite understandable and shared by all: most of the dogmata are indeed no longer comprehensible to us'[61] was his first reaction to the unusual but patently sincere second-year student's paper. Summing up the ensuing debate, Popov concluded that 'the speaker has shown a spirit of Christian filial respect as opposed to the all too common emphasis on the servile torpor into which we [the teaching Church] have fallen'.[62] This was fair enough. Florensky had chosen to set before his colleagues and teachers the premises from which he had moved to become a son of the Church, but his feelings about the Merezhkovskys and their adherents were already mixed and he had, indeed, warned that he would feel bound to oppose them if they persisted in denigrating and rejecting it.[63]

Indeed, though he continued to base his arguments on Symbolist thought and poetry, Florensky appears, by the middle of his second year at the Academy, to have lost his close ties with the Symbolist press. An article on Hamlet which originated as a school essay and had then been offered to *The Balance* and undergone preliminary editing in 1903 remained unpublished but was reworked in 1905 and dedicated to Troitsky. Florensky saw Shakespeare's hero as a religious type, not so much as indecisive and passive as a tragically split personality, actively engaged in a Promethean struggle to call God to account for the evils of the world. 'Shakespeare', he wrote, 'lays bare deeply hidden processes in the development of the spirit at which, though we experience them, we scarcely dare to guess and sometimes prefer not to guess.'[64] Caught on the cusp of a changing world, engaged in a hopeless yet mandatory struggle to set right disjointed time, Hamlet knows that it is against his tragic duty to opt out by taking his own life. It is laid upon him to do what he can, though as a true tragic hero he is pitted against forces more powerful than himself and fated to succumb. We should not, Florensky concludes, dropping the scholarly mask as he drops it at the end of 'On types of growth' and addressing himself directly to the 'quiet friend' who is *not* divided against himself, refuse the poor Prince the only help we can offer – our prayers.

On a lighter note, at the beginning of the Hamlet article, Florensky relishes the ineptitudes of the eighteenth-century author Sumarokov's adaptation of Shakespeare's play. Ophelia, Claudius and all the evil-doers suitably dispatched, is preparing, in a most implausibly 'happy' end, to wed Hamlet and sends her triumphant bridegroom to greet his rejoicing people whilst she, anon, retires 'to give Nature its due'. To Sumarokov, this meant to attend the obsequies of her father, but the snort of laughter the phrase provokes in Russian no less than in English is of a piece with the Rabelaisian sense of the absurd which undoubtedly contributed to the fun of collecting the *chastushki*. Florensky complained in his preface to the collection that the censorship had most regrettably forbidden publication of verses which were considered excessively bawdy. The peasant habit of calling a spade a spade was, he considered, a healthy habit in comparison with the vogue for pornography and innuendo which was setting in among the intelligentsia after the 1905 Revolution: 'In the sense of frankness of expression and absence of euphemisms, the *chastushki* speak out with such total frankness that there is nothing left for the singers to imply: everything has been roundly called by its own name.'[65]

Florensky's flashes of ribald humour and unshockable addiction to plain-speaking have, in some recent criticism, earned him a reputation for 'scurrility',[66] but this is too 'academic' a perception of a trait in his make-up which served as a safety valve. At Tolpygino, he wrote an 'Elegy on the dulling of P. Florensky's wits': 'Alas, alack, unhappy P. Florensky has forgotten Kant and Hegel over gingerbread and pancakes, he eats and drinks so abundantly he has forgotten "the question of faith", has fallen on his bed and lies there like a collapsed crocodile!'[67] Such occasional outbursts are understandable, at times even endearing, in a subtle scholar and scientist always straining to live and work at the limit of endurance; still more so in a somewhat inhibited, rootless young man in search of salvation but in love with Russian frost and forest, log huts, home-cooking and the stamp of dancing feet ...

Florensky's frequent visits to Tolpygino led him to invite his friend Troitsky to spend part of the 1907 summer vacation with his family in Tiflis. Ol'ga Pavlovna found Sergei easier to talk to than her own son and the whole family welcomed him with open arms. He reciprocated and, having completed his course at the Academy, decided that autumn to take up the offer of a teaching post in the Georgian capital. As to Florensky himself, the slow process of his metamorphosis into or reversion to the type of traditional Orthodox *Batiushka*[68] represented by his paternal ancestors, never totally completed, now took a more painful turn. Though very busy with his new teaching commitments and working hard on his dissertation, which we shall examine in greater detail in its published forms in the next chapter, he was lonely without his friend in the high-vaulted cell which served as his study-bedroom and, at times, depressed.

The winter of 1907–1908 was one of loss and deprivation. On 22 January Aleksandr Ivanovich Florensky died. However much he may have criticised his son's decision to enter the Theological Academy, he had been a kindly father and an appreciative correspondent who understood Florensky's maths-speak. In a letter of July 1936 from Solovki, Florensky recalled how he was sitting at his table by the window at twilight and somehow lost all sense of having grown up, as though he were still in Tiflis:

> Next to me on my left sat Papa, watching attentively as he used to when I was doing my homework, saying nothing. I was so used to this that I paid no attention, only felt glad. Suddenly it came to me that I was not in Tiflis but in Posad. I raised my eyes and looked at Papa. I saw him quite clearly. He looked at me, evidently waiting for me to understand that it was indeed him and that this was surprising, then suddenly his visage faded, as if drained of colour, and disappeared – did not leave, did not dissolve, but began very swiftly to lose reality, like the fading of a photograph. A few hours later I got the telegram telling me of his death. (*S* IV, p. 502).

On 4 February the natural father was followed by the spiritual; at 11 o'clock that night, Father Isidor, having sent away the young monk who had looked after him during the last days of a long, wasting illness, met his Maker as he thought fit, in solitude. Florensky composed an affectionate and appreciative *in memoriam* 'Salt of the earth', written in popular form and serialised first in the journal *Khristianin* then published as a book by the Trinity St Sergius Monastery.[69]

Pavel Aleksandrovich completed his course of studies at the Academy with highest honours as the best student of the year in the summer of 1908. Yet his graduation was an anti-climax.

The heady excitement and optimism of the Revolution was dying away, and this was to be felt in Church circles no less than among the intelligentsia and on the street. Stolypin was firmly in power and, however talented an administrator he may have been, his policies in 1908 were deliberately repressive. The Tsar had not called a Local Council and was now unlikely to do so. Approved by the State, Bishop Antonii (Khrapovitsky) had instituted a methodical crackdown in the theological academies.

As for the Christian Brotherhood for Struggle – it had gone into self-destruct mode. Sventsitsky, though he was later to repent, had involved himself in a series of scandalous quarrels and sexual misdemeanours crowned by the publication of a novel[70] in which he pilloried himself as the demonic, authorial hero and depicted characters clearly resembling Ern, Bulgakov and other 'brothers' as religious and revolutionary mountebanks, so plunging the whole movement into disrepute and disarray. Ern withdrew into marriage, philosophy and, increasingly, ill health. During a brief spell of imprisonment he had caught cold sleeping on a hard stone floor and suffered an inflammation of the kidneys which became chronic and which, in 1917, was to claim his life. 'Brothers' from the priesthood either conformed or – sooner or later – were defrocked. Some, like Stalin's old schoolmate at the Tiflis Seminary Brikhnichev, were drawn towards the more literate, sectarian peasantry and new careers in publishing and journalism. Others founded their own breakaway congregations such as the harsh Golgotha Church led by Bishop Mikhail (Semenov) and briefly embraced by Marietta Shaginian. El'chaninov, whose involvement with the Brotherhood had been peripheral and eirenic, drew closer to Florensky and spent much time with him in Sergiev Posad, but the old dream of a gentle, idealistic, anonymous order, active for reform within a benevolent, receptive Church, lay in fragments about their feet.

Everywhere, the civic freedoms granted by the October Manifesto of the autumn of 1905 were being eroded. The experiment in secular parliamentarianism represented by the first two impractically radical Dumas had failed and the Third Duma, elected on a more limited franchise, was felt by many to be an ineffective talking-shop. Bulgakov, the only one of Florensky's immediate circle to have offered his services as a deputee, was disillusioned with practical politics and religious speculation. As early as 1906 when his newspaper *Narod* (*The People*) had been shut down in Kiev he had felt this to be providential, because of his and his friends' religious inexperience. The Merezhkovskys and their circle now seemed to him no better than refined Sectarians and he, like Florensky, had begun to feel strongly that the Orthodox Church represented the only real way forward, but, for him, its continued subjection to the State remained an insurmountable barrier to entering the priesthood.

Florensky, too, did not see the way ahead at all clearly. His commitment to the Church was irrevocable but the next step, to take holy orders, was conditional upon either choosing a suitable bride and entering the married priesthood or taking monastic vows. Bishop Antonii still firmly opposed his spiritual child's desire to pursue the latter course and Florensky had no inclination to marry. So, without much enthusiasm, as a stop-gap, he accepted the offer of a teaching research fellowship. In the autumn of 1908, after two trial lectures on 'The cosmological antonyms of Kant' and 'The roots of idealism in human nature',[71] he was officially installed at the Moscow Theological Academy as a research fellow (*dozent*) and lecturer extraordinary on the History of Philosophy.

# 5

# The Quiet Mutiny

There was a time: I thought to rise
Upwards in a jet like a fountain
But, having attained the crest,
I am cast down from the height.
...
Perdition is near, – God is far
And, in my soul, I dare not pray
To Him. I have not the strength.
I keep silence with lowered eyes.

You, meek one, lamb of God,
You pray, if you can,
Say a prayer in chaste humility
For those who are sick at soul.

Pavel Florensky
16 March 1907[1]

Vladimir Ern, who had been present at Florenky's well-received trial lectures at the Theological Academy in September 1908, wrote to his wife that Pavlusha had presented them with an elegance that matched the content and, having allowed his hair to grow and fall in curls before his ears, was looking exotic and impressive – 'in general, something of an Ancient Egyptian effect'.[2]

All the more poignant is the contrast of Florensky's self-portrait for that autumn, perched on a wooden crate which served him as both seat and work-table, cold, lonely and rather hungry. At the beginning of term the young lecturer had moved into a detached wooden house that stood in its own little plot of land with three birch trees in the street of St Peter and St Paul.

It was especially creepy in the evenings. It would grow dark. The rain would begin to spot, knocking lightly on the tin roof. Then, suddenly, it would come on more heavily, – drawing out the dry sound of the ticking clock. And – the rain, – came down in sheets. The roof shuddered in mortal anguish and cold despair. There was a hard pitter-patter like chunks of frozen earth on the lid of a cheap board coffin. It felt as though my chest was bare and the cold rain was trickling down into my tired, discouraged heart. That cold autumn rain breathed gloom and unease. In the whole house there were but two living beings, myself and the clock; except that now and again a fly would buzz feebly against the black, gaping maw of the window. Ah, I was even glad of the fly.[3]

Eight years is not, by any standards, a long apprenticeship. Florensky, who always insisted he mastered new disciplines only at the cost of dogged application and a slow process of grinding ingestion, had, over this period, completed two university courses with distinction, greatly improved his knowledge of modern languages, Latin and Greek, acquired Hebrew and fluency in Church Slavonic, established an easy command of Theological and Philosophical terminology, written a thesis on the cutting edge of mathematical research and learned to use mathematical formulae, a shorthand in which he felt at home, for the theological and philosophical ideas on which he was endeavouring to found a holistic world view. The publications, diploma works, poetry and preaching of his Academy years were but froth on the surface of the constant flow of thought which went into the writing of the theodicy which he sought to communicate in 12 'letters' first and foremost to his other half, his friend and brother in Christ Sergei Troitsky.

In this friendship, sealed by a vow of brotherhood taken in Church before shared Communion according to an early Christian rite not unlike the sacrament of marriage, Florensky felt he had approached that state 'when two or three are gathered together in My name' and the Kingdom of Heaven can begin to be re-established in the hearts of fallen human beings. It was, we see from the date of the poem which serves as an epigraph to this chapter and from Florensky's private letters, a state of striving rather than of serene achievement, a kind of voluntary, often painful, ascetic pilgrimage, joyfully undertaken in the light and warmth of true love. The relationship was, he felt quite overwhelmingly, his way to Salvation. He wanted to clothe Sergei in heavy, natural linen garments like an angel. He loved to listen to the 'mild, quiet, cordial voice'[4] as his friend welcomed peasants from his home village to the Great Monastery or exhorted some simple-minded wastrel to reform for the sake of the image of God in which he was made; it gave him pleasure to watch Sergei eat and drink (always sparingly as he came from a poor family and liked to have money put aside to help those poorer than himself, but with the uninhibited enjoyment of one to whom feast and fast were second nature); he had been touched to the heart by the young man's imaginative response to other people which took in their taste in books and pictures; by the skilful carpenter's hands; by the confident, pure singing voice which had, from childhood, praised God in his father's choir throughout the Church year; and by the generous indignation with which Sergei reacted to the more repressive policies of the Synod in the years of revolution and his enthusiasm for enlightenment in their work together to build up a library for the Tolpygino peasants. It had been, in part, Sergei's anguish at the Church's sanctioning of the reintroduction of the death penalty which had prompted Florensky's sermon 'The cry of blood'.

Troitsky's decision to accept a teaching post in a Tiflis school had been dictated by his disaffection with the reactionary climate in the Church itself after 1906 and by what he called 'my painful problem regarding marriage'.[5] His heart's desire was to become a country priest like his father before him, but the Russian Orthodox Church discourages celibacy in the clergy: the choice for would-be ordinands is between marriage and monastic vows. On completing his course at the Academy, Sergei had not felt ready to commit himself to either. What he really wanted, he confided in a letter to a Tolpygino friend, was to live the contemplative life with his brother in Christ in an izba in the Kostroma district, earning bread by the sweat of their brows but surrounded by books in every language and albums of great art. 'Pavlia and I have sometimes talked ourselves into a state of hallucination describing such a life to one another.' Yet, during the visit to the Florensky family in the summer that he completed his studies, Troitsky was drawn to Georgia: 'these peaks towering above the clouds, this heat, these people with their ardent hearts'.[6] The Church chants were as full of longing as in the Kostroma forests; in the ancient Armenian churches he felt himself back in the first centuries of Christianity. So, when Florensky returned to complete his studies in Sergiev Posad, Troitsky stayed on in his friend's home-city to become a favourite with his family and a much-loved teacher of Russian literature with a gift for making pupils think for themselves rather than swot up the critics and a reputation for independence in relation to the educational bureaucracy.

For Pavel Aleksandrovich, Troitsky's absence during his last year at the Academy was a melancholy but inspiring factor in the composition of the 'letters' which were to compose his Master's thesis. Writing had become a means of communication, and of what should he write to his beloved but of that which was nearest to both their hearts: the problems of belief in the modern world? Living alone in his narrow, vaulted cell during his last year as a student and then, as a young lecturer, in the small, new, wooden house with a vegetable garden which, once he had acquired some furniture and made himself at home, was much envied by Ern and El'chaninov who came to visit him from the bustle of their Moscow lodgings and, in El'chaninov's case, to share for long periods his life of study and his simple, virtually vegetarian board, Florensky was absorbed in creative work on the dissertation and on his ever-expanding course of lectures on the history of philosophy.

However, like Troitsky, Florensky longed for the priesthood and was faced with the same dilemma. He had no desire to marry and, indeed, felt that, were he to found a family, it would distract him from the service of God.[7] Bishop

Antonii, his spiritual advisor, still held out firmly against Florensky's ambition
to become a monk and energetically encouraged him to pursue his intellectual
interests. Lonely and disorientated, Florensky felt betrayed and abandoned
when Troitsky entered into a betrothal with his own younger sister, Ol'ga
Aleksandrovna, known for some reason to her family and friends as Valia, a
sensitive artist who was at the time in the process of becoming close to Zinaida
Hippius, Dmitrii Merezhkovsky and their essentially un-Orthodox religious
circle.[8] The ideal, advocated by Florensky himself in letter 4 of *The Pillar and
Ground of Truth*, painfully, experimentally incorporated in the domestic lives
of the Merezhkovskys and their circle and – more controversially – into the
erotic private life of Viacheslav Ivanov and his wife Lidiia Zinov'eva-Annibal,
that love between two human beings should be open to include a third and
thus all mankind, did not seem to work out for any of them in practice. When,
in January 1909, Ol'ga and Sergei were married in Tiflis, Pavel, heart-broken,
angry and, in his own high sense of the word, consumingly jealous, did not
attend. Ol'ga's gossamer pencil sketch, showing her brother and husband
walking together through a flowering meadow and entitled 'brothers-in-Christ',
shows that she, too, was acutely aware of the unhappiness caused. She and
Troitsky would have liked to include Pavel in their own 'religious' relationship.
In the summer of 1909 the newly-weds went to stay with the Merezhkovskys at
their *dacha* and Hippius refers to them as 'Olia Florenskaia and Serezha – her
brother-husband – Troitsky'.[9] In his diary for 27 November 1908, Sergei had
noted very much as Florensky had written of him in 'Types of growth': 'I would
wish to be a virgin. That is not the same as to be celibate, but to be *pure in heart*.'
Love, he felt, was probably granted by God as a revelation of how things might
be, but to experience it in one's own life a special grace was needed.[10] Yet there
were moments when Troitsky had felt his problems would only be resolved by
death – a premonition rather than a self-destructive wish. At such times he
wondered with nervous diffidence whether he might not at least hope to be
accounted a worthy sacrifice.

The premonition came true. On 2 November 1910 Sergei Troitsky was
stabbed to death outside his school by a deranged, expelled 17-year-old, Shalva
Tavgeridze, a Georgian aristocrat and nationalist. 'They were putting the knife
into me, so I knifed one of them', he said defiantly at the trial, having escaped
lynching at the hands of his victim's pupils only thanks to Sergei's agonised cry:
'Unhappy boy! Why? What for?' and, as his life blood gushed from horrific
wounds to throat and stomach: 'I forgive him everything! God be his judge!'

The trauma, for Florensky, had been his friend's deviation to his sister rather
than the bloody shambles of his murder. Already in the course of his first year
as lecturer (1908–1909), he had embarked on his 'quiet mutiny', reminiscent
of Alyosha Karamazov's rebellion after the appalling disillusionment of the

onset of decay in the Elder Zosima's body and the ugly triumph of Zosima's ill-wishers.

Working long hours with stubborn resolve, Florensky continued to shoulder the burdens laid on him by the Theological Academy, compounding the exhaustion of his student years. This kept him busy but, without the promise of that wholeness of spirit he had thought to attain with his brother in Christ, without the comforting presence of his confessor Isidor, the Academy no longer seemed to him the secluded refuge of 'labour and chaste delights' of which Pushkin had once dreamt, but an increasingly reactionary institution peopled by pompous priests he longed to poke in their majestic stomachs and by well-drilled, respectful students, who filled him with a wild desire to slide down the banister as he left the lecture room.[11] The rough company which had delighted him in Tolpygino was now much more to his taste – and not to take a glass of vodka in such company was a discourtesy. Christ, he explained to a shocked and deeply concerned El'chaninov, had not only come to save those who were lost but had, most probably, *preferred* the company of publicans and sinners, because the righteous (Pharisees, who retain only the moral law and devotion to ritual) are such a bore. Drinking, Florensky said, left him with a remarkably clear head on the following day and was the best of cures for self-conceit. Besides – how was one to lecture on the origins of philosophy in Dionysian rites if one had never known intoxication? According to his new best friend at Sergiev Posad, Vasilii Giatsintov, he even, like Dr Jekyll, tried out experiments on himself with hashish and opium.[12] Naturally, Moscow was abuzz with gossip, fuelled by a certain physical deterioration evident in the young lecturer's dullness of eye and generally unkempt appearance no less than by his opinions, highly unconventional in a would-be ecclesiastic and stringently expressed in private conversation, more decorously in *The Pillar and Ground of Truth*. The sexual instinct, Florensky told El'chaninov, was a part of creativity and its rigorous suppression in theological writing was one reason for the sterility of much of the Church's teaching.[13]

For many months, Pavel Aleksandrovich, though he continued his allegiance to the Academy under obedience to his confessor, shrank from consulting him about his rebellious state of mind. He would not, he told El'chaninov, go to talk to Bishop Antonii, because he knew in advance what he would say and had no mind to follow his advice. The only salvation he could envisage for himself was in a monastic community because salvation, for him, was only attainable, or, indeed, desirable – 'together'. He did not even want to be saved alone, though he admitted half-humorously that his friends' prayers might conceivably bring this about without his cooperation and he did not object to El'chaninov telling their spiritual director of the state of his soul. 'Early, early, early', muttered the good bishop, shaking his head distressfully as he heard his spiritual child was seeking comfort in the bottle. 'Tell him', he said impetuously, 'that I implore him to refrain until he is thirty. He must exert all his strength. After that the danger is over. The blood is in ferment up to the age of thirty, but the years just before that are particularly dangerous.'[14]

Florensky, though, in spite of the new close friendship with Vasilii Giatsintov, a young man of similar background to Troitsky, but more placid and practical by nature, was in a state of weightlessness, filled with the lightness of despair. At one moment he would load himself with work to such an extent that he would be grateful for El'chaninov's help to meet deadlines, at another spend an entire day on skis, willing himself to live in the present, playing the fool with the abandonment of a child. His attitude to the opposite sex was equally unstable. After a visit from young ladies of the Moscow intelligentsia, who disgusted him by their 'porous' capacity to soak up other people's ideas, he suggested to El'chaninov it might be a good thing to get a priest in to hold a special service to clear the air in the house, protesting that, much as he respected feminine women, the *mind* was an attribute of the male gender. Yet at another time he asked merrily how one set about making oneself agreeable to girls, and he could be animated and amusing in mixed company when the mood took him.

Always more ready to condemn himself than others, El'chaninov was aware that his own lack of commitment to an exclusive friendship had been, at least in part, the cause of Florensky's first schoolboy bout of depression, and observed his friend's relationship with Vasilii with interest:

He has so much tenderness, capacity for affection, for love. I never knew him to be the first to grow cold towards others, begin to tire of a friend, to seek change, freedom. When he takes someone to his heart he puts everything into the relationship, he wants to draw his friend into every detail of his life and enters wholeheartedly into their life and interests; he'll abandon his own business, his acquaintance, pressing work, if his time is needed (or if it seems to him that his time is needed) by his friend. He and Vasia eat from one bowl and not for anything will he sit down to dine without him, however late he may be; he goes to talk to his doctor, helps him with written work, in general doesn't leave him time to draw breath. That is what true friendship should be like, but only given total reciprocity; otherwise it's an insupportable burden, I know that by my own experience. He often says he wants to leave the Academy. He had almost decided to do so this summer [1909], but Vas[ilii] Mikh[ailovich] dissuaded him. Yet he's still in a black mood.[15]

Deeply concerned, El'chaninov had broached the question of homosexuality or, as he put it less clinically in his diary of 7 July 1909, 'Pavlusha's indifference to ladies and frequent falling in love with young men'. He writes:

For a long time we muddled along in search of explanations,' he writes, 'then P stumbled upon the following hypothesis. A man seeks an object sufficiently passive to receive his energy. For the majority of men, such objects are women. There are insufficiently masculine natures who seek their complement in masculine men, but there are also hyper-masculine men, for whom the feminine is too yielding, as yielding as a cushion, for instance, to a steel blade. That kind seeks and loves simply men, or insufficiently masculine men.[16]

They were, of course, still under the spell of Plato, though Florensky had added the 'hyper-masculine' to the three genders proposed by Plato's Aristophanes. It seems probable that Sergei was by nature insufficiently masculine, whereas El'chaninov and Vasia were 'simply men' though men of rare spiritual quality and, in the case of El'chaninov, with his radiant smile and readiness to listen to others, charm. It was the astute, earthy strength of Vasilii Mikhailovich, however, which was to help Florensky steer his bark through the storms and doldrums of his 'quiet mutiny', and it was for Sergei that he wrote the *Pillar and Ground of Truth*.[17] It is against the background of their essentially poetic but far from serene relationship that the biographer must look at the book – and, indeed, at its reception. Florensky himself never entered into polemics with his critics and, owing to the abnormal situation obtaining in the Soviet Union from 1917 onwards, remained ignorant of much of the controversy to which the full text of his book, published by Morozova's Put', in 1914, continued to give rise amongst émigré theologians.[18] These controversies, therefore, are for the most part and on the deepest level peripheral to his biography.[19] The book itself, however, is central to it. It is Florensky's major opus of the pre-revolutionary period, the justification of his spiritual journey from agnosticism through a long and troubled apprenticeship to the practice of Christianity in his daily life according to the rule of the Orthodox Church.

Florensky set out, quite deliberately, to write his 'justification of God' in a manner that would interest and seduce his uncommitted contemporaries. In an age of individualism, he adopted a personal approach through the epistolatory form, inviting the reader to identify with the addressee of the 'letters', to negotiate with the author the stumbling blocks of the impossibility of rational proof and the incompatibility of belief in a merciful, all-powerful God with the concepts of Sin and Hell, and to accompany him on a meandering but ultimately purposeful voyage of discovery through the beauty and wonder of the more than half-forgotten world of ecclesiastical culture.

In an age of aestheticism, Florensky gave thought to the form of the book, its appearance and stylistic unity. At a time when Europe was rediscovering the Ancient World, he drew freely and with fresh insight on those 'origins of philosophy' in ancient cults which were the subject of his lectures and deployed, as in his lectures, a platonic strategy, seeking to create an atmosphere of heart-to-heart discussion, which allowed for digressions into the most various disciplines, or simply for pause to investigate the fascination of what Max Müller called 'fossil words', to admire the beauty of a text, an icon or the natural world. The letter form allowed him to slip from discourse to free association, to vary pace and mood and to generate a confessional tension, at times somewhat exhausting in so vast a work and certainly unsettling for the modern reader in an era which tends to regard the author as a construct of the text. This book was not written by a construct but by a slight, sallow young convert with a big nose and an extravagant hair-do engaged, as the author himself admits, unsystematically over a long period of time, in a titanic, solitary struggle to communicate to twentieth-century readers the revelation of Truth and Beauty he had found in the Russian Church and, at the same time, to face up honestly to the difficulty of committing mind and body to this Institution, which he had acknowledged – once and for all – as the Pillar and Ground of Truth.

In style and presentation, Florensky's book was unprecedented in the annals of theology – most certainly of Russian Orthodox theology. The colours of the jacket were symbolic, chosen from the Novgorodian icon of Sophia, the Holy Wisdom; the dedication was 'to the most sweet-scented and pure name of the Virgin and Mother'. The title page is an engraving from the book *Amoris Divini Emblemata* published in Antwerp in the seventeenth century. It depicts, under the title *The Pillar and Ground of Truth*, a pillar from the top of which rise or grow two three-quarter-length angelic or cherubic figures, winged and resplendent, heads inclined to one another and arms entwined behind their backs in tender love so that they appear to have been grafted together. At the foot of the pillar lie a discarded quiver full of arrows and a Cupid's bow. In the background is a great sweep of sky and a severe classical building, standing like the pillar itself on a paved embankment and topped by a small cross. Beneath the picture is the Latin legend: 'Finis amoris, ut duo unum fiant'.

Smaller engravings from another book *Symbola et Emblemata* embellish every chapter heading, and the author's intention to give of himself is indicated by the exquisite vignette of a pelican over the Introduction, which begins where his first paper for the MDA Philosophical Society left off:

> Living experience is the only legitimate way of understanding dogmas – that is how I would express the general aspiration of my book, or, more exactly, my tentative studies, written at various times and in various moods.[20]

The style, for a serious academic dissertation, was as unheard of as the form, and left some readers speechless with indignation, whereas others were torn between admiration for its baroque elegance and disgust at its occasional infelicities. Yet the spontaneity of Florensky's invitation to join in his exploration of the long buried treasures of ecclesiastical culture, dark and even fearsome as these may now appear to the uninitiated, was irresistible precisely because, like a man with a spluttering taper in a catacomb, he was discovering them for himself as he went along. At first, he says, he had wanted to write only in his own words, then he was tempted to quote more and more until it seemed he would have done better to allow the Church to speak for Herself. 'And if nonetheless I attach some significance to these letters of mine, it is only as a preparation, for the catechumens, for as long as they are unprepared to receive direct nourishment from the hands of the Mother.'[21]

To be prepared, it is necessary to belong to the Church and there is no defining what this means in the abstract; it is a way of life, life itself, a state of being.

The first 'letter' is called 'Two worlds' and begins with a description of the world of everyday in which the author is writing, the solitude of his room and life in Sergiev Posad, an autumnal lament for the absent and the dead and his own countless petty sins of omission. It is precisely this state of loss and contrition which compels him to seek support in *The Pillar and Ground of Truth*.

But, he asks, how are we to approach this Truth? – and he chooses to do so through Christ's words recorded in Matthew 11.27–30, read over and over again in the monastery at services of intercession at the coffin of St Sergius, words which, he maintains, are about gnosis itself:

All things are delivered to me of my Father: and no man knoweth the Son, but the Father; neither knoweth any man the Father, save the Son, and he to whomsoever the Son will reveal Him.

Come unto me, all ye that labour and are heavy laden, and I will give you rest.

Take my yoke upon you, and learn of me; for I am meek and lowly in heart: and ye shall find rest unto your souls.

For my yoke is easy, and my burden is light.

The familiar words have added poignancy for those accustomed to pray before an icon of the Saviour holding a book open at 'Come unto me ...'

This chapter, most effective in its brevity and simplicity, appears to have been forgotten by the majority of Florensky's critics by the time they reached the end of the book. He does not, he concludes almost sheepishly, wish to proselytise but rather, like the pelican in the vignette, to feed his readers from his own heart.

The second 'letter', which has provoked far more discussion, is headed 'Doubt'. It is about the undoubted existence of Truth, attested by the etymology of the word itself, and its inaccessibility to 'subjective' reason or the 'objective' evidence of the senses or, indeed, 'subconscious' mystic intuition. None of these provide proof of truth, as required by Plato and Aristotle before we can claim knowledge, and we are left with absolute doubt, hell to those who love and desire Truth and, ultimately, the negation of mind itself, madness and despair.

Truth is *coincidentia oppositorum*, eternity in the moment, unity in diversity. It is everything and everything is in it, so that, although we cannot 'know' or 'prove' it for ourselves, we are justified in seeking it always and are ourselves, inescapably, part of it. It is not, therefore, beyond our reach, as Kant's image of the transcendent, the sky, is beyond the reach of the mountaineer. Truth is that in which we live and move and have our being. It is the contemplation of Self through another in a third: the three hypostases of the Trinity, each of which confirms the absolute Being of the Other.

'Three in One' is the title of the third 'letter', which moves to a consideration of the term *homoousios*, the Nicene Creed and the 'mathematical precision' of Athanasius the Great's formula – which, does, however, require us to abjure reason (for how can Three equal One?), no less than Christ was required to abjure His will for the Father's in the Garden of Gethsemane. 'The Faith by which we are saved is … the cross and co-crucifixion with Christ.'[22] Either we make the leap of faith or we abide in scepticism and unknowing – 'tertium non datur'.[23] When we set foot on the bridge of faith we are supported only by Hope and Love. One is reminded here of Florensky's strange 'intimate' photograph in which he stands before the Cross on the wall of his study with lowered eyes and an expression of total submission. Co-crucifixion, for Florensky the scientist, was not ascetism in the more usual sense of the word, but renunciation of his own will to prove Truth exclusively by scientific method: not my will, but Thine be done.

The chapter ends with another etymological excursion, this time into the word for Faith in various Indo-European and Semitic languages. The root meaning of 'trust' (whether trust in the reliability of Truth, in God, or interpersonal trust) – brings him to the next 'letter': 'The light of truth'.

The very thought of Faith and Trust brings the author back to the recipient of this 'letter' – who, of course, like the writer himself is not altogether a literary construct. He writes:

> Only I alone am beavering away here in my cell and it seems to me as though I have been dead a long while. In these careless, rapid lines is all my link with life; if I haven't altogether died it is thanks to this conversation with you, it is thanks solely to you, my quietly radiant Guardian, the very thought of whom cleanses and raises me …[24]

Faith, through love, is beginning to work for him. He is beginning to escape the deadlock of the law of identity, the solipcism of I=1. When he prays – and here

Florensky topples disastrously into a morass of metaphor: 'For some reason I want to compare my state to one in which it is as though my whole body has become soft wax and all my veins flow with milk.' Again, one is reminded of the 'intimate photograph', even as one is aware of the dead metaphors 'as wax in his hands' and 'the milk of human kindness'. Florensky himself admits disarmingly: 'my simile sounds comic, but I can't think of a better'.[25]

Indeed, this self-disparagement leads to the discovery that God is not just loving but is Love itself and that the reason the author had thought to renounce is still an inalienable part of his being. The act of knowing presents itself to him in the biblical sense of a union between the knower and the known. The knowledge of God is only possible through the beauty of Love – in Communion, transfiguration, divinisation. Of the three hypostases, Christ incarnate is the hypostasis of Divine Love, and Florensky quotes Jacob Boehme, calling Him 'the Heart of the Father'.[26]

Conditioned by Leibniz's concept of the monad which 'has neither doors nor windows'[27] it is hard for the modern heart to understand Love ontologically as union with another Being rather than as a pleasant psychological state of general benevolence towards an agreeable object distinct from oneself. The merging of Love and knowledge is a creative process: one has to work at the kind of Love Christ speaks of in St John's Gospel, and which is invoked in the Liturgy of the Faithful: 'Let us love one another, that we may with one mind confess ...' Only when 'idea' and 'reason' replace 'concept' and 'ratio' can we achieve this ontological synthesis of loving and 'being of one mind'. It is at this juncture[28] that Florensky propounds the theory that two joined together in God can attract a third and that third can in turn open themselves to another close-knit fellowship of three, an idea suggested by Bugaev's doctrine of monads capable of becoming diads and triads, but also very much 'in the air' at the time in Symbolist circles.

Love, Florensky continues, is synonymous at this level with light, the light of Mount Tabor which the saints perceive as the manifestation of God; for those who have known the Truth of Love as light and beauty there will, as for Saint Augustine, remain 'no doubt at all any more'.[29]

Having thus resolved doubt through Faith and Love, Florensky proceeds in his next 'letter' to conjure up the conversations he had with his distant, but eternally close friend as they last walked through the Russian forest in late August, talking of religious antonyms and the Holy Spirit. The chapter is headed 'The comforter' and, according to the author, represents only the dried flowers of these talks. 'It is', he confesses, 'the reason why I write "letters" to you instead of composing "an article" – because I am afraid of *making assertions*, and prefer to ask questions.'[30]

In one of his remarkable metaphors from applied science, Florensky says that any attempt to be too definite about the Holy Spirit is rather like trying too hard to develop an under-exposed film: the longer you hold it in the solution, the mistier it becomes. This is what is happening for those of the 'new religious consciousness' who preach a Third Testament of the Spirit and, indeed, for all charismatic sects from the intellectual Gnostics to the grossly physical *Khlysty*: the Spirit veils itself from those who seek to perceive it clearly without having attained the requisite sanctity. Neither can the Spirit be 'possessed', even by the saints, because it is essentially outside time, associated with the Coming of the Kingdom and with the 'moment' of Pentecost which has now become, like the platonic anamnesis, a memory occasionally stirred through sacrament, fasting, ascetic striving towards absolute love and beauty. Startlingly, he associates this doctrine of the Spirit with Nietzsche's 'Gay Science'.[31] To seek to rationalise or harness the power of the Spirit, as Tolstoy and, to some extent, the new religious consciousness does, is a sin. Even the Church is vague about the Spirit, unclear about its relationship to the Father and the Son, not to mention to the Church Herself and to Sophia, the Divine Wisdom – which last, as Florensky says elsewhere, are not *persons* of the Trinity yet are a part of its unity in diversity. Even the liturgical texts are of little help: even the third kneeling prayer for the Sunday of Pentecost (Trinity Sunday in the Orthodox calendar) is addressed to the Son rather than to the Spirit.

What is certain is that even the Church thinks of the Spirit as of one who is to come rather than as one who was and is in Glory, like the Father and the Son. Yet expectation within the Church is meek and peaceful and it is, therefore, through the Church and the insights of the Fathers (he quotes specifically St Gregory the Theologian, Maximus the Confessor and Irenaeus of Lyons) that the 'light of Truth' will eventually shine out from Christ in Glory and illumine us all.[32]

The sixth 'letter', entitled 'Contradiction', examines the dangers encountered on the descent from the heights by those who have been caught up in the Spirit: the descent into time on the personal level, into space on the social. Our transient, relative understanding cannot encompass or prove the existence of the Eternal, yet we can show it forth in symbols and, as creatures created creative, we are bound to try ...

We can, however, only express the Truth if we foresee the extreme expression of all the contradictions inherent in it, from which it follows that Truth itself encompasses the ultimate projection of all its invalidations, is antonymic and cannot be otherwise.[33] Over the next ten pages, Florensky plunges into formulaic expression of his argument, based on Euclid's 'reductio ad absurdum', which he says has long been employed *de facto* in philosophy, thought and fiction (he mentions an argument in Turgenev's *Rudin*) but has only recently been formally recognised in philosophy.[34] The expression 'antonym', however, which originated in jurisprudence and theology, was first used in philosophy by

Kant in his *Critique of Pure Reason*, 1781, for which the German philosopher deserves eternal fame, even if his examples are open to criticism. Antonyms are implicit in the thought of Heraclites, the Eleatics, even Plato, whose dialogues are essentially dramatisations of the dilemmas they pose. Further he evokes Nicholas of Cura, Hegel, Fichte, Schelling, Renouvier and the modern pragmatists, beginning with James.

All these go to support the conviction that antonyms should be accepted. 'If the world is cracked, and we cannot mend the crack, we should not paper it over.'[35] The Book of Job and 'all the Church services, especially the canons and stikhera, are bubbling over with the endlessly-seething wit of antithetic juxtapositions and antonymic assertions'.[36] This is because our earthly reason can only deal with fragments. What they are saying is neither 'Either this or that is not true' nor 'neither this nor that is true'. What they are saying is: 'Both this and that are true, but each in its own fashion; reconciliation and unity – are above reason.'[37] It is when we try to separate the antonyms contained in all dogmas and to maintain the truth of one side against the other that we get heresies. It requires 'a psaltery with many strings to play on eternity', says Andrei Bely.[38]

In Holy Writ itself contradictions are presented like fighting stags with locked antlers by the literary device of 'asyndeton', missing out connecting words as in St Paul's Epistle to the Romans, 'that explosive anti-reason bomb, loaded with antonyms'.[39] But antonyms belong to the very essence of experience, as inseparable from it as the petals of a flower are inseparable from the pigment which colours them. They are also of the essence of belief and will only cease to be so when Faith and Hope pass away and nothing is left but Love. Only in Love does 'I' become 'not I' (or 'a = not-a', to return to the original alogical proposition which Florensky here reasserts as both 'impossible' and 'beyond doubt'). 'True Love is the renunciation of reason.'[40]

The relevance of Florensky's exposition of his doctrine of the antonymic nature of Truth, the philosophical as well as the structural centre of a book which shocked many of his sympathisers among the intelligentsia by the implication that it is not for mere man to reason about religious dogma, springs almost certainly from his own genius for applied science, the intellectual inheritance from a father who had used Euclidean geometry to build the bridges of which his children had been so proud. Contemporary discoveries in the sphere of non-Euclidean geometry and higher mathematics excited Florensky and were not, of course, beyond his intellectual grasp, but were precious to him precisely as intimations of the real existence of a complex, eternal reality beyond the law of cause and effect, as symptoms of imminent Apocalypse.[41] Though 'true', they would not necessarily work in time and space as we know them, and it was very much a part of Florensky's genius that he had a remarkably clear

instinct for what would.[42] The method which 'worked' for him was to investigate each phenomenon according to its own laws and within its own limits,
and to seek ultimate harmony through the ascetic life rather than by harnessing
human reason to probe the secrets of a God ineffable by definition for Whom
'all things are possible'.[43]

From the problem of gnosis Florensky passes, in the seventh and eighth
'letters', to the fundamental dichotomy of every theodicy, which had provided
his own chief argument against Christian belief in his pre-school days in
Batumi and which, in 1904, El'chaninov had advanced against his acceptance
of the Church: the existence of Evil, Sin and Hell in a universe designed by an
all-powerful and loving God.

Sin, Florensky says in the seventh 'letter', is not a matter of choosing a
right or wrong path as it is sometimes depicted in allegory. It 'is the moment
of disintegration, of the falling apart and ruin of spiritual life'.[44] Later, he was
to use the word 'enthropy' of the falling apart of society. He calls to mind the
old-fashioned term 'a lost woman' and applies it, surprisingly and to the intense
indignation of many subsequent readers, to post-Renaissance Europe and to the
smile of the Gioconda, the sceptical, self-sufficient smile of a lost soul in whom
the image of God has disintegrated.

How can such disintegration come about? Above all by pride, as we see from
many ancient, not necessarily Christian mythologies: the foolish desire to storm
the heavens, to be 'as gods'. The symptoms of pride are rootlessness, foolishness,
ratio without reason,[45] superficial vulgarity (the untranslatable Russian word
*poshlost'*), lack of self-control. Sin, like Goethe's Mephistopheles, is something
of a clown. It is a state of chaos – wholly negative. This is also true of sexual sin
which is the misuse of the genetic sphere of our being that belongs to the dark,
instinctive, impersonal roots of our nature and, given a face and put on display,
upsets the balance of the whole person, takes over will-power and makes a
mockery of personality – which is why the devil is often depicted with a face in
place of his genitals or, by those who have not fully grasped the implications, of
his stomach.

Sin is the opposite of *tselomudrie* – the Russian word for chastity which has
connotations of wisdom and wholeness. Its tendency to infinite, progressive
disintegration is shown in the parable of the Gadarene swine.

The blessed are held in the 'eternal memory' of God and it is the aspiration
to remain a part of this eternal memory which inspires not only the rites for the
dead but the creativity of life, the teaching and engendering of children, the care
of friends. Etymologically, the word for memory has the same root as the word
for thought. Sin is forgetfulness of the Divine. Ultimately, Sin can only work on
that which is capable of being perverted and destroyed. This does not include
'eternal memory'.

Yet, in the eighth 'letter', 'Gehenna', Florensky feels bound to pursue the fate of the sinner. Can it be that we, who were made in God's image, can fall out of His eternal memory, His thought, His providence?

Tentatively, and with considerable anguish, out of the depths of experience and invoking not so much the understanding of his brother in Christ Sergei as the memory of his Father in Christ Isidor, to make a confession to whom had been like 'confessing to the universe', Florensky affirms from his own experience the real possibility of falling into outer darkness, of banishment from the Presence of God, and the consuming temptation to hide from God in the smoke and flame of lust. All people, though, are subject to temptation. It is by our fruits we shall be judged.

Here, he suggests that that immortal part of us which is made in the image of God really cannot and will not be rejected or destroyed, but that our evil works and their consequences will indeed be consumed by fire, a process which cannot but entail great anguish, both of regret that we did not contribute anything worthy of Eternal Life and of the pain of amputation: for judgement, like the sacrament of penitence, cannot condone only burn away our sins. The cleansing fire, however, is neither punitive (as in the juridical concept of purgatory) nor eternal, as this would indeed be irreconcilable with all we know and believe about our Creator, and about 'the unconditional divinisation of human nature in the person of Jesus Christ' which is 'the foundation common to us all'.[46]

This powerful, learned letter disturbed the Academy as being overly close to Origen and Pelagius – Florensky even has the audacity to argue with St John Chrysostom, albeit on a matter of the exact interpretation and usage of the Greek word for 'trial', which the saint interpreted juridically, the scholar academically in the sense of 'experiment', 'examination' or 'test'. The chapter on Gehenna was among those Florensky was recommended *not* to submit to the Synod for his candidate's degree.

Letter 9, entitled 'Tvar'' which normally means 'the creature' but has here also the sense of 'The Creation', is the theologically acceptable lead-in to the more doubtful 'Sophia' chapter, and provided the conclusion of the dissertation 'O dukhovnoi istiny'. In a sense, it is a revival of Florensky's adolescent 'natural philosophy', illumined by tenderness and reverence for the fallen Creation which is, nevertheless, of divine origin and divinely redeemed. The lyrical introduction conveys a sense that the author is here turning away from the individual towards the general. To the strains of one of his beloved *chastushki* singing of a last meeting and imminent separation, the author, the gloom of depression intensified by the melancholy spectacle of the setting sun, contemplates the seeming indifference of teeming, seeding nature. Furiously, he scolds himself for his self-indulgent subjectivity: life is for God, he must learn to live objectively, to do without … And to live objectively means to acknowledge the reality of God's creation, to endeavour to peel away the rind of Sin and to perceive it as God intended it to be when first He saw that it was good.

The way to do this is the same as the way to knowledge: the ascetic life. And here Florensky likens asceticism to orthopaedic surgery, 'the correction of deformities in bones or muscles', according to the Oxford dictionary.

The ascetic begins with the body[47]; the etymology of the word in Greek and Sanskrit indicates that the concept has its origin in something whole and healthy. The *hesychast* acknowledges the role of the body in mysticism (the prayer of the heart) – and it is through the body that we are involved in the life of creation as a whole, not in the pantheist sense that 'all is full of the gods', that ensouled nature is daemonic and chaotic, a multiplicity of forces to be feared and propitiated, but in the Christian sense of partaking in the life of the fallen world and in the work of preparing the Coming of the Kingdom.

'The providence of God and the freedom of creation, as antonyms, form a single dogma, – the dogma of the love of God, i.e. of 'the gift to the Creation of its own independent being.'[48] The study of 'the Wholeness of Creation – not the elemental wholeness of indifference but the organic wholeness of harmony – is the prelude to Science'.[49]

God loves his creation and suffers for it, is tormented by its sinfulness. God extends His hands to His creation, pleads with it, calls it, awaits the return of the Prodigal Son. And mankind, the head of creation, answers to God for it, just as one human being answers for another.[50]

To deny the body or, by extension, the physical world, as Tolstoy does, for instance, in his *Kreutzer Sonata*, or the Eastern mystic in his struggle to be free of the cycles of being, is not Christian. The Christian Church, on the contrary, thinks of the body as the 'brother' of the spirit (St Andrew of Crete, St Francis), tends it in death, blesses it in marriage, accepts its link to the 'winged ecstasy' of ascetic mysticism[51] and praises 'all creation in its primal triumphal beauty'; the Christian heart, to quote Isaac Sirin, has compassion on all created nature.

Essentially, trimmed of the lyrical digressions, these were the 'letters' (with the exception of the meditation on Gehenna) which Florensky presented for his Master's degree on 5 April 1912 and which earned him much praise and two prestigious prizes from the Moscow Theological Academy. The further chapters on Sophia, Friendship and Jealousy were written at the same time as part of the same work ('Jealousy', the last, in 1909, when the author's 'quiet mutiny' was at its height). Their confessional character and close association with pre-Christian and Gnostic thought led his well-wishers at the Academy, and notably the Rector, Bishop Fedor, to advise him against presenting them as part of his candidate's thesis, because this had to be approved by the Synod, once again firmly installed as the Directory of Church Affairs and none too well qualified in matters spiritual, though always on the watch for original thought which might turn out, on closer examination, to contain seeds of heresy or sedition. Florensky bowed to his examiners' good sense, but published the blocked chapters which, more than any others, were to earn him the title of 'Theologian of the Silver Age', together with the rest of the text with restored lyrical passages and with extensive appendages enlarging on his mathematical arguments, with the Moscow publishing house Put' as *The Pillar and Ground of Truth* in 1914, the year he was eventually awarded his Master's degree by public examination on the basis of the truncated earlier version.[52]

It is the order of letters and illustration in this second book that we have so far been following. The 'letter' about Sophia is here the tenth. It treats of a concept which originated with the Wisdom of the Old Testament, was taken up and developed into a whole new mythology by Valentinian Gnosticism but was also enshrined in the liturgical texts of the Early Church, particularly those relating to the cult of the Theotokos. The great Eastern Churches at Constantinople, Kiev and Novgorod were dedicated to Sophia, the Divine Wisdom. The concept of a creative Female Spirit distinct from the Saviour, the Theotokos and the Church yet present in all three is inherent in Russian Orthodox iconography.[53] Florensky, influenced in part by Vladimir Solov'ev and Andrei Bely but also by close study of ecclesiastical sources had, since his first year at the Theological Academy, been intrigued by the idea of a Holy Being who manifests herself on the borderline between the spiritual and the material. It seemed to him that Sophia reveals Herself through human personality when the physical is illumined by the spiritual, just as She manifests Herself in the finest dust of the Earth's atmosphere, illumined and coloured by the setting or the rising sun, and in the merciful azure which cloaks the blackness of outer space. Following the meditation on the sanctity of the Created World, the 'letter' on Sophia is at once a painstaking study of a difficult, elusive concept and a hymn in its praise. It concludes with the thought of the significance of Sophia as a manifestation of the Spiritual in the material granted in 'the sincere, personal love'[54] of two individuals who, thanks to the breakdown of the boundary between 'I' and 'thou', provide 'that environment in which begins the revelation of truth'.[55]

Letter 11, about friendship or ideal love, develops this theme and is directly addressed to Sergei: 'Distant friend and brother!' It is further contextualised by the opening description of the onset of winter, whereas letter 10 had opened with the passage on loneliness and autumn rain quoted at the beginning of this chapter. The mood of the 'letter' on Friendship is no longer supine and hopeless. Snow and darkness bring back fond memories of a winter pilgrimage to the Skete of the Paraclete; the stumble through drifted snow and down into the dim underground church; the old monk who reminded the friends of St Sergius; the young monk, Father Pavel, gaunt from fasting and with the mark of death on him, who had indeed since died; the shared Communion and Father Isidor quoting from Proverbs 18.12. 'Brother strengthened by brother is strong as a city.' The memory awakens thoughts of love and death, how love conquers death, and death ... the passions.

Heine, Florensky continues, wrote that 'love is an earthquake of the soul'. A different kind of love, to be sure, than the attribute of the Godhead of which he had written in the fourth letter, although, in the life of the individual, such an 'earthquake' can be a presentiment of this divine love, because it rends the monolith of our self-sufficiency in such a way as to admit a break-in of Paradise, an experience which can give direction for a lifetime: 'Beyond the moment of Eros, in the Platonic sense of the word, comes the revelation of *philia*, – the highpoint of earthly experience and the bridge to heaven.'[56]

In as far as in the soul of the Friend, the Other (in Russian the words are variations on a single root), we are granted an albeit momentary revelation of new-created beauty, we have already escaped solipsism. In this revelation of 'being of one essence' with Another is the promise of Truth.

But to talk about love one needs the right words. Florensky weaves a complex pattern from the ancient Greek *eros* (passion), *agape* (respect or veneration) and *philia* (brotherly love) to the New Testament Greek usage. From the Old Testament he recalls the love of David and Jonathan and, from the New, the absence of the word Eros and the interaction of *agape* and *philia*, whose meanings become closer, noting the use of different verbs in Christ's threefold 'Lovest thou me?' to Peter after the Resurrection and in Peter's response. By *philia*, Florensky explains, he means the love which makes two become as one being, 'one soul'.[57] Friendship is not so much psychological or ethical as ontological and mystic: 'the contemplation of self through the Friend in God'.[58] This is not, however, the contemplation of a mirror image. Friendship is not unison, but harmony; the friend is my opposite and the way of friendship is not heart's ease but hard-won fidelity, nourished by dogged endeavour to remain true to that higher vision of self and the Other granted at the moment of choice. 'Tears are the cement of friendship',[59] 'to give oneself is difficult'.[60] He describes the "natural sacrament" of brotherhood which gives grace for the thorny way of philial love. Like all Church ceremonies, he maintains, the blessing of sworn friendship is both personal to the individuals involved and a micro-event in the community.

Finally, Florensky introduces the theme of Jealousy perceived as a positive force which maintains and energises every close relationship, whether between man and wife, friend and friend, spiritual director and disciple or even parish and priest.[61]

Jealousy is the theme of the twelfth and last 'letter', written in 1909 and clearly bound up with painful personal experience. Jealousy, Florensky pleads, is neither possessiveness, that half-comic sense of proprietary ownership of another human being which is pilloried and deplored in world literature, nor the deadly sin of envy, covetousness. It is not morally reprehensible in any way. The word proceeds from roots which carry connotations of zeal, energy and ardour and is, of course, used of the God of the Old Testament. Divine jealousy, wounded, misprised love, is to be felt in the parable of the wedding guests – invited but too busy with their own affairs to respond – and in Christ's lament 'O Jerusalem, Jerusalem...' To be jealous is to demand of those we love that they remain true, not just to us but to their ideal selves. Jealousy is 'the watchdog and keeper of God's laws'; not our love of others only, but 'our aspiration towards the Pillar and Foundation of Truth is activated and preserved through jealousy, a facet of our nature despised and suppressed by the contemporary mind'.[62]

So, in full rebellion still, not against the laws of God but against what he saw at this moment of his life as the lamentable inadequacy of the mindset of the contemporary world, Florensky concluded his last letter on a piercingly personal note. The epistolary form was not only a literary device, but was suggested by circumstances and deployed with genuine passion, *de profundis*.

The Afterword which concludes the book bears the hallmarks of exhaustion. If one were to follow the bad practice of some reviewers and skim through it in the hopes of obtaining a summary of the ideas expressed in the preceding 482 pages of complex and concentrated thought, it might indeed appear that all the author had to offer was 'a Christianity without Christ', a book written 'from despair'.

In his summary, Florensky returns to Kant, whom he here calls 'that Copernicus of philosophers'[63] and who had been the first, in the very midst of the Age of Reason, to demonstrate the inadequacy of Pure Reason to cope with the antonyms inherent in it. Either, Florensky maintains, one must remain with Kant in the Gehenna of doubt, scepticism, unknowing, *epoché*, or one must accept the ontological way offered throughout the ages by the Christian Church, the way of asceticism, motivated by love and by the miracle of friendship.[64]

'The Pillar', he affirms, is the Church Herself which teaches the self-proving Truth of the Holy Trinity and through which we know that 'with God all things are possible'.

'The Ground', common to us all, 'the unconditional divinisation of human nature in the person of Jesus Christ' of which Florensky wrote on p. 230 of the chapter on Gehenna, is not recalled in the conclusion: neither is the brief and beautiful first 'letter' 'Two worlds'.

Instead, Florensky concludes on a note of high pathos, carried away at the end of his long task by a certain poetic inertia, with the Cherubic Hymn to the Holy Trinity:

Holy, holy, holy is the Lord!

Possibly he felt, with some justification, that this covered everything ...

*The Pillar and Ground of Truth*, as Father Sergei Bulgakov declared in his moving memorial tribute to his friend Father Pavel Florensky, was 'for all that it made his name in theology, a youthful work and by no means his last and only word'.[65] Nevertheless, the book, untidy, overloaded with erudite footnotes and, as some thought, affected, sentimental and lacking coherent form, was a milestone for his generation. Florensky's mathematician friend Luzin, who visited him several times in 1908, looked wonderingly through his friend's schoolboy notes on physics which, he told his wife, envisaged the possibility of wireless telegraph before Popov and, more doubtfully, at his 'teasing', 'elusive' but 'compelling' mathematical ideas, and was shown the 'intimate photograph', did wonder in passing whether Pavel Aleksandrovich had not hidden himself away in the Theological Academy because of some 'sub-conscious, infernal pride', but nevertheless wrote that talking with his friend at this time had saved him from thoughts of suicide, and considered his book 'a battering-ram' which broke down all previous materialist certainties. For him, and for many of his generation, this was a book which treated 'the most fundamental principles of life' and which opened up the possibility of faith to the educated scientific mind. By illumining the problems of the literary and scientific intelligentsia and – with utmost frankness – his own personal problems in the light of the teachings of the Russian Orthodox Church to which he, to the best of his understanding, had submitted his whole life, Florensky had, by the time he turned 30, made a unique if flawed contribution to the thought and sensibilities of his own generation. He had also succeeded in saying much about knowledge, faith, love and man's stewardship of the created world which has lasting resonance.

By the summer of 1910, Florensky was fighting his way back towards light. On a visit to Vasia Giatsintov's home in the village of Kutlovy Borki, in the province of Riazan, he had met his friend's sister Anna, a modest school-teacher who rather took his fancy and awoke in him a new kind of feeling, compassionate and protective. Though he did not immediately see his way to shouldering the responsibilities of a family man, he set out to please her and wrote her letters when he returned to Sergiev Posad. He also resumed his relationship with Bishop Antonii and accompanied him to Zosimovo Pustyn. Berdiaev, who happened to make the pilgrimage at the same time, recollects how, during the long Vigil service, he had suddenly become aware of Florensky standing behind him – in tears. 'I was told he was going through a very difficult period.'[66]

# 6

# The Four-leafed Clover

Awake, O my soul, be as courageous as the great ones of the Patriarchs, that thou
attain action with knowledge, that thou gain a mind to see God, and reach to the
impenetrable darkness in contemplation, and become a great merchant.
The great one of the Patriarchs begat the twelve Patriarchs, secretly establishing
for thee, O my soul, the ladder of rungs for thy actions, the children as steps, the
foundations, as rungs, all wisely laid down.
The Great Canon of St Andrew of Crete, Ode 4, vv. 9–10.1

In a letter of 27 July 1912 to his friend and colleague the religious thinker
Valentin Kozhevnikov, Florensky defines three stages in his spiritual pilgrimage:
*catharsis*, or the process of purgation from contemporary positivism undergone
after conversion; *mathesis*, or apprenticeship, the intellectual labour of incor-
porating religious experience into a holistic world view; and *praxis*, or positive
asceticism and active love within the sacramental life of the Church.

> One has to grow a great deal to win out beyond the *mathesis*, and it is necessary to suffer
> greatly to attain the mystery, the *praxis*.[2]

The beginning of Florensky's *praxis* was hallowed by the sacrament of marriage,
celebrated on 25 August 1910 in the remote village of Kutlovy Borki by the
bride's brother Father Aleksandr Giatsintov. This in turn opened the way for
the sacrament of ordination as deacon then priest of the Russian Orthodox
Church (celebrated by Bishop Fedor, rector of the Theological Academy, on 23
and 24 April 1911). This is not to say that Florensky's entry into the 'honourable
estate of Holy Matrimony' was undertaken in blind obedience to his spiritual
father, who had long foreseen and encouraged the step, still less as a calculated
move in an ecclesiastical career. As with everything else this unpredictable man
undertook, the motivation was idiosyncratic, almost whimsical, although, again
most truly in character, stubbornly faithful in execution.

> I married quite simply to fulfil the will of God, which I understood from a sign [wrote
> Florensky, recalling an aimless, disconsolate stroll through the countryside around
> Sergiev Posad] ... Mechanically, I can't remember why, I stooped down and closed my
> hand on a little leaf. I picked it and saw, to my surprise, that it was a four-leafed clover

– 'happiness'. The thought immediately struck me (and I felt it was not my thought) that this was a sign – the will of God. At the same time I remembered that ever since I was a child I had looked for a four-leafed clover, peered and poked through whole meadows, examined clump after clump, but in spite of all my efforts had never found what I sought.[3]

The marriage was a rude shock to Pavel Aleksandrovich's friends.

Pavlusha has got married [wrote Ern to his wife on 2 September 1910]. I called in on him as dusk was falling, we embraced and without a word he showed me his ring. I was thunderstruck, but he called out 'Anna!' and introduced us. Vasen'ka appeared, we sat down to tea, everything so easy and simple, and I sat there in amazement, trying to take in the *fait accompli*. She behaves affectionately to Vasia and calls him 'Thou'. I look at her face: his sister! It's three days since she arrived from Riazan and when they were wed I don't know. Pavlusha is quiet, calm and merry, natural and tender with his wife without any sign of being in love, as though they'd been living together for 20 years. And so – it's happened! But all my fears are dispersed. Nothing tragic. Everything very simple and good. The old, complex Pavel has died down and it seems he took this step without forcing himself. There will be children to whom they will be devoted and there will be one more close-knit family in Russia. She is very like Lilya [one of Florensky's sisters], not pretty at all, but obviously unassuming, good-natured, simple and perhaps very beautiful in soul. I liked her attitude to Pavlusha. Again, very natural, as though she were his sister, respectful and loving. That was my impression ... But, in spite of everything, I was a bit sad for Pavlusha. There is so much self-abjuration and humility in what he has done which I doubt I would have been capable of, I even feel a kind of admiration for him. But, at the same time, there's something vulnerable about him and [indecipherable word], and through the quiet merriment glimpses of deep sadness ...[4]

Most probably, Ern was not just writing of his friend's known aversion to marriage. The logical next step, to take the cloth as a simple priest in pre-revolutionary Russia, where only monks rose to the higher ranks of the Church, was, according to their mutual friend Sergei Bulgakov, who himself stemmed from the hereditary priesthood, the act of a simpleton, a holy fool.[5] It was to lose caste – socially and intellectually. Florensky's marriage to this plain if pleasant-faced girl of peasant origin was an act of identification with those humble ancestors of his who had served the Church as priests and deacons in the far forests of the Kostroma district, and a potential renunciation of his birthright as one at home in the world of art, music and science and of the luxurious merchant-princely heritage of his Armenian forebears. It was also a declaration of intent and, just as his entry into the Theological Academy had been, an act of total commitment. Most impressive in the story of Florensky's marriage is not just the quiet mutual care and tenderness which distinguished his relationship with Anna and his paternal devotion to their children, but the fact that he shared his home amicably with Anna's and Vasilii's illiterate mother, in her own way a bearer of the oral culture of the traditional Russian peasantry, and that his wife was accepted and respected by his own mother and sisters and, until her own death in 1973, continued to be sought out, loved and honoured by his friends. 'We are one person', he wrote to Anna from his first exile in Nizhni Novgorod,[6] and this was indeed how he understood marriage, even as he had once understood 'brotherhood' ... as an indissoluble fusion, at least in this life.

Yet, in spite of his great need for love and life 'together', Florensky was undemonstrative to a fault in his letters and speech, and the evidence we have of his relationship with his wife is largely second-hand. Some, notably Bulgakov in jealous mood, found it 'stylised',[7] others – touchingly harmonious and serene.[8] However, in Florensky's essays on *Names*, for all that he is careful to stress that given names confer only potential, and profoundly antonymic potential at that, to be developed for good or ill by the bearer, there are often clues to be gathered as to his perception of people to whom he had been close. Of 'Alexander', his father's and El'chaninov's given name, he writes that Alexanders, most harmonious of beings, 'can share their worldly goods without pause for thought. But they are not much inclined to share themselves and that, given a close relationship, makes for a feeling of mutual detachment.'[9] 'Vasilii' is distinguished by will-power, an organising mind, a sense of duty and a suppressed sensibility which occasionally finds release in strong drink. 'Pavel' reads almost like a self-portrait: he is essentially an eccentric, a holy fool (*iurodivyi*), obsessed by the need to embody the principle of spirituality in life, often abrasive, impatient of human warmth and tenderness because they deprive him of the cold bliss of contemplation and sap the will to action: 'Nourished directly from the well-spring of earthly sorrow, Paul yet sees that the root of being is Good, not evil.'[10]

Of 'Anna' Florensky writes with the pen of a poet: Anna is rooted in Grace, her subconscience touches on the subconscience of the World Soul; all that is instinctive and elemental in her is somehow objective. Because of this impersonal wealth of being she often, as an individual, seems poor – to herself and others. Her great gifts she feels *as* gifts, not as achievements. She is mistrustful of intellect which, it seems to her, may distort 'pure experience' and 'for this reason plan, style, even punctuation all seem to her something secondary, artificial, insincere'. In the same way, she has no need to cultivate appreciation of art and music:

> that which is conferred by art is in a sense more profoundly and fully familiar to Anna than anything one can obtain from art ... Precisely that which music can bestow on us Anna possesses in full measure without having to make the least effort.[11]

Florensky, in a word, had found his own antonym, his ideal female complement, in this unpretentious, sometimes unaffectedly childlike woman, whose very being, as it seemed to him, was tuned in to the natural harmonies of Grace. From family photographs and letters it is clear that Anna not only kept the young priest's house and garden and minded his children, but that she sat beside him at his work-table, knew where he kept his papers, stood behind him at the piano and had a special, twinkling half-smile for a shared joke. When his son Vasilii married, Florensky wrote to him from Solovki: 'I would wish you to find in Natasha at least a quarter of what your Mama has been for me over the last 25 years.'[12] Yet perhaps the most romantic passage in his letters to Anna herself was ten lines of his own translation from a beautiful, tragic poem by the Persian poet Hafiz on undying fidelity 'under the press of fate and sorrow rotated by the turning of the world.'[13]

For the first years of their marriage the couple found a new home, a modest three-window, izba-type building, known as 'Ozerov's house' on Shtatnaia ulitsa[14], which Anna kept spotlessly clean, quiet for Florensky's studies yet welcoming for his guests. He enjoyed the domesticity, the ordered, unfussy, self-sufficient housekeeping which required ample store of supplies so that there need be no frenetic dashing down to the shops in the case of unexpected guests, but rather a modest abundance of traditional food in keeping with the requirements of the Church calendar. For Anna and her mother, who shortly after the marriage became an integral part of the family and shouldered responsibility for cooking and catering, this was the natural order of things. They enjoyed preparing festive dishes but were undismayed by the required austerities and Pavel Aleksandrovich himself, putting his boyhood botanising to more mundane use, loved to grow and to gather. On 24 March 1912, in the night of Good Friday to Holy Saturday when the last preparations for the Easter Feast are under way in the home and the orphaned world breathlessly awaits the Resurrection of Christ, Florensky wrote to his friend Sergei Bulgakov: 'this is the time when "all flesh falls silent" and when, in our home, some are asleep and others go silently about the housework ...'[15]

So Florensky's family life dovetailed into the liturgical year. He worked late, making full use of the quiet small hours when others slept, and rose early to attend to his ecclesiastical duties, but always appeared alert and clear-headed, achieving a quiet, active sobriety at the heart of a lively, steadily increasing family and amidst the turmoil of war and revolution which were soon to engulf his life and work. The laying on of hands at ordination was an intense spiritual experience. It was also a coming home: 'I have returned to my forefathers', Florensky wrote that day to another friend, the maveric St Petersburg writer and religious thinker Vasilii Rozanov.[16] He was given the parish of the Annunciation in the village of Blagoveshchensk two and a half kilometres north-west of

Sergiev Posad. Here, in the beautiful but homely seventeenth-century church, he found inspiration and consolation in the celebration of the liturgy and administration of the sacraments, which he performed with reverence and simplicity, if at first rather inexpertly. It was as a priest before the altar, Father Sergii Bulgakov was to recall on hearing of Father Pavel's death, that he was most truly himself. Rozanov, for his part, seeking the operative word to describe one friend to the other, wrote simply to Bulgakov: 'He is a priest', using the high Greek word (ἱερεῦς).[17]

Absorbed by the *praxis* of his vocation, Florensky seems to have shed his former somewhat irritable impatience with the ethos and traditions of the intelligentsia, particularly within his own family. On 3 June 1911, the birth of his first child Vasilii set the seal on his new identity as *pater familias*. It was natural for him to perceive himself and others as offshoots of a family tree and it was a profound joy to feel that, in his and Anna's offspring, he now had an heir of his body and a new mind and soul in his care. 'You will always be my own beloved little Vasia', he was to write to the eldest son who had shouldered his role as family provider after his father's arrest – and regretted the busy schedule which had made him a somewhat remote parent, not given to organising time-consuming, special treats and, perhaps, unduly stern when rebuking Vasia's enthusiastic attempts to build houses with his library books.[18]

On 14 December 1915 Vasilii, according to Sergei Bulgakov a brilliant lad,[19] was followed by Kirill, of whom Father Pavel was eventually to think of as his own most likely intellectual successor. The first daughter Ol'ga, nicknamed Olen' (Stag), was born on 21 February 1918; and after her Mikhail (Mika, 1922), a delicate child but with all a small boy's passion for hunting and exploring, which culminated in an adventurous career in the far east of the Soviet Union; last but not least, on 11 October 1924, came Maria (Tin-a-Tin or Tika, 1924), still small enough during the years of Florensky's imprisonment for him to send polite messages to her dolls and pretend to get news of her from migratory seagulls.

Naturally, the changing rhythms of Father Pavel's life were to have a profound effect on his work, but this is not immediately apparent from the chronology of his publications, as the peaceful early years of marriage were devoted to consolidating achievements already alien to him as yesterday's concerns: the publication and defence of his thesis separately from the immensely time-consuming preparation of *The Pillar and Ground of Truth*, in which last he received much help from Bulgakov and by which he appears to have set so little store that he was soon without so much as a single spare authorial copy.[20]

Even before the award of his Master's degree, Florensky had to combine his new duties as priest with an ever-increasing workload at the Academy. In June 1912 Bishop Fedor made him acting editor of the MDA journal *Bogoslovskii vestnik* and the appointment was confirmed at the beginning of the academic year. Bishop Antonii (Florensov), under obedience to whom Florensky, as he wrote in the dedication of his speech in defence of his dissertation, had first entered the Theological Academy to study then stayed on to teach, feared for the young couple's health ('what your wife thinks is very important') and encouraged him to give up his beloved village parish and, after a period serving in the Academy Church within the monastery, on 29 September 1912, to take up the less exacting and distracting cure of the St Mary Magdalene House Church at the Sergiev Posad hostel for retired Red Cross sisters, a function which he continued to fulfil until their disbandment in May 1921. Father Pavel was particularly struck by the fact that the altar here faced west, not east, and took this as in some way emblematic of his continued involvement with the world of pagan antiquity. The appointment brought Florensky into contact with the patroness of the hostel, the Grand Princess Elizaveta Fedorovna, and brought him and his family an actively benevolent friend in the person of the Directress Natalia Kiseleva.

Nominated Professor Extraordinary in 1914, Florensky took on new lecture courses at the Academy, examining duties and supervision of research students. He published no less than 24 reports on candidates' theses in *Bogoslovskii vestnik* between 1910 and 1916 and, as editor of that journal, encouraged contributions from lay religious thinkers alongside those of professional theologians and, a startling innovation in a Church periodical at that time, even published some female authors.[21] For Volume I, 1913 he reworked, under the title 'The limits of gnoseology (the basic antonym of the theory of knowledge)', a variation of the 1908 introduction to the course of lectures on the philosophy of the ancient world which he read from the year of his graduation until the academic year 1917/1918.[22] The course itself was under constant revision right up to the year 1916/1917 and it is against the background of this ongoing updating of bibliography and, occasionally, reconsideration of content that we should seek to understand Florensky's contribution to classical studies – not to mention the cupids cavorting above the fireplace in his dining room and the anomalous preponderance of framed photographs of antique sculptures of nymphs and heroes which sometimes shocked newcomers to his priestly study. For all the simplicity of his family life and the joy of homecoming to his Kostroma ancestors, Florensky never felt entirely at ease with his fellow-theologians and ecclesiastics, who, indeed, barred him from the teaching of theology *per se* and occasionally riled him by their entrenched resistance to his unconventional genius.

The clergy [he complained to his steadfast friend and patron Bishop Fedor on 7 November 1913] in their capacity as those in authority in the Church, in part by right, in part by usurpation, tend more than any others of the powers-that-be to identify the Church of Christ and Her attributes with the traditional priestly [he uses the derogatory *popovskii*] way of life, manners and interests. I don't take it upon myself to say *popovstvo* is bad in itself, but I do say in no uncertain terms that it is not just alien to me, but I see no reason at all to conform to it. Yet from it there emanates a load of petty requirements made as though in the name of the Church but fearsome and quite incomprehensible for anyone not raised in that atmosphere.[23]

However, the cross his spiritual father had appointed him to bear was tolerance within a community of jealous academics and zealous priests, rather than monastic, ascetic feats or the idyllic simplicity of 'the life of a village priest', and Florensky devoted himself to his work in the Ancient World with untiring energy. Not content to repeat a course, he would often rewrite lectures into the small hours of the day in which he delivered them.[24] In a letter to Vasilii Rozanov, he wrote on 25 November 1913:

I am plunging ever deeper into antiquity. Greece – there we have the prelude to Orthodoxy, 'our own', a strikingly deep and organic link, both formal and external and, more importantly, in spirit, in essence ... Greece ... she is we ourselves, she is our own soul.[25]

Student reaction varied. Some found their teacher's excursions into the realms of archaeology and costume, his leaps from myth to etymology, from logic to intuitive interpretation of symbols and from mathematics to aesthetics hopelessly confusing, while others were mesmerised and enchanted. The lecturer appeared to be puzzling things out from source as he spoke and some pupils, used to being told what to think and instructed how to justify foregone conclusions, were bewildered and resentful. 'A lecture is not a tram to take you from one place to another', Florensky informed these last, 'but a walk with friends. It is the walk that's important, not the destination.'[26] He wanted his students to learn to research primary sources, to notice significant detail, to accompany him on his excursions into the mind of the past. Many responded. Below is one description:

The largest lecture room is overflowing. There are people standing between the benches, along the walls, sitting on the windowsills, crowded about the doors ... Florensky, though his voice was rather low, without resonance, painted pictures with words and not only painted but awoke a kind of musical resonance in the soul ... I felt eager to live, meditate, think, create. He would open our eyes to the minutest details of the world about us, of nature and people, beauty took on lustre and caressed us with its lucent clarity, evil appeared as shadow, as the absence of beauty. Evil ceased to be threatening ...[27]

But others merely shrugged him off: 'Was there anything anybody didn't understand?' he once asked rashly. 'We understood absolutely nothing' came the reply.[28] Some regarded their lecturer's simplicity and modesty as affectation and spiritual pride. As Master of Theology from 1914, Florensky wore only the priest's plain pectoral cross, never the more elaborate ornament to which his academic status entitled him.

Naturally, Father Pavel had now to play his part as examiner for higher degrees, in which capacity he showed himself a formidable but benevolent 'opponent'. A case in point is the immensely detailed critique composed for the examination of A. M. Tuberovsky's Master's thesis on 'The Resurrection of Christ', submitted to the Council of the Imperial Moscow Theological Academy and discussed first on 2 May 1916, on which occasion the candidate was required to make considerable amendments to the version of his monograph he had already published. Florensky, in spite of the severity of his critique of style and content, recommended that the author should nevertheless be awarded the degree he sought on the grounds that the thesis showed a sincere desire to serve the Church and promising evidence of wide reading, and that the candidate himself might well turn out to be 'an ugly duckling'.[29] He found himself, however, in a minority of two and earned no gratitude from Tuberovsky who – apparently unacquainted with Andersen – deeply resented the 'ugly duckling' label and regarded Father Pavel, who had been a year junior to him at the Academy, as the author of his failure. He appealed the decision which, at an acrimonious debate during the frenetic summer of 1917, was reversed. Tuberovsky was awarded the same Metropolitan Makarii prize of 289 roubles which had been granted to Florensky for his *On Spiritual Truth*.

The background to the dispute was the rise of the Renewal Movement (*Obnovlenchestvo*) within the Church, which was sufficiently socially radical to make a comparatively easy accommodation with Bolshevik officials working on the 'divide and rule' principle after the Revolution. This led, in the 1920s, to open conflict with more traditionally minded hierarchs, and to the infiltration, loss of integrity and, eventually, disintegration of the so-called Living Church, many of whose members had once been merely liberal advocates of renewal. In 1916, however, this naissant movement was but one of the cross-currents of opinion within the Church, strongly influenced by the more radical lay thinkers of the new religious consciousness and by fashionable Western intuitivism and pragmatism, particularly by Bergson and James.[30]

Tuberovsky himself took no part in the development of the Renewal tendency in Soviet times but, after the dissolution of the MDA, retired to his native village where he took holy orders and served as a priest alongside his own father until his death in 1939. Perhaps in order to distance Florensky from the Renewal Movement, it has been suggested that, in criticising Tuberovsky's highly personalised and modernising approach, Florensky was doing battle with his old self as author of *The Pillar and Ground of Truth*, but in fact the blistering and detailed critique shows him rather as distancing himself from an inept vulgarisation, amounting at times to caricature, of his own attempts to write of Christian dogma as contingent on experience and to use a vocabulary familiar and agreeable to educated, even primarily scientifically educated contemporaries. Language was important to Florensky, and he was genuinely pained by Tuberovsky's pretentious neologisms, use of everyday commercial terminology to explain the 'economy' of Redemption, overworking of frequently misapplied technical terms such as 'dynamic' and 'static' and clumsy attempts to russify catchwords from foreign books on psychology and the natural sciences. As a trained scientist, Florensky was revolted by Tuberovsky's description of the Resurrected Body of Christ as 'excluding' those organs of which we shall have no need in the after-life. Either, he says sharply, we admit we do not know, or we use our knowledge of anatomy as a guideline and do not invent monsters with a normal head and a body made of empty skin blown up like a balloon![31] He also makes mincemeat of Tuberovsky's use of Latin and Greek and of misunderstood references to the Classics. The fact that Florensky objects to such combinations of words as an 'intimately-individual appreciation of the Resurrection'[32] does not necessarily imply a renunciation of the personalism of a younger, more impetuous self. The one firm statement he makes against subjectivity in theology is not a denial of the importance of lyrical, subjective feeling as a starting-point for meditation (which is the function of such feeling in *The Pillar and Ground of Truth*), nor yet a denial of the role of the subject in the act of cognisance, which he always maintained was to achieve synergy with the object, but rather a rebuttal of the notion that 'pietistic getting on intimate terms with the Lord God' should be considered a desirable methodological technique, considering that 'the task of theology is not in the least to make one's *own* (possibly quite worthless) experience the object of our theologising, but to acquire that higher spiritual experience which leads one's consciousness out of the subjective sphere into the ontological.'[33]

This last word, 'ontological', is very much the key to Florensky's mature thought. Under his editorship, *Bogoslovskii vestnik* became known as the organ of the Ontological School of theology. The meaning of the word, though, is not the opposite of 'subjective' but rather comprises subjectivity (also an existential fact) as a fallible but necessary check on 'objective' methods of cognisance:

The basic self-awareness of humanity, that 'I live in the world and with the world', presupposes the existence, the real existence as reality, of both myself, humanity as such, and that which is outside myself, which exists apart from me or, more exactly, independently of human awareness ... In the act of cognisance it is impossible to separate subject from object; cognisance is at once the one and the other; more exactly, it is precisely the cognisance of the object by the subject, a unity, that is, in which the one can be distinguished from the other only in the abstract, yet at the same time the object is not obliterated by the subject, neither is the latter dissolved in the object of cognisance exterior to itself. Moreover, once unified, they do not engulf one another even though, while maintaining their mutual independence, they are no longer divided. The theological formula without confusion and without separation is fully applicable to the cognitive interrelationship of subject and object …[34]

'Ontology', the Oxford Dictionary tells us, is a 'branch of metaphysics dealing with the nature of being'. This takes us back to the chapter in *The Pillar and Ground of Truth* dealing with the nature of 'true God of true God' and the Russian word *istina* (truth), which is, Florensky maintained, etymologically close to the verb 'to be'. If God is 'that which truly is', then it is indeed imperative to escape 'the subjective sphere into the ontological' in order to gain a higher spiritual insight into the Divine Nature; but this Florensky had always known, from the days of his childhood 'Eros' for the laws and exceptions of the natural world. The person, on the other hand, is equally a partaker of the absolute being of God, Creator and Redeemer, and it is no denial of the person as such that Florensky, having shaken off a long-drawn-out spiritual adolescence, could once again, as in childhood, begin to investigate the world around him rather than the process within … and to look more deeply into literature, art, culture and science from the point of view he had achieved as a celebrant of the Holy Sacraments and a priest of the Church, i.e. of one who touched in his daily life on the ultimate reality of Divine Incarnation and Redemption.

It is of this orientation from *within* the Church that Florensky spoke in the address pronounced in honour of his teacher Aleksei Vvedensky's quarter-centenary of service in the Theological Academy:

scholarly work does not become ecclesiastical because it treats various specifically theological subjects but rather because it takes an ecclesiastical approach to any object it undertakes to study … Or, to express the same thought in a different way, one might say your appeal was not to the field of study which describes how the world looks at the Church but to that which teaches how the Church looks at the world, and at Herself.[35]

This field of study, into which Florensky had both found his own way and, to some extent, as he acknowledged in this speech, joined with other disciples of Vvedensky,[36] was a search not just for one's own truth but for *the* Truth. In another speech on the occasion of the fortieth day after the death of the distinguished Slavophile Fedor Samarin, who died on 23 December 1916, Florensky suggested a division of writers into plagiarists, for whom every truth has to be *my* truth, and 'pseudo-epigraphists', happy to ascribe their best formulations to some other name in order the more vividly to encapsulate the truth at which they have arrived. It was, of course, Samarin who Florensky designated as a 'pseudo-epigraphist', but the quaintly pedantic label suited his own later manner to a nicety. At the same time, he believed that thought, emanating from the practice of the Orthodox Faith and the attempt to see with the eyes and understand with the mind of the Church, would open up the possibility of a particularly 'Russian' school of philosophy, since

> the philosophy of every nation, in its deepest essence, is the discovery of the people's faith, emerges from that faith and strives towards it. If a Russian philosophy is possible, then only as an Orthodox philosophy, as the philosophy of the Orthodox Faith, as a precious garment of gold (reason) and jewels (results obtained by experiment) for the Holy Orthodox Faith.[37]

This pursuit of a specifically Russian 'philosophy of the Orthodox faith' did not alienate Florensky from that Russian religious renaissance of which he himself was a part. His ongoing schoolboy attachment to Ern brought him into the orbit of Viacheslav Ivanov, to whom Ern had become deeply attached while living abroad and in whose Moscow flat on Zubovsky Boulevard he stayed for long periods as a house-guest after the poet and his family took up residence there in 1913. Together, Ern and Ivanov attended Florensky's defence of his Master's thesis and, on one occasion, Florensky spent several nights talking of the nature of artistic and mystic ecstasy with the almost entirely nocturnal Viacheslav. 'I went to bed and left them to it', Ern reported back to his wife.[38] It was to Viacheslav Ivanov 'with friendly greetings' that Florensky dedicated his elegant scriptural exegesis of the much-disputed verses from the epistle to the Philippians, 2.6–8: The argument was based on a shared view of ecstasy, founded on a sub-Schegelian schema enlarged upon by Nietzsche in *The Birth of Tragedy from the Spirit of Music* and delineated by Ivanov in the influential 1913 lecture (published as an article in 1914) 'On the limits of art', originally read as a lecture in the Moscow Philosophical Society. It posited ascent through Dionysian ecstasy to the moment of Apollonic revelation or inspiration, followed by descent back through and to the material world necessitated by the urge to communicate, to embody that which had been perceived in words, sounds or artistic visual form. Florensky interprets the Slavonic *ne voskhish-chenie nepsheva*, usually understood, as in King James Bible, as 'thought it not robbery [to be equal with God]', as 'not thanks to ecstatic vision (transport, visionary elevation)'. Christ, being 'of one substance with the Father', did not need to achieve rapture to know that He was one with God. Florensky's far-ranging etymological excursions into the use of the Greek words of the original drew an enthusiastic, though not uncritical, response from Ivanov in a letter dated 7 October 1915, from which it is clear that, though poet and theologian might differ on matters of detail, the two thought along the same lines and took a shared delight in applying their knowledge of Ancient Greece to the interpretation of the Scriptures.[39]

Florensky's increasing inclination to speak from within the Church did, however, give a certain edge to his relationship with those representatives of the 'god-seeking' intelligentsia who had wandered furthest from Russian Orthodoxy and from the nostalgic populism which had been so powerful a stimulus to the desire for dialogue with the Church at the turn of the century. The Merezhkovskys, for instance, had wearied of the attempt to reconcile modernist culture with the People's Church and, after two years' discreet retirement in Paris to avoid political backlash after the quelling of the 1905 Revolution, had returned to declare that there was nothing more to be hoped of the 'historical Church', of which they quietly ceased to be practising members, preferring to 'celebrate' with friends in the intimacy of their home. Florensky, not surprisingly, put considerable effort into weaning his tragic sister Ol'ga (Valia), who was to die from the family nemesis of tuberculosis at the age of 24, four years almost to the day after the murder of Troitsky, from her friendship with Hippius, incurring the hostility of the latter, as 'jealous' a friend as he was himself, and he appears in Hippius's memoirs as a somewhat sinister figure, the cleverest and 'most cruel' of the priests.[40] Marietta Shaginian, another admirer of Hippius, who had gravitated towards the Golgotha Church, also found Florensky unsympathetic and over-zealous and complained to Bely, whose inclination towards theosophy and later Steiner's anthroposophy took him right out of his old friend's orbit for many years and who replied that Shaginian should simply ignore 'Florensky's saying foul things'.[41] Berdiaev, the apostle of spiritual freedom and an unrepentant aristocrat married to a Roman Catholic, took a personal and, according to Bulgakov, somewhat envious dislike to the soft-voiced young priest with his downcast eyes, encyclopaedic erudition and 'stylised orthodoxy'. Florensky, he thought, was seeking to stifle the agonies of intellect under an assumed cloak of humility[42] – not a virtue Berdiaev admired – and it was not until religion and idealism came under fire from a new, anti-Christian tyranny that he again began to recognise how much they had in common.

Sergei Bulgakov, on the other hand, once Berdiaev's close ally and fellow-Marxist-turned-idealist, whom Florensky had originally encountered through the Christian Brotherhood for Struggle, became a firm friend and a frequent visitor to the family home in Sergiev Posad. Though Sergei Nikolaevich retained sufficient anti-authoritarian zeal to resist the call to take Holy Orders until the post-revolutionary dissolution of the Holy Synod and subsequent emancipation of Church from State, he was nevertheless moving steadily towards recon-ciliation with the Church based on a lively sense of his own personal 'religious inadequacy'. Bulgakov shared not only theological and intellectual affinities but the joys and sorrows of fatherhood with his friend Father Pavel who, after his own family, he loved 'more than anything in the world, with wonder, reverence, adoration, as a schoolboy his teacher'.[43] The friendship, however, was based on contrasting character: intellectually, Bulgakov's forte was sociology and economics and, though he shared Florensky's interest in the spiritual in art, he had little feeling for the *laws* of music, art and poetry *per se*. Temperamentally, too, they were opposites. As the self-critical Bulgakov wrote to Florensky as early as 7 July 1908:

> It is true, you are right, I'm always getting worked up over something or other, hysterical sensitivity and religious weakness are the basis of my empirical 'temperament', not to mention the fact that, in some circumstances, I distrust the over-consistent cultivation of the calm attitude which you consider to be the norm.[44]

Yet this contrast in temperament undoubtedly strengthened rather than undermined the relationship between the two men. The energetic and persistent Bulgakov was a faithful ally who ardently embraced Florensky's Christianisation of Solov'ev's cult of Sophia[45] and was always ready to assist or indeed initiate plans which went against Synodal guidelines, such as Florensky's 1913–1916 serialisation in *Bogoslovskii vestnik* of a *Study of the Apocalypse* by Archimandrite Fedor (Aleksei Bukharev), which had been banned by the Synod in 1862,[46] or to involve his friend in his own projects, such as the publication of manuscripts of diaries and other works by Anna Nikolaevna Shmidt, an admirer of Vladimir Solov'ev's who claimed direct mystic contact with the Divine Wisdom. Living in Moscow, Bulgakov was in constant contact with Medtner's Musagetes, Novoselov's 'Religious-Philosophical Library' and Morozova's Put' and did his best through these contacts to further Florensky's efforts to publish Serapion Mashkin and to place their joint review of Sergei Solov'ev's new edition of his uncle's *Works*,[47] eventually published by Florensky himself in *Bogoslovskii vestnik*.

In general, Professor Bulgakov kept his reclusive friend in touch with the capital, persuading him to accompany him to view Shchukin's collection of Picasso paintings or exhibitions by Nesterov and Ciurlonis and sharing his and Viacheslav Ivanov's indignation at the exclusion of Rozanov from the Religious Philosophical Society, albeit on a purely personal rather than ideological basis. Merezhkovsky, the most ardent advocate of expulsion, had, Bulgakov considered, come out badly from the affair and Bulgakov only refrained from writing in defence of Rozanov because the piece he envisaged began to sound like a denunciation of his opponent and 'I've never made personal attacks'.[48] He did, however, share Florensky's and Rozanov's interest in the *Kabbala* and in the

Jewishness of St Paul and thought their now much execrated correspondence on the subject interesting and profound.[49]

Bulgakov, like Florensky, was an active associate of Mikhail Aleksandrovich Novoselov's Circle of Seekers after Christian Knowledge and of his work as publisher of a series of books on religious questions of contemporary interest, printed in Sergiev Posad under the imprint of the Religious-Philosophical Library (1902–1917).[50]

The Circle of Seekers after Christian Knowledge thus had firm links with Sergiev Posad. Florensky found Novoselov a *dacha* where he spent most of his summers, and maintained close contact with the latter in Moscow through his ex-pupil and friend Fedor Andreev, not yet in holy orders and always ready to oblige, whether to help his teacher move house or to act as go-between between *Bogoslovskii vestnik* and the Circle, whose discussions in Moscow Florensky himself attended when he could find time. There was no hard-and-fast line between the more 'liberal' Vladimir Solov'ev Society, the Morozova-Trubetskoi circle about the publishing house Put' and the Circle of Seekers after Christian Knowledge, though Berdiaev and Shagynian found the last too ecclesiastically orientated for their taste. Florensky, for his part, emancipated by his commitment to the priesthood from the fear of being drawn back into and reabsorbed by lay society, moved freely between these microworlds of the Russian religious renaissance and was respected by all for his capacity to discuss the essence of a problem in its own terms.

The working relationship with the Circle of Seekers after Christian Knowledge was, however, particularly close, stimulating and businesslike. As Florensky wrote to Rozanov on 7 June 1913:

> Or course, the Moscow ecclesiastical fellowhip is the best thing we have and in this friendship we find a complete *coincidentia oppositorum*. Everyone is free and everyone is bound, each in his own way, yet each like the others ... We don't give talks, we discuss, and don't even so much discuss as communicate ... The ongoing task of a Novoselov, a Bulgakov, an Andreev or a Tsvetkov etc. etc. is – for me, for everyone of us – not *their* business, the task of some rival (the worse it goes for him, the better for me!), but my *own* business, at least in part my own ...[51]

In those busy pre-revolutionary years this was perhaps the nearest Florensky came to finding that brotherhood, that togetherness which had been so inherent a part of his dream of the monastic life, or, before that, of 'anonymous' cooperation on some future Symbolist journal.

Indeed, Florensky did write a number of anonymous introductions to volumes of the Religious-Philosophical Library which involved him, not infrequently against his better judgement, in some of the most controversial questions of the time. A case in point is the *imiaslavtsy*[52] controversy, thanks to which he and Novoselov found themselves, somewhat to their own confusion, in head-on confrontation with the Holy Synod.

The controversy (also known as the Athonite Rebellion) centred around the practice of the Jesus prayer as expounded in *The Way of the Pilgrim* by a Monk of the Eastern Church (first published in English) and in a book in Russian by Father Ilarion, the disciple of an ex-Athonite monk who had retired to a hermitage in Georgia, entitled *In the Caucasian Mountains*, first published in 1907 and reprinted in 1910 and again, in Kiev, in 1913 under the patronage of the Empress's sister, the saintly Elizaveta Fedorovna. This book enjoyed great popularity on Mount Athos as a devotional aid among Russian monks of the St Andrew Skete, a filial of the predominantly Greek monastery Vatopedi, and of the Nea Thebais Skete, a filial of the Russian Monastery of St Panteleimon. To both monastic authorities, however, the book's orthodoxy appeared suspect and, after a negative internal review and much debate, its use by the largely simple and theologically naive community in the St Andrew Skete was forbidden by their abbot, Ieronym. The abbot was immediately ousted by an indignant brotherhood, who appointed one of their number, Brother David, in his stead. The appointment, however, was not recognised, which led to open insubordination, rioting, letters of complaint, a blockade of the Skete, the excommunication of the rebels and an appeal to the Russian Government by the Athonite authorities to send in soldiers to control their monks. This was done and the unfortunate brothers, many of whom had long since lost all ties with their families and lay employment, were shipped back to the motherland, exhorted to recant and, when they proved stubborn, imprisoned or disbanded, excommunicated from their Church and abandoned to their own devices. Sympathy for these rather brutally treated contemplatives was lively in certain circles at court and within the Church itself and also among the religiously minded intelligentsia, particularly the Novoselov group. As so often, this rift between holy and well-meaning men, concentrated on matters by definition beyond the scope of human reason, aroused quite unholy passions. The *imiaslavtsy* found a vigorous, if academically ill-prepared, defender in Father Antonii (Bulatovich), a well-connected priest-monk who had taken vows and joined the community on Mount Athos after a distinguished career in Russia, Abyssinia and China as an officer of the Hussars. In the autumn of 1912, Novoselov undertook to publish Bulatovich's *Apologiia* for the beliefs and practices of his protégés and asked Florensky to write an introduction as from the editors of the Religious-Philosophical Library and to edit the ex-cavalry officer's somewhat bellicose, theologically hit-and-miss text. Disciplinarians, indignant beyond measure at the organised rebellion of the monks and the temerity of Bulatovich's public challenge to authority, counter-attacked; the Holy Synod called for expert opinions. These were provided by Sergei Troitsky, an academic theologian, Archbishop Nikon, who had been sent to Athos by the Synod to re-establish order, and Metropolitan Antonii (Khrapovitsky), who had already launched a ferocious pre-emptive onslaught on the *imiaslavtsy* in a review of *In the Caucasian Mountains* (which, as Florensky pointed out in his introduction to Bulatovich's *Apologiia*, he had not even read)[53] condemning its adherents as ignorant mystagogues, no better than the sectarian *khlysty*.[54]

Novoselov and his friends, to whom the ancient practice of the Jesus prayer was an object of veneration and who had no difficulty in believing, with Florensky, that the 'The Name is God, but God is not the Name'[55] took the zeal of the *imiaslavtsy* for a welcome sign that the Russian Orthodox Church was still a live volcano fed by the fires of the Spirit and, given the fact that *In the Caucasian Mountains* had gone through three editions without trouble from the ecclesiastical censor, underestimated the virulent reflexes of the great and the good whose authority has been challenged, as they saw it, by a handful of ignorant peasant monks. True, Florensky did have qualms when he considered the prevalence of positivism and the distinctly anti-mystical intellectual climate of the Theological Academies, but he had thought the Synod too torpid to reassert the righteousness of its judgements with any vigour. He had had neither time nor opportunity either to correct Bulatovich's text with the cooperation of its author as he would have wished, or to formulate his own considered defence of the practice of the Jesus prayer and was overwhelmed and shamed by the flood of correspondence for and against the Bulatovich publication which, via a rather shaken Novoselov, whose forthright criticism of Rasputin had already made him vulnerable to attack from above, now landed on his desk in Sergiev Posad. It was not that Florensky's own academic position was threatened. Even the forthright old disciplinarian Khrapovitsky, when he eventually grasped that Father Pavel, whom he had always thought a model of erudition and piety, albeit too mystically inclined and too little concerned with straightforward morality, was the anonymous author of the impertinent preface, held no grudge against him for, as he saw it, being led astray by 'sympathy for that villain and nihilist Bulatovich'.[56] What upset Florensky was rather the awareness that he had collaborated in stirring up an acrimonious debate about profound and sacred matters which were now being bandied about before an indifferent or hostile public. Ivan Scherbov, a lecturer in theology at the St Petersburg Theological Academy, who had afforded lodging and protection to Bulatovich when the latter came to plead his cause in the capital, was striving to broker an agreement (albeit for the sake of 'economy') to patch over the confrontation, and sent Florensky Professor Troitsky's counter-arguments or 'antitheses' to the *Apologiia* (with which Bulatovich was prepared, for the sake of reconciliation with the Church, to agree). Father Pavel replied unhappily:

I am so weary of all the fuss and rows because of the Name that it seems I am ready to agree to absolutely anything just to be left in peace – to agree outwardly, that is, with all that is required ... So we must hope the opponents will consent to these [Troitsky's] antitheses and hope that it will merely be an act of 'economy' ... I admit, *in my heart*, I blame the *imiaslavtsy* very much, and even M[ikhail] A[leksandrovi]ch [Novoselov] ... It is unbearably painful to me that *Imiaslavie* – an ancient, sacred mystery of the Church – has been dragged out into the market place and tossed from hand to hand by people who have no right to so much as touch it and who, by their whole make-up, are incapable of understanding it ... It's the fault of all those who raised the question to begin with, of Father Ilarion and of Ioann of Cronstadt.[57] But if Fathers Ilarion and Ioann spoke of the spiritual in a spiritual way, then Father Antonii, seeking to justify himself and his teaching to those before whom it would have been better to keep silence, has already begun to *rationalise*, already stripped Ilarion's thought, that ancient thought, of its sacred cloak of mystery. Father Antonii *adapts the doctrine of the Name to the mentality of the Intelligentsia*, but hasn't quite succeeded in doing so ... Christianity is and should be sacramental.[58]

Unfortunately, the Synod almost immediately pre-empted the intended 'economical' solution to the dispute by publishing the reports of their experts in the official *Tserkovnyi vestnik* and proclaiming all unrepentant *imiaslavtsy* heretics. The rift was temporarily healed on the eirenic advice of the saintly elder German of Zosima Pustyn when, at Easter 1914, at the express request of the Tsar, the *imiaslavtsy* were given an 'Easter present' and readmitted to full communion with the Church until the matter should be properly debated by a Church Council. Upon the outbreak of war that summer, Bulatovich, true to his upbringing, resumed his priestly office and went off to minister to troops at the front, which he did with considerable panache until the end of the war, and it was not until after the Revolution that the Church reneged on the agreement, maintaining that, in fact, the *imiaslavtsy* had only been readmitted as an act of 'mercy' and the underlying theological dispute about whether or not the Name of God was God indeed had never been properly resolved. It appointed a Sub-Commission to look into the matter, in which both Bulgakov and Florensky were to play an active part. Florensky, who had made a close study of the 'theses' of the so-called *imiabortsy*[59] responsible for the reports to the Synod, but had refrained, at the time, from further involving either *Bogoslovskii vestnik* or Novoselov's publishing house with the vociferously polemical Bulatovich, now prepared a considered defence of the *imiaslavtsy's* position, working hard towards reconciliation. It was owing entirely to the Bolshevik dissolution of the All Russian Church Council ('a plague on both your houses' indeed) that the Commission never met and the matter remained unresolved.[60]

During the truce which had followed on the 1914 'Easter present' to the *imiaslavtsy*, Florensky's attitude was best expressed in a letter refusing to publish a renewed attack on them by Khrapovitsky, with whom he was personally on good terms, on the grounds that he would not be permitted to reply in print. 'The only thing I would like to see happen and which would entirely satisfy me', he wrote to Khrapovitsky on 29 December 1915, 'is an authoritative admission that, in the questions touched upon in this matter, there is something extremely important, as yet unresolved and deserving of maximal attention.'[61]

In this way, Florensky's association with the Circle of Seekers after Christian Knowledge acted as a powerful irritant which prevented his settling too comfortably into pastoral, familial and academic seclusion. The case of the *imiaslavtsy* also convinced him, for all his loyalty and determination to work within the Church, that the Institution had lost its way in the world of *realpolitik* and rationalism and stood in need not so much of reform as of spiritual purgation.

Even the homely neo-Slavophile ambience of the Novoselov group, of which Florensky was widely supposed to be the ideological inspiration, was not altogether cloudless. In 1916, Florensky published an extensive meditation 'Around Khomiakov',[62] in the form of a review article on the two volumes (in three books) on this central figure of nineteenth-century Slavophilism by Vladimir Zavitnevich. The review attracted the ire of Berdiaev and, as Florensky complained to Bulgakov, a good deal of criticism in the form of 'womanish whisperings' behind his back from within the Circle of Seekers after Christian Knowledge. In his review, Florensky insists with some rigour on the importance of Khomiakov's actual relationship to the Russian Church of his time, insufficiently illuminated, he complains, by Zavitnevich's rambling exposition of his thought. For Khomiakov, Florensky suggests, the Church is first and foremost identified with the principle of *sobornost'* (conciliarity, brotherly love), and this is more important to him than Her position as the authoritative guardian of ontological truth, in particular of the truth of the Sacraments of the Eucharist and the doctrine of transubstantiation which touches on the essence of Being. The article contains a long digression on the possible Old Testament source of Blood Sacrifice, in which the blood of the sacrificed animal (the *life* of the animal) was poured out before the Lord and only the meat consumed. This Old Testament tradition Florensky sees as a possible reason for Roman Catholic Communion being given only in one kind (a practice which Khomiakov considered degraded the laity) and, at the same time, he makes it very clear that, in his view, the ancient rites of blood sacrifice symbolised an ontological reality which is not denied but fulfilled in the Bloodless or, as the latest English translations have it, Unbloody Sacrifice of the Eucharist. He also makes it clear that he suspects Khomiakov of leaning too far towards Protestantism in his critique of authoritarian Roman Catholicism thus, by implication, undermining the spiritual authority of his own Church. It was this upholding of authoritarianism, with its implied support for the ideal unity supposed to exist for Orthodox Russians between the Tsar, his people and their Church, which Florensky's critics, and even some of his friends, interpreted as a reactionary political statement. Novoselov, indeed, spent almost a whole night with Florensky, arguing against the latter's 'Romanising-magical' tendency, and exacted a promise to refrain in future from theological speculation.

As Florensky himself protested, the stance he had taken up had more to do with his increasing feeling for the 'illusory' nature of an essentially secular civilisation, which had gradually lost all sense of the connection between ultimate reality and everyday life, than with political ideology – to which he consistently professed himself totally indifferent. He loved Khomiakov and never tired of praising the purity of his intention, the transparency of his character and the beauty of the structure of his thought. But he also looked long and critically at all that was 'around Khomiakov'. Could he, as a member of the landed gentry in Western-educated, nineteenth-century Russia, really be considered 100 per cent Orthodox in his opinions? Zavitnevich's book, Florensky protests, fails to situate the Slavophile ideologist either in his society or in his family. Florensky here employs a favourite word – *entelechy* – to signify Khomiakov's status as the embodiment of the ideal of his kindred, just as elsewhere he calls the Trinity St Sergius Monastery the *entelechy* of Russia and, in conversation with friends, the butterfly the *entelechy* of the caterpillar. The family tree, he explains enthusiastically, can show the individual either as the product of his ancestry, as he grows from it, or as a vessel into which heredity flows. Much can be learned from studying the ramifications of the tree, especially in the case of the Slavophiles 'who were all interrelated' and tended to live as one big, mutually supportive clan 'which we do not find in westernising circles'[63] and which, perhaps, he thought, explains Khomiakov's intuitive preference for free association as exemplified by family ties over compulsive structures such as the authority of Church and State:

> Projecting their studies, their drawing rooms and their dining rooms onto the world at large, they would have liked to see all the world organized like a family, like one vast tea-party of affectionate kinsfolk, who have come together at the close of day to have a natter about some uplifting question.[64]

As in the critique of Tuberovsky's dissertation, Florensky is extraordinarily thorough, adding to his review an extensive appendix of facts about Khomiakov not to be found in Zavitnevich's compendious study: from the titles of missed-out poems to anecdotal information, such as the story of two frustrated burglars who waited all night for the light to go off in a room where the master of the house was to be seen deep in prayer,[65] or the extract from Nikitenko's diary

about a meeting with him at the house of a government minister, where the
Slavophile leader had appeared in traditional peasant costume and 'talked
without pause for breath and mostly in French – as befits a representative of
Russian populism'.[66] As ever, Florensky, alongside the most exhaustive pedantry,
shows a happy flair for revealing, often gently ironic detail!

Blood sacrifice and the importance of genealogy were all very well when
Florensky was writing about the Christian churches and his beloved Slavophiles,
but his interest in such things took on a very different complexion when he
ventured to write about the Jews. His critique of Professor Daniil Khlvolson's
denial of the practice of blood sacrifice in ancient Israel and his 'Letter from the
Caucasus', which were published by Vasilii Rozanov in the latter's inflammatory
'Sense of sight and smell in the Jews' attitude to blood',[67] have only comparatively recently been definitely attributed to Florensky, as has his introduction to
Novoselov's collection of articles *Israel in the Past, Present and Future*,[68] signed
with a Greek letter and in more closely guarded anonymity than the preface
to Bulatovich's *Apologiia* – for fear, as Florensky explained when asking for
Rozanov's discretion, that he would be attacked 'from left and right' should he
venture to put his own name to thoughts involving the role of Israel in world
history ... more particularly at a time when the *cause célèbre* of the Jewish
artisan, Beilis, falsely accused of the ritual sacrifice of a Christian boy, was
shaking Russian society to its foundations. The accusation was exploited in
Russia by the Black Hundreds to whip up pogroms and, by the liberal press at
home and the European press abroad, to excoriate Russian backwardness and
superstition. Florensky, as he made clear in the Khomiakov review, did not
consider the idea of blood sacrifice superstitious, and his involvement in the
debates on Judaism sparked by the Beilis case was not a deliberate attempt to
precipitate action against Jews.

Many members of the Religious Philosophical Society in St Petersburg,
however, clamoured for Rozanov's exclusion for his insistence on the possibility, indeed the probability of Beilis's guilt. They succeeded in obtaining
majority support for a motion of censure disassociating themselves from the
stomach-turning descriptions of Jewish customs and rituals Rozanov elected
to publish in the notoriously anti-Semitic newspapers *Novoe vremia* and
*Zemshchina*, together with the untimely suggestion that the murdered boy,
Iushchinsky, should be proclaimed a martyr. Rozanov felt himself forced to
resign. He had, however, many personal friends and admirers amongst the
intelligentsia ... among whom was Florensky, who backed him up and launched
into an eager discussion of the intriguing subject of blood rituals, to which
he too attached mystic significance. 'Blut, das ist ein ganz besonderes Saft',[69]
murmurs Mephistopheles as Faust prepares to sign away his soul in it. So it

seemed also to Florensky: life-blood. He would refer deliberately to the consecrated Communion wine as 'the blood' and was convinced that, as the blood
of God-become-man, it had ontological and cosmic significance. Had he been
a priest in Ancient Israel, he had once said to his sister Ol'ga, he would have
had no hesitation in taking part in the mystery of blood sacrifice.[70] At the time
of his first published letter on the subject to Rozanov, Florensky was painfully
embroiled in the *imiaslavtsy* controversy and had just returned from arranging
a family funeral in Moscow, where the handsome and only slightly elder cousin
David Melik-Begliarov, with whom he had spent time in Germany at the age
of 15, had died of tuberculosis and been buried in the Armenian cemetery. He
spoke out against those who scoffed at the whole idea of blood sacrifice and
blamed the lawyers and 'Jewish press' (whom he lumped together as Yids, not
true Israelites) for the superficial liberalism and positivism to which so-called
Christian society now so easily subscribed.[71] One of his letters to Rozanov ends:
'These are just thoughts I wanted to write to you … I could not find proper
expression for everything but I was trying to say something about my wonder
at the tragedy and mystery of the world and at the higher logic of everything
that goes on in it.'[72] Rozanov valued precisely this spontaneity – his own literary
technique was based on jotting things down just as they came into his head and
on publishing intimate details from correspondence not intended for the public
eye. Nevertheless, Florensky knew this and permitted him to publish not only
letters, but a whole dialogue about 'The Jews and the fate of Christians' to which
his contribution is, if anything, more intolerant than Rozanov's. Throughout
Rozanov's career as a writer, which is inseparable from the private life which he
chose to draw upon, this flawed but deeply fascinating thinker demonstrated
a highly ambiguous love–hate relationship with the Jews, their customs and
religion, whereas Florensky, in this correspondence, is concerned primarily
with the case against equating them with everybody else. In a sense though, it
is also a love–hate relationship which Florensky ascribes to St Paul, on whose
writings he based his introduction to the Religious-Philosophical Library's *Israel
in the Past, Present and Future*. As he wrote in yet another letter to Rozanov:
'Although I have absolutely no doubt that blood sacrifices do exist in the general
way, this particular trial [the Beilis case] has, it seems, brought together scoun-
drels from all the world, and there is absolutely no disentangling who is right
and who is wrong from here, from the sidelines.'[73] Nina Simonovich-Efimova's
notes of conversations with Florensky confirm that he persisted in his distrust
of the Jews,[74] yet he does not appear to have been amongst the many representatives of the Old Regime in Soviet times who blamed the Jews for the Russian
Revolution. Half Armenian and deeply fascinated by his own lawless ancestry
in Nagorno-Karabach,[75] Florensky could by no stretch of the imagination be
considered a 'Russian nationalist'. He does, however, use the expression 'we

Aryans' in the sense of 'we non-Jews', in the letter to Rozanov and some other terms which have since become associated with the run-in to the Holocaust. Yet nowhere in Florensky's family letters or elsewhere in his life or his written work, as far as I have seen them, are there traces of anti-Semitism. The interest in genealogy he shared with Rozanov, which now appears suspect to some of his critics, perhaps because, using the vocabulary of the time, they wrote in terms of blood and seed rather than of genes and DNA, was compounded, like so much of Florensky's thought, of poetic imagination and well-grounded scientific intuition. There is no evidence he was worried about his own ancestry. Indeed, in one of his first letters to his friend on this theme, he speculates that his mother's surname, Saparyan, might have a Semitic root in the word 'saphar' (to write).[76]

The years leading up to the First World War had seen mounting unease and painful attempts at self-identification throughout European Jewry. Were European Jews to assimilate culturally and linguistically to the host country, not just as fellow-children of the Enlightenment and contributors to, as well as enthusiasts for its culture, but potentially, as patriots ready to fight and die for their adoptive nation-states? Or were they to valorise their cultural difference, their Yiddish folk culture and their Ancient Hebrew mystic and religious heritage? If Florensky had been a Jew, he would certainly have adhered to the latter camp. 'I think a Jewish Kabbalist would have explained [The Hebrew Scriptures] more or less as you have done had he wished to enter into a discussion', Tikhomirov wrote to him in 1914.[77] Florensky's attitude expresses his conviction that Europe (and even the Russian Church in its present 'enlightened', rationalistic opposition to the 'peasant' mysticism of the *imiaslavtsy*) was experiencing a kind of ontological drought, a withering of real roots which were everywhere being replaced by abstract schemae – today we might say by virtual reality. This passionate conviction found expression in his correspondence with Rozanov, where it was contaminated by the racial terminology of the day in a way that makes it distressing reading in the shadow of the obscenities to be perpetrated against Jews of all persuasions only 20 years thereafter. To put Florensky's position in context, however, we should look carefully at the declaration which concludes his introduction to *Israel in the Past, Present and Future*:

> It is not the political and not the socio-economic aspect of Judaism taken as such but the spiritual sense of the Divine Destinies which are in process of working themselves out that is the object of this book. We here are not suggesting any programmes, but are anxious only to clarify the spiritual relationship of the forces now locked in struggle in world history.[78]

'We here' includes Novoselov, the publisher of the series in which the book appeared, and such contributors as: Nikolai Berdiaev, Vladimir Solov'ev, Bishop Ignatii Brianchaninov, Blaise Pascal, Ivan Aksakov, Fedor Dostoevsky, Andrei Bely, Vasilii Rozanov, Johann Gottlieb Fichte, Houston Stewart Chamberlain, St John Chrysostom and Feofan the Recluse – a mixed bag of saints and sinners from down the ages, including a few birds of ill omen and a scattering of Florensky's most brilliant contemporaries and predecessors.

The very fact of Rozanov's close friendship with Pavel Aleksandrovich Florensky is an enigma which, in simple human terms, involved an ongoing reconciliation of opposites. Rozanov, an apologist for sex, not for the disembodied Platonic Eros of the Symbolists but for sex as procreative life force, is perhaps best known in English letters for having earned from D. H. Lawrence the accolade of being 'the only interesting Russian' of the period. He was also labelled a 'Russian Nietzsche, a dangerous opponent of Christianity'. He and Florensky struck up a correspondence, probably through El'chaninov, who had visited Rozanov as a student in St Petersburg, when Florensky was still a would-be monk.

As has been said, they shared an interest in genealogy, family roots. The relationship took on a warmer, more human dimension with Florensky's marriage and priesting. Rozanov's common-law wife was a priest's daughter[79] of whom he stood somewhat in awe and, for all the anti-Christian pathos of much of his writing, he was essentially an *anima religiosa* who loved the Church and, more especially, the married priesthood, both as a section of the population with whose manners and customs he felt at ease and for their mystic power as celebrants. He specifically recalled that it was under the influence of his 'friend', Varvara Dmitrievna, Tsvetkov and Florensky that 'I made my peace with Christianity'.[80]

Florensky was drawn to Rozanov by the power and the poetry of his writing, of which, however, he was far from uncritical, and by the antonymical thrust of his intellectual speculation, which knew no forbidden themes, eschewed consistency and pursued modern psychological insights down the labyrinths of ancient cults in a way the scientist-priest found deeply fascinating. Also, like many others, Florensky was attracted by Rozanov's warmth and human curiosity, to which his own reserved nature responded as to kindly sunshine. You always felt, said one of Rozanov's colleagues, Aleksei Remizov, that Vasilii Vasilievich really had time for you. So when the older writer lost a major source of income with the closure of *Novoe vremia* by the Provisional Government in the summer of 1917 and sought refuge from the shortages and disorder in St Petersburg with the seriously ill Varvara Dmitrievna and their numerous children in Sergiev Posad, Florensky helped find them lodgings, arranged for the paid employment of a grown-up daughter, acted as go-between for Rozanov with possible Moscow publishers, offered to co-author a book on numismatics based on his fabulous collection of ancient coins and undertook, though never completed, the onerous task of editing a posthumous *Collected Works*. In all this he acted more as Rozanov's colleague than as father confessor, Rozanov preferring for this function a simpler priest, but it was Florensky who said the prayers for the dying by his friend's bedside. In his last book, *The Apocalypse of Our Time*, Rozanov blamed the Church's neglect of the things of this world for the triumph of militant materialism in Russia, and there was much speculation as to whether he died a Christian. Florensky, who had at the time tried to dissuade him from publishing *The Apocalypse*, bore witness that, though Rozanov never renounced or repented his love of the older religions, he had somehow, in parallel, as it were, or in some deeper strata of his being, made his peace with Christ at the last.[81]

One way and another, Florensky was granted neither time nor leisure to work systematically on his own specifically 'Russian philosophy'. War intervened in the summer of 1914 and Father Pavel, like other idealistic patriots, felt called to the service of his country and set out for a short spell as an army padre on a hospital train for the wounded. The expressed opposition of his spiritual director, always, it seems, out to quell Florensky's more quixotic starts, together with a combination of family events, led him, after a few months, to renounce this initiative, which he had found interesting and challenging, and to renew his commitment to the Academy and Sergiev Posad in a new house on Dvorianskaia ulitsa.[82] The move coincided with the birth of his second son Kirill and with his mother's and youngest sister Raisa's removal from far-away Tiflis to Moscow, where they had taken up residence in a flat he had found for them after Ol'ga's death not far from Viacheslav Ivanov's on the corner of Novokoniushennyi pereulok and Dolgii pereulok.[83]

The war did nothing to slow down Florensky's involvement with cultural life. The new, larger house, with its enfilade of rooms through the nursery, the hospitable dining and music room on to the inner sanctum of his study, the tiny room for Anna's mother by the stove off the kitchen, large verandah and secluded courtyard and garden, made it easier for him to receive visitors concerned with matters spiritual and intellectual. Amongst these was a whole group of vociferous Futurists, headed by the poet Velimir Khlebnikov, who engaged their host in an absorbing mathematico-poetic discussion on the Laws of Time and invited him to join the *317 Chairmen of the Globe*.[84] An eccentric after Florensky's own heart, Khlebnikov, etymologist, mathematician and poet by the Grace of God, was also a kind of modern troubadour, a wanderer on the face of the Earth, a 1920s backpacker. As theoretician of Russian futurism, he shared Florensky's passion for etymology, words, sounds and language, and was innovative with an inventive playfulness that amounted to genius. In spite of the boisterous presence of Khlebnikov's followers, there was a brief moment of intense affinity between priest and poet.[85]

Language and sign were, at the time, central to Florensky's creative thinking and, by 1917, he was involved with two other poets, Max Voloshin and his old friend Andrei Bely, in discussion of a *Symbolarium*, work on which was eventually begun and aborted in the troubled year of 1925, leaving, as Florensky's contribution, a brilliant disquisition on that most multivalent of symbols, 'The Point', which has no area by definition, yet signifies large, inhabited areas on the map, marks the moment of appearance and vanishing, and acts always as a differential.[86]

It was in 1916 that Father Pavel began making notes towards and dictating scraps of the memoir *For My Children* and so, at the very time he was juggling words with the most sophisticated literary intellects of the day, he was in practice striving towards a new simplicity, on the assumption that anything worth explaining should, if one could only find the right words, be perfectly comprehensible to an intelligent child. This showed in the style of a projected book of lectures 'First steps in philosophy' as well as in a wide-ranging cycle of articles on culture, art, language, genealogy, philosophy, astrology, the natural sciences and mathematics, perceived at once as real phenomena and as symbols of his more profound noumenal experience as a priest. This cycle, already in gestation and intended for the elaboration of Florensky's Orthodox 'Russian philosophy', was to be included in a new book, 'On the watersheds of thought'. Typically, Florensky, that most unhistorical of thinkers, conceived of a new and, as he termed it, 'medieval' flowering of culture in terms of space rather than of time: a mountain pass opening up onto new vistas waiting to be discovered. Never published in its entirety during his lifetime, the new religious philosophical compendium towards which he was striving became available to contemporaries only in fragmentary form: lecture notes, typescript copies corrected in Florensky's hand, articles prepared for print, then withdrawn and the printset scattered by government *fiat*, conspectuses and approximate plans.

These component parts have, however, now been published in the four-volume *Works* and, before that, in various unsystematic, posthumous publications, beginning from the late 1960s. These appeared not only in theological journals and academic periodicals but in widely read 'monthlies', where their idiosyncratic yet stringent approach to technical problems and profound religious content were to prove a revelation to Soviet readers brought up on dialectical materialism and socialist realism. Florensky's mature style, while retaining the dialectic subtlety and poetic shimmer which always charac-terised his work, shows him to have mastered and digested his own erudition to a degree which made it possible to obviate the copious notes and baroque superstructures and excrescences of his earlier writing. It is also free from the occasionally cloying sentimentality of his youthful lyricism. Naturally, however, the register differs according to the intention of the author: many pieces were written for oral delivery while others are encyclopaedic and factual; still others bear the hallmarks of raw research and are speculative, unfinished, occasionally repetitive. Some, such as the largely anonymous pieces on the Jewish question or the *imiaslavtsy*, were sparked off by major publicistic controversies, though Florensky invariably seems to have found these burdensome and reached out towards realms higher and deeper than the *faits-du-jour* to which he was originally responding.

If the subject of Florensky's first *magnum opus*, *The Pillar and Ground of Truth*, is the way of a young, early twentieth-century scholar of mixed ethnic origin and secular upbringing to the heart of the Russian Orthodox Church, the subject of this second period, which comes to fruition largely within the compass of the next chapter, is his new perception of culture and science from within that Church. The keeper of his archive and first biographer, his grandson Igumen Andronik (Trubachev), sees the first period as one devoted to 'the justification of God' ('theodicea', as *The Pillar and Ground of Truth* is subtitled), and the second to 'the justification of man' ('anthropodicea', a term used by Florensky himself to indicate the direction of his later work).[87] There is, however, no learned introductory discussion of the justification of man, whether by works, faith or grace, or of the hallowing and divinisation of human nature through the incarnation of Jesus Christ, though the latter is implicit in the discussion of sacrament, cult and the 'hallowing of reality' featured in the 1918–1924 lectures. Neither do we have an authorial summing-up of conclusions. We do not know whether Florensky contemplated any such conventional philosophical structure.

We do, however, have a remarkable 'statement of intent' as to the organisation of 'On the watersheds of thought'. Here Florensky envisages his second *magnum opus* as the philosophical equivalent of the score of a heterophonic choral symphony in which, as in Russian folk song, 'each voice more or less improvises yet does not break up the whole but, on the contrary, ties it in more firmly, for the common sound is knitted into one by *every* performer in a multiplicity of repetitions and variations'. In such a way, the envisaged weave of themes and ex-prompts would seek to become the philosophical expression of 'the soul of the Russian people as expressed in song'.[88]

Essentially, then, Florensky remains too intensely individual yet wide-ranging an author for us to impose a coherent overall plan on the glowing 'threads and patches' of his mature work. Each piece deserves to be read and pondered for its own sake, in context, as it was written. For, though drawn from the well of silence which is scholarship and contemplation, the lectures and occasional pieces which were to have gone to make up 'On the watersheds of thought' were very much products of the evil of the day, written by a trained, spiritual athlete in rare moments of undisturbed concentration over a time of and often in response to intense and violent historical upheaval. Read in this way, without any rigidly imposed schema, his 'Unfinished Symphony' is more likely to recombine as an essentially harmonious whole, organised by the rhythms of that inner music which, Florensky maintained, sounded for him and within him almost to the end of his life.[89]

# 7

# Catastrophe 1917–1926

Therefore thou art inexcusable, O man, whosoever thou art that judgest: for
wherein thou judgest another, thou condemnest thyself; for thou that judgest doest
the same things.
But we are sure that the judgement of God is according to the truth against them
which commit such things.
And thinkest thou this, O man, that judgest them which do such things, and doest
the same, that thou shalt escape the judgement of God?
Or despisest thou the riches of goodness and forbearance and longsuffering; not
knowing that the goodness of God leadeth thee to repentance?

(St Paul, Romans 2.1–32)

In essence, bolshevism is the logical conclusion of bourgeois culture.

P. A. Florensky[1]

The February Revolution had immediate repercussions within the Church. The
call for the convening of a Local Council to restore the Patriarchate was at last
crowned with success and those of the clergy who had resigned themselves
to the subordination of Church to State under the Synod were ousted from
positions of authority. On 1 May 1917 Bishop Fedor was dismissed as Rector
of the Theological Academy after a vituperative meeting at which not only
rebellious students but members of his own staff subjected him and his tenure
to scathing criticism. Florensky confided to Novoselov that, had he not been
a priest, he would have gladly challenged his colleagues to single combat in
defence of his bishop and their mutual friend Aleksandr Dmitrievich Samarin
but, since this option was not open to him, all he could do was to stage a
demonstrative walkout and, two days later, to resign his own post as editor
of *Bogoslovskii vestnik*. It was not, he added, that he objected to liberalism,
but he did consider it incumbent on members of the Church to show human
decency.

These events followed on a visit from the ex-Procurator of the Holy Synod
Vladimir L'vov, which left Florensky so firmly convinced that a time of persecution was at hand that he began a letter to his 'children' (at that time comprising,
rather touchingly, his wife Anna, Vasilii and the two-year-old Kirill), advising
them how to live in the event of his death, how to preserve all that was best of

the past (and his own memory) in the firm belief that God would require such stewardship of them and of their descendants and that he himself would always be with them in spirit. The letter, written up at intervals between 1917 and 1923, eventually included Ol'ga and Mikhail and spoke tenderly to each 'child' in turn.

Possibly, this mindset to envisage the worst from the moment of the fall of the autocracy actually contributed to Florensky's inner serenity. Had not Vladimir Solov'ev, he himself and his fellow-'Apocalyptics' foreseen just such a time of tribulation? Had not his beloved Father Isidor spoken of days when Christians would have to hide from their ill-wishers, and had not these shared premonitions been at the very root of his ecstatic, ascetic relationship with the friends of his youth? And should he not recall the song of those that had gotten the victory over the beast at the time of the seven last plagues: 'Great and marvellous are Thy works, Lord God Almighty, just and true are Thy ways'?[2] It was that very month of May 1917 that the artist Mikhail Nesterov painted his 'The Philosophers', the remarkable dual portrait of Florensky and Bulgakov pacing the fresh grass against the leafy, transparent backdrop of Florensky's springtime garden, deep in talk: Florensky, calm and absorbed, the white cassock flowing easily about his slender form, Bulgakov storm-tossed but sturdy in his stiff civilian garb – it was not until June the following year that he finally committed himself to the priesthood, an occasion at which Father Pavel was present at the laying on of hands and to co-celebrate his first Liturgy. For so long a rebel against authority, Bulgakov welcomed the emancipation of Church from State, but found it harder to wait for the chaos to subside (even contemplating seeking refuge with Rome) than did his apparently more apolitical and pliable friend. 'Sometimes, he seems to me – a saint', noted Rozanov, by that time already resident in Sergiev Posad, 'Higher than Pascal ... On a level with the ancient Plato.'[3]

Yet, oddly, Florensky's detachment was due precisely to the clarity with which he perceived the breakdown of the old, structured edifice of Orthodoxy and autocracy, to which he had deliberately chosen to submit a free spirit and a fearlessly probing mind. This breakdown, as he saw it, came from within, from the infiltration of Russian theological academies by first an authoritarian Roman Catholic then a Protestant rationalistic and moralistic ethos which had left no place in the hearts and minds of the hierarchy of the Church itself, not to speak of educated society as a whole, for the sacred mysteries of the Christian life. The controversy over the Jesus prayer, which now resurfaced with the promise of a Church Council with power to decide whether or not its avowed practitioners could continue as priests and monks of the Orthodox Church, was again a point at issue ... and a deeply symptomatic one. Between 29 July and 15/17 August 1917, at a time when the Russian intelligentsia as a whole were racked with hope and fear for their fragile, new-born democracy, Florensky composed a 'civic confession' (why not, he jibed, since 'civic marriages' and 'civic memorial services (*panikhidy*)' were fast becoming all the rage?) to his ex-Marxist, ex-revolutionary fellow-philosopher Bulgakov.

Elected power, Florensky wrote, takes away my freedom because it obliges me to bow down before myself, whereas the old rough-and-ready discipline of 'the sacred knout'[4], being transcendent rather than imminent in relation to myself, leaves me free. And here, forgetting his God-fearing, priestly, paternal ancestry, Florensky chose to recall his 'brigand' maternal forebears in a fierce hymn to Karabach:

From this comes my – I'll say it in plain words – my contempt and hostility towards all the contemporary world … Evlach, a small town now, but then – *nominem nudum*, where I was born, is situated in the Transcaucasian steppe, bounded to North and South by snowy mountain ranges. The Caucasian range and the Armenian mountains are like diamonds, their sparkling sharpness quite beyond the imagination of those who have no experience of mountains, the ultimate perfection of their distant outlines thrusting up into the eternal, unquestionable, incorruptible, eternal in a way those who have no experience of mountains simply cannot conceive, into the depths and velvety infinity of the azure sky. And amidst these mountains lie the torrid open spaces, all woven from the metallic, resonant trills of cycadas and grasshoppers, from an abundance of growing things, fish, game, beasts of the hoof, predators, poisonous insects, snakes and sweet scents, famous for their karabach horses, the best in the Caucasus, and their dashing brigands, the most desperate in all Transcaucasia. In the free space of my soul there are no laws. I do not want law and order and set no value on it, for I know myself to be a brigand to the core of my being, who should not be sitting in a study but galloping through the stormy night, galloping with the whirlwind, without purpose … I want to take possession of the Azure, to embody it in myself. Yet never to forget that the Azure is ABOVE me, the Kingdom of Eternal Peace, a calm, serene Kingdom that pours itself into my soul. And, submissive only to the Azure, I still need symbols of my limits. It is the snow-peaks that frame the steppe which make me aware of my freedom and of my limits. The snowy peaks thrusting up into the Azure situate it closer to me – and further away … I will not come to terms, cannot come to terms with anyone who shuts off my view of the peaks with wooden fences or obscures them with smoke. Authority – fatherland – kingdom – priesthood – powers spiritual – these are the snowy peaks of my conscious being …

For authorities issuing forth from the belly of Leviathan I have no recognition other than the toe of my boot. But it is precisely the *immanent* that is springing up now from every nook and cranny. The Church Authority, the sacraments, the meaning of dogma, God Himself – have all become immanent, are all losing every vestige of real being outside ourselves, are becoming projections of ourselves. Everyone is busy undermining the heights, misting over the earthly firmament, piercing the Azure.[5]

It was this insistence on the ontological reality of the Christian cosmos and this tragic concept of self as one engaged in a vigorous but, in the short term, hopeless struggle against encroaching chaos that armed Florensky for the 'long defeat' which lay ahead. Perhaps it was the death of his old friend Vladimir Ern which had released the spate of imagery from their shared Caucasian boyhood. Father Pavel officiated at Ern's funeral and wrote a warm memorial tribute, full of mountain air and remembered sunshine, read aloud by Bulgakov at a gathering of the Religious-Philosophical Society on May 26 and published in *Khristianskaia mysl'*, 1917, No. 11–12, pp. 69–74, although the volume of articles in memory of Vladimir Franzevich which the friends co-edited failed to find a publisher.[6]

Publishing, indeed, had suddenly become very difficult. Everyone, including the publishers, were living from hand to mouth and from day to day. In the Church, those who had been in high favour with the Synod now found themselves in ill odour almost everywhere, and the gruff, old conservative Antonii (Khrapovitsky), whose article against the *imiaslavtsy* Florensky had turned down because he would not, at the time the controversy was raging, have been permitted to print a proper answer, but who was now ousted from his Chair at the Kharkov Theological Academy and from the editorship of *Vera i razum*, turned to *Bogoslovskii vestnik*, not realising that Florensky had resigned the editorship, in the hopes his erstwhile opponent, having shown such staunch support for his own Rector, Bishop Fedor, might find space for an article on 'The dogma of atonement'.

'Your Holiness, gracious Arch-Pastor and Father', replied Florensky with quite unwonted devotion. 'I am no longer editor of *Bogoslovskii vestnik* and have handed over my office to Mr Tareev, the new editor. I resigned helter-skelter, not having the least desire to propagate the ideology of the new Hamocracy.'[7]

Novoselov's Religious-Philosophical Library was on its last legs financially and its editor too deeply involved in day-to-day developments within the Russian Church to have time for books. He was elected member of the Temporary Council of all Moscow Parishes on 30 January 1918 and immediately became embroiled in resistance to the confiscation of Church property. Also, having taken up residence in the Donskoi Monastery, Abba Mikhail, as he had long been affectionately nicknamed, was moving towards the monastic life.

The years 1917–1918 were, in fact, a time of such rapid change that the only apparently relevant reading was the daily paper. Books simply went out of date before they reached the shops.

Yet it was precisely over these years that Florensky made maximum progress towards the planning and completion of his next major opus, 'On the watersheds of thought', originally contracted for publication with Morozova's still extant *Put'*, and intended to change the emphasis from the justification of God to the part to be played by man in building the Kingdom of God 'on Earth as in Heaven'.

In the following account of Florensky's writing towards 'On the watersheds of thought' I have, for the sake of clarity, abandoned the strictly chronological approach usually required of the biographer and chosen to follow the scrupulous endeavour of the editors of his *Works* to reconstruct the sequence of articles and lectures as the author wished them to be presented in his great unfinished book, rather than to give an account of his day-to-day development as a thinker. The grand plan, after all, was already there in his head, *in statu nascendi*, as he might himself have said, ever since his consecration to the priesthood, and the way he subsequently arranged the 'pieces' is probably more important than the exact order in which they were written – frequently on demand or as a response to extraneous pressure.

Thus Part I, tentatively entitled 'The Image and the World', consists of texts mainly taken from the 1917 History of Philosophical Terminology course, and shows the human being as a contemplative in search of a way to reunite himself and his fellows with the reality of being and how he goes about it: through word and deed, language and instruments. In science, Florensky had long maintained, words were all-important and terms an essential tool – both for teaching and research. Throughout 1917 he sought to apply this principle to the elaboration of a coherent, theocentric world view capable of replacing the discredited certainties of post-Renaissance rationalism, determinism and subjectivism, beginning with a special course on the history of philosophical terminology, which he delivered during the September–November semester, under the shadow of the Bolshevik seizure of power, to a colloquium of third-year students of the Moscow Theological Academy. Lectures on 'The term', *Homo faber*, the instrument or tool as a projection of bodily organs, the symbolism of dreams as linked to bodily functions, macrocosm and microcosm, proper names, the *Kabbala*, the meaning of Idealism, Plato, Aristotle and what Florensky called 'concrete metaphysics' came tumbling from his pen 'to provoke a game – which is a method of acquiring knowledge',[8] as he wrote in a projected introduction to 'On the watersheds of thought'. From the beginning of 1918 he elaborated a further course which, together with works just enumerated and the later 'Reverse Perspective', was intended to become the first section of the book: 'Science as symbolic description'.

The thrust of this first section is concerned with re-establishing Florensky's old dream of Natural Philosophy, a philosophical attempt not to deny the discreet elaboration of theory through mathematical symbols in pure science but, in philosophy, to cross borders, to deny 'the scientific method in all that is most essential – deny, challenge and smelt its rigidity in the heat of eros for that which truly is'.[9] Dialectics, together with the philosophical method of question and answer, stimulated new questions about the antonymic nature of language itself, questions which Florensky approached very much in the spirit of Russian

Symbolist thought, through Humboldt and Potebnia. Interested, as always, in facts rather than theories, he explores the contrast between invented languages like Esperanto and, with much greater sympathy, transrational sound-languages such as Zaum, both of which, he maintains, arise from mistrust of the concept of Logos, the Word as embodiment of Divine Reason 'which was at the Beginning'. This leads him to venture an answer to the eighteenth-century dispute between Church and Englightenment as to whether language is God's gift to man or the creation of the peoples who speak it and the individuals who use it. Florensky's take of this dispute is conciliatory:

> it is precisely in this contradiction, and in its extreme acuity, that language as eternal, steadfast, unchanging Reason, as pre-human Logos, is in fact conceivable as something at the same time infinitely close to the soul of each one of us, affectionately supple to the heart, personal in its every moment, its every movement and expressive of utmost individuality.[10]

Part II, 'The embodiment of form (action and tool)', is again largely taken from the History of Philosophical Terminology course prepared in 1917, yet is clearly the product not only of Florensky's years at the Faculty of Mathematics and the Theological Academy, but also of the intense engagement with experimental work in the Heath Robinson domestic laboratory of his boyhood – and it bridges the way to his resumption of service in applied science.

The first lecture, *Homo faber*, begins with a resounding reprise of the nihilism once favoured by Florensky as a schoolboy with quotations from Laplace and Büchner: 'I have searched the heavens and nowhere have I found one trace of God', says the former, and the latter adds naively: 'Why did the Creative Force not sign his name in stars?' These, Florensky says, are excellent take-off points for the modern theologian, for they force us to come to grips with the simple yet extremely complex fact of the existence of antonyms. Both the Book of Being and the Book of Culture are deserving of study and both, in the last analysis, show forth True Being – but not to those who attempt short cuts by ignoring differences. Scientists, for instance, did not sit back and wait for the law of gravity to appear blazoned in stellar letters in the night sky. Being has meaning and meaning has being, but it is no good pretending they are the same thing. Yet, in the study of nature, as in the study of culture, there is one common factor, one absolute requirement: the need for language – words, terms and names – to enable our understanding. Terms are the 'tools' we require to understand the physical world but, being words, they are also a bridge between science and the humanities.

There is no biological proof that man is, indeed, *Homo sapiens*, one who knows, who is endowed with Reason. On the other hand, as Bergson says, we have sensual evidence that man is indeed *Homo faber*, a doer and a maker, capable of adjusting to and mastering his environment with the help of handmade tools – the only material proof that distinguishes him from the animal kingdom. At the beginning of his next lecture, Florensky quotes Benjamin Franklin: 'Man is a tool-making animal'. The Greek etymology suggests the word for 'tool' has the same root as 'member'; Herbert Spencer defined tools as extensions of our sensory organs. With his usual love of the 'concrete' detail, Florensky provides a stream of examples of scientific experiments and exact observation comparing the performance of various instruments such as weighing machines, metal and water detectors, microscopes etc. to functions of the human body – not forgetting to cite anecdotal cases of extreme human sensitivity: the water-diviner, the wine- or tea-taster, the mind-reader. True to his old passion for exceptions, Florensky looks also at instruments sensitive to phenomena to which our bodies, our sensory organs, are not normally receptive, such as the electro-dynamic phenomena, recounting in some detail Lord Lindsay's doubts as to the zero results of his early experiments on the effect of electro-magnetic waves on the human organism and the polemics engendered as much by the occult implications of electro-magnetic experiments as by their purely scientific interest. Florensky's own opinion was that, although electro-magnetic forces have hitherto appeared 'blind' to our physical presence, meeting no resistance, instruments have been invented to measure degrees of galvanisation which are not only of great potential use but which imply the possibility of inventing tools that do more than project the efficacy of our own organs, instruments capable of handling 'physics hidden from our sensual perception'. Nevertheless, citing the eighteenth-century Ernest Kapp's 'Philosophy of the Technical', he is inclined to accept the idea of tools and instruments as, basically, extensions of our sensory organs and borrows the term *organoproektsiia* as the title for the next lecture.

Here, Florensky introduces the highly contentious word 'magic' to define 'the art of extending the border of the body beyond its usual location',[11] which differs from technical activity only in so far as it is an instinctual rather than a reasoned and creative response to a natural craving. He does not, however, agree with Bossuet that the body, like the man-made machine, presupposes an intelligent Creator. Rather by providing the 'form' for technical ideas, it presupposes the idea that the body itself has a form. The body is comparable less to a machine than to a dwelling place (house, temple or toolshed) where, whether or not we are aware of it, for some of our organs are as yet rudimentary, the potential of all technology is already stored. In this way, the study of technology and biology is mutually supportive, not in a mechanistic, but in a symbolic fashion.

The next lecture, on the symbolism of vision, explores the synergy of two or more realities which are revealed in given, not invented symbols. The symbol, always greater than itself, is like a hall of mirrors which shows me myself, a single being seen from countless points of view, the self subliminal and the self spiritual without which there could be no physical self nor such projections of our physical self as the tools and instruments needed by *Homo faber* for his work in the world. These have their origin in subconscious urges, the key to which is often the study of dreams and hallucinations, as in the Viennese School (he mentions Scherner, Volkert, Wundt and Freud). In this context it would be interesting, he says, to research the genre and history of the old popular manuals on dream interpretation, which also stress the close connection between our physical organs and projections of the psyche.

Science, religious creativity and the arts differ from dream and vision in that they are more subject to our conscious mind and will, more systematic and socially orientated. Religious symbolism, for instance, is accepted by whole peoples and, indeed, to some degree by all people. To a lesser extent so are scientific and philosophical symbolism. Artistic symbolism is a degree more personal, dream symbolism still more individual and fortuitous – but all spring from the same source. Culture is the incarnation, the materialisation of dreams and visions – as is The Economy (the title of the next lecture), which is the achievement of the technological equipment we have dreamt up to satisfy our needs. We inhabit only those parts of the world we have been able to master and our economy reflects ourselves.

At this point Florensky advances a strongly felt, religiously based philosophy of the environment. To master is to control, and we control what we have understood, 'named', 'grasped' and made our own. The world is a projection of our spirit and of the body to which the spirit is so intimately connected. Adam lost his God-given mastery of the world when he lost control of himself, bringing division. But even in his fallen state man has not lost the magical power to control the world through the lower magic of technical mastery and science and the higher magic of philosophy and art – and through the theurgy of religious (ascetic) effort, which involves first re-establishing control over the microcosm of the body. For the body is our threshold of awareness, more important by far than the materialists and positivists on the one hand, or the spiritists on the other, care to think: 'mathematics, astronomy, physics, etc. etc. not to mention art, are luminous reflections of spirit illumining, ordering, organising, assimilating and revivifying the albeit sin-shattered body'.[12]

It is still in the context of the economy, but in the ensuing lecture entitled Macrocosm and Microcosm, that Florensky reintroduces the concept of Sophia, thought of as the Bride of Christ the Man, the World Soul. It is for human beings to 'husband' the world as a man cares for his wife. In this context:

> Thrice criminal is the predatory civilisation, which knows neither pity nor love for the creation but which seeks from it only gratification, which is not motivated by the desire

to help Nature manifest her hidden culture but imposes violent forms and aims from without ... in raping the Environment, Man does violence to himself and, sacrificing Nature to his selfish greed, sacrifices himself to the elements brought into play by his passions. This is inevitable, for Man and Nature resemble one another and, at heart, are one and the same. Man is the little world, the microcosm ... The Environment is the macrocosm ...[13]

The thought is not new, he admits, but thoughts founded on the latest scholarly novelty soon go out of date 'like a comic old-fashioned hat',[14] whereas religion and folklore alike support the idea of symbiosis between man and nature.

A supplement to this lecture printed in the form of a letter Florensky addressed to Professor Vladimir Vernadsky on 21 September 1929 introduces a discussion of the terms 'biosphere' and 'noosphere' used by the professor and, in a slightly different sense, by Teilhard de Chardin. Florensky, very tentatively, suggests adding the concept of 'pneumosphere', the interpenetration not just of mind and matter but of matter and spirit, linked in his mind very practically to his own scientific work on the transition from steam to electricity to the technology of sustainable energy:

the thought of the existence in the biosphere or, perhaps, above the biosphere of what might be called the pneumosphere, that is of the existence of a particular part of matter involved in the cycle of culture or, more precisely, the cycle of the spirit. The irreducibility of this cycle to life in a general sense is hardly open to doubt. But there is much data, not yet sufficiently studied, it is true, that would seem to indicate a special kind of durability in material formations permeated through by the spirit such as works of art. This makes one suspect the existence of a corresponding particular sphere of matter in the cosmos. At present it is premature to speak of the pneumosphere as a field for scholarly research. Possibly, the question should not have been touched on at all in writing. Only the impossibility of talking to you personally has induced me to air the thought in a letter.[15]

This letter, which was not published until 1984, when it engendered animated discussion, demonstrates, as the editors of Florensky's *Works* doubtless intended it should, the importance that Florensky wished to place on the indivisibility of matter and spirit, on the relevance of the biosphere to the spiritual man. It is our duty, he says, to continue in study and, always, to prefer an honest 'Don't know' to the imposition of an apparently rational, well-rounded, mechanistic explanation. We do not now know all about Kant's 'starry heaven above and moral law within' but we do know that this does not necessarily place them forever beyond our cognition: on the contrary, they interact in the biosphere (noosphere, pneumosphere), and this is all a legitimate field of close study.

The next section of 'On the watersheds of thought' opens with 'The concept of form', a continuation of the same 1917 course on the history of philosophical terminology. Still looking at culture as the creation of man the toolmaker, Florensky sees it as a Janus-figure: man, the living, changing organism looks into metaphysical time; but his world of tools and instruments, which have no power of change in themselves, looks into metaphysical space. Man and his machines, in fact, face in opposite directions, but are linked by a shared physical form to constitute 'a whole', a word which, in different languages could mean also something 'perfect' and 'complete' (Hebrew), 'healthy' (Greek), 'full' (Latin) or 'whole' with all these connotations in the modern Russian. Such a 'whole' is always the sum of its parts, never a simple, single, large thing. In its multiplicity, the 'whole' implies balance; often, as in a magnate, a syllogism, an electric force-field, a balance of opposing forces, essentially antonymic:

> The idea, essentially single, manifests itself as a harnessing of antonymically opposed poles – as antonym.[16]

Yet such a whole is not formed by juxtaposing mutually interchangeable polarities. It is formed in accordance with the Golden Section, a progression where each number is the sum of the preceding two numbers as in 0, 1, 1, 2, 3, 5, 8, 13, 21, 34, etc., any pair from which roughly corresponds to ideal proportion, whether we are thinking in terms of architecture or the human body, of space or time, of the biological life cycle or the trajectory of the entelechy of a living organism from and into Eternity through the brief span of mortal life (for 'the biographical past of *every* organism is *infinite*, each has its own, biographical eternity').[17] All these things relate harmoniously to one another according to the pre-existent law of ideal form which, Florensky asserts, is not, as its nineteenth-century German proponents originally considered, a law of aesthetics but an ontological law expressing the relationships of parts to the whole. Precisely because of this, the greatest works of artistic and religious creativity also – demonstratively – observe it: and Florensky illustrated his thought for his students with diagrams of the structure of Greek tragedy and the Liturgy – unfortunately virtually illegible as reproduced from the typescript of the old 1917 lectures in the *Works*.

The next section of Florensky's second major opus was largely written in 1921 and has come down to us in the form of rough notes towards an unfinished series of lectures on the cultural-historical place of the Christian world view delivered to students of the Moscow Theological Academy in the Petrov Monastery between 11 August and 18 November 1921 and of typed-up versions of the students' conspects of what he said with some corrections in his own hand, clearly made with the thought of incorporation in 'On the watersheds of thought', but insufficiently edited to produce a truly harmonious balance, to eliminate repetition and to redress polemical exaggerations which cannot but strike a discordant note for what was surely intended as an essentially poetic, philosophico-cultural treatise. In this section, Florensky continues to pursue the essentially Greek idea of the primary importance of form, but very much in the context of the renewed polemic surrounding the Name of God controversy and of the recrudescence of a holistic, ontological world view in science, theology and philosophy which was making support for the 'ignorant monks' intellectually acceptable. To Florensky, this dawning of what he termed the New Middle Ages was marked by a revulsion from the dominance of the Kantian system, which he saw as the acme of post-Renaissance thought, a lofty way of thinking, already presaging the return to such 'medieval' insights as Original Sin and the importance of antonyms, but one which puts man rather than God at the centre of being; in terms of ethics, aesthetics and, above all, epistemology. The Middle Ages were for Florensky the Platonist, as was Ancient Greece for Keats the poet, an epoch

> When holy were the haunted forest boughs,
>   Holy the air, the water and the fire.
>
> (John Keats, 'Ode to Psyche')

All things, from this theocentric point of view, were rooted in ultimate reality and thus interconnected, everything in Nature part of a hierarchy divinely ordered and proportioned, with man (the person, rather than the species) as its steward. Symbolist art and music and, above all, the drama and poetry of cult, reflect the multisignificant, poetic resonance of Being.

This vision of the world, Florensky contended, had been virtually lost not just to post-Renaissance Europe but, as already stated at the beginning of this chapter, to the Teaching Church in Russia, which had succumbed through years of scholastic (Roman Catholic) and positivist (Protestant) teaching in the Theological Academies to a rationalistic, subjective view which gave human reason and morality precedence over ascetic striving for real communion with the Divine Energy. The reason for the Church's condemnation of the *imiaslavtsy* was, he now iterated in so many words, unacknowledged docetism, the failure to understand the basic doctrine of the Incarnation of Jesus Christ, Who took on flesh to enable the reintegration of the material and the Divine and Whose main opponents, in His lifetime, had been the Pharisees who, like the theologians of today, preferred their law to His freedom. For Christ had taught 'not "honesty", not "duty", but the will of God. Suppleness.'[18]

Florensky's historical critique of Russian Orthodox theological teaching originates here from Archimandrite Fedor, whom he regarded as a pioneer of the new medieval way of thinking, but he finds allies both within and without the Church in his old mentor Serapion Mashkin, his spiritual directors Isidor and Antonii (Florensov) and in the gentle, charismatic figure of Father David of the *imiaslavtsy*, as well as in modern biology and psychology (Myers, James, Starbuck, Ognev, Pavlov and Freud). As with Carl Jung, who, curiously, Florensky does not mention, the profound conviction that all things are inter-linked in the individual and communal night-world of the sub-conscious leads to an interest in the 'secret sciences' of graphology, hypnotism, alchemy, astrology and telepathy. Florensky borrows terms such as 'astral body' appar-ently uncritically and speculates in a manner which, in the pre-Fascist context, may appear irresponsible but which should also be considered in the light of contemporary medical research, on the importance of genes and blood-lines. However, his thought on the occult and the subliminal is everywhere contained by emphasis on ascetic method, 'the effort to cultivate oneself', and by clear awareness of Original Sin.

Indeed, he regarded theosophy and anthroposophy as more dangerous to Christian cultural thinking in his own day than the outright atheism of the Marxists who, with their emphasis on the primacy of being over consciousness and on the need for radical transformation of man and the world were, in a sense, symptomatic of the New Cultural Epoch – in so far, at least, as they rejected the self-satisfaction of the post-Renaissance era. Even the curious Utopian heresy of Fedorov, which posited man's destiny to be the technically achieved resurrection of the dead and the population of new stars by directing the Earth like a spaceship about the Universe, even the 'magic' Titanism of Scriabin's dream of writing a symphony which would transform the world, even what he called the 'German' Actualism stemming from Schelling, Goethe and Nietzsche ('who misunderstood himself, strove towards Christ and failed to solve His mystery because we stood in the way'),[19] Florensky perceived as symptoms of the dawning of a new age – albeit rogue symptoms. Theosophy and anthropology, on the contrary, were last-ditch attempts by the Age of Reason to impose its methods on the recrudescence of faith.

This is not to imply that Florensky was, or taught his pupils to be, a fellow-traveller, Fascist sympathiser or hubristic believer in the Superman. On the contrary, the acute awareness which had come to him of standing literally 'on the watersheds of thought', looking back over the whole post-Renaissance landscape of scientific humanism and forward to the perils and promise of the new age with its daunting vistas of Perfect Freedom, filled him with a sense of awe and responsibility. Several times in the notes towards these lectures and once in his plan for an introduction to 'On the watersheds' he borrows the words of the nineteenth-century Russian poet Tiutchev:

O, soul oppressed with second sight,
O, heart with fell anxiety brimming,
O, how you flutter on this height –
The threshold of a dual Being![20]

It was not as a conservative Slavophile reactionary or as an adherent of any of the strange new cults sprouting up all around him, but as a pilgrim-priest and teacher, responsible for his students, that Florensky looked out from the watersheds to the pitfalls and discoveries through which he was called to guide his little flock.

He would not, for instance, have them subscribe too credulously to the popular superstition that our 'contemporary events', which he perceived merely as symptoms of cultural crisis, were necessarily the work of Antichrist, preliminaries to the Last Days. We need, he advised soberly, to remember in everyday life as we do during the brief times we spend in church, that we inhabit both Time and Eternity. It is right, however, without specifying times or seasons, to maintain an awareness that the world *will* have an End, though the symptoms of this are evident rather in the discord growing up between Man and Nature than in the activities of advocates of rationalised mysticism or painful social panaceas. Meanwhile, the fact that man has ceased to hearken to and learn from the world about him and has concentrated his energies on the exploitation of the environment will, inevitably, lead to loss of contact with the elements, to disintegration and, eventually, entropy. 'That is a sign of the End.'[21] As usual, Florensky, never afraid to learn from the past, to seek, to discover and preserve eternal truth, was ahead of his time.

It was, he told his listeners, not helpful to wonder whether or not they were fortunate to live at a time of cultural crisis. It was up to them to build the new, Christian culture, to cleanse their minds of the prejudices and limitations of the old 'deterministic' world view and to accept the multiple breakthroughs of the new science. To do this they should try to see objectively, not just from their own point of view in time and space. It is to this subjective point of view that we owe the 'law' of perspective and the concept of continuous, gradual evolution without pre-existent form or qualitative leaps. Now there is a great need to cultivate the objective, Christian viewpoint, in which we can be helped by such apparently 'physiological', 'material' things as diet, bodily posture, even costume, or indeed sex-life, confession (which he compares to the removal of splinters and to psychoanalysis, only that different cures are prescribed), partaking of the sacraments.

It has become evident that man is the

creative centre and not just an eye peering through a crack at the world, not a passive spectator situated outside the world but an active participant within it. Man has become aware of himself as the world's physician, as creative substance.[22]

The Christian mind moves not from the general to the particular but from the particular to the general, from 'thisness' to 'thatness', as Duns Scotus would have said. The Christian's cult is the cult of the Person of Christ, and his God, as according to Pascal, is not the God of the philosophers but 'the God of Abraham, Isaac and Jacob'.[23]

> Jesus Christ, an individual, contains in Himself all other individuals, all are in Him, every action of ours, every judgement; the whole fullness of variety of that which was, is and is to come are contained in Him. Everything should be considered from the take-off point of Christ. This is in direct opposition to post-Renaissance logic. Contemporary thought has basically overcome the Rennaissance world view in that it has acknowledged primal metaphysical form as complex, whole, concrete.[24]

This approach through the 'concrete' (in Florensky's sense of 'real' and 'particular') is that of 'a little child' and is the foundation of the sciences, of history, of our understanding of human prototypes in literature as universal categories. This is the same principle as that by which

> The life of Jesus Christ can be projected onto history and even the Cosmos, just as can the whole of world history.[25]

This way of thinking, perfectly proper to the educated man, in terms of 'concrete' images and poetry, is natural to the individual family man who sees himself as part of nature rather than as a member of some group or political party for which 'God' is merely a 'hypothesis' in the creation of disembodied schemes to control the world. The scientific way of thinking 'reaches conclusions not contained in science itself',[26] whereas the medieval, symbolic mindset is always open to new revelations, 'can trace all kinds of cross-sections and discover new links'.[27]

From this point the coherence of the course is lost. There were to have followed lectures on St Sergius as the 'Russian Dante', on Fedor Bukharev and on the Name of God. The transcripts tail off into question-and-answer sessions and pastoral teaching eminently relevant to the situation of students faced with hostility and upheaval, into reprises on Kant, the symbol, particularly the symbolism of the 'Iconostasis', the lasting importance of the Platonic ideal of the Symposium which Florensky still associates with the ideal of monastic community, cosmic harmony as expressed in music and mathematics, and the dream of the compilation of a Book of Permanent Symbols, on which they break off.

Not surprisingly ...

Even the sheltered world of the Academy in Sergiev Posad was shifting under the feet of its inhabitants. The town had always centred round the monastery and its dependencies which, for a while, abiding by the rule of service and hospitality, became a refuge for undernourished writers, intellectuals and displaced *ci-devants*. The Moscow Theological Academy was uprooted soon after the Bolsheviks came to power and, from October 1918, continued to drag out a precarious existence in the shelter first of the Danilov Monastery (1918–1919), then of the Petrov Monastery, both situated in Moscow, and, eventually, on a semi-clandestine basis, at private gatherings in various people's flats until its final suppression in 1928. Florensky not only continued to teach at these ever-shifting venues, stopping in the capital overnight on a truckle bed in his mother's kitchen when need arose, but supplemented his much depleted income as editor and lecturer by undertaking courses on physics, mathematics and geometrical method, astronomy and the history of material culture at the Sergiev Pedagogical Institute, where he had charge of the physics laboratory. He also continued to minister to his little parish of nursing sisters until they, too, were disbanded in May 1921.

In spite of all this disruption and increased family responsibility with the birth of his first daughter, Ol'ga, in 1918, Florensky experienced a sustained burst of creative activity. Apart from, though very much in parallel to, the plans towards the new book at which we have just been looking, he embarked in May 1918 on a series of incandescent lectures on the philosophy of cult: 'The fear of God' was followed by 'Cult, religion and art', 'Sacraments and rites', 'Features of the phenomenology of cult' and 'The hallowing of reality' – all written and delivered during the month of May, the last month the Moscow Theological Academy would spend in its ancient home until after Russia's victory in the Second World War. This new cycle of lectures he completed as and when he had occasion to deliver them: 'The deduction of the Seven Sacraments' on 22/29 December 1919; 'The philosophy of cult' 16 April/4 June, 1922; 'The historico-cultural situation and fundamental assumptions of the Christian world-view' which was the full title of the course read in the autumn of 1921 in the Petrov Monastery; 'Witnesses' (or 'Martyrdom', 5/17 June 1922); and 'Verbal devotion. Prayer' (28 August/12 September 1922). The double-dating throughout reflects the necessity to keep to the Old Style Calendar still in use to this day in the Russian Orthodox Church and to the New Calendar which would have defined Florensky's teaching timetable in the Pedagogic Institute and elsewhere outside the Theological Academy.

Clearly these lectures, some of which appear to have been written very quickly, others, possibly in snatches, over a rather more extended timescale, were the product of a period of incubation which had begun with Florensky's service as a priest and were intended, in some form or other, for incorporation in 'On the watersheds of thought' or in a more loosely envisaged *Collected*

*Works*, for which there are several plans. Igumen Andronik, the editor of the posthumous *Works* now in process of publication, quotes a passage which defines their aim as being to show the centrality of the church order of worship to all Christian life, thought and action and to demonstrate how all things that afterwards became laicised in culture have their origin in cult: philosophy, science, forms of social life, art. 'Cult', writes Florensky, 'and its foundation, the sacrament of the Eucharist, is the sacred and sole foundation of living thought, creativity and the social order.'[28] Such was, indeed, his profound conviction, yet it is well to remember that Florensky's technique was always to proceed from the evidence rather than the conclusion: to follow his thought process is always to embark on an absorbing, if often demanding and circuitous, voyage of discovery. His vocation was to explore and to guide, not to hammer home his conclusions, and this is also a reason why it is now so difficult to reconstruct the unfinished 'Anthropodicy'.

Meanwhile, another way in which Father Pavel continued to fulfil his function as lecturer extraordinary to the Theological Academy was by illuminating world literature through ecclesiastical texts. This he accomplished with a sensitivity that allowed a real dialogue to develop between secular and sacred. 'It is not enough just to lay texts side by side', he wrote of one student's efforts to establish such a dialogue. 'The art lies in getting them to speak to one another.'[29] Even at his most patristic, Florensky remained faithful to the ideal of the Platonic Symposium.

From 1917 onwards, he extended his teaching activities far beyond the auditorium provided by the gradually expiring Academy. Intellectual life was, in those early years, still vibrant in revolutionary Russia, and on 12 June 1917 Bulgakov and Florensky 'founded' a Religious Philosophical Academy for the study of religion in its 'concrete' historical context, to which the terminally ill Valentin Kozhevnikov was to leave his books but which, in the chaotic instability of the post-revolutionary world, never really took off before Bulgakov, a little more than a month after his ordination, departed for the Crimea on 31 July 1918. Other religious philosophical associations, however, enjoyed a brief but vivid flowering and Florensky was invited by his old opponent Berdiaev to speak at a new Free Academy of Spiritual Culture,[30] one of several initiatives to compensate for the suppression of religion and, to some extent, to celebrate its corollary – the emancipation of religious speculation. At the invitation of a new friend, Vladimir Favorsky, with whom Florensky shared an intense interest in the philosophical implications of contemporary theories of multiple geometrical space and their translation into new approaches to the handling of pictorial space, he was invited to conduct a course of two-hour lectures on the subject at the Higher Art and Technical Studios,[31] the nursery of the left-wing, often aggressively materialistic Russian Avant Garde, with whom he already had some acquaintance, having been on visiting terms with Liubov' Popova, whose circle included Vladimir Tatlin, since 1914. Florensky continued to teach at Vkhutemas until 1924.

The preoccupation with pictorial space, together with the course on new approaches to geometry at the Pedagogical Institute, put Florensky in mind of an unpublished university paper he had been working on while still a student at the Mathematical Faculty in 1902, which now suggested to him a whole plethora of astronomical, literary and pictorial implications. In 1922, he published *Imaginary Points in Geometry*,[32] with two appendices, one on the cosmological implications for Dante's *Divine Comedy* and another on the representation of a fourth dimension on a flat surface in the 'Explanation of the cover', to which we will return in the context of Florensky's association with Favorsky. The publication called forth protest from conventionally educated Soviet critics, to whom it appeared the retrograde product of a typically 'medieval' (in the perjorative sense) priestly mentality. In spite of this, however, Florensky was invited in the early twenties to contribute to a new Soviet Encyclopedia of Mathematics and to lecture to the all-Russian Union of Engineers. He appears to have picked up applied science without effort at the point at which he had left off on entering the Academy in the autumn of 1904, not just shouldering an ever-increasing workload to boost the family budget but, as is clear from the luxuriant sprouting of *Imaginary Points*, rediscovering abundant stimuli to an ever-active mind engaged in the Promethean task of explaining the macrocosm of physical being to the human microcosm – a task he had long since acknowledged to be 'impossible without God'.

The pursuit of truth for its own sake was still Florensky's overriding preoccupation and politics – ecclesiastical and civic – concerned him only in so far as they infringed directly on his expectation of decent conduct amongst his fellows. He felt no inclination, for instance, to join the intelligentsia's initial boycott of Soviet institutions and did not see putting his mind and erudition at the service of the Bolshevik State – whether in education or in practical scientific projects – as a compromise. On the contrary, he welcomed every opportunity to contribute to the spiritual and material well-being of a war-torn Russia which, he devoutly believed, would outlive and outgrow its crisis-ridden present. He did, however, make it a rule not to compromise in matters of conviction, eschewed the *Obnovlentsy* and took no part in the desperate politicking through which various representatives of the Church hierarchy, in various ways, were seeking an accommodation or at least a *modus vivendi* with a hostile government, while at the same time refraining from judgement and preserving canonical fidelity to the elected Patriarch and his successors. Where his ideas met with resistance, Florensky retreated into 'discreet' science, making no attempt to adapt his admirably lucid writing on religion and culture to an increasingly repressive censorship for the sake of publication. 'Remember, one compromise involves another, and so on, *ad infinitum*', he admonished himself in his diary in 1920.

Although critical of the direction of the majority of Orthodox theologians, Florensky unhesitatingly performed the tasks laid upon him by the Church and avoided faction and confrontation, unlike his friends Novoselov who, as Brother Mark, became active in the Catacomb Church, or Fedor Andreev, who, working as an ordained priest in Petrograd, was, at the time of his death in 1929, a prominent Iosiflianin, totally opposed to the declaration of loyalty to Soviet power made by the Locum Tenens Metropolitan Sergii (Starogorodsky) and to that power's perceived interference in Church appointments. On 9/22 March 1918, Florensky was asked to participate, with Novoselov, Bulgakov and other Moscow Slavophiles, in work on the section of the Local Council of the Russian Orthodox Church on Education and the types of pastoral instruction suited to prepare a priesthood now envisaged as representatives of a disestablished Church. Also, with Novoselov and Bulgakov, he was given the opportunity to prepare a reasoned defence of the *imiaslavtsy* for the Sub-Commission of the Council appointed to adjudicate on the question of whether or not their beliefs constituted a heresy. In connection with this he became a member of the Aleksei Losev circle, which supported their doctrine, lectured and preached vigorously and worked closely with their eirenic Moscow leader David towards full reconciliation. Bulgakov, for one, was confident this could be brought about, but the Council was dissolved by the Government before the Commission got beyond two preliminary meetings. Florensky's definitive essay on the cardinal importance ascribed by the *imiaslavtsy* to the Name of God was, together with frequent references to the problem in the 1921 lecture course, included in his plan for 'On the watersheds of thought', and he undoubtedly considered acceptance of their belief in the indwelling presence of God in His Name as an important step towards the establishment of the new epoch of thought 'beyond the watersheds'.[33]

More momentously still for the direction of Florensky's creative work, he was appointed on 22 October 1918 to the Commission for the Preservation of Art and Antiquities in the Trinity St Sergius Monastery, on which he served until its dissolution in 1920. This appointment proved not only extremely onerous (all the treasures of the ancient Monastery had to be described and catalogued and Florensky, most suitably for one who loved clothes and believed they exercised specific influence over the wearer, bore particular responsibility for the historic collection of ecclesiastical robes), but both inspiring and dangerous. Other members of the Commission were Count Iurii Ol'susev, Il'ia Bondarenko, Nikolai Protasov, Mikhail Boskin, Pavel Kapterev, Tatiana

Aleksandrova-Dol'nik, Sergei Durylin, Sergei Mansurov and Mikhail Shik, both of which last subsequently took holy orders. Rozanov's daughter, Tatiana Rozanov was, thanks to Florensky's good offices, employed as a secretary. This distinctly *ci-devant*, predominantly Slavophile committee was directly responsible to Patriarch Tikhon, which involved them in finely calculated navigation between the Scylla of an intransigent protector of Church property and the Charybdis of a hungry state, eager to requisition and sell off ecclesiastical treasures and actively opposed to religion as such.[34]

Their position was not strong. In 1918, the monastery had been officially nationalised and this was followed at the end of March 1918 by the expulsion of the Moscow Theological Academy then, at the end of April 1918, by the opening of the casket containing St Sergius' relics for 'scientific examination'. This sacrilegious act by the State was pre-empted, on the instructions of the Patriarch, by Florensky and other leading members of the Commission who, under oath of secrecy, removed the saint's head, substituting that of a long-dead prince, and hid it in various places of safekeeping until the rest of his body was restored to the Church and the shrine again became an object of pilgrimage and a centre of worship after the Second World War. The cloak-and-dagger concealment of the blessed relic – at first in the monastery wardrobe administered by Florensky himself – appears to have gone undetected at the time by an authority so concerned at the prospect of popular resistance that, before opening the coffin, they confiscated the keys to the bell tower to prevent an attempt to sound the alarm and rouse the people. From November 1919, the monks were gradually dispersed, those remaining until the last being evacuated to the nearby Gethsemane Skete in May 1920. Several defrocked brothers subsequently found employment with the Commission as keepers of the Trinity Sergius Museum established by a decree of the Bolshevik Government personally signed by Lenin on 20 April 1920. Until 1928, when a campaign was mounted by press and police against ex-members of the Commission and all their works, the great complex functioned more as a memorial to the spirit and splendour of its past than, as had been intended, as an 'anti-religious museum'. The Cathedral of the Trinity was, nevertheless, closed for worship and sealed on 31 May 1920 and the bells dismantled in 1930: the three great bells, the largest bell in all Russia, the Tsar, dating back to 1742 and the still more ancient Tsarborisov and Karneukhii, were dropped one upon the other and broken up for scrap, and only the smallest, oldest and most true in tone, Lebedok was preserved for posterity. Florensky, with the composer Pavel Ippolitov, foreseeing the possibility, made a musical annotation of their individual notes and characteristics to complement the article by Mikhail Shik for the splendidly illustrated report of the Commission, edited and introduced by Florensky and submitted on 11/20 April 1920.

The report, ironically enough subsidized by the government, was printed but was not published until 2007. In 1920, the typeset was broken up, ensuant on an outcry in the press against the waste of best-quality, state-issue paper and the overly reverend, lyrically apologetic tone of the articles. Fortunately, a few copies survived.[35]

These articles for the report and others written by Florensky in defence of his beloved monastery have left their mark on the history of art as well as on that of Christian material culture. His inspiration overflowed the brief period during which the Commission continued to function but the spate of eloquence was undoubtedly struck from him by the threat to all he held most dear. In these articles, Florensky speaks of the historical and spiritual importance of the Trinity St Sergius Monastery as the 'entelechy' of the Russian land, describing the beauty of its services and symbolic significance of its treasury: 'The Trinity–St Sergius Lavra and Russia', 'The Church Service as a Synthesis of the Arts'; 'The most venerated icons of St Sergius'; 'Celestial signs' (a meditation on colour symbolism and its religious significance); 'Reverse perspective'; 'Amvrosii, fifteenth-century master-carver of the Trinity Monastery'; 'Iconostasis'.[36]

The first of these articles was written specifically as an introduction to the report, under intense pressure. Florensky dictated it in one night (24/25 October / 6/7 November 1918) to Ivan Vvedensky, who took it down directly on a typewriter to be read at a meeting of the Commission scheduled for 27 October/9 November. It defined the aim of the Commission as the preservation not just of walls and artefacts, but of sounds, scents and atmosphere, all the elusive material symbols of the essential spirit of an historic site. The article on the icons of St Sergius was dictated to the same, to I. A. Vvedensky and his brother, the two working with the author 'all night long' over 27/28 November, and read out, after some editing, on 23 January 1919 at the thirteenth meeting of the Commission, which intended to publish it as a separate brochure illustrated by photographs of the icons described. Less creative but no less exacting was a systematic description of the collection of *panaghia*[37] in the wardrobe of the monastery, Florensky's particular responsibility. The meditation on colour symbolism, 'Celestial signs', completed 7 October 1919, though not directly connected to work for the Commission, was first published in No. 2, 1922 of the art journal *Makovets* (allied to the spirit of St Sergius by the choice for its title of the name of the little hill on which he first founded his monastery) and is undoubtedly an offshoot of the aesthetic concentration of this period. It is also among the most beautiful and illuminating of Florensky's short pieces.

'Reverse perspective', the most discussed of all Florensky's aesthetic studies and one of the first to be reclaimed for posterity (in Iurii Lotman's semiotic journal *Trudy znakovoi sistemy*, III/198, Tartu, 1967) was originally written for the Commission in 1919, but, on the invitation of Pavel Muratov, was delivered as a lecture to the Byzantine Section of the Moscow Institute of Historico-Artistic Research and Museum Study where, though not published at the time, it actually got as far as the stage of printed proofs. The paper was a by-product of the close study of icons in which work for the Commission had involved Florensky and was influenced by a German essay by Oskar Wulff: 'Die umgekehrte Perspektive und die Niedersicht'.[38] Having defined the technical means by which icon painters highlighted rather than concealed the use of reverse perspective and multiple viewpoint (i.e. the depiction of objects, buildings and even the human face as though perceived from several angles simultaneously), Florensky concludes that not only were these so-called 'primitives' consciously employing a spatial system different from the single point, geometrical perspective (which, beginning with Giotto or, as Florensky suggests, somewhat earlier after Vitruvius, under the influence of Anaxagorus's treatise on stage design, became increasingly *de rigueur* in high-Renaissance and post-Renaissance art), but that they were employing this system in order to achieve specific aesthetic, cognitive and, indeed, religious effects and insights. The Renaissance, in other words, did not 'discover the laws of perspective', but each epoch employed its own system to express a world view, as did the great civilisations of the Ancient World: Egypt, China, for example. The system obtaining in European art from the Renaissance until the early twentieth century was, Florensky maintained, simply the one best suited to express an increasingly rationalistic, subjective and superficial mentality which preferred the illusionist, stagey effect obtained by the artist confining himself to a single viewpoint and scaling what is depicted according to distance from the beholder rather than intrinsic importance. The great artists did not adhere strictly to this tyranny of 'optical illusion', but allowed themselves a certain freedom to exploit the symbolic possibilities of spatial relationships in which artists of the 'reverse perspective' epoch had enjoyed such remarkable creative autonomy. At the time, in a society brought up to identify the introduction of perspective with 'progress', Florensky's concept was truly shocking and even today, presumably because the Renaissance and all it entailed only reached Russia in the late seventeenth century, it is sometimes seen as reactionary and 'anti-Western',[39] an apologia for superstitious artist-monks who did not know their geometry. But Florensky, of course, did know his geometry and was indeed a step ahead of all those who had not made a special study of non-Euclidean space, which gives his arguments a persuasiveness that thrilled his first auditors in 1919 as it did his first readers in 1967. It was essentially liberating to be presented with reasoned proof that naturalistic representation of form (as imposed by socialist no less than nineteenth-century realism) is, in fact, a geometrical nonsense, and Florensky's debunking of the single viewpoint, in spite of its thorny technicalities, was welcomed as a riotously subversive *reductio ad absurdum*. The article, which is one of the cornerstones of Florensky's call to move on from the post-Renaissance epoch, was scheduled for inclusion in the first part of 'On the watersheds'.

The much longer 'Iconostasis' is relevant both to the lectures on the philosophy of cult and to the Commission for the Preservation of Art and Antiquities. It was possible to complete so major a work in the hectic post-revolutionary years thanks to the fact that it had been in the writing since 1912, when the author first began to make notes towards a meditation on the function of icons. The text of 'Platonism and icon painting' which forms, as it were, the kernel of the treatise, was completed in the night of 24/25 August 1919. Having disposed of the philosophic dimension, Florensky homed in on the function of the icon screen as safeguard and revelation of sacred space, which he discusses in the introduction, at which he is known to have been working off and on from June 1921 to January 1922. He finally edited the whole work in the form in which it has come down to us over the summer vacation of 1922 between 8 July and 29 August. 'Iconostasis' was thus originally undertaken as part of Florensky's ongoing plan to show art and culture from the point of view of the Orthodox Church and to explain the symbolic riches of cult against the material background of ecclesiastical buildings and artefacts, but the work undoubtedly gained greatly in intensity and expertise from the author's direct involvement in the defence of the treasures of his monastery. Like so much else he was writing at this time, 'Iconostasis' was published posthumously, many years after his death.[40] Florensky, it is said by friends, students and colleagues, never sought academic acclaim. His reputation in the early twenties rested almost entirely on *The Pillar and Ground of Truth*,[41] on the spoken word and on personality, the impression of sheer strength radiated by this frail, scholarly dreamer with the encyclopaedic mind, for whom 'culture' was a synonym of ascetism and who, it seemed, never tired and was 'never ill'.[42]

What distinguishes these articles from Florensky's earlier academic writing is that they are not products of solitary meditation addressed to kindred souls, or occasional pieces undertaken for a readership of fellow-theologians and religious thinkers, but attempts to communicate directly with a wider audience, embracing not only the artistic and scientific intelligentsia, with whom the circumstances of Florensky's life were once more bringing him into close contact, but even Marxist officials who had the power to preserve the St Sergius Monastery, as Florensky briefly hoped, as a *living* museum (monks and all), an idea he advocated with a sophisticated persuasiveness clearly drawn from the turn-of-the-century discussions of the function of museums and exhibitions as *Gesamtkunstwerk*[43] or, as he himself put it, 'a synthesis of the arts'. 'True art', he argues, 'is a fusion of content and of the means by which that content is expressed', and he declares that, whereas he would have understood a fanatic demand to annihilate the monastery as an affirmation of the triumph of materialist socialism, he did not understand the profane mentality of the *Kulturträger*, who seeks to preserve icons, frescoes or architectural ensembles out of context. By 'context' he means not only spiritual context, but the whole sensual ensemble of wavering candlelight, the glittering coloured glass of the *lampadki*,[44] the wreathing blue smoke and sharp scent of incense, the measured, choreographed movements of the celebrant and the black-clad figures of the monks. To collect and exhibit ecclesiastical artefacts in the sterile atmosphere of the Museum would be, he maintained, 'a sin against life'.

> A work of art, we repeat, is artistically viable only in the setting considered essential at the time it was brought into being ... Aphrodite in a bustle is an intolerable thought and so is a seventeenth century marquise in an aeroplane.[45]

At the time, of course, Florensky and the Commission did not succeed in their quixotic attempts to avert the closing down of the monastery, but they did ensure the preservation of its carefully catalogued ecclesiastical treasures for the Russian State[46] and, for some years at least, of the whole complex of monastic buildings in relative peace and dignity, albeit no longer in 'Sergiev Posad' but in 'Zagorsk': the Soviet State enthusiastically adopted Machiavelli's advice to his conquering Prince to change the sign system, eradicating as far as possible old associations in nomenclature, coinage, civic monuments and iconography.

Florensky, never afraid to appear inconsistent, later admitted that the Vladimir Mother of God and other great icons actually took on a new, more austere and compelling beauty on the unadorned walls of a museum:

> Now there is neither gold nor glitter of precious stones in their vicinity. No candles, no *lampadki*. Yet this stark poverty rings out louder than rustling robes. This poverty speaks more directly to our hearts – that which is 'not of humankind' in the Vladimir icon sings on in a voice that will never fall silent, whether in Church or museum.[47]

In spite of all the lost battles, Florensky remained serenely confident that the war, as such, could not be lost. 'The most important thing', he wrote to Anna Mamontova, heir to the cultural artistic complex of Abramtsevo, 'is the spiritual idea, which is indestructible. I'll say worse. If Abramtsevo were to be physically destroyed, even then, though its destruction would be a monstrous crime against the Russian people, if only the idea of Abramtsevo lives on, then not everything will be lost.'[48] Florensky believed ardently that nihilism, which he understood as St Augustine understood it as the denial of the divinity of Christ and with Him of all creation, would eventually run its course and break up on its own inner emptiness so that, in his beloved mother country, 'hearts and

minds will turn again, not idly and half-heartedly but with the avidity of deprivation, to the Russian idea, the idea of Russia, Holy Russia'.[49]

The pathos of Florensky's identification of the Trinity St Sergius Monastery
with the birth of Russia as a self-aware nation with her own 'idea' may well have
exercised a belated influence on the decision to restore the shrine of St Sergius
and to reopen the monastery and the Moscow Theological Academy as a gesture
of conciliation by the Soviet Government towards the Russian Orthodox
Church for the patriotic stand it took during the Second World War. Eloquent
and poetic, Florensky's articles in defence of 'the spirit of Russia', though power-
fully worded, are not confrontational. On the contrary, they are overwhelmingly
positive. Instead of anathematising the militant atheists, Florensky accepted
what was happening in his native land as a judgement on a culture which had
already become deracinated from the 'cult' on which it was founded. Believing
implicitly in the Church's abiding, ontological greatness and sanctity, he sought,
at this moment of Her humiliation, to bear witness, with all the cultural range
and lyrical feeling at his command, to the beauty of Her adornments, songs and
rituals, to the imponderable profundity of Her Sacraments and to the homely
radiance spread from the sanctuary of the holy places throughout the Russian
lands. Drawing on the well-spring of systematically cultivated memory, innate
aesthetic sensibility and the energy of his religious praxis, Father Pavel applied
an alert, formidably concentrated mind to the task of encapsulating in words
the essence of what could be salvaged from the present shipwreck. At the same
time, he sought to puzzle out the infinitely complex past, present and future
relationship between cult and culture, to diagnose the entropy of encroaching
chaos and to proclaim the entropic power of Christ.

Head of Pavel Florensky by N. Vysheslavets, 1922.

Florensky's mother, Ol'ga Pavlovna Saparova (Saparian) (1859–1951) in the 1870s.

Ol'ga Pavlovna, Aleksandr and Iulia Florensky with the two eldest children, Iulia (nicknamed Liusia), on her father's knee, and Pavel, on small chair.

Pavel Florensky as a school-boy, 1887–1889.

Pavel Florensky in the uniform of a student of Moscow University
(1900–1904).

„Бѣлые къ сердцу цвѣты я
Вновь прижимаю невольно."

(А. Бѣлый – „Знаю")

Andrei Bely (B N Bugaev, 1880–1934), pastel drawing by
Ol'ga Florenskaia, 1912.

The Monastery of St Sergius, wood-engraving by Vladimir Favorsky, 1919.

Pavel Florensky and Sergei Troitsky with Florensky's family in Tiflis, 1907.
From left to right, standing, back row: Sergei, Pavel, Pavel's brother Alekandr;
seated: Elizaveta Pavlovna Melik-Begliarova, Liusia (christened Iulia),
Aleksandr Ivanovich, Ol'ga Pavlovna, Repsimia Pavlovna Tavridova;
seated on floor: Andrei, Raisa (nicknamed Gosia), Ol'ga (nicknamed Valia),
and Elizaveta.

Pavel Florensky, 1909.

Vasilii Mikhailovich Giatsintov, Anna Mikhailovna Giatsintova (Florenskaia) and Pavel Florensky 1911.

The Florenskys' new home in Sergiev Posad, 1915.

Mikhail Nesterov, "The Philosophers", Pavel Florensky and Mikhail Bulgakov
in the Florenskys' garden Sergiev Posad, Spring, 1917.

Florensky in his office at the State Experimental Electrotechnical Institute GEEI, Moscow, 1925.

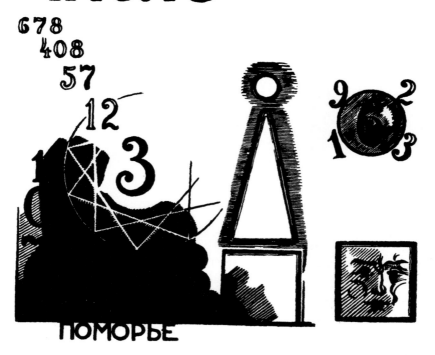

VI Favorsky, cover for Number as Form, wood engraving.

Florensky picnicking with his family near Zagorsk towards the end of the twenties. Seated from the left to right Father Pavel, Mik, Ol'ga, unknown woman in white headdress, Maria, Anna Mikhailovna; kneeling behind them: Vasilii and Kirill.

Pavel Florensky and some of his dependents in 1932. Florensky seated
on steps in centre with Maria. Standing from left to right: Ol'ga Pavlovna,
Nadezda Giatsintova:, Mik, Iulia Aleksandrovna, Anna Mikhailovna. Strictly
speaking, it was the other sister, Gosia (Raisa) who was dependent at least in
part on her brother until her death from the family scourge of tuberculosis.
Iulia worked as a psychiatrist.

A shared joke with Anna and Mik, 1932.

Florensky at the piano, 1932

Police photograph of Florensky after his arrest, 27 February, 1933.

Florensky with P N Kapterev in Skovorodino at the Permafrost laboratory, 1934.

"When you look out of the window you can imagine yourself in Italy", view from the window of the old forge by the Holy Lake, photograph of 2002.

# 8

# Diversification – Art, Music and Science 1919–1933

> For some reason this has always been the way of my life: all the questions, books, research projects which particularly moved me have eluded me, squeezed out by more alien matter, undertaken for the sake of present duty, and always it was necessary to put off till some future day all that most deeply and genuinely occupied my thoughts.
>
> P. A. Florensky[1]

Gradually, as the grip of militant atheism tightened, Florensky's intellectual activities were forced into new channels not directly concerned with theology or the Church. Throughout this period, however, he practised what he had preached to his 'children' in the 'Testament' letter of 19–20 March 1921:

> Get into the habit, train yourselves, to do whatever you are doing conscientously, with elegance, with distinction, don't blur your work, don't do anything in bad taste, all anyhow. Remember that you can waste a whole lifetime on all anyhow, whereas in measured, rhythmic activity even things or tasks of secondary importance may help you discover much that may later serve you, perhaps, as a most profound source of new creative insights … Thought is God's gift and requires cultivation. To be clear and precise in thought is the guarantee of spiritual freedom and delight in thinking.[2]

Florensky's growing preoccupation with questions of aesthetics was much stimulated by a close friendship which arose indirectly from his work for the Commission for the Preservation of Treasures of Art and Antiquities. Vladimir Favorsky, xylographer, monumentalist, teacher and theoretician of art, newly demobilised from the Red Army, set up house with his wife and children in a wing of the Trinity St Sergius Monastery in 1919 – and remained resident in the town of Zagorsk until 1938. Favorsky's father Andrei Evgrafovich worked on the Commission with Florensky, and his father-in-law, Baron Vladimir Derviz, was to become the first director of the Sergiev Art-Historical Museum. This musical, artistic, highly cultivated but natural and unpretentious Christian family soon became close friends of the Florenskys. Favorsky drew the Florensky children, Kirill, Ol'ga and Maria. His brilliantly gifted elder son Nikita, born, like Kirill, in 1915, became a schoolfriend of Kirill and Ol'ga. The youthful musical coach of the Favorsky children, Sergei Trubachev, son of one of Father Pavel's students at the theological academy, who had written a thesis for him on 'The cosmic in church services' and at whose wedding he had officiated in 1918, eventually married Florensky's daughter Ol'ga, authored a luminous series of reminiscences about life in Sergiev Posad and founded a dynasty devoted to ordering and publishing his father-in-law's archives. Maria Vladimirovna, Favorsky's wife, became firm friends with Anna Mikhailovna (in spite of the yawning gap in social status) and also left vivid reminiscences of the Florensky household. Favorsky himself, who had studied with Holoszy before the Second World War and, with N. B. Rozenfeld, had translated A. Hildebrandt's book *Problems of Form in Figurative Art* (Musagetes, Moscow, 1914) and K. Voll's *Experiments in the Comparative Study of Pictures* (Moscow, 1918), found Florensky a most stimulating interlocutor and, as we have seen, invited him to read a course of lectures on pictorial space and perspective in Vkhutemas (1921–1924). The resultant conspectus of the lectures was, as had become almost the norm for Florensky's works of the early 1920s, published from archive posthumously under the title 'Analysis of space and time in the visual arts', but the graceful introductory lecture, in which the speaker salutes the artist as the seeing eye of humanity, disclaims any intention of interfering with this inborn gift but promises, like a devoted nurse, to see that the eyes of his charges are free from dust and infection accumulated from the prejudices of the past, took on a life of its own and surfaced, somewhat earlier than the bulk of the course, in a Soviet art journal in 1982.[3]

Although Florensky's worn, white cassock attracted the occasional provocative question from this new, fierily left-wing audience, his lectures awoke nothing but respect among his students, for, though preceded by moments of intense private prayer, they were entirely concerned with the primary importance of 'organising space' in all branches of art and with the various technical ways in which the artist works on the passive material or, if his 'material' be words or sounds as in poetry and music, on the imagination of his public. At a time when easel painting was being declared an art of the past, Florensky talked of the difference between line and daub, between the sculptural, hewn from resistant material, and the plastic, moulded from more yielding substances. He distinguished between the energy of movement and the celebratory gentleness of contemplation. Pointing out, as always on concrete examples, how these material and spiritual elements combine and vary in artistic practice, Florensky simply annihilated the concept of 'progress' in art, the notion that cave-paintings, Assyrian art, Egyptian bas-reliefs, Ancient Greek sculpture, Byzantine frescoes and the Renaissance rediscovery of what he called 'illusory perspective' represented a 'progression' from primitive ignorance to a more sophisticated, 'realistic' and 'scientific' way of representing the world. The task of the artist has always been to reveal the essence of reality through the organisation of space and, although the accepted conventions differed at different times, the recalci-trance of problems arising from the resistance of the material has remained the same from age to age and has to be wrestled with anew by each individual artist in his own way. Florensky may, as he says elsewhere, have been looking at art through the eyes of the Church but, in his parlance in these lectures, that eye is a biological sense organ, a nerve through the agency of which we contemplate the exterior world, just as we feel that world through our skin. The body itself is an instrument; the artist's instruments are a projection of the body; the artist works with matter on matter. True ... there is matter and matter: the solid environment created by the application of paint, for instance, as opposed to the intangible force fields which arise in the curves of space between dynamically outlined objects. Both, however, will dissolve chaotically into their component parts without the energy exerted by the artist's will to impose an integrated whole. This exercise of will, Florensky maintained, leads inevitably to a certain deformation of what is seen, a deformation which he calls 'illusion', a term he is careful to differentiate from the derogatory 'illusory art' which he applied to stagey realism of the post-Renaissance variety. The task of the artist is not to duplicate reality but to perceive and show the workings of its architectonics, its material being and most profound inner, essential meaning.[4]

In other words, Florensky's lectures on art, though grist to the mill of the world view to be set out in "On the watersheds of thought", were not founded on an *a priori* theological schema, but on a close investigation of the psycho-physical perceptions needed to depict a world in which what is seen does not necessarily coincide with what is known. They are set out, moreover, in terms of the different possibilities afforded by different media in the attempt to synthesise the evershifting 'illusions' of multiple space and relative time.

Florensky's ideas interacted well with Favorsky's more simply expressed teaching,[5] but the priest invested the artist's careful exposition of theory and practice with a dazzle of mathematico-physical speculation and deep metaphysical rootedness which delighted and inspired the artist. He made three portraits of Florensky, two drawings and an engraving on bone, redolent of the intellectual acumen and intense concentration he so admired, and produced woodcuts for the dust jackets of *Mnimosti v geometrii* (*Imaginary Points in Geometry*) (Pomor'e, Moscow, 1922) and 'Chislo kak forma' ('Number as form') (1923) which are quite remarkable graphic expressions of mathematical thought. The former, in particular, which elicited the author's enthusiastic 'Explanation of the cover', shows, in abstract terms which are yet as far as may be from diagram, the possibility of another dimension 'beneath the surface of the paper', the flatness of which is indicated by lettering as in a geometrical figure but undermined by curving lines promising, as in Florensky's university thesis, the possibility of breaks in continuity: here by means of shading, cross-hatching and the judicious use of white spaces and areas of intense black. The 'Number as form' cover, which like the book for which it was made long remained unpublished, uses the shapes of Arabic numerals to suggest the organisation of space and time, not as a continuum but into distinct, finite forms, subject to count: the date '1923' spins lightly around a sphere anchored by the large, black, perfect number '6'; a triangle mounted on a square topped by a circle, shaded to convey an illusion of solidity, occupies the central space, but in no way obtrudes upon the black, billowing cloud of chaos which dominates the left-hand corner. This area of unorganised space is bounded on the extreme left by vertically stacked cardinal numbers '1', '0' and '7', and gently invaded from the right by the segment of a circle, subdivided into shaded triangles and dominated at centre by a triumphant curlicued '3', while the circumference is marked by a half-solid, half-transparent '12', from which other numbers, flickering between black and white, 'real' and 'imaginary', 'finite' and 'transfinite', mount steadily stepwise to the left edge of the woodblock, above the cloud: '57', '408', '678'. Like a signature in the lower right-hand corner is a playful reference to Florensky's discussion of the difficulty of representing the Earth's globe on a flat surface – a human face of considerable dignity and wisdom mapped out as a square.

So Favorsky produced an apparently effortless visual reaction to 'Number as form', only two chapters of which have been published to this day.[6] These tend, in the manner of all Florensky's works destined to contribute to 'On the watersheds of thought', to suggest that the new mathematics and science were leading away from Kantian constructivism and out into unchartered distances which are yet recognisably adumbrated in the thought of the Middle Ages and the Ancient World, where numbers are perceived not as milestones along the continuum but as self-contained wholes, capable of giving form to discreet phenomena and, indeed, having form in themselves. Florensky saw it as the task of the modern thinker to reinvest numbers with rhythm, to rediscover their long-forgotten Pythagorean music.

Delighted by Favorsky's pictorial response to his cloistered thought, Florensky was also very taken with the ex-libris his friend devised from the family crest of a knight transfixed by an arrow, discovered in the course of research into the Florensky family tree. The knight on the ex-libris, alert and vigorous in spite of the arrow through his heart, rests one hand on his sword and the other on a shield depicting a diagram of a bare, aspiring tree divided into sections towards the crown. It bears the legend 'From the books of the Priest Pavel Florensky' and, dominated by the word 'Priest', suggests a nice combination of asceticism, romanticism and science – with a hint of cosmic depths beneath the flat surface in the black splodge behind the knight's white shield, a visual quotation from *Imaginary Points*.

Through Favorsky and Vkhutemas, Florensky met the artist Nikolai Chernyshev who, together with Pavel Pavlinov, Nikolai Chekrygin and others involved him in the group active from 1921–1927 under the name of Makovets. Their aim was to promote, through exhibitions and a journal (edited by Florensky's artist-sister Raisa (Gosia) from their mother's flat in Moscow), a deeper realism, opposed to the naturalistic and illusory but also to gratuitous distortion as in Picasso's 'Demoiselles d'Avignon', and capable, as Florensky felt true realism ought to be, of expressing a trans-sensual reality behind and beyond the material of art.[7] It was Florensky who linked this group to the Trinity St Sergius Monastery by suggesting the name and Favorsky who designed the programmatic cover for the third number, which should have contained his friend's essay 'On realism'. The cover, like the essay, suggests a fine balance between art and life: a framed human figure which is itself a frame containing centripetal emblems of the biosphere (a flower, a bird, a tree, a horse, a comet and, where the heart should be, the sun itself), detaches itself from its own outline to step vigorously out of the rectangular frame and the emblems leap and fly outwards with him into the free space of a greater world: microcosm and macrocosm, art and life on one page. As Florensky explains:

> Even as the seed contains the whole life-cycle of the tree that will grow from it, so the cover should be the seed of the journal. Then it will function as a link between individual articles, allowably quite disparate if published separately, even polemical. The thoughtful observer will see in this the spiritual FORM of the journal in all its many-faceted content.[8]

For Florensky, membership of Makovets involved realism in Viacheslav Ivanov's sense of 'from the real to the more real'. The artist-members, he maintained, had one thing in common: their thought was concentrated 'on reality itself, not on its secondary reflection. In this way, all draw from the same well, res rather than notio, vita rather than ars, which allows for maximum diversity in theory and artistic practice.'[9]

Other close friends whom Florensky proposed for membership of 'Makovets' were the sculptor Ivan Efimov, who also taught at Vkhutemas, and his wife, impressionist painter and puppeteer, author of a number of Florensky portraits and vivid reminiscences, Nina Simonovich-Efimov. Florensky was a frequent visitor at their home in Moscow and they at his in Zagorsk, where once they even staged an outdoor puppet-show for the locals and their children. To the scholarly Father Pavel, the expertly manipulated, exquisitely carved and costumed puppets, which seemed to take on a life of their own in the hands of their dedicated creators, touched on those deeply hidden childhood strata of the personality through which, and only through which, we can 'enter the Kingdom of Heaven'.

The Puppet Theatre has the high distinction of not being illusionist. Yet, while neither being 'true to life' nor pretending to be so, the puppet in fact creates a new reality. It fills the space freed up for it with a life of its own in a festive frame. The chorus of spectators are united by the puppet and, through the puppet-master, invest it with their own most profound emotions – which might seem inappropriate to everyday life.[10]

So Florensky wrote in an introduction to Nina Efimova's *Notes of a Puppeteer* (Moscow, 1925) which, like so much he undertook in these years, was blocked for publication.

In 1927, at the house of his erstwhile pupil Fedor Konstantinovich Andreev, now no longer an ever-helpful presence in Sergiev Posad but a priest in Leningrad, Florensky met another important figure from the world of art, the tempestuous virtuoso Maria Yudina. Yudina, a concert pianist of genius who had turned from Judaism to Christianity through reading St Augustine and Florensky's *Pillar and Ground of Truth* as a young student, became a greatly valued family friend and member of the Efimov-Favorsky-Florensky circle. After the Second World War, she and Favorsky were publicly to stand godparents to Ol'ga Pavlovna's and Sergei Trubachev's first daughter – to the detriment of both their teaching careers. During Florensky's lifetime, Yudina took every opportunity to meet and converse with him, often played for him at his own home, where she immediately broke her host's antique piano and had to make do with the more plebeian modern instrument, or at the Efimovs' Moscow flat. The strong, concentrated figure seated at a concert grand piano lives on in Favorsky's art.

Yudina, who often gave talks at her recitals, found Florensky's thinking on the synthesis of art and religion, on science, nature and the Ancient World, extremely stimulating, valued his response to music and drew confidence from his compassionate approval of her as a human being and artist. Their temperaments, of course, were complementary: she so elemental and spontaneous (only 'half-christened', according to the rather rigid Fedor Andreev[11]), he so quiet and self-contained: 'the transparent calm, like liquid in a crystal cup, the quiet calm of his personality' was what she most particularly remembered.[12] She loved the atmosphere of the Florensky home: the pink-washed, wooden house on the hill overlooking the great monastery, where the family lived retired behind closed gates that opened from the street onto a backyard with outbuildings and a door into the kitchen; the high-fenced, grassy 'garden' with its silver poplars, young lime trees and dark firs that was only to be reached through the French windows in the dining-cum-music room. There was, in these dangerous years, a certain guarded reclusiveness about this sanctum, but those who penetrated it were, as it were, taken to heart. Yudina was awed and honoured to be given a bed for the night in Father Pavel's study. She shared with her host a passion for the music of Bach, Mozart, Beethoven and Schubert. 'Bach climbs majestically to the heights like a pious aspirant', Yudina would quote Florensky, 'whereas Mozart is always at home there. Mozart is a world apart to which Bach is only teaching us the way'.[13] Of course, Florensky had his own 'medieval' take on this clearly post-Renaissance music which so delighted him. There is a delightful story how Olechka Florenskaia, a partisan schoolgirl accustomed to her father's 'light, pure and transparent' rendering of Mozart, informed Yudina, whose interpretation of a sonata had seemed to her overly tempestuous and impulsive, that her Papa played it better. 'I love and respect your Papa very much', retorted the virtuoso firmly, 'But nevertheless *I* play better.'[14]

'As for me, I've no pretensions to sanctity, my problems are different – art ... What I so infinitely appreciate in you (what was indwelling and radiated from Father Pavel) is your profound understanding of the variety of human activity and culture in general ... The combination is so rare', wrote Yudina to Anna Mikhailovna in 1961 and, on Florensky's name-day in 1967 to Ol'ga: 'Again I can only write the same unforgettable and eternal truth: that for me there is no-one in the world greater than Father Pavel and there never has been.'[15]

Given the scattering of the Novoselov circle, the exile of a whole coterie of religions philosophers including Berdiaev in 1922 and of Sergei Bulgakov from the Crimea where he had been living since 1919, the disappearance of Viacheslav Ivanov first to Baku and then to Rome, the restless peregrinations of Andrei Bely between the Berlin and Moscow anthroposophists and the virtual dissolution of the Moscow Theological Academy, these Olympian friendships with creative people who loved him and his family and took inspiration from his thought as he did from their art and music must greatly have supported Florensky in the exhausting, itinerant existence he came to lead between his peaceful home and ever-growing family in Zagorsk, the shifting, semi-clandestine venues of intellectual life in Moscow and the reactivisation of his expertise in mathematics and applied science.

Over these post-revolutionary years, Florensky's spiritual and physical resources appear to have been quite inexhaustible and it is touching to read how, in 1921, visiting Archimandrite David, the revered leader of the *imiaslavtsy* in Moscow, he asked the good father's prayers as sole reward for his efforts toward their reconciliation with the Orthodox Church – not for himself, but for his wife Anna and their yet unborn child Mikhail, and of how Anna felt the power of the prayer he had requested in her restless body as she lay wakefully beside him that night. 'Mika' turned out a delicate child, his health in early life affected by shortages and parental anxieties, but he came through and was followed into the wildly uncertain world of New Economic Policy Russia by the buoyant Maria, cheerfully nicknamed Tin-a-Tin after a fairytale Georgian princess, and her father's particular delight. Neither did he lose touch with Vasia, his first-born, or with clever Kirill, who had once – to his father's lasting, tender amusement – wept bitter tears because he would never grow a furry tale like a cat. When, in 1925, Florensky was commissioned to compose a report on possible Soviet exploitation of the mineral wealth of the Caucasus, he took these two eldest with him to show them the land of his own childhood. Subsequent letters to them from the camps reflect a certain disappointment at his failure in the course of this trip to recreate the lost paradise of the seashore and wild mountain country round Batumi which he had recorded for them in *To My Children* in the early summer of 1921. The little boys, exhausted by the long train journey and, of necessity, left much to their own devices by a preoccupied father, were, however, enthused if not by the irrecapturable past then by his present occupation and conceived the ambition to become mineral geologists, an ideologically neutral speciality in which both managed to pursue successful careers, and to support their mother and siblings after Florensky's arrest, while still, in a sense, following directly in their father's footsteps and retaining a common language.

Florensky's notebooks for the previous year, 1924, mention a 'crisis at the age of 42', which would appear to indicate that the apparent serenity with which he faced up to what amounted to an enforced change of profession was not easily achieved. This was the last year of his lectures at Vkhutemas. The Theological Academy had lost its last foothold in the Petrov Monastery and he had requested but not received permission to retire from professional duties. Since the dissolution of the Red Cross Sisterhood, he had become a priest without a parish and the practice of his profession had taken on an episodic character as visiting priest to such churches as Ilya Obydennyi and Saint Nicholas 'on chicken's legs' in Moscow or celebrating occasional services in the homes of friends or, on special occasions as when, in February 1924, he conducted a *panikhida*[16] together with Patriarch Tikhon for his spiritual father Bishop Antonii.[17] The loss of his own, beloved parish was a hard blow which Father Pavel saw as the interference of malign, other-worldly forces in his own personal fate. He lost not only the altar at which he formerly celebrated, the west-facing chapel, the cure of souls and, presumably, the stipend. The Red Cross was, of course, an international body which had brought him the occasional visitor from abroad, including an American representative who took out an article by Florensky's ex-teacher Lopatin on possible progress towards ecumenism together with Florensky's own supportive and explanatory 'Christianity and culture' and a separate 'Note on Orthodoxy', which were partially published in William Temple's *The Pilgrim* in 1924.[18] These contacts faded and, as Soviet suspicion of the outside world grew, Florensky became careful, no doubt for the sake of his family but also from an inherent dislike of duplicity, to abrogate all further approaches from foreign-based publishers.[19] At the same time, as book after book, article after article towards 'On the watersheds of thought' remained unpublished or were met with opprobrium and abuse, he was beginning to face up to the fact that he would never be able to honour the 1922 contract he had concluded with the publishers Pomor'e after the collapse of Put'. The artist Lev Zhegin came to see Florensky at his workplace in the Glavelektro Institute where, in that same year of 1924, he had just been elected a member of the Central Electrotechnical Council. Seeing a pile of proofs delivered to his desk, Zhegin enquired whether this were not 'On the watersheds of thought':

> 'How could it be 'On the watersheds of thought'!' with something as always calm but at the same time, as it seemed to me, despairing in his eyes. 'You understand', he said next time we met. 'They'll allow you to state your basic thought, but they won't allow you to substantiate it – and in a form like that it loses all meaning.[20]

The proofs Zhegin had seen were those of Florensky's new textbook: *Dialectrics and their Technical Application*.[21]

Strong Florensky undoubtedly was, but the constantly increasing workload he had been taking on in the field of applied science cannot but have been a contributory factor to his conceding defeat on the grand project of 'On the watersheds of thought'. The years 1917 to 1925 saw a profuse flowering of his philosophical thought, but it was a flowering of desert blooms which shrivelled back into the dry earth to await the rains of a more temperate future. His works passed from hand to hand, people hung on his words, but he was granted neither time nor encouragement to see them into print.

Since 1920, Florensky had been working with Professor I. F. Ognev, a neighbour in Sergiev Posad, at the Histological Institute of Moscow University on an experimental type of ultra-microscope. This was not altogether alien to his humanitarian interests. As always, science fed his philosophical thought and it is not difficult to find cross-references to histology in his reflections on man as toolmaker. On a personal level, Sofia Ogneva, the professor's wife, was a staunch friend who took down much of Florensky's best works ('Iconostasis', *For My Children*) at his dictation, taught his daughter Ol'ga French and, in general, was a pillar of reliability to the whole family in difficult times. Nevertheless, it was an extra-academic appointment, as was Florensky's involvement as consultant, then director of testing, production and technico-scientific research at the Moscow factory Karbolit. He was engaged by Karbolit in the autumn of 1920, in curious tandem with an appointment by the Sergievo Historico-Art Museum, as the Trinity St Sergius Monastery had by then become, as their resident expert on silver and fine metalwork.

At the beginning of 1921, Florensky was co-opted to 'full time' research in Glavelektro VSNKh RSFSR (later SSSR), the Commission for the Electrification of Russia and, from 9 January 1921 to 1924, he continued to work there in various departments: the Carbolite Commission, the departments of mechanics and chemistry, the sector investigating high-voltage technique and at the State Experimental Electrotechnical Institute. It was in connection with the last appointment that Florensky, as rumour had it at the express invitation of Leon Trotsky, astonished delegates to the eighth Electrotechnical Conference to discuss the GOELRO plan by addressing them in his priest's cassock. Trotsky had suggested he should conform to the more normal professional two-piece suit and modify the beard and flowing locks, but accepted his explanation that, although without a parish, Father Pavel was still a priest and was bound by his vows.[22]

Yet this stubbornly exotic, exceptionally articulate person had clearly a genuinely valuable contribution to make to the economic and technical self-sufficiency of the Bolshevik's newly acquired empire that stretched, with one line of rail and but few roads, from the fair fields, woods and castles of Belarus to beyond the Urals, across vast expanses of tundra and desert, brushing the northern foothills of the Himalayas and the frozen shores of the Arctic, all the way to the Pacific Ocean and the misty island of Sakhalin. In 1924, the crisis year, Florensky was elected a member of the Central Electrico-technical Soviet at Glavelektro and began work in the Moscow United Committee of Electrotechnical Norms and Rules known as MOKEN. His work on the Special Commission for the improvement of quality of production was experimental, hands-on and involved original research (laboratory work had been one thing he had missed sorely after entering the Theological Academy), but Florensky tells his children, in the memoirs he was still, in his spare moments, dictating to Sophia Ivanovna Ogneva,[23] that the creative tension involved was nothing like so intense as his disinterested, schoolboy attempts to extend the bounds of physical knowledge. The work was, however, salaried and involved publications which must have helped the family budget: the already mentioned *Dialectrics and their Technical Application* (Moscow, 1924); an article on 'Supplies of world energy' for the journal *Electrification*, No. 1, 1925; a published paper on 'The achievements of O. N. Iablochkov in the study of elements', *Electricity*, No. 12, 1926, presented as a talk to the Russian Technical Society in Petrograd on 12 December of that same year. Also, he managed to arrange a post for his old and close friend, Anna's brother, Vasilii Giatsintov. Mundane considerations, perhaps, but important to a man committed to the support of five children, his wife and her mother, his own mother and his consumptive artist-sister.

Florensky was a natural manager of people and a woman who worked with him recalls his checking her for criticising a colleague with the words: 'As far as I am concerned there are no bad members of staff. We need to stimulate the good inherent in each person and assuage the bad in them.'[24]

Almost in spite of himself, Florensky the electro-technician was proving as relentlessly successful as Florensky the Master of Theology. His quiet study in Zagorsk saw a steady stream of visitors come to consult him in either or both these capacities as well as on broader questions of art and culture – and as a priest. Those who hesitated to disturb him at home would catch him in the street or in the train between Moscow and Zagorsk, or at Fedor Andreev's in Petrograd, or in his mother's flat, or at the Efimovs' in Moscow. Yet in his inner self he remained, as Bulgakov once wrote of him, 'as solitary as Mt Ebrus', slow to focus on the manifold claims on his attention, as though tearing himself away from problems on which his mind was currently concentrated.

Florensky was an enigmatic figure, and not the least problem he poses the biographer is how he found time to do all he did. From 1927 to 1934, he worked as editor of a new technical encyclopaedia, to which he contributed 127 entries, and 1928, the year of his first arrest and a brief period of exile in Nizhnyy Novgorod, saw the publication of a new monograph entitled *Carbolite: Production and Characteristics* (Moscow, 1928).

Florensky's first brush with the OGPU, as the interior police were called, was a comparatively civilised affair. Possibly hostile reviews of the publication of *Amvrosii, XV Century Master Carver of the Trinity St Sergius Monastery* (Sergiev Posad, 1927), co-authored with the *ci-devant* Count Iu. A. Olsuf'ev, had alerted the authorities to the continued activity of the officially defunct Commission for the Preservation of Art and Antiquities. After a vigorous campaign in the press deploring 'mandates in the hands of counts and barons' and the reverend way in which ex-monks employed by the management of the museum showed their awed visitors round the ancient premises, most of its members, including Florensky, were pulled in and accused of anti-Soviet, pro-monarchist activities. The arrests were, of course, also symptomatic of the pressure to conform exerted by Stalin as he began to jettison the New Economic Policy and embarked on the Five Year Plans. The nest of highly cultivated, devout and predominantly Slavophile people in the little town of St Sergius was clearly an anomaly. None of those arrested denied their deep disapproval of the anti-religious and, more specifically, anti-Russian Orthodox Church policies implemented by the State, but all categorically maintained their political innocence – and that of their friends. It was decided that the group, consisting as it did of well-respected and essentially patriotic and peaceable scholars and public servants, did not merit punitive action, but should, as a 'prophylatic' measure, be broken up.[25] Permitted to choose between various places 'minus five' of administrative exile, Florensky selected the great and comparatively accessible trading city on the Vol'ga, the site of the 1897 World Industrial Exhibition, then still known as

Nizhnii Novgorod, famous as the home-town of Maxim Gorky and later as the place of exile of Academician Sakharov, to which he was despatched 'for three years' from the beginning of June 1928. Those exiled in this way were put on the train under police escort but then left to travel alone – with the obligation to report to the local police on arrival. The first letter he wrote, actually from the train, to a family who had hoped to the last for his release without charge, contained a severe reprimand to Anna for having left the children to travel to Moscow and wasted money on prison parcels for him and obtaining the luxury of a prison visit ... to which Anna, with a certain wry and affectionate coquetry, replied that she had supposed he might actually be pleased to see her – and shyly offered to come to Nizhnii and help him settle in.[26] The first to come, however, was Vasilii, skinny and green from swotting for the exams which would decide his admission to the Institute at which he wished to study. Vasilii annoyed his father still more by telling him the smaller children were all fine (when, as he later learned, Mika had scarlet fever and Maria (Tika, Tin-a-Tin) a festering cut on her hand), and then grassed to his mother that 'papochka' was evidently desperately short of cash. The correspondence, humorously but rather desperately orchestrated by Anna, suddenly responsible for everything including fighting off an attempt to confiscate their home, is a model of the loving, mutual irritation of people who want nothing but one another's good. Florensky wrote to his wife:

> For me our house is not just a house, i.e. something profitable and habitable. If it was a question of twice or thrice the worth of it in money, I would face up to the loss almost with indifference – The children write that you cry every evening. Dearest Mummy, you don't know what those tears cost me, and if you knew – you wouldn't cry. You need to live a lot longer and not be manure[27] but help me, because you and I have become one being. The house just now is one of the essential conditions for a decent life, – not as property but as the psychological basis for scholarly work and for the upbringing of the children.[28]

And to his mother:

> I've heard from Anna that you are not accepting financial help and are very upset. Please don't add to my troubles. For as long as we have money, spend it – from what Anna handed over to you – and I am gradually getting things in control with my earnings, writing one or two things etc. Please, feed Gosia well and don't stint yourself, dear Mama, otherwise you only add to my worries.[29]

Florenky's first letters show a man thoroughly disgruntled by the difficulty of finding a place to live and work and to organise employment offered by the radio-laboratory in Nizhnii Novgorod founded in 1918 by Mikhail Bonch-

Bruevich – all of which was trammelled by red tape and the necessity of reporting to the police. He was also irked by separation from the reference books he needed to continue editing the *Technical Encyclopedia*, proofs from which were arriving thick and fast, and by the knowledge that piles of library books were due for return at home.

Yet he continued to teach and care for his children. An appallingly misspelt missive from the ten-year-old Ol'ga assuring him of her good progress in French and Anna's tales of Mika, deeply upset by his father's disappearances but drinking in all the grown-ups' talk and storing it away 'in his little heart' and of Maria-Tin-a-Tin-Tika haring about all day pretending to be a little boy but crying for her father at night, together with a message from Kirill, who was staying with his Aunt 'Lusia', that he was learning vegetarian cooking in preparation for a visit to his father, elicited affectionately pedagogic letters and vivid descriptions of the old, sixteenth-century, Venetian-built fortress (more in the style of the fifteenth), of the scent of flowering lime trees, the provincial calm, the beauty of the confluence of the great Vol'ga River and the Oka and the colourful excitement of the river traffic. Eventually, Anna Mikhailovna brought the two smaller children to stay in the cramped digs which Florensky's friend, Dmitrii Vvedensky, with whom he had been sharing, tactfully vacated. She wrote to Vasia:

> Papulia, of course, gets all het up. We really get under his feet … In the mornings we take tea and try to disappear somewhere for the whole day. But in the evening the supper has to be cooked, and tea, and the children put to bed. That's a lot of hassle. Sometimes Dmitrii Ivanovich sits with us in the evening and tells us about his childhood and the rest of his life, so that the evening passes peacefully in a family atmosphere, and then Papa and I are left alone together and he writes and writes, works very hard. Most often we go down to the Vol'ga, the children splash and bathe on the sandy bank. They're very tanned, even Mika is quite black. We had lovely weather, sunshine all the time, only today it rained … Somehow now we are with Papa all our cares have taken flight …[30]

Anna had not been idle before rejoining her husband in exile, but had interceded for him with Gorky's compassionate and influential ex-wife Ekaterina Peshkova who, distressed by the thought of five fatherless children and well aware of Florensky's newly acquired scientific eminence, had, together with the publishers of the hard-pressed *Technical Dictionary* and Florensky's colleagues on the various research committees to which he now belonged, won him a reprieve. To the delight of his friends, he was permitted to return home in the wake of his family at the end of August and immediately reinstated as head of the Department of Science Materials on GEEI (later, under the initials VEI, decipherable as the All-Union, rather than the State Experimental Electro-technical Institute).

Florensky returned, as he himself later wrote, 'from exile to hard labour'. In the course of 1929, he attended three scientific conferences on electro-isolating materials, mica and graphite, on which last he subsequently published an article illuminating its significance for the work of his institute.[31] On 5 January 1930 he was appointed assistant scientific director to the K. A. Krug All-Union Electrotechnical Institute, while VEI heaped on additional responsibilities for their technical sections on vacuum, x-ray, measurement and light. During this period and later, in the camps, Florensky was granted 12 patents from 47 applications concerning his own technical innovations. In 1931, he attended the second All-Union Conference on Electro-isolating Materials and was away from his family for the whole of May, June and July with another mineralogical expedition, this time to Marioupol in search of graphite, to Kerch for iron ore and to Tiflis and Chiatura for manganese. The journey provided some delightful reminders of Pushkin and glimpses of the ancient cultures of the Scythians and the Greeks:

> there's a little house with frescoes and a cupola, pomegranates and rose petals (the symbols of death and resurrection), a head of Demetra, the rape of Persephone – quite beautiful. You are shown round by an old man and an old woman like Philemon and Baucis. And they've planted a beautiful flower-bed before the house: – it's the department of the Eleusis mysteries.[32]

Florensky had not lost his inner sense of music nor his sensitive attunement to Nature and Antiquity, and the work on which he was engaged was, after all, not uncongenial. He had always had a 'fraternal' feeling for minerals, he was able to help and guide his two eldest sons, now following in his footsteps, and he genuinely believed that his 'hard labour' was contributing to the material reconstruction of his famine-ridden, war-torn country. The year 1932 saw the publication of numerous articles including 'Physics at the service of mathematics' in such journals as the in-house VEI *Generator* and *Socialist Reconstruction and Science*.[33] The ideological climate, however, was such that Florensky no longer wore the much-mended, white cassock and had cut his hair, thought it still curled luxuriantly around a tanned, bearded face and dangled over the severe professorial metal spectacles, the jutting nose.

As though all this peaceful, constructive activity was not enough, Florensky was co-opted on 27 February 1932 by the publishing sector of the Supreme Command of the Soviet Air Force (RKKA) to write a course on the electro-technical study of materials (for electro- and radio-technicians) and, on 4 May, became a member of the Commission for the Standardisation of Scientifico-technical Terms and Symbols set up by the Soviet for Labour and Defence. This association with the Ministry of Defence was later to call forth the distressful comment from Anna Mikhailovna that it was, perhaps, a blessing that her husband had been executed before the beginning of the Second World War – or he might well have found himself in some *sharashka*,[34] like that in Solzhenitsyn's *First Circle*, working towards the atom bomb.

Be that as it may, Florensky's usefulness to the State now entitled him to an official flat in Moscow, near the notorious Lefortovo Prison on Prolomnyi pereulok, House 43, Korpus 3, Flat 12, where there was room for Vasilii and Kirill who, at 22 and 18 years of age, had graduated to higher education in the capital. Florensky himself had no longer to doss down in his mother's kitchen but returned from the laboratory to a well-equipped study with books from floor to ceiling, space for his collection of minerals, privacy for a wash and change. Here he spent the working week, in superior bachelor quarters with his two student sons. On Friday evening or Saturday morning, he would escape to his beloved home in Zagorsk, as they now had to remember to call Sergiev Posad, to Anna Mikhailovna's welcoming smile,[35] long nature walks with the younger children, picnics, mushrooming or abundance of clean country snow according to season, to music, study, the prayerful quiet his heart always craved and the gentle evening light 'which always sounds in my soul ... the beginning of the life beyond'.[36] You could clearly see the Evening and the Morning Star on the way from the railway station to his home, from his home to the station.

It was in the official flat with the ill-omened address, on 25–26 February 1933, that the OGPU finally caught up with him.

# 9

# *Permafrost*

'And the evening and the morning were the first day' ... But it begins with evening
and ends with the morning of ever-lasting day. Even so the history of the world
– flowing through the murk of sin – is surely nothing but one single night, one
single, terrible dream, stretching from ages to ages – yet a night imbued with the
sad mystery of evening and pregnant with that awesome, joyous morning?

P. A. Florensky[1]

Florensky's arrest was not unexpected. He himself had anticipated it since 1917
and was well aware that the Sergiev Posad case of 1928 had passed off miracu-
lously easily. The secret of the removal and concealment of St Sergius' head
remained inviolate and, of those involved in the preservation of the monastery,
only one, an ex-Lieutenant-General of the Tsarist Police who had refused to
become a Soviet informer, had received a custodial sentence. Not all Father
Pavel's friends, however, had been so fortunate. Those who continued to serve
as priests were subjected to continual harassment. To take but one example,
Fedor Andreev was arrested several times in the late 1920s in Leningrad and,
when his health broke down under the strain and he died in office in 1928,
the OGPU turned their attention to his widow who was sentenced to three
years forced labour. Florensky and Yudina persuaded Peshkova and Gorky
to intervene for the unfortunate widow. Yudina even went to Gorky's house
to play for him: 'Did he cry?' asked Florensky. 'Yes', replied the great pianist.
'That's all right then', Florensky affirmed.[2] And so it was. Nataliia Nikolaevna
Andreeva was merely exiled to Al'mata. Andreev's adolescent twin daughters
were granted an interview with their mother before she left and went straight
from this harrowing farewell to the Florensky home in Zagorsk. Father Pavel's
family continued to support and succour them after his second arrest, when
the Andreev twins' grandmother who had taken them in was exiled in her turn
and they were able to stay at the Florensky home on their way from Leningrad
to Kuibyshev, where their mother, still forbidden Leningrad and Moscow after
her return from exile, had found work. Such odysseys, involving whole families,
were commonplace amongst those overtly loyal to the Church and the fact that
they supported one another without fear of contamination by association says
much for their moral stature and active charity.

Many people have shown us kindness and understanding beyond our deserts [Florensky
had written to his 'Children' in 1920] And you, my dears, always be kind and attentive
to other people. You don't need to go giving everything away, scattering broadcast your
belongings, your tenderness, your good advice, you don't need to 'do good works'. Just
try to keep your ears open and be sensitive and able to step in with real help when it
is needed by those God sends you who stand in need of your help. Be kind and give
generously.[3]

Apart from such peripheral involvement in the vicissitudes of the Church of
which he never ceased to be a priest, albeit without a parish, Florensky was
personally subject to attacks in the press, not only for his adherence to the
Commission for Preservation of Art and Antiquities in the Trinity St Sergius
Monastery, 'two-legged rats who scuttle away with valuable old items',[4] and to
the 'very crafty and insolent fellows' who write of 'events in the life of Jesus
Christ' and 'the beheading of John the Baptist' in their art books 'when every
young pioneer knows the legend that Christ existed is nothing more than a
priestly fraud',[5] but also for the book *Imaginary Points in Geometry*, published
back in 1922, against which a virulent campaign was mounted in connection
with the five hundred and fiftieth anniversary of the birth of Copernicus in that
year.[6] Indeed, Professor Florensky's position as a *spets*, a bourgeois specialist
temporarily useful but, in the eyes of the authorities, potentially disloyal and
certainly ideologically alien to the Soviet Union, now rendered him vulnerable
on an entirely new count.

Nevertheless, the catalyst for Florensky's arrest was a sequence of events no
one could have foreseen: the interrogation and forced 'confession' of a professor
of canon law, Pavel Gidiulianov, of whose very existence he had been unaware
until confronted with detailed testimony of their joint complicity in a national-
fascist centre for the Resurrection of Russia, the aim of which was to help Nazi
Germany take over Moscow and, assisted by revolutionary 'Soviets without
Communists', to establish a neo-Slavophile, anti-Semitic, crypto-monarchist
government of collaborators. Florensky was described as the 'ideologist' on the
right wing of this monstrous association and was, it appears, in direct contact
with an emissary of the Third Reich, a German Jesuit posing as an engineer
who promised to negotiate reunion of the Russian Orthodox Church with
Rome. In this capacity Florensky was supposed to be spreading propaganda
through *troikas* (cells of three) of Moscow priests and what monks were still
to be found in the environs of the capital. He and Gidiulanov, who, as a sign
of his 'great penitence', claimed the leadership of the conspiracy, were allegedly
assisted by various others who had furnished corroborative confessions, and,
more ominously, according to these depositions, by Florensky's colleague
Academician Chaplygin, director of the Hydro-Dynamic Institute, and his

university friend, with whom he had remained on the best of good terms, Academician Luzin who, having worked with Poincaré and being very much a part of the international scene in mathematics, was supposed to be in charge of foreign affairs. Naturally, Florensky began by flatly denying the whole fantastic farrago.

By an extraordinary quirk of fate, we have Gidiulianov's own detailed account of how he was worked upon, by sleep deprivation and mental and physical abuse alternating with kindness and promises of full exoneration, first to cooperate with his interrogator Shupeiko and, eventually, simply to 'confess' under dictation, almost anticipating his requirements:

> I was put in a cell with a certain agronomist called Kolechits, who justified the theory of self-disarmament. Kolechits aided me to correct my depositions, showing me what I should change, and he explained to me what he called the 'Aesopian language of the OGPU'. All of this meant that what they needed from me, when they said self-disarmament, was not the truth but something that had the appearance of the truth. As a specialist in the history of judicial procedure I could discern in all this a peculiar form of trial by confession. In the early Middle Ages this was termed the *purgatio vulgaris* and later, the *purgatio canonica* ... The suspect, in the medieval trial by confession, we should explain, was not considered innocent even when there was no evidence against him. He himself had to prove his innocence by performing acts that would re-establish his good reputation.[7]

The resultant 'literary composition', as Shupeiko called it, was a collaborative effort, signed by Gidiulanov as 'written in my hand in accordance with the truth', for which the unfortunate professor was promised his liberty and reinstatement at work. The promise was not kept and the account of the process by which his testimony was obtained, which includes the explicit statement that he had never in fact met Florensky before being confronted with him in prison, we owe to a letter of complaint he was brave or misguided enough to address to the Procurator's Office from a camp in Kazakhstan. The recipients merely arranged for it to be added 'for eternal preservation' to Gidiulanov's OGPU file, from whence, after the onset of *glasnost'*, it came into the hands of the investigative journalist Shentalinsky. Gidiulanov was eventually shot.[8]

Florensky, to judge by the dishevelled police photograph in profile and full face, was taken unaware. His glasses were lost or broken, his slender person manhandled if not actually beaten up, his flat ransacked, books and manuscripts pawed over in search of 'religion or pornography', the antique Caucasian broadsword, daggers and sabre, relics of the Saparov family, triumphantly confiscated as 'offensive weapons' and his rooms sealed. Faced with the network of testimony against him, uncertain who was taken and who still at liberty, Florensky's initial denials broke on a confrontation with Gidiulanov arranged by Radzilovsky, the head of the political department of OGPU. Gidiulanov's account is bald: 'I persuaded Professor Florensky to follow our example and sincerely admit his guilt, since he was hindering our release by his stubbornness.' Shentalinsky explains the immediate effect of this meeting on Florensky as Christian self-abnegation: 'When the release of several people from the hell of the Lubyanka and his own self-humiliation were weighed on the scales of his conscience, he could only choose the latter.'[9] Was he really so gullible as to believe cooperation would secure release – for himself or for others? At first sight it seems unlikely, but one must remember these were still, in Akhmatova's famous phrase, the 'comparatively vegetarian'[10] years of the terror. Florensky was well connected and previous brushes with the authorities had been mitigated for him and his friends by the efforts of influential well-wishers: Rachinsky, back in Tsarist times; Peshkova and Gorky in 1928. Even now Ludwig Martens, his editor-in-chief on the *Technical Encyclopedia* and an old Communist, was appealing to the head of the OGPU to look into the bizarre arrest, surely the result of a misunderstanding, of a scholar whose fate was 'of great significance for Soviet Science as a whole'.[11] It is, however, equally possible that Florensky simply perceived all too clearly that those of his 'fellow-conspirators' who had already committed themselves neither could nor would go back on their testimony, and that he himself was so inextricably enmeshed that all that was left was damage limitation: to avoid further compromising those already compromised by outright denial and, at the same time, not to incriminate others (Chaplygin and Luzin remained at liberty, possibly safeguarded by Stalin himself as valuable to the State, and there appears to have been no further ramifications of the case amongst the clergy and monks Florensky was supposed to be organising). By cooperation, he may indeed have hoped to ensure a quick if not a happy end to the affair and to minimise harassment for all concerned.

Be that as it may, at interrogations on 3, 4 and 5 March, Florensky became a co-author of the phantasmagoric Lubyanka scenario, even concurring in the name, Ludwig Stein, for the German engineer and papal emissary with whom Gidiulanov was supposed to have visited him. He took no particular care, however, to make his testimony sound like the truth. The whole plot, he wrote, being organised 'by scholars and scientists who had never been politicians nor taken part in underground or "above" ground activities ...' naturally came to nothing and he 'had no idea' whether the people incriminated in previous testimony had 'actually been involved'. He did not offer any new names. Asked to describe himself, Florensky wrote that he was 'a specialist in electrical engineering' but, as far as politics were concerned, 'a medieval approximately fourteenth-century, romantic'.[12] As Shentalinsky says, the language and style of the bulk of the text betray the alien authorship of these stained and tattered pages, written in various coloured inks, occasionally splashed with water in a hand that bears mute witness to various degrees of stress. Yet, even so, 'Florensky himself is occasionally to be heard through this nonsense, involuntarily voicing thoughts near to his heart',[13] as in the excerpts above or when he writes of the conduct of education or popular science in his 'ideal state'. If, as Gidiulanov explained in his letter from Kazakhstan, the interrogators welcomed the appearance of authenticity, then they would certainly have angled for such moments of self-expression, and it becomes clear why, after the none-too-satisfactory conclusion of the interrogation proper, they 'probably' suggested that, as the ideologist and spiritual leader of the Union for the Regeneration of Russia, 'he should set out his opinions in systematic form'.[14] 'Probably', Florensky was only too glad to do so to avoid further interrogation designed to incriminate others. Florensky himself left no record, apart from mentioning to Ol'ga the disorientating effect of sleep deprivation and bright lights, of precisely what went on between the first interrogation on 28 February, when he denied all accusations, through the elaboration of Gidiulanov's confession which he wrote out and signed on 3, 4 and 5 March to the completion of the outline of the ideology for 'a future state' which he signed off with an insertion on the conduct of foreign trade on 16 March. Forensically, this document, with its preponderance of red ink, splodges, torn edges and unsteady handwriting, was clearly part of the process of interrogation and formed part of the case against him. It was not, however, given to Shentalinsky when he inspected the archive but returned by the KGB in 1990 to Florensky's family, who published it as a serious Utopian project on the lines of Plato's *Republic* and included it among his *Works*. As with the depositions, Florensky's own voice can at times be heard, but the advocacy of the instalment of a 'beloved dictator' very much in the image of Vladimir Solov'ev's Antichrist has done incalculable harm to his posthumous reputation. Not enough attention has been paid to the way in which this dictator is to come to power, without exciting the attention of the world at large or interior opposition, by the gradual manipulation of cadres and breaking off of links with the outside world, precisely as Stalin was doing, or to the clearly OGPU-inspired fantasy of leading on the Germans only to use evidence of their predatory intentions in Russia to alarm the French. It is hard to share the credence accorded by Florensky's descendants to the *bona fide* of this 'politico-philosophical tract',[15] written as it was under extreme duress by this most apolitical of men in an atmosphere of total unreality in which all that was required was 'the appearance of the truth'.

Even the OGPU's successors, the MVD of 1958, in Florensky's official 'rehabilitation' document, admitted that:

There are no materials in the file that could serve as a justification for the arrest of Florensky (and other persons tried in the same case). Witnesses were not cross-examined, and those who carried out the investigation have been found guilty of falsification. Florensky (and other persons) were unjustly convicted without proof of their guilt.[16]

The only time we hear Florensky himself recalling the conduct of his case is when we read the denunciations of police informers reporting on conversations between him and fellow-prisoners on Solovki. Florensky, it seems from these incriminatory scraps, had little or no hope of liberation, either by amnesty or by serving out his time, because his interrogator had told him, after an exhausting session in which he had refused to incriminate any of the various people suggested as his accomplices, that, as a matter of fact, they were well aware that he was not – as yet – guilty of any crime against the State, but that the function of Soviet security organs was to foresee possible threats and act prophylactically. He was just the sort of person who *might be* used as a figurehead by reactionary forces or foreign powers and must therefore be neutralised before this could happen. Clearly there was no escaping such a rationale and one was better off in the camps than constantly expecting rearrest and being anxious for friends, family and colleagues. This clear-eyed hopelessness, which Florensky described to his son as 'optimistic tragism',[17] was acquired in the school of the Lubyanka.

The Florensky who emerged from the conveyor belt of round-the-clock interrogation was mistrustful, self-controlled and self-contained, unwilling to ask favours and dignified in his renunciation of false hope yet, as his letters show, fully alive still to love, beauty, the pursuit of knowledge – and undismayed in faith.

> There are ways of coming to terms with permafrost. [Florensky writes in the introduction to the poem 'Oro', begun in the first year of his life in the camps and dedicated to little Mik.] It conceals all kinds of bitterness and painful experiences. But one shouldn't poke about in its depths. The rigour of permafrost gives energy to master the disintegrating forces of chaos. Permafrost is Hellenism.[18]

Only his outward appearance was altered, the priestly beard shaven – for hygienic purposes, he assured Anna Mikhailovna, who objected to the change – the hair shorter, the smooth grace he himself saw as a corollary of the soutane yielding to a sturdier physical presence. And, like most prisoners, he had begun to smoke heavily.

Florensky's dreary incarceration in the Lyubyanka lasted until summer was at its height, when he was convicted by a special *troika* of the Moscow Region OGPU under Article 58:10–11 (anti-Soviet propaganda and adherence to a counter-revolutionary organisation) and sentenced to ten years in corrective labour camps. In August he was allowed a visit from his family after which he was dispatched by train to the Far East of the USSR ... a horrifying experience lasting all September during which political prisoners were entirely at the mercy of criminal convicts and robbed of such food, money or provisions as their families had been able to furnish them with.[19] Hygiene was non-existent and the only moments of relief were a halt at Sverdlovsk, where the convicts were deloused and fed and he was able to write and send letters, and a 30-hour delay at Krasnoyarsk, from where he wrote to little Tika, joking that it was now so long since he had seen a book she would have to teach him to read. He exhorted his elder sons to profit from a scientific expedition they were undertaking to the Tadzhik Pamirs and instructed Anna Mikhailovna to apply to the editors of the *Technical Encyclopedia* for monies owing to him. Only to Ol'ga Pavlovna does the *cri-de-cœur* escape him that it is fortunate his sister Gosia died when she did as she would not have found strength to bear all their present troubles. The 23 September saw the prisoners still journeying on in a dark cattle truck through the beautiful, scarcely glimpsed country by the Angara River beyond Lake Baikal, and only on 1 October did they eventually come to rest, at least temporarily, at a camp in the Altai hills called Stantsia Ksenevskaia; undulating country, yellow and mauve larch trees, frosty nights but sun so warm in daytime Florensky actually enjoyed a 'sun-bath'. His fellow-prisoners, he informed Anna Milhailovna, all look the picture of rude health and he has been issued with warm, padded clothing and felt boots so wants for nothing. She must not send parcels and he would be quite content were he not worried about how the family were doing without him and that the boys might have to evacuate the flat allotted him by the State for his work in VEI. Also, he adds, he would be better able to cope if only he had a pair of serviceable spectacles.

The prisoners' regime involved working from nine in the morning until the small hours of the next day, but with a break for dinner and a snooze between five and seven in the evening. From his letters, the work appears to have involved both physical labour, rudimentary engineering and bookkeeping. Although crowded conditions made it hard to concentrate and the lack of glasses meant that he must bend double over his paperwork, Florensky suggested that proofs of the *Encyclopedia* should be sent to him, which would only take a month there and back, so that he could earn some money for the family. If that was impossible, he wrote, let them publish his articles albeit anonymously, so long as they paid Anna Mikhailovna, for whom he was preparing a power of attorney so that she could receive his earnings outstanding from various technical publications. Worried about the curiosity of the younger children, he asked her to remove all acids, phosphorus and other dangerous chemicals from the top shelves in his study and give them to Vasilii for safe-keeping in his laboratory. Anxious to offer the children some little treat, he asked Anna to choose presents for them from his books. She herself must please drink from his porcelain cup and not hesitate to sell his personal belongings to provide for the family.

The first letters from home, which reached him in November, were reassuring. Vasia, wrote Iulia, Florensky's elder sister with whom, so long ago now, he had disputed the seat next to the coachman on their Caucasian outings, had taken on two jobs and was supporting the family. Kirill was distinguishing himself at his studies and keeping them all in good spirits. Ol'ga, however, was having difficulties at school because of the stigma of his arrest and little Tika-Tin-a-Tin-Maria was anaemic and still suffering from the shock of the farewell prison visit. Still, all the children loved and supported one another and Anya has grown slimmer and prettier and could well pass as the sister of her grown-up sons: 'She has become especially dear to us ... Her meekness and love for all around seem limitless. She has room in her heart for everyone. She's very energetic and spares no effort in standing up for her children.'[20] Typically, the only moment of disharmony had been between Vasia, too proud to allow his grandmother to feed him whenever he came to see her in Moscow, and Ol'ga Pavlovna, who had transferred her loving care from son to grandson and was determined to do so! The elder boys, for the moment, were still living in their father's flat with the two sealed-off rooms.

The news that Ol'ga must study on her own inspired the pedagogical direction of Florensky's letters to her, which provide a rich source for his thought on art, literature and music. From his own experience, he assured her that one could learn much more at home than at school. She should not swot, but read aloud to herself in French and Russian and collect and classify plants and stones, remembering their weekend botanising:

> In mathematics try not just to memorise what to do and how but take it in gradually, bit by bit, as though it were a new piece of music. Mathematics should not be a burden laid on you from without, but a habit of thought.[21]

From the moment he arrived in Ksenevskaia, Florensky found the energy to write personally to each child, exerting all the considerable powers of his pen which had formally gone into the preparation of lectures and articles to give them all he could of himself – not, as in the uncensored letters of 1917–1921 in case of his death, admonishing them in so many words 'to stand always before God', to take frequent communion and to eschew envy and ambition, but simply to eat well, to travel, to observe and study, to borrow anything of his that might be useful to them, to cultivate his most interesting friends. He advised on what they should read and why, how to make an exciting adventure of exploring the worlds of nature and scholarship, art and music. He told each individually all that might interest or amuse them about his life in camp – even joking with the scape-grace Mika that the high altitude of Ksenevskaia had all the prisoners scuttling helter-skelter to the latrines which, however, do not smell as nothing rots in the cold, bright climate. One could take a verse from the poem 'Oro' to characterise the change from ecclesiastic to natural imagery that yet involved no change in the thrust of Florensky's life-affirming thought:

> Here pliant ranks of larch are shaped
> By robes of royal purple drapes.
> No domes like St Sophia's glow
> But rather, clad in light and snow,
> Splendour of Tabor shines again
> From the Tungurusk Mountain chain.[22]

Except for the uncongenial work, Florensky appears almost to have enjoyed Ksenevskaia; his four room-mates were quiet, decent engineers and the commander of his section, a Russian German who had been a professor at the University of Leipzig, had immediately taken an interest and was responding to an initiative to get him transferred to an experimental project, where he would be able to use his scientific qualifications.

On 29 November, he was moved on to a camp in a town, ironically named Svobodnyi (Freetown), where he arrived on 2 December. The setting, 1,200 kilometres nearer the Pacific Ocean, a mere stone's throw in Siberian terms, was unattractive: the country comparatively flat, the climate parched, the soil sandy with a paucity of snow in winter. Florensky, however, was buoyed up by the possibility of a second transfer to the remote station of Skovorodino to study permafrost – a pioneering scientific project, which immediately engaged his imagination as important 'for all fields of domestic economics and for our understanding of the world'.[23] Meanwhile, in Svobodnyi, he was in demand to teach Latin to the medics at the camp and, for the first time, wrote to Anna that he would try to arrange for her to come to visit him, perhaps travelling with Lena Kaptereva, the wife of Pavel Nikolai Kapterev, the son of one of Florensky's colleagues on the Commission for the Preservation of Art and Antiquities in the Trinity St Sergius Monastery who had been arrested at the same time as he and with whom he had journeyed all the way from Moscow. Kapterev was also destined to work on permafrost and was eventually to write up his own and some of his friend's research in a book jointly authored with Nikolai Bykov, the head of the research station in Skovorodino, and published in 1940. In Svobodnyi, Florensky at last managed to obtain a new pair of glasses and the strength of the prescription, +9½, shows how helpless he must have felt without them since his arrest. Here, too, news reached him of the death of Andrei Bely, whose image, as he wrote to Ol'ga, 'lives on in me unchanged, although in life

Andrei Bely himself had become grey and dusty,[24] and he spoke at an evening devoted to the memory of the poet, as well as taking part in other prisoners' projects for self-education, particularly the scientific ones. As Solzhenitsyn was later to discover, the camps were universities in their own right, where the lucky *zek* (abbreviation of the Russian word for prisoner, *zakliuchennyi*) might find himself listening to the most distinguished professors – though one could never count on completing a course.

The letters continued: Florensky encouraged Mika to disect icicles but be careful not to cut himself, and he was entrusted with the good news that his father had received a present of raisins and olives from Mummy *on his birthday*. Tika got a description of the local horses: 'tiny, shaggy, with short ears and very wild'. On 6 February he wrote to Vasilii, together with copious advice on what to read about silicates, that a branch of rhododendron was actually in bloom in his room. By 18 February, he was buoyantly informing Anna Mikhailovna of a comfortable journey to Skovorodino, the permafrost station at the back of the beyond where his work now lay, and he was expecting her to visit, warning her not to overload herself and the children with things for him. He already had more clobber than he could easily travel with and a *zek* needs no more than he can carry:

> The station's on the edge of the village, behind there's a green field, so you feel you're at a *dacha*.[25] There are four of us here, and our room is only separated by a partition from the laboratory. The laboratory is organised on ground belonging to the experimental station – in a word, every convenience.[26]

Any complacency Florensky may have felt was soon shattered. It was at Skovorodino that he received the stunning news that Shupeiko and his crew had revisited the Moscow flat, when neither of the boys had been in, and 'confiscated' his entire library.[27] There was no 'self-disarmament' in the letter of protest he dispatched to the authorities:

> My whole life has been devoted to philosophical enquiry and scientific research. I never took a holiday or indulged in pleasures and amusements. Not only all my time but most of what money I happened to earn was devoted to the service of humanity (spent on books etc.). My library was not just a collection of books but a selection made according to planned and precisely envisaged projects. You could say that my works were in process of writing and already existed in the summaries I made of books, which only I know how to implement … This destruction of my whole life-work is far more intolerable for me than my own death …[28]

Needless to say, the protest went unanswered and worse was to follow. On 4 March 1934, Anna Mikhailovna wrote to her husband:

I told you your books were taken from the Moscow flat. Yesterday they came and took the books from Zagorsk. They took all the boys' books and Ol'ga's. In a word, anything can happen, you must do what you can. So far, they've taken 2,684 books without a detailed receipt and they're coming back for the rest on the seventh. I'm very upset and it's had a bad effect on Vasia and Kira, but we are all keeping cheerful and think that things could be worse …

Later that day, however, the good cheer was wearing thin.

All our lives we've tried artificially to practise self-denial and now it's being forced on us. We are longing to come and see you. The books they took are your and our favourites. It's very hard to see strangers going through your favourite things, but what can one do, we have to put up with it. Mika, poor little chap, cried all day for the books ('You know how he cries', she says in another letter, 'with a kind of pathetic squeak').[29]

Ol'ga's Pushkin was taken and when Anna Mikhailovna protested she needed it for school, the reply came merrily pat: 'Pushin's forbidden now. I was chucked out of school for Pushkin myself.' To her attempts to deny them her sons' books, they just said: 'No business of ours whose books. We were told "books", and that's that.'

Florensky, who received this letter quite quickly, in mid-March, was devastated: 'If only you could feel and understand how I love you all, how I suffer for you, you would feel better. But I don't know how to help you, I don't even know how to express my love …' He did what he could by sending symbolic sums of money he had managed to earn and by dissuading them again and again from sending him parcels, for, as in the Lubyanka, he has – he writes – more food than he could eat and is giving it away, with especial pleasure to hungry boys who remind him of his own sons. Desperate for a point of contact, he tells Anna at what times he looks at the stars (Orion's Belt) and that she should try to synchronise with him – although they are separated not only by space but by time zones.

By the beginning of April the permit for a visit by Anna Mikhailovna and the three youngest children came through and the anguished mood passed into one of expectation. Florensky, now totally absorbed in the mystery and beauty of the ice (not only its uncanny power to preserve life but what wonderful jewellery one could make of it if only it didn't melt![30]), could not, however, surpress a certain anxiety about the work to be done and how to maintain the reputation he and Kapterev had established for exceptional industry. They were trusted to go off for expeditions to do fieldwork in the hills and travelled without tickets on a goods train and back on a bone-shaking lorry full of petrol cans to the local provincial centre on the Amur River, where Florensky delivered a lecture on permafrost and was entertained to an excellent dinner – with dances, manners and songs all dating back to the late nineteenth century. His travelling companion, A. V. Gudzovsky, a half-Georgian type from Baku, provided a model for a character in the new poem 'Oro' about the Orochen people, whose language he was trying to learn, and he witnessed one of the great forest fires apt to rage unchecked in this vast wildnerness, which provided a colourful incident in the poem. The nomad Orochen themselves fascinated Florensky. He met up with a convoy of almost 100 camels returning from work in the forests to their summer pastures, herded by reindeer-riding natives who gave him lots of new words in their language and allowed him to take their photographs. In his enthusiasm, Florensky forgot his rule of never troubling his wife to send parcels and requested a Tunguz grammar as a model for a similar work on the Orochen language.

Anna Mikhailovna arrived with Ol'ga, Mika and Tika on 1 July. Florensky, overjoyed, helped them wash down and put the children to bed in a little house the Bykov family had arranged for her to rent – up the hill from the low-lying research station. The visit is best told in Anna Mikhailovna's own words in a letter she wrote from Skovorodino to Florensky's mother:

Papa comes to us for lunch and for the night, but in the morning at 7–7.30 goes off to work. He works a great deal. Is busy all day. At one o'clock he comes for dinner and after dinner immediately begins teaching Olya and Igor Bykov until 4–4.30, and then back to work until 10 in the evening. He talks to us over supper and at night. Smokes a lot, thin, but always cheerful and pleased with absolutely everything. I make dinner at home from food issued in lieu of his common rations and what we brought from home. They give us flour and I often make fritters or yeast pancakes. The children like it here very much, the forest is close by the house. They've been bathing two or three times in the Big Never, which is shallow here so that I can cross it without taking off my dress. The children splash about with great glee and it's a joy for me to watch them as I wash our linen. Ol'ga studies every day. She doesn't go off anywhere unless Papa can come too. Tinochka does her arithmetic and Russian lessons, but Mik spends all his time with Kolia Bykov. P[avel] N[ikolaevich] comes to visit us and some of Papa's other colleagues. They say they are so happy to be in a family atmosphere. Only Papa has his family here. I've met many good people and learnt a great deal and the most important thing, of course, is that Papa can relax a bit and enjoy some nice food. He takes no sugar at all in his tea, so I try to slip a little more in with the cooking. I often make compote. Pity I didn't bring more supplies with me, though. It's impossible to buy anything here, everything is very expensive. I do buy curds, though, and sometimes fresh milk. We went out mushrooming and had a fry-up. I hope we will gather berries for *kisel'*. [31] Today Papa has gone off on an expedition for five days or so. We plan to use the time to wash all our clothes and linen and scrub the floors. I'm busy mending his underclothes and doing what I can for sheets, towels and socks belonging to P[avel] N[ikolaevich] ... [32]

Somehow, Father Pavel found time to read aloud to his children from the book *Dursu Uzala* of which Kurosawa was later to make an unforgettable film, a book which tells the story of a Russian explorer's friendship with a native Siberian tracker.

The time passed all too quickly. On 16/17 August Anna Mikhailovna and her children were due to start the return journey to Zagorsk and the kindly Bykovs invited them and Florensky to a farewell dinner at their home – from which he was suddenly recalled under armed guard to Svobodnyi. To his daughter it had seemed as though the efforts of his friends to secure his release were about to bear fruit. It was a shock that they were the ones to see him off – back to prison in Svobodnyi. She remembered him standing at the door of the train with the guard behind him. 'Papa, when will you come back?' she asked. 'When you learn to play Mozart's "Turkish March"', he answered. 'But I never did learn to play it', she told her listeners more than half a century later.[33]

Ol'ga took home with her a list of recommended reading (mainly Florensky's Symbolist contemporaries, but also some spiritual literature) and the family eventually got back all her father's things and manuscripts left behind in Skovorodino. Kapterev made sure they received a 50-rouble premium which had been due to Florensky and a 124-page list of stolen books he had compiled for further complaint on the confiscation of his library. Bykov bitterly regretted the loss of a 'most distinguished scientific worker and a number of important projects he had undertaken, which, unfortunately, remained unfinished'.[34]

The camp authorities at Svobodnyi explained nothing. Arbitrary changes were a particularly tormenting feature of the Gulag nightmare. There was neither rhyme nor reason in what happened to you. From the productive work and poignant family interlude in Skovorodino, Florensky was thrust into solitary confinement without permission to write or receive letters, whence he was dispatched west under special convoy. In Medvezhaia Gora, he was again incarcerated in solitary for a further month, then sent on to the dreaded transit camp for the island prison of Solovki at Kem', on the shore of the White Sea. On arrival, he was robbed by armed convicts with axes. The prison was crowded and filthy, occupied by a variety of oriental types of largely criminal provenance. There was no chance of work of any kind and, as throughout the terrible journey from the Far East, he was cold and hungry. He was, however, at last able to send a letter informing his family of where he was and that he hoped to be sent on to Solovki.[35]

On the crossing to the islands the prisoners and their baggage were tossed about, bruised, contused, cold, wet and desperately sick in the darkness of the hold. It was at the very end of the navigation season. The next letter, numbered to ensure the family would know if any went missing, as were theirs to him, tells of Florensky's arrival at Solovki: 'my first impressions were very depressing, partly, most probably, from travel-weariness, the rough sea passage, not knowing what would happen next and general disorientation'. He longed for news of Anna and the children, but she was not to send parcels – a little money, perhaps, but not more than ten roubles.[36]

The prison camp of Solovki was situated in the burnt-out and ill-repaired fortress complex of a great monastery with outposts scattered, as in the days of the monks, at various points around the islands where there had once been hermitages, industrial or fishing outposts. The wealth of the monastery had come, even after the confiscation of its mainland holdings under Peter the Great, from salt-boiling, fishing, brick-making and the sale of artefacts from fur and leather. There was an abundance of freshwater and sea fish and the monks had grown enough root vegetables and crisp, sweet cabbage to feed themselves, their workforce, prisoners and hoards of pilgrims. For Solovki had served as a monastic prison since the time of Ivan the Terrible and as a stronghold of Russian power in the White Sea. The massive, lichen-covered battlements which surrounded the main monastic complex had been built for defence. They were not needed to keep prisoners in – a task performed all too well by the remoteness of the islands and the stormy, arctic seas.

Situated some seven hours' sailing time to the north-west of Archangel, in the shelter of the Finnish peninsular, the Solovetskie Islands had been created by the retreat of ice-age glaciers: granite, fresh and salt water, thin soil, sweeping sea winds. In spite of their position off the northernmost coast of Russia only 100 kilometres from the Artic Circle, the islands enjoy a comparatively temperate mini-climate, cool, damp and misty, though all but three short months of summer the sea is semi-frozen, winter days are short and dark and snow in summer is nothing unusual. Yet the straggling trees and lichens grow green, the meadows blossom and the sun circling the horizon in summer almost forgets to set. The earliest inhabitants, Bronze Age Saamis in flat-bottomed boats which moved as easily over ice as water, left stone labyrinths which had a ritual signifi-cance for their fishing, a livelihood they shared with whales, seals and raucous summer gulls. But no myths of an aspiring Prometheus or the search for the Golden Fleece attached to their bare rocks and no buildings but the strange, stone labyrinths had withstood the winds. Nothing could have been more unlike the ancient Colchis of Florensky's childhood, and he took an instant, patrician dislike to the glacial debris of so comparatively recent a geological and mythical past.[37]

Neither was Florensky enchanted by the eventful history of the great monastic community which, since the fifteenth century, had cultivated the islands, building the magnificent fortress-monastery with its towering, golden-domed cathedral, many churches, bell towers and the deeply venerated shrines of three saints – Savatii, the ascetic hermit-monk who, fleeing the spiritual perils of his fellows' admiration, had first sought salvation with but one companion on these perilous islands where no one, at least since pre-history, had dared to pass the winter; Zosima, who founded a community where Savatii had laboured in solitude; and Phillip, in the world Fedor Kolychev, a boyhood playmate of Ivan IV who sought refuge from the excesses of the Dread Tsar on Solovki and, as father superior, worked hard to further the economic and spiritual traditions of the monastery, preferring to dwell apart from the main korpus in a lakeside hermitage a couple of kilometres from the administrative centre – a hermitage which became known as Phillipov Pustyn', Phillip's Hermitage, where Florensky was to spend the most congenial months of his years on Solovki. Phillip, though, had not died peacefully on the island, but responded to an appeal from Ivan to assume the white cowl of Metropolitan of Moscow, at that time the highest office in the Russian Orthodox Church. He fell out with his one-time friend over the misdeeds of the Oprichnina, the much-feared force of 'men apart' which Ivan had created to subdue and terrorise the Old Nobility, to which Phillip belonged by birth. He was cast down, imprisoned and eventually murdered, for refusing to bless Moscow's wars on Pskov and Novgorod, by the infamous Maliuta Skuratov. Many years after his death the martyred prelate's incorrupt remains were translated to the monastery he had served and enshrined in one of the great churches, but reclaimed for Moscow by Tsar Aleksei Mikhailovich Romanov. Florensky's birthday fell on his saint's day.

The monastery, isolated for a while during the Intervention and Civil War, was nationalised somewhat later than the Trinity St Sergius Monastery. For a while, the monks stayed on working at the old industries and, as at the monastery, a Commission was appointed for the preservation of treasures and antiquities. It did not, though, as did the Commission of which Florensky had been so notable a member, have roots in the surrounding community – nor could it have done. Solovki had always been inhabited by monks, soldiers, a few prisoners and a strong but itinerant peasant workforce who gave their labour in lieu of the cash donation richer supplicants could afford in gratitude for answered prayer and hope of divine favour. There was no academy here, no religious-philosophical community. The Commission, brought in from outside, was weak. Though it did succeed in founding a museum, it could do nothing to withstand the removal of the saints' remains, or the disbandment of the remaining monastics, and little to prevent the reconstruction of the burnt-out monastic complex after a devastating fire to serve the requirements of the First Soviet Labour Camp.

Solovki had always offered a natural oubliette for political undesirables and heretics, but in Tsarist times these had come singly or in twos and threes, seldom more than 50 souls at any one time, whereas the Soviet Labour Camp SLON (the acronym spells 'elephant' in Russian) swallowed up thousands: priests, intellectuals, *ci-devant* aristocrats and Tsarist officials, smugglers, prostitutes and common criminals. This unqualified crowd of resentful, sick, half-starved prisoners was no substitute for the skilled, industrious peasant-monks and, although logging and plans to extract iodine from seaweed were added to the traditional local industries, the camp did not prosper. Towards the end of Florensky's sojourn it was declared economically unviable and became STON (Russian for 'groan'), with a T for *tiurma* (prison) rather than an L for *lager* (camp).

Solovki and its saints are still deeply revered by many believing Russians and heroic efforts are being made to reconstruct the majestic monastery, whose mighty ramparts have withstood the battering of history and nature. Yet Florensky's romantic heart and eager mind remained untouched by its history of heroic intransigence to foreign attack and domestic tyranny, and of cantankerous infighting among the brethren. Solovki, he felt, had never been his kind of monastery. There was, he complained to Anna Mikhailovna, more about economics than spirituality in the accounts of the place, and he was strangely unimpressed by the antiquity of his surroundings. Though, as a boy, he had dreamt of an island surrounded by the ebb and flow of tidal seas and, as a young man, of life in a monastery, the fulfilment of these dreams, as of the desire to sleep in one room with his laboratory experiments, had come with a bitter, 'monkey's paw' twist.[38] Life in Solovki was one long endurance test and only towards the very end, certain in his own mind that he was about once again to be moved, did he occasionally feel the fascination of those northernmost isles. For a long time he continued fiercely to resent the interruption of his research on permafrost and would have welcomed a transfer back to Siberia.

Nevertheless, he made the best of the hand the Lord God had dealt him, although the White Sea turned out to be 'dirty grey' and there could be no hope of further visits from Anna Mikhailovna who was travel-sick on a tram and would never have stood up to the rough crossing. Besides, visits on Solovki were regulated to two hours, monitored by prison staff. Not worth the terrible journey, even for one of the boys. He forbade them, but unbent sufficiently to send a modest list of desiderata in his second letter home: a cigarette holder; cheap cigarettes or tobacco and rolling paper; gloves; two or three exercise books or white writing paper; pens; cheap ersatz coffee; onions; vegetable oil to counter the shortage of fats; boots or shoes and, again, spectacles.[39]

The horrible 'quarantine' ward to which new arrivals were consigned housed up to 50 essentially incompatible prisoners in extremely cramped circumstances. Florensky was detailed to perform a variety of physical tasks such as digging and loading sacks of turnip and horseradish which he found extremely onerous: he was, after all, coming up 54 and, although a good walker and accustomed to stringent self-discipline, had pursued basically sedantary occupations for many years. There were, he informed Vasilii, interesting people among his fellow-detainees, more interesting than were to be met with nowadays outside, but it would be more exact to call them 'ex-interesting', because the pressures and dullness of the uprooted existence they were all leading made it hard to believe that they had ever been significant personalities. 'Probably I'm the same', he added, 'not probably, even, undoubtedly.'[40]

With escape from the 'quarantine ward' on 15 November the grinding-down process was temporarily halted. Florensky was transferred to work on obtaining iodine from seaweed, another childhood 'dream-come-true'. He explained in a letter to his wife that:

> In connection with this, I've been moved to another 'colonna' and therefore to another place. Now I am living with perfectly decent cohabitants and not with bandits and 'urki'[41], and there are not many of us; were six, now five ... The building where I work stands on the shore of the Bay of Content [*Blagopoluchiia* in Russian, another curious euphemism]. This small and ill-equipped workplace sports a grand sign on the door: 'LABORATORY'. But though it's only a sign it still gives me pleasure to read it as I go in. What is more, I sometimes get to work in a real laboratory, a bit small but respectable by Solovki standards.[42]

Though the situation of the 'laboratory' was very beautiful, Florensky's heart remained unresponsive to the eerie loveliness of Solovki. He was, however, pleased to be getting to grips with seaweed, which had fascinated him since childhood. Indeed, the next letter to his mother shows a marked rise in energy. He hopes to increase the yield of iodine and, as a sideline, has undertaken to catalogue foreign books in the camp library, to give lessons in Physics and organise a mathematics circle. The evidence of other prisoners suggests he had lost none of his old magic as a teacher. Roman Litvinov, a professor of chemical technology from Nizhniyi Novgorod, who was to become one of Florensky's closest colleagues and take out patents with him on new ways of processing seaweed, wrote in his letters home that same month that the lectures on physics gave him intense aesthetic pleasure. The friendship became deep, but was slow to mature. Florensky, though thankful to be in acceptable company, preserved the permafrost in his heart and kept his distance. He was aware, however, that some stimulation was needful for the mind and attended the camp theatre, though he only really enjoyed the vigorous performances of non-ethnic Russians such as his native Caucasians.

Before the year was out, Florensky's extraordinarily resilient mind was full of projects: how to harness wind and tide to supply energy for the islands' industries; how to obtain bromide from seawater; how to get not only iodine but agar-agar from the seaweed. Writing to Ol'ga took him away from science and back to aesthetics. Chernyshevsky, the nineteenth-century, materialist 'martyr' she was studying at school, was, he told her gently, quite wrong to say life is 'higher' than art, because art is a part of life as flowers are a part of a plant. He would have his children study his own childhood heroes, Goethe and Michael Faraday, great scholars who did not think

> in abstract schemae, in signs, but in images, concrete through and through, – thinking in terms of the typical. Ideas (Goethe's *Urphänomene*) are not abstract postulates. You can't love postulates, can't delight in them, but Goethe and Faraday loved the artistic images of their own thought and did delight in them … Those are the people who are close to me.[43]

The quiet interlude with only five others proved shortlived. By mid-January Florensky was again sleeping in a large cell with 21 'iod-prom' workers. As ever, he was irked by the absence of solitary concentration. Yet, taking stock on his fifty-fourth birthday, he was able to write to Anna Mikhailovna that he had never consciously done anybody any harm 'and there is no anger or malice in me',[44] and to apologise to Kirill for the devouring sense of duty which had made him such a distant father, at the same time regretting that he had been prevented from fulfilling his potential of service to society, adding, with a flash of the old, titanic pride: '… still, it's far from clear who is the loser, I or society …'[45]

In February, Florensky, Litvinov and two others were allowed to move out to actually reside in the laboratory at Phillip's Hermitage, two kilometres from the Kremlin, 'a quiet isolated place in the forest, so it will be possible to work'.[46] Here they introduced all kinds of home-made machinery to extract iodine with fewer fumes, urgently needed not just for the workforce but for the scientists themselves whose living room adjoined the three rooms set aside for laboratory work – an ideal arrangement according to Florensky as it enabled them to check experiments round the clock, very necessary as the temperature of the nitrate natria had to be kept at a steady 400°C on an erratic wood-burning stove and the mixture regularly stirred. The kitchen, bio-laboratory and attic of their building was also home to 12 rabbits, 8 guinea-pigs, 30 white mice and 1 cat, whose antics and remarkable fecundity provided a great source of news for Mika and Tika.

It was from Phillip's Hermitage that Florensky, for the first time, saw the aurora borealis, great pillars of light flaming in the sky and reflected in the lake.

Ol'ga, who was writing an essay on Tiutchev, elicited several letters on the poet's affinity with Goethe and Schelling and the difference between his Ancient Greek view of chaos as the mother of cosmos and Dostoevsky's more anthropocentric concept of chaos as depravity and moral disintegration:

He and Tiutchev are speaking of different things: while Tiutchev goes beyond the confines of the human into Nature, Dostoevsky remains within those confines and speaks *not* of the fundamental in Nature but of the fundamental in man. When he thinks as Tiutchev does he uses the term 'earth' for what Tiutchev means by 'night'.[47]

There is an echo of these thoughts in Litvinov's letters to his family, where he conjures a vivid picture of the hermit Phillip's successors sitting round the wood-burning stove with its seething pot of nitrate natria in their underpants, trying to dry out and mend an insufficient supply of trousers, while Florensky, needle in hand, expatiated sagely on the differences between Tiutchev's and Goethe's *Naturphilosophie*: 'We discuss all the poets and agree about almost all of them except Fet', Litvinov wrote enthusiastically. He had been more enriched by conversation with this particular fellow-prisoner than by any university course, he told his family, carefully refraining from mentioning names as did all the prisoners. They often talked on scientific subjects, of which his friend had 'a profound understanding', and sometime touched on 'the non-exact sciences'. All in all, Litvinov wrote, he regarded this acquaintanceship as a 'fine compensation' for many troubles.[48]

In the hermitage-laboratory, in spite of or because of the isolation, Florensky was much happier, absorbed in work, though conscious of separation and of a slipping grasp of the latest developments in science and technology. The good accord with Litvinov and some other prisoners was stilted by the inevitable presence of the odd stool pigeon, who would submit reports of their conversations to the camp authorities. Though valued for the constructive thought and energy they invested in production, which earned them the occasional monetary premium, decent rations and the privilege of sending off three rather than one letter home per month, critically thinking individuals such as Florensky and Litvinov were held to be potentially hostile to the State and singled out for specially close observation. The obverse side of their isolation was the sheer physical difficulty of getting 'into town' (as they described going to the Kremlin for supplies), especially in the winter darkness:

> You walk on, aware that for at least a kilometre all round you there are no people. Silence. The island is surrounded by ice-flows, then the sea, stormy and unpredictable. So you feel yourself cut off from the whole world and are particularly aware of this on the way back to the laboratory in the dark.[49]

There was little enough daylight anyway in the winter: 'nor day nor night, nor dark nor light', as Florensky wrote home, quoting Lermontov's description of the Demon, and the mini-climate brought about freak thaws which left hard-packed ice under new snow. Grigorii Kotliarevsky, a fellow-*zek*, recalls how, one stormy day in a heavy fall of wet snow, he encountered Litvinov and Florensky on their way 'into town'.

> The learned men staggered along with difficulty against the wind, supported by long staves. Their fur caps, beards and faces were all sticky with snow. They would stop to wipe their glasses and then go on, deep in conversation. Several times, bowled over by the gale, they slipped on the snow-covered ice.

Kotliarevsky helped them to their feet and 'Pavel Aleksandrovich jested about harnessing the wind'.[50]

The laboratory apparatus was primitive to a degree and Florensky compared their work to the efforts of Jules Vernes' characters in the *Secret Island*. However, both he and Litvinov took a certain satisfaction in making something out of nothing. In May, they were ready to mount an exhibition of their progress in obtaining not just iodine but the currently more valuable agar-agar. As the days lengthened the guinea-pigs sunbathed on the windowsills and the rabbits produced litters much coveted by the laboratory cat, but they were still profoundly isolated, and Florensky felt as though he were in a space capsule, oblivious to the recent past and reliving his childhood, very close to the dead: 'Gosia, Valia, Aunt Julia, Papa. Aunt Liza, David and Margarita'.[51] The white nights were more uncanny than the darkness, the 'ghost of a sun' illumining fresh-fallen snow in June, and still Florensky felt curiously alienated from the natural world around him, comforted only by the astonishing luminescence of the northern skies, which he described in great detail in his letters home and tried to picture in coloured crayon. He was also posing for a Leningrad artist and teacher of graphic art, Dmitrii Ivanov, who made two drawings of him, showing the curly hair and beard which had been allowed to grow again because he had been robbed of his shaving gear and to please Anna Mikhailovna.

In the letters, Florensky sought not only to dwell on all that was positive in his day-to-day existence on Solovki, but to comfort his wife with the lasting reality of memory.

> Die Rose, die dein auszer Auge sieht,
> Sie ist von Ewigkeit in Gott geblüht.

The quotations, like the dried flowers he sent to her from Solovki, are almost the only demonstrations of tenderness in Florensky's contentful, instructive letters. He responds with measured wisdom to her anxiety that Vasilii's forthcoming marriage to a distant relative on her own side of the family, Nataliia Zarubina, might estrange him from their own household, and scolds gently that she worries too much about the younger children's manners or marks at school, whereas she should rather be concerned to increase their self-confidence, to find more to praise than to blame. For himself, he sought strenuously as before to keep in touch with each individual child, entering into animated scientific discussion with Vasilii and Kirill, writing thoughtful, beautifully expressed mini-essays to Ol'ga on her reading and why she should keep up her music – not in order to become a professional performer but for the joy of playing to herself. In the same vein, he exhorts Mika to keep practising the piano, at the same time regaling him with accounts of how he is working outside in spite of the mosquitoes to boil down seaweed into glue and with tales of wildlife and hunting. Tika he tries to keep in line and obedient to her mother with humorous flattery:

> The other day in the Kremlin I saw a Mama-seagull perched solemnly on a table and, besides her in the bushes, a baby gull. He was big and fat and still yellowish-black, not like a seagull at all. The mother-gull was ticking him off about something and he turned away, not at all pleased. I could just catch that she was telling him about news she had heard from another sea-gull. The mother-gull was saying, in her own language, of course: 'Human beings have good children, and you don't do as I tell you. In Zagorsk there's a little girl ... who looks after her dolls and will soon be playing beautiful music, whereas you haven't even learnt to gobble like a turkey yet! She is embroidering a towel – and you haven't even learnt how to build a nest![52]

Another artist, Petr Pakshin of Novosibirsk, sketched Florensky, and he sent the drawing to Anna Mikhailovna for their wedding anniversary. 'The eyes look sad', she responded anxiously and he replied, ruefully: 'I don't see my own eyes, but really there's nothing for them to look particularly merry about.'[53] Nevertheless, when she wrote to him that summer of an offer from the Czech Government to give asylum to him and his family if the Soviets would commute his hard labour sentence to exile, he replied in the words of St Paul that he had learned to be self-sufficient in all circumstances (Phil. 4.11) and told her to stop all efforts on his behalf. When, the following summer, Masaryk, prompted by one of Florensky's spiritual daughters who had emigrated with his blessing in 1935, again enquired after the imprisoned priest through Peshkova, the latter appealed once more for his release, but not for his release abroad as she understood from Anna Mikhailovna that he did not wish to avail himself of the Czech offer of asylum. She was refused on the grounds that Florensky was a priest who had never renounced that office. Although unwilling to avail himself of the emigration option, Florensky did not condemn those who chose to do so.

The summer passed like a dream, the warning bells of the monastery acting as foghorns, the island wrapped in pearly, opaque mist, silvery and watery where the sun tried to break through, 'the ghost of suns'. And then, just as the latter-day hermits were planning to go mushrooming and gather the wild yellow raspberries and bilberries to supplement their home cooking, they were ordered to evacuate their laboratory dwelling for a less beautiful, less congenial site.

Autumn comes early to Solovki and the seagulls had already flown when, on 20 August, they moved to their new quarters and Florensky wrote to his wife:

> I am living in a new place. It is an old monastic building near the Kremlin. The walls of the ground floor are thick and the ceiling high with stone vaulting. It was once the monastery's blacksmith's forge. My living space is on the first floor with its own entrance by a decrepit outside staircase as for a dove-cote. There are two rooms. One I occupy together with the laboratory assistants and in the other one live the technical personnel who are almost always absent. We do our own cooking on an electric ring in the living room and eat almost exclusively vegetables, which is as I like it. The house is situated on the shore of the Holy [now the Kremlin] Lake. From the upstairs windows one has the impression it actually stands in the lake. You can imagine yourself in Italy or Switzerland.[54]

One of the most poignant letters to Ol'ga was written from this draughty eyrie above the lake. She was studying Serbian epics and the recollection of their Dostoevsky-style gloom prompted him to an unwonted disparagement of Slavic melancholy:

> There is no sun in the Slavs, no transparency, no definition! Clarity and serenity are lacking ... It seems to me this is meaningfully related to their failure to grasp Goethe's symbolic approach to life, to be able to see and value the depths of your immediate surroundings, to find the sublime in the 'here' and 'now' and not strain to seek it in the non-existent or the far-away.[55]

It was a wrench to leave the laboratory that he and Litvinov had worked so hard to make functional and there was no immediate replacement. Florensky busied himself in the Construction Office writing articles on what they had achieved, applying for patents and working with a chemical engineer, Nikolai Briantsev on a project for the manufacture of chemicals and the possibility of drilling for oil in the sea 'which quite eclipses the iodine'.[56] He pictures them for his mother as they compose

> countless reports on our inventions in the sphere of seaweed and peat ... Just now I'm sitting by the window, the lake laps the shore and the wind roams around my room in spite of the pillow stuck in where the glass and shutters are broken.[57]

By the end of September, however, Florensky and his team were moved again – back into the stink and incessant din of a large dormitory in the 'soulless and depressing' Kremlin with not so much as a table to write on. At least, he wrote, thankful for small mercies, his room-mates were a decent lot from the Project Bureau and there was a promise that he would be allotted a smaller room with only four or five others. Meanwhile, they were eating in the communal dining-room where the cooking was tolerable; meat, which he always made a point of giving away, was a rarity and fish comparatively plentiful. Though he shared out the content of parcels sent from home, they lasted a long time and his family, he wrote imploringly, must not deprive themselves in order to send delicacies to him.

On the minus side, Florensky was now unable to concentrate, even on a letter, and felt he had fallen so far behind in science that there was no point in his wife sending him periodicals. Grimly, he joked that a Persian fellow-*zek* was teaching him to tell fortunes from cats' tails, but that most cats on Solovki had no tails. To amuse the little ones he began, for want of first-hand impressions from nature, to retell prisoners' stories: advertisements, armadillos and albatrosses in America; Swedish circuses; Chinese food and English oddities such as 'mock-turtle soup' and 'mince pies', the flora and fauna, bushmen and boomerangs of Australia; the peculiarities of Persian and Japanese grammar. The Soviet Gulag of the mid-1930s flung its net wide indeed. To Kirill he wrote more seriously:

> Life is far from being one long holiday and diversion. There's much that is monstrous, evil, sad and dirty in life. Yet, knowing all that, it is essential to preserve harmony in one's inner eye and to try to make it a reality ... to formulate a new approach to nature, a new, concrete, realistic understanding of the world instead of a lifeless, abstract, illusory one.[58]

Lethargic and run-down from lack of privacy and fresh air, he was still struggling to introduce shape and meaning into the formless existence of this misty, sub-arctic penitentiary, where even the seasons were hard to tell apart, and to formulate in ever more simple terms, directly from experience, his ever more steadfast ontological convictions.

Meanwhile work had started up again with redoubled intensity. The production of seaweed extracts, including agar-agar, was taking on industrial dimensions. Florensky and his associates had been encouraged to found a 'bureau of inventions', to which he was giving three two-hour lectures every week. In spite of the smell of seaweed and a plague of escaped white mice and flies which reminded him of Beelzebub in the warm, damp, new laboratory, he was anxious to be allotted a room next to it where he would be able to work in peace.

As 1935 passed into 1936 Florensky was thrilled to hear from home that he was to become a grandfather, and delighted that Kirill had begun to publish his research, though anxious that he had mentioned the possibility of prospecting for gold which, he warned, was overvalued and aroused undesirable passions. Ol'ga was reading Shakespeare whose works, he told her

> are instinct of profound intelligence, but it is an imminent intelligence (inwardly present) to the characters and speeches, so that you do not see the writer's mind behind the images. In general, you do not see the writer himself – that is the enigma of Shakespeare.[59]

On 20/21 February Florensky and four colleagues, one from the days of Phillip's Hermitage, at last moved into a room next to the laboratory, from which they could constantly oversee their experiments. Ethnicly, it was a diverse team preponderantly from Udmuria – Ivan Burdiukov, a Russian chemist born in Udmurtia, Kuz'ma Chainikov, a writer whose real name was Kuzebai Gerd and who is said by his family to have acquired faith in God while working in the seaweed laboratory, Konstantin Iakovlev, also an ethnic Udmurt, one Ukrainian and one Komi. Unfortunately, the cramped accommodation and its situation in the Kremlin did not give the peace they had enjoyed at the hermitage, but there was nevertheless more time and space to concentrate on work, write home and observe the Northern Lights.

The building they had been allotted was a compilation of sixteenth, seventeenth and twentieth-century architecture. The laboratory, in the oldest part under stone vaults, looked like a witches' kitchen with hand-made machinery of medieval appearance and wooden chests shaped like coffins. The machines groaned and creaked amidst billowing steam and an open birchwood conduit drained the seaweed-smelling water from the stone-slabbed floor. 'All that's missing', Florensky wrote to his wife, 'is a stuffed crocodile hanging from the ceiling.'[60] They worked a 24-hour shift system, Florensky rising at 8 a.m. and, after breakfast, working through the day, analysing results and dealing with constant crises in the hand-made machinery, until dinner at 6 p.m., then snatching a couple of hours sleep until 9 o'clock, when he would be on duty again until four or five in the morning, then go to bed – subject to no extraordinary emergencies in the laboratory. The factory was at some distance from the Kremlin dining room and one passed up to 40 acquaintances on the way, so – he wrote to Anna Mikhailovna – it was really impossible always to doff one's hat – though witnesses remember Florensky doing precisely this with a polite, priestly bow.[61]

The grinding regime banished all possibility of new creative work and Florensky, in a moment of frustration, begged Anna Mikhailovna to persuade Nikolai Ivanovich (Bykov) to publish his findings on permafrost as they stood as he had neither the books nor the time for revision:

My lifework is destroyed and I will never be able or willing to take up again the labour of fifty years. I will not want to, because I was not working for myself or my own advantage and, if humanity, for whose sake I never knew a personal life, has considered it possible completely to annihilate all that was done for its sake and only awaited the last finishing touches, then all the worse for humanity, let them try to reconstruct what they have destroyed for themselves ...[62]

Various people, he says, are working blindly on a variety of subjects that had become clear to him.

I know enough of history and the historical development of thought to foresee the time when people will begin to gather up the pieces of what has been destroyed. But that does not so much comfort as exasperate me: detestable human stupidity, spun out from the beginning of history and, no doubt, intent on continuing to the end. But that's enough – all this about myself is really uninteresting ...[63]

The resentment, however, was but the obverse of the renewed vitality of Florensky's mind. In this same letter to Anna he passes from his 'uninteresting' self to associations between Odysseus and geographical placenames, then goes on to write to Ol'ga of the unfathomable mystery of genes and their relationship to tragic guilt: 'Greek tragedy is the most edifying, profound and perfect part of world literature'[64] which is why there has been no true tragedy since; mission accomplished. Leaping from the Greeks to Russian Futurism, he laments that he never had the chance to talk to Khlebnikov, whom he would have loved to know better, about the Orochen. On 3 April, Florensky directed a letter through Kirill to his teacher, Academician Vernadsky, in which he overcomes his anger at 'human stupidity' and tries to reformulate the cornerstone of his philosophy: the *reality* of time and space. Thought of by rationalists as an abstract way of organising our perceptions and by the sensualists as subjective delusion, for Florensky space and time are the key to understanding and

the most weighty proof of the reality of space-time is the fact of the existence of asymmetry in nature and of irreversibility in the temporal ... Asymmetry in time is irreversibility. To be is to be in time, to be in time is to be irreversible, that is 'historical'.[65]

We cannot, as the cinema can, turn time around and have the splash before the dive. We cannot, in real space, lay triangles one exactly on top of the other: i.e. two triangles cannot coexist in one and the same two-dimensional space. 'Physical space-time cannot be thought of other than as potentially immense in compass yet endowed with distinct content. And that leads to the assertion of the curvature of space-time.' Different sections of the curve have different surfaces: a rough surface wears more slowly, a jutting corner weathers faster. We cannot conceive of the border between the inner and outer body as flat. Thus time itself can be measured differently in different spatial conditions.

These hypotheses, Florensky tells his son and through him his son's teacher, still out there and able to study and publish in the world of science, may be proved wrong tomorrow but will surely be proved right the day after and he needs to record them. So the free mind, struggling in the weary body amid the white mice, winter flies and billowing steam, still fought to communicate, to leave some trace ...

Not that this made Florensky indifferent to the task in hand. It is such a shame, he writes, that he had never seen seaweed growing, never had the chance to solve the problem of how it holds to the rock without roots, and goes on to explain how it is harvested not from the sea but from the wrack 50cm high and 1m wide around the coast of the islands.

He was still giving the occasional lecture; on one occasion, for instance, he spoke on radio-geology to an appreciative audience, and he was training replacements for whom he had to organise examinations on seaweed. He tried to see his pupils as members of his own family – not in the sense of universal brotherhood or dutiful philanthropy, but as individuals, quite literally as his own children, parents, brothers, sisters – which did not stop him longing for communication with his own family and friends.

To Mika he sent a starfish and the dedication of the poem 'Oro':

> Parted from you yet again
> I can but give my fancy rein
> To spin a tale on the night-shift –
> Of powerless love the worthless gift.[66]

Vasilii he advises to compose a table of the history of the biosphere 'or I'll just send you mine' and enthusiastically discusses names for the expected baby, eventually accepting with a good grace the decision to call it after himself. Breaking with his usual rule of writing only to the family, he allowed himself a letter to Yudina, in which he confides that, although the pressures of the time compel him towards 'the spicy, the broken and the turgid ... I do not want to permit [myself] capriccio, I do not want Schumann, I do not want CAPRICE: In conformity with law there is freedom, in arbitrary caprice – necessity.'[67] Musical salvation, for Florensky, was still Mozart.

In early summer, just as he was beginning to feel he was mouldering away without the consolations of live music or nature, there was some relief from the grinding factory routine. On 20–21 May, Florensky was taken on a tour of the island in search of anfeltsia, the seaweed which yields agar-agar, and he drank in the sight of well-kept roads and houses, forest and moorland, the freshwater lakes and the sea that smelt of his childhood. The landscapes reminded him of early Nesterov paintings – but were still more dreamlike and insubstantial. Suddenly the sense of being on an island pleased him, for Florensky had inherited from his father an irrational fear of unbounded, unmanageable space.

In July he and his fellow-workers were awarded a premium for their rationalisation of production at the factory which had cut costs by 8,000 roubles and there seemed to be some hope of investment in equipping a real factory. Florensky felt a sense of achievement. From 13–18 July he was sent on a geological-mineralogical expedition from island to island. It was, he wrote, 'like a picture of the first day of creation'[68] to see pools and streams welling up from ancient rock formations, far older than the glacial granite.

In August there was another expedition to islands closer inshore on a Japanese-type, flat-bottomed steamboat, the 'Kavasaki', and back again in a tiny boat under sail, which made him feel like Robinson Crusoe – or Odysseus. They sighted waving forests of anfeltsia a metre below the surface of the sea at high tide. 'It's important ecologically', he wrote to Anna, 'but of less value than what I had hoped to give when working on permafrost.'[69] He showered the family with exquisite drawings of the various types of seaweed and even sent them two filmy strips of agar-agar to make jelly. By November he had worked out a way of producing these as rolls. For Christmas he obtained permission to send home a box of delights from Solovki: dried seaweed which had to be looked at in water; gulls' eggs; eiderdown; rose quartz; crabs; and more starfish. As usual, though, he scolded the family ungratefully for sending him a Christmas hamper he felt they could ill afford, and begged Ol'ga not to take on dead-end jobs at the toy factory in Zagorsk or the *Technical Encyclopedia* in Moscow just to start earning money. At the New Year he confided to Vasilii that the centre of his life was now not himself but the family: 'That's why the only thing I really wish for is that you and Mama should be all right and living life to the full, aware of its richness and value.'[70]

Even the summer expeditions had been unable entirely to renew Florensky's personal vitality. A young aircraft designer, P. A. Ivensen, whom he helped with an experiment on an early version of the hovercraft (which of course like most other things on Solovki was curtailed without further result), reports that he looked like an old man and had difficulty in walking. Solovki, he had written to his mother on 28–29 June, was a realm of silences:

not literally, of course, there is more than enough irritating noise and you want to hide yourself away somewhere quiet. But you don't hear the inner resonance of Nature, you don't catch the inner voices of people. Everything slides by like a shadow-play, and the sounds intrude like an irritating invasion of noise, a discordant accompaniment. It is very difficult to explain why nothing has resonance, why there is no music of things or of life. I don't properly understand it myself, but nevertheless there is no music.[71]

Since boyhood, Florensky had heard music, responding like a finely strung instrument to the world about him. As with the poet Aleksandr Blok, this slow plunge into inner silence was the harbinger of death.

Death, arbitrary, absurd and merciless, was creeping up on Florensky, as it was on all his 'family' of helpers, on the artists who had drawn him, on the Urdmut engineers, on Litvinov with whom he had talked poetry and science – exact and non-exact.

In spite of the success of the factory, the camp economy as a whole was failing. As in a terrible fairytale, the prisoners, having achieved prodigies of productivity with primitive instruments, were set a double norm – with no further investment in machinery. Iodine was pronounced non-competitive against imports from Japan (with whom Russia was so soon to be at war) and production was switched to agar-agar. When, in April 1937, they failed to meet the impossible target imposed upon them, this was used as an excuse to close down the factory altogether and those who had worked there were stripped of privilege and allowed fewer letters home. The exhausting wind-down continued, the prisoners being made to feel guilty for decisions taken elsewhere as to the viability of Solovki as a labour camp. In May 1937, SLON was renamed STON, reduced to the far more horrible status of prison: no work; no freedom of movement; tighter rations; fewer letters and, as when Florensky had first arrived, little or no distinction between political prisoners and common criminals – although he did at least share a room with 40 or so ex-iodine production workers – for which he was duly thankful.

What none of them knew positively but many felt instinctively was that, precisely for the more educated and thus politically undesirable prisoners, Solovki was now a death camp. An order signed by Ezhov required that the population of STON be decreased by 1,200 people, all to be properly bureau-cratically processed and done away with extraterritorially, as though they were simply being moved elsewhere. In the meantime, they were expendable. Litvinov's last letter of 19 September 1937 records a desperate shortage of food and money for the prison shop.

At the end of October 1937, this twilight existence came to an end. There was a hurried evacuation of more than a thousand men to the mainland. A witness recalls seeing Florensky, Litvinov and Kotliarevsky among the lines of four who were marched out to the Bay of Content.[72] Weighed down with cases and rucksacks, they could only nod as they passed. They were conveyed to the so-called Workers' Island where Florensky, with 12 others, was brought up before a *troika*, accused of counter-revolutionary Trotskyite propaganda and condemned to be shot.

On 25 November the condemned were moved near Leningrad, where they were delivered to a Major Frenikov, who carefully checked each one against his photograph. On 8 December Florensky's turn came. He was shot with two others whose fate had had no previous connection with his own and the bodies tipped into a communal grave. Aleksandr Romanovich Polikarpov, the officer commanding the shooting squad subsequently committed suicide because of difficulties at work, leaving a letter defending his unblemished record in the service of his country.

From the letters of that last desperate year Florensky's voice reaches us still ... telling Tika how he came upon the night-watchman at the factory, a gym-master before his arrest, talking to a little cat he had folded into his jacket and

> remembering how he'd cradled his one-year-old daughter that way and carried her round with him, but she had wanted to be put down on the floor. And I remembered my little daughter who I used to carry about with me too and who was afraid of the forest.[73]

'It was as though humanity and homeliness had not yet been invented or had already passed away', he writes to his wife of one of his last journeys across the island.[74] One of the rooms he briefly occupied during the many moves of that last year reminded him of the monastic cell he had slept in as a research student at the Academy in Sergiev Posad, and it was not until he found himself back in one of the big dormitories that he confessed to 'inner anxiety and a confusion of feelings'.[75] In one of the last letters he wrote to Ol'ga about his own reading, Florensky remarks sadly that Hume's *History of England*, with its record of wars, executions and powerful predators, is oppressing him with the thought that little has changed for the better. Humanity has 'become outwardly more decent, disguising violence in less vivid forms, i.e. ones that don't make effective tragedies, but the essence has not changed'.[76]

Though he never complained of hunger, the letters tend to dwell more often on vegetarian dishes with fresh herbs that would benefit the children and he confides that he has lately taken to eating seaweed – better than sour cabbage and even rather like asparagus! The closure of the factory he accepted as only natural:

> In my life it is always so, as soon as I have made a subject my own I have to give it up for reasons which have nothing to do with me or it, and to begin some new task, again from the foundation up, to blaze a trail I am not destined to tread. Probably there is

meaning in this since it has happened again and again throughout my life – a lesson in disinterestedness. But, nevertheless, it is tiring.[77]

As the prison walls closed about him, Florensky bade his other half get out in the fresh air, just a step from the house to hear the larks or see the corn come into ear, or, more especially to 'go for a stroll as evening falls and think of me'.[78]

One task he was still allowed to perform – that of night-watchman in the now useless factory. Even in June it had been too cold to work:

> the desperate cold in the dead factory, the bare walls and the howling wind that bursts through the broken glass of the windows are not conducive to study and you see by my handwriting that it's even impossible to write letters with frozen fingers. But I think of you all the more, worry about you. Life has gone quiet and at this time we feel ourselves more than ever cut off from the mainland ... It is six o'clock. Morning. Snow falls on the stream and a wild wind whirls it about. Broken windows flap in the abandoned building, groaning from the onslaught of the wind. You can hear the anxious crying of the seagulls. With all my being, I feel the insignificance of man, his works, his efforts.[79]

Yet, again and again, he rallies, exhorting Kirill to continue his work, Ol'ga to be and not to seem, Anna to seek solace in nature ... seeking to amuse them with tales of his neighbours on the prison bunks, an Armenian peasant on one side and, immediately above him, a fierce Chechen mullah who says Florensky would have made a good Muslim.

The mullah, too, was shot in 1937. From early June, the flow of Florensky's letters home dries up, though the prisoners continued to receive mail from their families. What happened next we know only from outside sources. There was to be no 'effective tragedy' and, if this was martyrdom, it was the very twentieth-century, existential martyrdom of a sentient, living human being, ground down to silence and consigned to an anonymous grave.

# Chronology

All dates until 1918 Old Style (OS) unless otherwise stated.

1882    9 January (OS). Pavel Florensky (further F) born near Evlach in Elizavetopol'skaia gubernia (now Azerbaijan) where his parents lived in tents and railway carriages for the first 18 months of his life.

1883    Family moved back to Tiflis, Nikolaevskaia ulitsa 61.

1884    1 July (OS). F's sister Julia (psychiatrist) born.

1886    7 May. F's sister Elizaveta (artist and art teacher) born.

1888    7 March. F's brother Aleksandr (geologist, mineralogist and art historian) born.

1886–1891    (approx.) The family live in Batumi where F's father is constructing the military railroad from Batumi to Akhaltsyk. They are accompanied by Aunt Julia Florensky who has been living with them in Tiflis and is now in charge of the elder children. F shows intense interest in the natural world and absorbs elements of science from his father.

1891    19 February. F's sister Ol'ga (artist and poet) born.
        Move back to Tiflis and F begins preparation for school.

1892    Formal education begins at the Second Tiflis Classical Gymnasium, having been prepared by Aunt Julia for the obligatory religious observance and instruction which F regards as a waste of time. Throughout school years he pursues a rigorous parallel programme of self-education in the study of nature and physical problems, tossing off homework in the breaks and easily maintaining position as top of the class. Friendship with fellow-pupils Ern and El'chaninov.

1894    16 April. F's sister Raisa (artist) born.

1897          June–July. Trip to Germany with aunts on his mother's side Repsimia and Elizaveta. Visits Dresden, Leipzig, Bonn and Cologne. Buys Rühmkorff coil for his laboratory. The family move to a house of their own where F has his own room with two large tables for apparatus and experiments.

1 December. F's brother Andrei (engineer) born.

1899          F writes first papers for accepted publication 'On electric and magnetic phenomena of the Earth' ('O elektricheskikh i magnitnykh iavleniiakh zemli') in *Izvestiia russkogo astronomicheskogo obshchestva 8* and 'An experiment in nebulae simulation' (Opyt vosproizvedeniia tymannykh piaten) in *Izvestiia russkogo astronomicheskogo obshchestva 4–6*, 1900. Hagemeister mentions one earlier publication on the glow-worm in a German nature journal, but this remains unidentified.

Break-up of F's relationship with closest friend Sasha El'chaninov the previous year and disillusion with the prospect of pushing back the boundaries of research in physics lead first to depression and then to a spiritual crisis, which makes him contemplate radical change in his whole way of life. At the Students' Philosophical society there is much discussion of Lev Tolstoy and Vladimir Solov'ev.

1900          June. F graduates from the Second Tiflis Classical Gymnasium with gold medal and top of class. Under the influence of Tolstoy's *Confession* F is barely dissuaded by his parents from abandoning further education at their expense and 'going to the people' to earn his own living by physical labour. On vacation helps his father look after Andrei at a Caucasian resort and begins to read *The World of Art* (*Mir iskusstva*), at that time the flagship of Russian Modernism.

September. Enters the Physico-Mathematical Faculty of Moscow University in the Department of Higher Mathematics and, after a brief period lodging with relations of his father, moves into a shared room with Ern at one of the university student hostels.

1900–1904  Studies mathematics and works towards a 'world-view', in part under the influence of Professor Nikolai Bugaev's arythmology (which he finds liberating) and monadology, of Cantor's set-theory and discussions of infinity, and of the new geometry, which he complements by wide reading in the natural sciences, continued interest in Plato, self-education in music and art and attendance at

Prince Sergei Trubetskoi's seminar on ancient philosophy and Lev Lopatin's lectures on psychology. F founds and acts as secretary to an undergraduate subsidiary of the Moscow Mathematical Philosophical Society.

1901–1902    F compiles an edition of Bugaev's lectures on integral calculation (*Integral'noe ischislenie. Lektsii ekstraordinarnogo Professora N B Bugaeva*, sostavleny i izdany Studentom P. A. Florenskim i A But iaginym, Moscow, 1901) and of I. A. Kobukov's course on organic chemistry (Organicheskaia khimiia. Konspekt lektsii privat dotsenta I. A. Kobukova, Moscow, 1902) and writes *Imaginary Points in Geometry*, which he finally publishes with revisions and additions in 1922. He is too busy to become involved in undergraduate unrest leading to boycott of lectures and violently repressed demonstrations, though he writes to the university authorities of his sympathy with student grievances and readiness to share in their punishments. The authorities, however, appear to have protected him as no such compromising statements are to be found in his student dossier.

1903    Professor Bugaev dies and F calls on his son the Symbolist poet Andrei Bely. A friendship is founded.

1904    January. Bely introduces F to various Symbolist literati including the Merezhkovskys, Blok, Bal'mont and Briusov. F finds they, too, are in full rebellion against what he calls 'the tyranny of the continuum' (obligatory thinking in terms of cause and effect) and are in search of intuitive insights which do not preclude an educated view of religion. He begins to write for the Symbolist Press, placing a 1902 article 'On superstition and miracle' with the Merezhkovskys' *The New Way* ('O sueverii i chude', *Novyi put'*, 8, 1903), an article on Cantor 'On symbols of infinity' ('O simvolakh beskonechnosti', *Novyi put'*, No. 9, 1904) and a review of a long poem entitled by the editors 'Spiritism as anti-Christianity' ('Spiritizm kak antikhristantsvo', *Novyi put'*, No. 3, 1904), and contributing to *The Balance* a philosophical piece 'About one assumption towards a world view' ('Ob odnoi predposylke mirovozreniia', *Vesy*, No. 9, 1904).

    In the course of this academic year F writes a dissertation on discontinuity on curved lines accompanied by an introduction stressing the philosophical importance of 'discontinuity', 'Ideia preryvnosti kak element mirosozertsaniia' and embarks on a review of Bely's as yet unpublished book of poetry *Gold in Azure* (*Zoloto v lazure*) and on a narrative poem of his own, an eschatological fantasy in the style of Bely's symphonies originally to have been entitled 'St Vladimir'.

March. Bely introduces F to Bishop Antonii (Florensov), who refuses his blessing to their aspiration to enter a monastery, but encourages F to put his new religious vocation to the test by learning more about the Church.

F takes Bishop Antonii at his word and, having graduated from the university with a first-class degree, turns down his professors' Zhukovsky's and Laktin's offer to remain in the Mathematics Department as a dotsent. Instead, to the dismay of his parents, he arranges to enter the Moscow Theological Academy (further MDA), leaving the secretaryship of his Student Mathematico Philosophical Society to his lifelong friend Nikolai Luzin. In June that summer he writes an apologia for this decision, 'On the empirical and the Empyrean', in the form of a dialogue loosely based on correspondence with El'chaninov which, however, remained unpublished during his lifetime.

1904–1905 (academic year)   The increasingly acute revolutionary situation in Russia sets off repercussions in the Church. Students and staff at the MDA are impatient with conservatism in Pobedonostsev's Holy Synod and, on the periphery of the Church, F's friend Ern, together with a new-found ally Sventsitsky, founds the Christian Brotherhood for Struggle for ecclesiastical reform. F, as always deeply concentrated on study, which now involves new disciplines including Hebrew, Greek, Latin, Church Slavonic, the scriptures and the Fathers of the Church, is not active in the Brotherhood but maintains friendly relations with his old friends. The divergence of interests between him and Bely leads to decreased contact, especially after the tragi-comic incident of the latter's 'poetic duel' with Briusov in which F figures as Bely's spiritual 'second'. The Church and the peace of the Trinity St Sergius Monastery where, as a student of the MDA, F is now living, his friendship with a priest's son one year his senior at the Academy Sergei Troitsky and their shared reverence for the saintly *starets* Isidor at the Gethsemane Skete combine to wean F away from turbulent Moscow life. The liberal mood at the MDA is congenial to his ongoing search for Truth in a blend of secular science and Christian wisdom.

28 August–5 September 1905. F visits the Optyno-Pustyn Monastery, where he works on the manuscripts of Archimandrite Serapion (Mashkin) – a monk who, like himself, had been seeking to found a theocentric world view on mathematics – with whom he had been in correspondence, but who passed away before they could meet. This work yields a report dated 4 September 1905 but published only posthumously as 'Otchet o zaniatiakh P Florenkogo nad rukopisiami Arkhimandrita Serapiona Mashkina' in the journal *Simvol*, No. 26, 1990 and several later works, though F never succeeded in editing the chaotic bundle of over 2,000 pages of manuscript inherited from Mashkin for publication.

Other works written in 1905 were a paper for an undergraduate philosophical society on 'Dogmatism and dogma' (dated 26 September 1905 and published in the journal *Khristianskaia mysl'*, No. 1, 1909) and a piece revised from his earlier contribution to a university student circle, the introduction to his translation of Kant's dissertation on 'Physical monadology'. The translation remains unpublished but the introduction appeared as 'Ot perevodchika. Vstupitel'naia stat'ia k perevodu: Immanuil Kant. Fizicheskaia monodologiia' in the organ of the MDA the *Theological Herald* (*Bogoslovskii vestnik*, No. 9, 1905). Also written in July 1905, while on vacation in turbulent, revolutionary Tiflis, was 'On the sprouts of growth', a curious mixture of mathematical logic and intensely lyrical self-expression ('O tipakh vozrastania', *Bogoslovskii vestnik*, No. 7, 1906). Also for *Bogoslovkii vestnik* (No. 4, 1906), was an introduction to an article by El'chaninov on 'The mysticism of M. M. Speransky'. A piece on Hamlet intended for *The Balance* remained unpublished during F's lifetime, as did the extensive coursework 'Ecclesiological materials: the concept of the Church in Holy Writ'.

1906    The onset of reaction brings unrest in public opinion and in the MDA to boiling point.

12 March. F helps edit an open letter to the bishops calling on the Church to speak out against repressions and pronounces a Lenten sermon 'The cry of blood' ('Vopl'krovi') against capital punishment, specifically the execution of Lieutenant Shmidt, which is immediately printed by his fellow-students and distributed by the Christian Brotherhood for Struggle. On 23 March he is arrested and imprisoned, but pardoned and allowed to return to

the Academy for Easter at the intervention of the Rector of the MDA and G. A. Rachinsky.

A less contentious sermon pronounced this year is on the occasion of the hallowing of a new church (published as 'Khram dukha sviatogo' in 1986). Another memorial piece on Archimandrite Serapion came out in the periodical *Voprosy religii*, No. 1, 1906, entitled 'K pochesti vyshego znaniia' and F undertook a translation from the German of the first volume of Sohm's learned work on Canon Law. On holiday at Troitsky's home in the Kostroma region he continues enthusiastically to collect popular jingles known as *chastushki* and to work at an introduction for their publication.

1907      Undertakes auxiliary lecturing at the MDA and completes a work on 'Sacred changes of name' ('Sviashchennoe pereimeno-vanie' not published at the time). F's poems, which appear in the journal *Khristianin*, No. 1, 1907, are bound and republished privately under the title *In the Eternal Azure* (*V vechnoi lazure*). A sermon pronounced 7 January 'Eternal joy' (Radost' na veki) is only published posthumously, but *Khristianin* brings out a series of documentary studies of various individual's experiences of the sacraments ('Voprosy religioznogo samopoznaniia', *Khristianin* Nos 1, II and III and later, in 1909, as a separate publication). Also in *Khristianin*, No. 1 appeared F's translation of 'A Prayer by Simeon the new theologian'. His 'Philosophical introduction to Christian dogmatics' came out in the journal *Vek* ('Filosofskoe vvedenie k khristianskoi dogmatike', *Vek*, No. 9, 1907).

Troitsky graduates from the Academy and accompanies F to Tiflis in the summer vacation, where he remains as a teacher of Russian literature.

1908      22 January. Aleksandr Ivanovich, F's father, dies.

3 February. Death of *Starets* Isidor. F publishes a tribute to the latter ('Sol' zemli, to est' skazanie o zhizni startsa Gefsimanskogo skita ieromonakha avvy Isidora, sobrannoe i po poriadku izloz-hennoe nedostoinym synom ego dukhovnym Pavla Florenskogo', *Khristianin*, Nos 10–12, 1908 and Nos 1 and 5, 1909).

June. F graduates from the MDA, as usual top of his year. His candidate's dissertation 'O religioznoi istine' (an early version of his eponymous Master's dissertation 'On religious truth' and of the book *The Pillar and Ground of Truth*, already in the writing at this time in the form of personal letters to Troitsky) is awarded the A. I.

Nevostraev Prize and he is offered a position as acting lecturer to the MDA on the 'History of philosophy'.

August. He moves out of the monastery into a small house on Petropavlovskaia ulitsa in Sergiev Posad.

23 September. After presenting two trial lectures on the 'Cosmological antonyms of Kant' and the 'All-human roots of Idealism' (published Sergiev Posad, 1909), he embarks on his new career as lecturer and, presumably to help contribute to the family budget after the death of his father, undertakes to teach mathematics and cosmography at the Girls' High School at Sergiev Posad.

6 November. He pronounces an address on the burial of Georgii Kharalampiev 'Pap-Kharalampiev'. The first eight 'Letters to a friend' which were to form the larger part of *The Pillars and Ground of Truth* were published in periodicals ('Stolp i utverzhdenie istiny. Pis'ma k drugu', *Voprosy religii*, No. 2, 1908 and 'Stolp i utverzhdenie istiny. Pis'mo vos'moe', *Religiia i zhizn'*, No. 2, 1908). An early pointer towards F's increasing interest in material culture was an article on a phallic monument in the Kotakhevsky Monastery ('Fallicheskii pamiatnik Kotakhevskogo monastyria', *Zhivaia starina*, No. 1, 1908).

1909    Sergei Troitsky's marriage to F's sister Ol'ga precipitates a bout of depression exacerbated by uncertainty as to his academic calling. Still drawn towards the religious life, F is again discouraged from taking monastic vows by his confessor Bishop Antonii and has no wish to marry, a necessary condition of ordination as a priest of the Orthodox Church who is not a professed monk. Unsettled without Isidor and Troitsky in what now seems to him the pharisaic atmosphere of the Academy, he is supported through a difficult period by his old friend El'chaninov and his new friend Vasilii Giatsintov. With El'chaninov, F writes an article on 'Orthodoxy' for the *History of Religion* which comes out that year under the former's editorship. He sees into print the collection of *chastushki* with his own introduction 'Neskol'ko zamechanii k sobraniiu chastushek Kostromskoi gubernii nerektovskogo uezda'. More abstract is an essay on 'The limits of gnoseology' ('Predely gnoseologii. Osnovnaia antinomiia teorii znanii', *Bogslovskii vestnik*, No. 1, 1913) and a review of a book on Russian grammar by A. Vetukhov, *Bogoslovskii vestnik*, No. 5, 1909.

1910    F composes a lively defence of his Platonic teaching methods in 'Lektsia lectio' instead of an introduction to a self-published course of lectures on religion in Ancient Greece, published separately in *Bogoslovskii vestnik*, No. 4, 1910). His doubts on his theological vocation are only resolved by his unexpected marriage on 23 August to Vasilii's sister, Anna Mikhailovna Giatsintova, a village schoolteacher and daughter of a country priest. They move into the slightly larger 'Ozerov's house' on Statnaia ulitsa. On 2 November, Troitsky is murdered by a deranged Georgian student who, in spite of the family's pleas for clemency, is executed. F is reconciled with his sister Ol'ga and his friend's memory.

1911    On 23 and 24 April F is ordained deacon, then priest by Bishop Fedor (Pozdeevsky), the Rector of the MDA and allotted the country parish of Blagoveshchensk near Sergiev Posad while continuing as lecturer. His first son, Vasilii (a geologist), is born 3 June. The last, profoundly personal 'letters' of the *Pillar and Ground of Truth* on 'Friendship' and 'Jealousy' are published 'Druzhba. Iz pisem drugu. Prilozhenie. Ekskurs o revnosti', *Bogoslovskii vestnik*, Nos 1 and 7, 1911.

1912    On 5 April F submits the revised text of *On Spiritual Truth* to the MDA as a Master's dissertation but, on the advice of his supervisor Bishop Fedor, excludes the lyrical passages directly addressed to Troitsky and four chapters on Hell, Sophia, Filiia (the chapter on Friendship) and Jealousy and (as he was afterwards to confess for financial reasons) much of the wide-ranging annotation to the published 'letters'.

28 September. F is confirmed by the Rector as editor of *Bogoslovskii vestnik* (1912–1917).

Finding academic obligations leave him little time for his out-of-town parish, F reluctantly renounces this and accepts, with the approval of Bishop Antonii, to serve first occasionally in the Trinity St Sergius churches and then the cure of the St Mary Magdalene House Church, attached to a home for retired sisters of the Red Cross and patronised by the Tsar's widowed sister-in-law Elizaveta Fedorovna (subsequently canonised), where he continues to serve until 1921.

F's address on the occasion of the twenty-fifth anniversary of Professor Aleksei Ivanovich Vvedensky ('Iz adademicheskoi zhizni 25-letnei iubilei Alekseia Ivanovicha Vvedenskogo', *Bogoslovskii vestnik*, No. 2, 1912) confirms his integration into the ontological school of thought at the MDA and also a new direction of his thought away from the position of catechumen approaching the

Church from the outside (embodied in *The Pillar and Ground of Truth*) towards contemplation of man's place in the world from within the Church.

1913    Over the previous years, from 1906 onwards, F had become increasingly involved with Sergei Bulgakov, who helps him prepare the cumbersome text and notes for the publication of *The Pillar and Ground of Truth* by Put' and involves him in the intellectual and artistic life of Moscow and with the Circle of Seekers after Christian Knowledge, which has evolved around Mikhail Novoselov and his series of books under the imprint of the Religious-Philosophical Library. F, attracted by the fact that content was more important to members of the Circle than individual success, agrees in this year to write anonymous introductions to two highly contro-versial volumes: priest monk Antonii (Bulatovich), *An Apologiia for Faith in the Name of God and the Name of Jesus*, published that year, and the compendium *Israel in the Past Present and Future* published in 1915. His interest in the Jewish question was stirred by correspondence on the subject of blood sacrifice and the Beylis case with Vasilii Rozanov who published anonymously as 'A letter from the Caucasus' a letter F wrote to him on the subject on 28 September and, in notes to *Sakharna*, further letters of October–November on 'Professor Khvol'son and ritual killing' and 'Jews and the fate of Christians'. The introduction to Bulatovich involves F in an ongoing polemic (which he much disliked and endeavoured to render as restrained and impersonal as possible) on the practice of the Jesus prayer, which lasts spasmodically into the 1920s. He is also energetically absorbed in the editorship of *Bogoslovskii vestnik*; in No. 1 he publishes excerpts from his own lectures 'On the limits of gnoseology' and begins the serialisation of A. M. Bukharev's 'Studies of the Apocalypse' (serialised through until 1916), a nineteenth-century work long forbidden by the Synod. To No. 6 he contributes an article on 'The stratification of Aegean culture'.

Unpublished remain his notes to Archbishop's Nikon's attack on 'The great temptation about the Most Holy Name of God' and an article about the foundation of the Trinity St Sergius Monastery 'Na Makovtse', written May–June and intended to serve as an introduction to his next book which he has already named 'On the watersheds of thought' (U vodorazdelov mysli).

Published Master's thesis *On Spiritual Truth* (*O dukhovnoi istine*, Opyt pravoslovnoi teoditsii, Moscow, 1913).

1914            Triumphant oral defence of *On Spiritual Truth* attended by
                Bishop Antonii, Ern, Viacheslav Ivanov and other distinguished
                Muscovites on 19 May leads to the award of a Master's degree and
                confirmation of F's appointment to an extraordinary professorship
                in the Department of the History of Philosophy. The publication
                of *The Pillar and Ground of Truth* (*Stolpi i utverzhdenie istiny*, Put',
                Moscow, 1914), the fuller version of *On Spiritual Truth* complete
                with lyrical passages, copious notes and four missing chapters,
                confirms F's status as one of the leading religious thinkers of his
                age and provides a bridge for many waverers from secular culture
                to acceptance of the Orthodox Church.

                Other publications are his own speech in defence of his Master's
                thesis ('Razum i dialektika. Vstupitel'noe slovo pred zashchitoi
                na stepen' magistra knigi: "O Dukhovnoi Istine", Moscow,
                1913 skazannogo 19ogo maia 1914 goda', *Bogoslovskii vestnik*,
                No. 9, 1914) and a further publication from Mashkin's archive
                ('Pis'ma o Protoiereia Valentina Nikolaevicha Amfiteatrova k
                Ekaterine Mikhailovne i k o Arkhimandritu Serapionu Mashkinu'
                *Bogoslovskii vestnik*, Nos 7–8, 1914).

                August. Declaration of war.

                November. F's sister Ol'ga dies of tuberculosis in Tiflis.

1915            24 January–23 February. F serves at the front as padre to a Red
                Cross train but is discouraged from continued active service by
                Bishop Antonii and by ever-increasing family responsibilities.

                20 April. F and family move to a new house on Dvorianskaia
                (later Pionerskaia) ulitsa, Sergiev Posad.

                Summer. F installs his mother and youngest sister Raisa in a flat
                in Moscow on Novokoniushnyi pereulok (now Ulitsa Burdenko
                16/12, apt. 51). Both these residences are still in possession of his
                descendants.

                14 December. Birth of F's second son Kirill (geo-chemist, astro-
                geologist and mineralogist).

                'The meaning of idealism' ('Smysl' idealizma', *V pamiáti stoletia
                (1814–1914), Imp. MDA Sbornik statei*, T II, Sergiev Posad) is
                published in a centenary collection of articles for the MDA and an
                article sparked by discussion of mystic inspiration with Viacheslav
                Ivanov on the exact meaning of Philippians 2.6–8 ('Ne voskhishchenii
                a nepsheva (Fil. 2.6–8). K suzheniiu o mistike', *Bogoslovskii vestnik*, No.
                7, 1915). Novoselov publishes the collection *Israel in the Past, Present
                and Future* with F's anonymous introduction, based largely on St Paul.

1916     Publications include a controversial pamphlet-review on a new book about the Slavophile Khomiakov (*Okolo Khomiakova*, Sergiev Posad, 1916), which leads to some disagreement with Novoselov and his circle, an obituary for Fedor Dmitrievich Samarin, a founder-member of the circle, ('Fedoru Dmitrievichu Samarinu nekrolog', *Bogoslovskii vestnik*, Nos 10–12) and an article on number symbolism ('Privedenie chisel. K matematicheskomu obosnovaniiu chislovoi simvoliki', *Bogoslovskii vestnik*, No. 6). Unpublished until 1993 was a detailed critique of A. Tuberovsky's Master's thesis 'On the Resurrection of Christ'. The conspect for a lecture on history, genealogy and heredity ('Imia roda: Istoriia, rodoslovie, i nasledstvennost'. Ob istoricheskom poznanii') was first published in the four-volume *Works*. In September–November F begins dictating his memoirs *For My Children*, to which he was to return at intervals for the next ten years.

    That autumn the poet Khlebnikov, on a visit to F at Sergiev Posad, appointed him one of the 'Chairmen of the Globe'.

1917     January. F visits the artist Nesterov with Novoselov, Bulgakov and other Christian thinkers. In May, in the aftermath of the February Revolution, which causes immediate upheaval in Church as well as State, Nesterov paints F and Bulgakov as 'The Philosophers' in the former's garden at Sergiev Posad.

    3 May. F resigns as editor of *Bogoslovskii vestnik*, shocked by the Church's potential for self-destruction evidenced, among other things, by attacks on Bishop Fedor, who was demoted from the Rectorship of the MDA. In the same month he writes the furious 'civic confession' to Bulgakov and, alarmed by the pessimism of L'vov, briefly Procurator of the Holy Synod, begins a series of letters to wife and children, in case the persecution of Christians they already foresee should entail his own death.

    May–June. F adds to his normal academic load a series of lectures on 'The philosophy of Cult' for the Society of Teachers in Moscow.

    Later that summer Vasilii Rozanov, devastated by the closure of the newspaper *Novoe vremia* (his main source of income) and by wartime shortages, seeks shelter with his family in Sergiev Posad. F does all he can to help both materially and spiritually.

    15 August sees the opening of the First Local Council of the Russian Orthodox Church for 217 years. F and Bulgakov are

involved with committees preparing to discuss education of clergy and reconciliation with the Glorifiers of the Name.

22 October. F is invited to join the Commission for the Preservation of Art and Antiquities of the Trinity St Sergius Monastery, on which he serves as learned Secretary and accepts particular responsibility for the Vestiary.

The October coup F regards not so much as the stifling of nascent democracy as the logical outcome of the February Revolution and, indeed, of the whole previous development of bourgeois humanist society.

His last publications in *Bogoslovskii vestnik* mark a return to the unfinished task of propagating the life and works of Serapion Mashkin ('Dannye k zhizneopisaniiu arkh. Serapiona Mashkina' and 'Khronologisheskaia schema zhizni otsa arkhimandrita Serapiona Mashkina', *Bogoslovskii vestnik*, No. 2–3). Cooperation with Sergei Bulgakov produces a publication from manuscripts left by Anna Nikolaevna Shmidt, an eccentric admirer of Vladimir Solov'ev, to which F contributes an introduction (A. N. Shmidt, *Iz rukopisei Anny Nikolaevnoi Shmidt*, Moscow, 1917). Reminiscences of F's friend Vladimir Ern who died that spring appear in the autumn ('Pamiati Vladimira Frantsevicha Erna', *Khristianskaia mysl'*, No. 11–12, 1917) as does a sermon on the Dormition of the Virgin ('Zemnoi put' Bogomateri. Slovo na den' Uspeniia Devy Marii Bogoroditsy', *Vozkhozhdenie*, No. 10, 1917).

A posthumously published essay on 'The term' marks a growing interest in signs, terms and symbols. Unpublished too during F's lifetime remained 'The concept of form' ('Poniatie formy') and an MDA in-house piece on a dispute ('K istorii odnogo disputa v Moskovskoi Dukhovnoi Akademii'').

1918        This year sees the nationalisation, in accordance with the decree of 20 January (12 February), of the Trinity St Sergius Monastery which entails the expulsion of the MDA, for which F continues to lecture first at the Donskoi, then at the Petrov Monasteries in Moscow. On 29 March (11 April) the State orders that the casket containing St Sergius' remains should be opened and confiscated for scientific examination. This last cannot have been too rigorous as on the 28 March (10 April) F and other select members of the Commission, sworn to secrecy, substituted the head of a contemporary prince for that of the Saint, which was concealed (originally in the vestiary) and restored to its proper place when the holy relics were returned and the monastery reopened after the Second World War. Meanwhile, F's work for the Commission consists in the cataloguing of treasures, preservation of sacred artefacts and preparing as smooth a transition as possible from working monastery to State museum. Over the next two years this work inspires (directly or indirectly) some of F's best-known pieces on art, cult and culture, none of which unless otherwise stated below were published during his lifetime. Written in 1918 were 'The Trinity St Sergius Monastery and Russia' ('Troitse-Sergieva Lavra i Rossiia' in the book *Troitse-Sergieva Lavra*, Sergiev Posad, 1919); 'A project for the Troitse-Sergieva Lavra Museum' (written 26 February, first published 1984); 'Paths and points of concentration' ('Puti i sredotochiia', first published 1986); 'Church Service as a synthesis of the arts' ('Khramovoe deistvie kak sintez iskusstv', *Makovets*, No. 1, 1922); 'Dialectics' ('Dialektika', revised 1922, first published 1999); 'Symbolic description' ('Simvolicheskoe opisanie', *Feniks*, No. 1, 1922); 'The antimony of language' ('Antinomiia iazyka', first published 1986); and six articles written in May for the cycle 'The philosophy of Cult', first published 1977: 'The fear of God' ('Strakh Bozhii'); 'Cult and philosophy' ('Kul't i filosofiia'); 'Cult, religion and culture' ('Kul't, religiia i kul'tura'); 'Sacrament and rites' ('Tainstvo i obriady'); 'The hallowing of reality' ('Osviashchenie real'nosti'), plus an article on the seven sacraments ('Deduktsiia semi tainstv').

21 February. Birth of F's first daughter and third child Ol'ga Pavlovna (botanist, m. Sergei Zosimovich Trubachev in 1946).

1919  F continues to lecture and to prepare for the Church Council. In spite of the fact that the session of the Council from 19 June (2 July) until 7 (20) September 1918 was to prove the last, it is still hoped that Patriarch Tikhon will be able to foregather further sessions in 1919 and 1920, a hope shattered by Bolshevik confiscation of Church lands, funds and property and by the fluctuating fortunes of Civil War and extreme hardship and disruption undergone by all sections of the population during the period of War Communism. The question of reform in Theological Institutes of Higher Education was thus never discussed for lack of time, and the Committee to consider the Name of God controversy never met, but F continued work on both these questions into 1920. To support his ever-increasing family, he takes on work at the Sergiev Institute of Popular Education, teaching junior physics, managing the laboratory and organising courses in geometry, maths, astronomy and the history of material culture.

The spate of publications on religion and art continues. He completes the article 'Venerated icons of St Sergius' ('Molennye ikony prepodobnogo Sergiia', first published 1969) begun the previous year, writes the seminal 'Reverse perspective' ('Obratnaia perspektiva', first published 1967) and the beautiful 'Celestial signs' ('Nebesnye znameniia. Razmyshleniia o simvolike svetov', *Makovets*, No. 2, 1922) in October. From March to April he continues dictating reminiscences of his childhood, first published by the journal *Literaturnaia ucheba* in 1988 then in *For My Children* (*Detiam moim*, 1992).

The year also sees the first of many publications on applied physics, a hectograph entitled 'Vychislenie vektora elektricheskogo polia na vilkakh obmotki transformatora', Moscow, 1919 ('Calculation of the electric field vector on the coils of transformer windings').

1920      20 April sees the enactment of Lenin's decree 'For turning the Trinity St Sergius Lavra into a museum'. As secretary to the Commission for Preservation of Art and Antiquities F prepares a report on their activities ('Doklad k kommissii po okhrane pamiatnikov iskusstva i stariny Troitse-Sergeevoi Lavry', first published 1984) for the Department for the Affairs of Museums and Preservation of Works of Art and Antiquities of Narkompross (People's Commissariat for Education) where A. S. Kocharsky is acting Commissar for the preservation of the monastery, which is also cared for by the Byzantine Section of MKhIM (Moscow Historico-artistic Research and Museums). A book sponsored by these departments and prepared by the commission is, however, banned and the typeset broken up.

May–July. F continues dictating his memoirs (the chapters 'Pristan' i bul'var' and 'Osobennoe') and, over the summer, works with Professor I. F. Ognev on the uses of an ultramicroscope in the Histological Institute at Moscow University.

14 September. F is appointed specialist on silver and artistically wrought metal at the new Lavra Museum and at about the same time begins work as consultant to Carbolit as head of the department of experiments in production at their factory and, in general, of scientific and technical experiments. Begins work in Moscow as instructor on higher scientific research courses.

All this time he continues to lecture at the MDA, constantly renewing and updating the content of his lectures, and in June–July he writes a key article on language 'The word as magic' ('Magichnost' slova', not published until 1988).

1921      On 9/22 January F transfers to the State Planning Commission for the Electrification of the Soviet Union (Glavelektro VSNKh RSFSR – further Glavelektro), where he is occupied in research. That October he attends the Thirteenth Electrotechnical Conference to discuss the plan submitted by GOELRO wearing his usual cassock. At the instigation of his friend the artist Vladimir Favorsky he is elected to read weekly lectures on 'Analysis of space in art works' in the radical Higher Art and Technical Studios (Vkhutemas), where the cassock sparks a mocking couplet from Vladimir Maiakovsky. His autumn course of lectures for the MDA, now in the Petrov Monastery, is entitled 'The cultural-historical place of the Christian world view', notes towards which are published in *Works*. For one of these places of employment he compiles a curriculum vitae (first published in 1982) and he completes a report on the Name of God controversy for the Church Council which never met ('Ob imeni Bozhem', first published in *Works*). The hectograph published in 1919 is accepted under a slightly modified title by Glavelektro's *Bulletin*: 'Calculation of the electric gradient on the coils of transformer windings' ('Vychislenie elektricheskogo gradienta na vitkax obmotki transformatora', *Biuleten' texnicheckogo otdela glavelektro*, Seriia IV, Moscow, 1921).

October 26. Birth of F's third son Mikhail (Mika) (a geologist).

1922      Continues to work for Carbolit in various departments (mechanical, chemical, sector of high-voltage technology and experimental) and to lecture in Vkhutemas and joins the art group Makovets.

In January he finishes the long article 'Iconastasis' on which he had been working since 1917 ('Ikonostasis', first published 1969). F also returns to the unpublished university study 'Imaginary points in geometry' and publishes this with a cover by Favorsky and appendices, an explanation of the cover and a reconsideration of Dante's arrangement of space in the *Divine Comedy* in the light of the new geometry (*Mnimosti v geometrii*, Pomor'e, Moscow, 1922).

The independent publisher Pomor'e announces the preparation for publication of F's new religious-philosophical book 'On the watersheds of thought' and it is towards this book that, over the summer and on into the autumn, he writes a series of articles which embody his current range of interests considered from the point of view of a practising Churchman. He returns once more to the Name of God question ('Imiaslavie kak filososkaia predposylka', first published 1988), writes remarkably on martyrdom in the article 'Witnesses' ('Svideteli', first published 1977), and on linguistics and religion ('Slovesnoe sluzhenie. Molitva', first published 1977; 'Stroenie Slova', first published 1972 and 'Itogi', first published 1974). Another series on man as toolmaker and man in the Economy, material and divine, was completed this year ('Homo Faber', first published 1984; 'Prodolzhenie nashikh chuvstv', first published 1992; 'Organoproektsia', first published with Commissions in 1969, completely in *Works*; 'Khoziaistvo', first published 1992; 'Makrokozm I mikrokozm', first published in 1983). 'Pythagoran numbers' ('Pifagorevye chisla' written in October 1922, first published 1971) also inspires a cover by Favorsky to a book they intend to call Number as Form (Chislo kak forma) but which does not materialise. Collaboration between artist and thinker also result in two pencil portraits of F and an ex-libris.

1923          F finishes the 'Will' or 'Letters to my children' he had begun in 1917 (eventually published in *For My Children*, 1977) and works hard on his memors, completing chapters on 'Religion' and 'Nature' in April–May and on 'Science' in November–December.

A belated fruit of his work with the Commission is a detailed description of the Lavra's collection of Panagii, ornamental pendants with relief depictions of the Theotokos, or Christ, or, occasionally, Saints of the Church worn by priests (*Opis' panagii Sergeevoi Lavry XII - XIX vekov*, Sergiev Posad, 1923). An article 'On realism' ('O realizme', first published in *Works*) shows an ongoing concern for artistic questions and the brilliant introduction to a 'Symbolarium', projected but never realised with Bely and Voloshin ('Symbolarium (Slovar' simvolov). Predislovie', first published 1971). More directly concerned with Church affairs are 'Note on old ritualism' ('Zapiska o staroobriadchestve', first published 1990) and 'Meditations on the death of Father Aleksei Mechev' ('Rassuzhdenie na sluchai konchiny otsa Alekseia Mecheva', first published 1966).

14 May. A visit from a representative of the American Red Cross, Mr Coulton, offers a chance to make the voice of Russian Christian culture heard in other parts of the world and F gives

him, to accompany an article by his old teacher Lopatin who had died in 1920, an article on Orthodoxy ('Zapiska o pravoslavii', first published in *Works*) and another on 'Christianity and culture' which was published in Coulton's translation in *The Pilgrim*, No. 4, 1924, a journal edited by William Temple, then Bishop of Manchester.

In this year F begins work on 'Names' ('Imena') and publishes two technical articles: 'On the formulation of the laws of electromagnetism' and 'Experimental studies of electric fields' ('O formulirovke zakonov elektromagnetizma' *Elektrichestvo*, No. 11 and 'Eksperimental'noe issledovanie elektricheskikh polei', *Elektrichestvo*, 1923, No. 7/8).

1924        Spiritual crisis. The closure of the retirement home for Red Cross sisters has left F without a parish and, though he continues to concelebrate in various Moscow churches, he is no longer in a position to support his family as a priest. In applied physics, however, he goes from strength to strength, and this year, is forced to face up to the fact that he will not complete or publish 'On the watersheds of thought' (to which so much of his recent work was to have contributed) under Soviet rule and should therefore devote his energies to the activities for which he is in demand. He is elected member of the Central Electrotechnical Soviet at Glavelektro VSNk SSSR, begins work in the Moscow United Committee of Electrotechnical Norms and Rules (MOKEN) and participates in a Special Soviet for Improvement of the Quality of Production.

June. F completes a piece on Father Aleksei Mechev (first published 1990) and continues a meditation on art which has occupied him since 1921 *The Law of Illusion* (*Zakon illiuzii*, first published 1971). Of more immediate benefit to his household are the book on the technical application of Dialectrics (*Dialektriki i ikh tekhnicheskoe primenenie*, Moscow, 1924) and two articles for technical journals: 'Space, mass and medium' and 'Ultramicroscope with shear' ('Prostranstvo, macca, sreda', *Elektrichestvo*, No. 8 and 'Ultra-mikroskop so sdvigom', *Tekhniko-ekonomicheskii vestnik*, No. 5).

He stops teaching at the Vkhutemas.

11 October. Birth of last and fifth child Maria (Tin-a-Tin) (chemist).

In this year the artist V. A. Komarovsky makes three portraits of F.

1925          Appointed director of the Department of the Science of Materials (Materialovedenia) in the State Experimental Electrotechnical Institute (GEEN) and, in early summer, is sent by GEEN to the Caucasus to investigate the possibilities of producing sintered basalt, taking with him the two elder boys. August–September he returns to dictating his reminiscences, the chapter ('Obval', ('landslide') first published 1977) and finishes writing up the course of lectures on pictorial space for Vkhutemas (*Analiz prostranstvennosti v khudozhestvenno-izobrazitel'nykh proizvedeniiakh*, first published 1993). Preaches a sermon on the occasion of a memorial service for soldiers fallen in war ('Slovo pered panikhidoi ob usopshikh voinakh', published only in the book by S. L. Kravec, *O krasote dukhovnoi. P. A. Florenskii: religiozno-nravstvennye vozreniia*, Znanie, Moscow, 1990). As usual, technical publications fare better and include 'World energy resources' ('Zapasy mirovoi energii', *Elektrifikatsia*, No. 1); 'New research in electrochemistry of cells and rechargeable batteries' ('Novye raboty v elektrokhimike elmentov i akkumuliatorov', *Elektrichestvo*, No. 6); hectograph on 'The preparation of sintered basalt' ('Proizvodstvo plavlennogo bazal'ta', Moscow, 1925); 'Technical standards on insulating materials (composites) for filling cable-boxes of strong-current cables for low- and high-voltage up to 11 K volts'. ('Tekhnichoskie usloviia na izoliruiushchie sostavy (kompoundy) dlia zalivki muftkabelei sil'nogo toka nizkogo i vysokogo napriazheniia', *Elektrichestvo*, No. 9).

1926          Continues work for GEEN, which he represents at a conference from 9–11 November 'On sources of electric current', where he reads a paper on electric cell manufacturing ('Po elementnomu delu' published in a hectographed book of the proceedings, Moscow, 1927). On 12 December spoke in Petrograd at a solemn congress to mark the fiftieth anniversary of the Iablochkov electric cell and published a paper on Iablochkov's achievement ('Zaslugi P. N. Iablochkova v elementnom dele', *Elektrichestvo*, No. 12). He continues work begun in 1924 on names (*Imena*, first published 1993) and concludes an 'Autobiographical note' for the *Encyclopaedic Dictionary* of the Russian Bibliographical Institute ('Avtoreferat', *Entsiklopedicheskii slovar' russkogo bibliograficheskogo Instituta*, 1927, published here with some excisions).

1927    Begins work for the *Technical Encyclopedia*, to which, from 1927–1934, he contributes according to some sources 127, to others 134 entries, and acts as co-editor to vols 1–12 and to vol. 26.

On visits to Fedor Andreev in Petrograd makes friends with pianist Maria Iudina.

The publication of a book co-authored with Count Olsuf'ev, one-time chairman of the Commission for Preservation of Art and Antiquities in the Trinity St Sergius Monastery on 'Ambrose, fifteenth-century wood-carver in the Trinity Monastery' (*Amvrosii, troitskii rezchik XV veka*, Sergiev Posad, 1927) provides ammunition for a virulent campaign in the press against the Commission and all its works, particularly the further involvement of ex-members ('various counts and barons') in the running of the museum.

Less controversial publications include 'Hailstones the size of a hen's egg' ('Gradi s kurinnogo iaitsa', *Priroda*, No. 7/8) 'On the porocity of insulator porcelain' (*Poristost' izoliatornogo farfora*, Moscow, 1927); 'Sunspots during an eclipse ('Solnechnye piatna vo vremie zamenia', *Priroda*, No. 7/8); 'Table for functional classification of galvanic elements and batteries' ('Tablitsa funktsional'noi klassifikatsii galvanicheskikh elementov i baterei', *Vestnik standartizatsii*, No. 6).

1928    F continues work on Volumes 2–4 of *Technical Encyclopedia* as author and editor.

In the spring the press campaign against ex-members of the Commission leads to a series of arrests under suspicion of a Church-sponsored, counter-revolutionary, monarchist plot. The Piatnitskaia and Vvedenskaia churches, served by ex-monks of the monastery, are closed down and the close community of sympathisers scattered, exiled to various parts of the Soviet Union. F offered the choice of all places 'minus five', selects Nizhnii Novgorod, where he lives and continues to work during the months of June, July and August. At the intervention of E. P. Peshkova, warmly supported by editors of the *Technical Dictionary* and functionaries of GEEN, the three-year term of exile is lifted and in September F is restored to his position as director of the Department of Science Materials.

Publishes the book *Carbolite: Its production and properties* (*Karbolit. Ego proizvodstvo i svoistva*, M, 1928); contributions to the *Technical Encyclopedia* and (on asbestos and asphalt and antiseptics for wood) in the *Large Medical Encyclopedia*. 'Some comments on product quality control' ('Neskol'ko zamechanii ob otsenke kachestva produktsii', *Vestnik teoreticheskoi in eksperimental'noi electrotekhniki*, No. 11); with A. Slavatinsky 'New "deposit" of meteorite iron' ('Novaia "zalezh" meteoritnogo zheleza', *Priroda*, No. 14); 'New data on cosmic rays' ('Novye dannye o kosmicheskikh luchakh', *Priroda*, No. 11); 'New thermoelement containing selenium' (Novyi termoelement s cerelom', *Priroda*, No. 12); 'On the economy of electric-battery zinc' (Ekonomiia elementnogo tsinka', *Vestnik teoreticheskoi i eksperimental'noi elektrotekhniki*, No. 1).

1929      F jests that he has returned from exile to forced labour, so intense are the pressures of his scientific work.

            15–19. Takes part in first All-Union Conference on Electro-isolating Materials.

            June. Conference on graphite.

            July. Further conferences.

            Publications include volumes 5–9 of the *Technical Dictionary*, 'From the history of non-Euclidean geometery' ('Iz istorii neevklidovoi geometrii', *Priroda*, No. 3); 'On streamlining of mounting and filling of cable-boxes' ('K voprosu o ratsionalizatsii montazha i zalivki kabel'nykh muft', *Vestnik eksperimental'noi i teoreticheskoi electrotekhniki*, No. 1); 'On the dialectric constants of dialectrics being unaffected by ionising radiation' (Nezavisimost' dielektricheskogo ko-effitsienta dialektrikov ot radioaktivnogo vozdeistviia', *Priroda*, No. 5). With N. D. Niuberg', 'A new technique for estimating the brittleness of pressed electroshag' ("Novyi metod otsenki lomkosti elektrotekhnicheskogo presshaka', *Vestnik teoreticheskoi i eksperimental'noi elektrotekhniki*, No. 2); 'Triboelectricity in metals' (Triboelektrichestvo metallov', *Priroda*, No. 4); with V. M. Moiseev '[Electric] cell electrodes with reduced surface' (Elementnye elektrody sokrashchennoi poverkhnosti', *Vestnik teoreticheskoi i eksperimental'noi elektrotekhniki*, No. 2); with A. S. Slavatinsky 'Electrode coals' ('Elementnye ugli', *Vestnik eksperimental'noi i teoreticheskoi elektrotekhniki*, No. 6).

1930      5 January. Appointed assistant scientific director to K. A. Krug in scientific matters for the All-Union Electric Institute.

            Continues to work in the Department of the Science of Materials in GEEN (now VEI) and takes over leading roles in the technical departments dealing with vacuum, x-ray, measurement and light.

Publications include: Volumes 10–12 of the *Technical Encyclopedia* (for all but the last of which he was the responsible editor and to which he made many contributions):

- an article in the Proceedings of the 1929 Conference of 15–19 May with N. German and M. Mantrov on 'The importance of surface effects for the durability of mica' ('Znachenie poverkhostnykh iavlenii v sluzhbe sliudy', *Voprosy izoliatsii v elektotekhnike. Trudy Konferentsii po elektro izoliruiushchim materialam*, Moscow-Leningrad, 1930;
- 'Observations concerning surface properties of mica' ('Nabliudeniia v oblasti poverkhnostnykh svoistv sliudy', *Vestnik elektrotekhniki*, No. 2);
- 'Studies on graphite at the All-Union Electrotechnical Research Institute' ('Raboty po grafitu vo Vsesoiuznom elektrotekhniche-skom nauchno-issledovatel'skom institute', *Gornyi Zhurnal*);
- with N. Z. Dnestrovsky 'Splicing of iron [electric] cables ('Srashchivanie zheleznykh provodov', *Vestnik elektrotekhniki*, No. 9/10;
- with N. D. Niuberg, 'Temperature limits for using iron-nickel alkali rechargeable batteries' ('Temperaturnye granitsy primen-imosti shchelochnykh zhelezenikalevykh akkumuliatorov', *Vestnik eletrotekhniki*, No. 3);
- with P. A. Kremlevsky, 'Feroxyl test of reliability of nickel and tin protective films on iron surfaces' ('Feroksilovoe ispytanie nadezhnosti nikelevykh i olovianykh zashchitnykh plenok po poverkhnosti zheleza', *Vestnik elektrotekhniki*, No. 9/10);
- with K. T. Metel'kind and V. V. Maksorov 'Electrochemical method for preparing anthrahydroquinone' ('Elektro-khimicheskii sposob polucheniia antragidrokhanona', *Vestnik elektrotekhniki*, No. 11/12).

1931    20–24 February. F takes part in All-Union Conference on Electro-isolating Materials.

May, June, July. F travels with a VEI expedition to study deposits of graphite in Marioupol, iron ore in Kerch and manganese in Tiflis and Chiatura. Publications include:
- entries for Vols 13–15 of the *Technical Encyclopedia*;
- with M. A. Tserevitinov a piece on the porosity of isolating porcelain which is a conspect of a paper sent to the Second International Conference on Energetics in Berlin, 1930 ('Poristost' izoliatornogo farfora. Kratkoe izlozhenie doklada

na 2-oi mezhdunarodnoi Konferetitsii po energetike v Berline',
*Elektrotekhnicheskii zhurnal*, No. 3/4);

- with R. A. Andrianov, also on 'The stability of organic dielectics towards acids' ('Kislotostoikost' organicheskikh dielektrikov', *Elektretekhnicheskii zhurnal*, No. 3/4 and No. 5/6);

- 'Manganese ore for galvanic elements' (Margantsevaia ruda dlia galvanicheskikh elementov', *Eletrotekchnicheskii zhurnal*, No. 9);

- with B. V. Maksorov, 'New material for preparation of plastics for surrogating ebonite (using sawdust and slate sand)' (Surrogatirovanie ebonite pomoshch'iu drevesnogo i slant-sevogo peskov' *Elektrotekhnicheskii zhurnal*, No. 3/4);

- with K. A. Andrianov and V. Maksorov 'New material for the preparation of plastic mass for surrogating ebonite' ('Novyi material dlia izgotovlenia plasticheskikh mass, surrogat-iruiushchikh ebonit'), in the book of conference proceedings Programma i tezisy 2-i konferensii po elektro-izoliruiushchim materialam 20–24 fevralia', Moscow, 1931;

- with K. T. Metelkin, 'On electro-catalytic oxidation of anthracene to anthraquinone' ('Ob elektrokalichiaticheskom okislenii antratsena i antrakhinon', *Anilinokrasornaia promysh-lennost*, No. 8);

- with N. V. Aleksandrov and N. M. Shul'gin, 'Experiments on wood modification' ('Opyty oblagorazhivaniia drevesiny', *Elektrotekhnicheskii zhurnal*, No. 5/6);

- with N. V. Vorontsov, 'On manufacturing special lighting coal [electrodes] giving intense ultraviolet radiation' (Proizvodstvo spetsial'nykh osvetitel'nykh uglei, bogatykh ultravioletovymi luchami', *Eksperimental'nyi zhurnal*, No. 11/12);

- 'Decomposition of cable-impregnating substances, Voltaisation, drilling for isolating oils', ('Razlozhenie propitki kabelei vol'talizatsiia, proboi izoliatsionnykh masel', *Vestnik Elektrotekhniki*, No. 5/6);

- and with M. I. Mantrov and D. Z. Budnitskii, 'Electrical breakdown properties of Soviet ores' ('Elektricheskaia krepost' soiuznykh rud', *Vestnik Elektrotekhniki*, 5/6).

1932      27 February. The editing and publishing sector of the management of the Soviet Air Force (RKKA) signs a contract with F to publish a course on electrotechnical material science for electro- and radio-technicians' (*Kurs elektrotekhnicheskogo materialovedenie dlia elektro i radiotekhnikov*).

On 4 May F is included by the Soviet of Labour and Defence in their Commission for the Standardisation of Scientifico-technical Terms. He is now living during the week with his sons Vasilii and Kirill in a flat provided by his employers on Prolomnyi pereulok, House 43, Korpus 3, Flat 12, Lefortovo, Moscow and, even in the train to and from Sergiev Posad (or Zagorsk as it is now called) is remembered as invariably deep in conversation, engrossed in books or correcting proofs.

Volume 16 of the *Technical Encyclopedia* comes out co-edited by F and 17–18 with many entries by him. He contributes to a *Compendium of Data on Cotton and Fibre for Isolation*, Leningrad, 1932 and publishes articles: 'Physics in the service of mathematics' ('Fizika na sluzhbe matematiki', *Sotsialisticheskaia rekonstruktsia i nauka*, Issue 8). Other publications are:

- 'Rechargeable battery containers' ('Akkumuliatornye baki', *Generator*, No. 5(36), 15 April);
- 'Asbestos for rechargeable battery containers' ('Asbest dlia akkumuliatornykh bakov' in Issue I of *Sbornik tsentral'noi akkumuliatornoi laboratorii*);
- with M. Voronov, 'A cheap source of ultraviolet radiation' ('Deshevyi istochnik ultravioletovoi radiatsii', *Sotsialisticheskaia rekonstruktsia i nauka*, Issue 3);
- with M. I. Mantrov, K. A. Makarov and I. G. Machina, 'On the subject of turbine generator disasters' ('K voprosu ob avariiakh turbogeneratorov', *Teoreticheskaia i eksperimental'naia elektrotekhnika*, No. 3);
- 'New materials from maize waste' ('Novye materially iz otkhodov kukuruzy', *Plasticheskie massy*, No. 1);
- with M. Voronov, 'On manufacturing special lighting coal [electrodes] giving intense ultra-violet radiation' ('Proizvodstvo spetsial'nykh osvetitel'nykh uglei, bogatykh ul'tra-filetovoi radiatsiei', *Novosti tekhniki*, No. 2);
- with M. Shik (also a priest), 'Standards of chemical composition and physico-chemical constants in the USA' ('Etalony khimicheskoi sostavi i fiziko-khimicheskikh konstant v SA SSh', *Sotsialisticheshiia rekonstruktsia i nauka*, No. 9/10);
- and two reviews of German technical publications: 'Anwendungen der matematischen statistik auf Probleme der Massenfabrikation', Verlag von J. Springer, Berlin, 1930 and N.

Stäger, 'Elektrotechnische Isoliermaterialen', Stuttgart, 1931 in
*Sotsialisticheskaia rekonstruktsia i nauka*, Issue 3 and Issue 1
respectively.

1933      Night of 25–26 February. F is arrested by order of OGPU at his flat
in Lefortovo, Moscow.

26 February–8 August. F is held in the Butyrka Prison.

4–6 March. Signed confessions made by F to trumped-up
charge of acting as ideologist to a monarchist-fascist conspiracy
preparing to invite and cooperate with a German take-over of the
Soviet Union, supported by monks, priests and 'Soviets without
Bolsheviks' ...

16 March. Completed *Presumed Organisation of the Future
State* which represents as it were the manifesto of the conspirators
but has been published by *Literaturnain ucheba* in 1991 and again
in *Works*.

26 July. F condemned by a special *troika* of judges under Article
58 to ten years' hard labour.

8 August. F dispatched for Eastern Siberian camp at Svobodnyi.

17–21 August. Halt at Sverdlovsk.

21 August–16 September. Transport continues from Sverdlovsk
to Irktusk.

23 September–1 October. Move from Irktusk to Ksenevskaia.

1 October–29 November. At camp in Altai hills, Ksenevskaia.

At Ksenevskaia, where the possibility of working on permafrost
is first mooted, F conceives the idea for a long poem about a son of
the Syberian people, the Orochen', later called 'Oro' and dedicated
to his youngest son Mika, on which he continues work until 1937.
First published by Paideia, Moscow, 1998.

12 December. F arrives at Svobodnyi where he is temporarily
housed in *barak* No. 4 and remains until February of the following
year while a direction that he is to work on an experimental
station researching permafrost for the scientific department of
Bamlag is duly processed.

Martens, the editor-in-chief of the *Technical Encyclopedia*,
intercedes in vain for F, but his articles continue to come out
in volumes 19–22 as does an article 'Calculation of the electric
gradient on the coils of transformer windings ('Vychislenie
elektricheskogo gradienta na vitkakh obmotki transformatora',
*Zhurnal tekhnicheskoi Fiziki*, 13, Issue I) and a review of another
German book, *Organ der Gesellschaft deutscher Naturforscher*

*und Arzte und Organ der Kaiser-Wilhelm Gesellshaft*, J. Springer, Berlin, 20 Jahrgang, in *Sotsialisticheskaia rekonstruktsiia i nauka*, Issue I).

1934      10 February. F sent to the permafrost experimental station at Skovorodino.

20 February. F arrives at Skovorodino where he remains until 1 September.

February/March/April. F works intensively with his friend, colleague and fellow-*zek* P. N. Kapterev on two papers 'On the freezing of water in laboratory experiments' and 'Observations on the freezing of water in natural conditions' ('O zamerzanii vody po laboratornym opytam' and 'Nabliudeniia nad zamerzaniem vody v prirodnykh usloviiakh') which are dispatched to the Academy of Sciences.

April. F begins to write the poem 'Oro' and to collect materials towards a dictionary of the Orochen' language.

10–18 April. F sent from the Skovorodino station on the Baikal-Amur (BAM) line of rail to study lake and river ice and the effect of permafrost on prospecting shafts in gold-mining, on minerals and on trees. Delivers seven lectures and conducts five seminars on permafrost.

End April–early May. Second journey to Strelka on the BAM line of rail.

1 May. F lectures on permafrost at an official reception at Strelka.

May–June. F works on ice formations and towards a book *Permafrost and Building thereon* eventually published under the names of P. N. Kapterev and N. I. Bykov (the head of the Skovorodino station) as *Vechnaia merzlota i stroitel'stvo na nei*, Moscow, 1940.

July–August. Helped by E. P. Peshkova, Anna Mikhailovna brings her three youngest children to visit F at Skovorodino. There is real hope that, if the Soviet Government could be persuaded to release him abroad, F and his family would find refuge in Czechoslovakia, but he himself discourages these negotiations.

16/17 August. F recalled under escort to Svobodnyi.

17 August–1 September. F in solitary confinement in Svobodnyi.

1 September. F dispatched for Solovki.

12 September. F detained in solitary confinement in Medvezhaia Gora.

13 October. F arrived at Kem' where he remains until 23 October.

23 October. F arrives at Solovki where he is detained in the 'quarantine quarters' until 15 November.

15 November. F dispatched to work for Iodprom (the processing of seaweed for iodine) at their 'laboratory', where he introduces work on agar-agar and for which he produces more than ten patented discoveries and inventions. Remains at the laboratory in comparatively tolerable conditions until the following year.

Volume 23 of the *Technical Encyclopedia* comes out this year still with entries by F. He requests his family to negotiate with publishers to bring out any works of his in their portfolios anonymously but to pay monies owing to his wife and meticulously contributes any small premiums earned in the camps to the family budget.

1935    10 January. F delivers a lecture on the problems of the seaweed industry on Solovki and that same month gives several lectures on mathematics to the prisoners' mathematical circle.

16 January. F moved back into large cell for 21 people in Kremlin.

30 January. Trial of apparatus for filtering iodine invented by F.

16 February–29 August. F quartered in the chemical laboratory situated in Phillipov Pustyn (Phillip's Hermitage) in relative peace and quiet with other scientists.

29 August–27 September. F is moved to the Old Forge outside the Kremlin.

27 September–1 October. F back in a large cell for 32 people in Kremlin.

1 October–20 February 1936. F in a small cell for 4–5 people in the Nikol'sky Korpus of the Kremlin.

1936    20/21 February–15 December. F lives in a room for 5–6 people above the Iodprom factory with windows onto a lake called Bannoe Ozero. He is constantly on duty to tend the Heath Robinson machinery but finds time in March for a course of lectures on the technology and chemistry of the seaweed industry and to organise a special course for his workers.

15 December. F is moved into a separate room with view over the Kremlin in an old wing of the Agar Factory (previously the Leather Factory).

Towards the end of the year, production targets are set impossibly high and no more improvements are made to the machinery in preparation for the closure of all productive work and the transformation of the Solovki Labour Camp to a prison.

1937   13 June. The factory is closed down and F is moved to a cell for 40 fellow-ex-Iodprom workers, who, as he tells his wife, he tries to think of as his children, his only 'place' a bunk bed between an Armenian farmer and a Chechen mullah. With the cessation of production, rations get tighter.

3–4 June. Family informed that he has been resentenced to 'ten years without right of correspondence'.

19 July. F's last letter to his family from Solovki is received.

25 November. A special *troika* of TsNKVD of the Leningrad region condemns him to death. With other condemned prisoners he is moved again to Keleinyy Korpus at Sel'diany Gates.

2–3 December. F and 1,115 other condemned men are moved to the mainland.

8 December. Sentence is carried out. As one of three-at-a-time executions F is shot in the back of the head in a cellar used for this purpose and his body buried in a mass grave in Toksovo, 30 kilometres from Leningrad. Executed with him were Kornilii Timofeevich Stoliarov, a priest's son (b. 1892) and Khasan Abdulkadyrov, a Chechen (also b. 1892), who had served as a lieutenant in the Tsar's Army.

His family were not informed.

1958–59   F was rehabilitated by Moscow Town Judiciary and Archangel Regional Judiciary, the original case against him being declared without basis in fact and fundamentally flawed in the way it was conducted.

1958   The Nevsky ZAGS (for registration of births, deaths and marriages) gave his family an erroneous date of death 'for unknown reasons' 15 December 1943.

1989   24 November. F's family are finally issued with a death certificate for 'Citizen Florensky, Pavel Aleksandrovich, d. 8 December 1937 ... cause of death – 'execution by shooting'.

The certificate, issued by the ZAGS of the Kalinin district of

Moscow, made it possible for researchers to gain access to the now well-known prison photograph and Xerox copies of some pages of the transcript of the investigation in 1933. Gradually, energetic research has produced the details of Florensky's last days recorded above, the absence of which, like all unexplained 'disappearances', had by then already created a web of legend.

# Glossary of Names

**Ageev, Konstantin (1868–1919)**, liberal priest involved with the Circle of 32, the Union of Church Renewal and the Christian Brotherhood for Struggle.

**Akhmatova, Anna (real name Anna Andreevna Gorenko) (1880–1966)**, Russian poet.

**Aleksandrova-Dol'nik, Tatiana Nikolaevna (1882–after 1934)**, member of the Commission for the Preservation of Art and Antiquities of the Trinity St Sergius Monastery 1918–1920, Specialist on and restorer of antique embroidery, later worked for the Tretiakov Gallery. Precise year of death not established.

**D'Almeida, Joseph Charles (1822–1880)**, French physicist renowned for his contributions to the theory of photography. Founder-editor of the *Journal de physique théoretique et appliquée* from 1872.

**Anatolii, Prepodobnyi (Potapov, Aleksei Alekseevich) (1855–1922)**, *starets* of the Optyno-Pustyn Monastery.

**Anaxagorus (*c.* 500–*c.* 428 BC)**, Greek philosopher, scientist and astronomer, tutor of Pericles and Euripedes.

**Andersen, Hans Christian (1805–1875)**, Danish writer of fairytales.

**Andreev, Fedor Konstantinovich (1887–1929)**, member of the Circle of Seekers after Christian Knowledge and pupil of Florensky's at the MDA. After ordination he served as a priest in Petrograd, where he adhered to the so-called Iosifliane, who opposed the Locum Tenens Metropolitan Sergii's compromises with the Soviet authorities. Thought by some to be the author of the controversial 'O Bloke' attributed by others to Florensky.

**Andreeva Natalia Nikolaevna (1897–1970)**, wife of **Fedor Andreev**.

**Andronik, Igumen (Aleksandr Sergeevich Trubachev) (b. 1952)**, son of Florensky's daughter **Ol'ga**. Active in research on his grandfather's heritage, author of *Teoditsiia i antropoliditsiia v tvorchestve Pavla Florenskogo*, Vodolei, Tomsk, 1998 and *Obo mne ne pechal'tes', zhizneopisanie sviahchennika Pavla Florenskogo*, Izdatel'skii Sovet Russkoi Pravoslavnoi Tserkvi, Moscow, 2007.

**Antonii, Bishop (Mikhail Semenovich Florensov) (1847–1918)**, Bishop and *starets* living retired in the Donskoy Monastery where **Bely** met him in 1903 and introduced Florensky to him in 1904. Advised Florensky to study in the Theological Academy and remained his spiritual advisor until his death.

**Antonii, Metropolitan (Aleksandr Pavlovich Khrapovitskii) (1863–1936)**, Metropolitan of Kiev and Galich 1917–1918. Conservative but independently minded hierarch, theologian and administrator. Rector of the Kiev Theological Academy in the years between the revolutions and editor of their journal *Vera i razum*. On good terms personally with Florensky, they took opposite sides in the 'Name of God' controversy. Emigrated in 1920 and became head of the Russian Church in Exile from 1922–1936.

**Antonii, Metropolitan (Aleksandr Vasilievich Vadkovskii) (1846–1912)**, liberal churchman and supporter of the Religious Philosophical Meetings in 1901–1903 while Metropolitan of St Petersburg.

**Antonii, Priest-monk (Aleksandr Ksarevich Bulatovich (1870–1919)**, Athonite priest-monk, ex-officer of Hussars, who became spokesman for the *imiaslavtsy* and whose *Apologiia* was published by **Novoselov**'s Religious-Philosophical Library with an anonymous introduction by Florensky in 1913.

**Aref'ev, Gavril Andreevich (18??–*c.* 1882)**, first husband of **Vladimir Ern**'s mother and his natural father. Vladimir was adopted by Franz Karlovich Ern after his marriage to the boy's mother.

**Aristotle (384–322 BC)**, Greek philosopher. Though a pupil of **Plato**'s, he questioned his master's teaching on the separate existence of the Idea (or Form) and set more value on the evidence of observation. Aristotle's influence was predominant in medieval and modern Western Europe.

**Bach, Johann Sebastian (1685–1750)**, German composer and keyboard player. Last great exponent of counterpoint.

**Bazarov, Evgenii Vasil'evich**, fictional hero of Turgenev's novel *Fathers and Children*. Medical student and prototype of the new materialism of the 1860s.

**Beelzebub (*Lord of the Flies*)**, Old Testament soubriquet for the Devil.

**Beethoven, Ludwig van (1770–1827)**, composer and pianist, profoundly deaf towards the end of his life. Epitome of the Romantic, creative artist.

**Beilis, Menachen Mendel' (1874–1934)**, Jewish artisan, falsely accused of ritual murder in the *cause célèbre* of the Russian boy **Iushchensky**.

**Bely, Andrei (real name Boris Nikolaevich Bugaev) (1880–1933)**, Symbolist poet, novelist and theoretician. Son of mathematician **Nikolai Bugaev**. Close friend of Florensky's from 1903–1906.

**Benois, Aleksandr Nikolaevich (1870–1960)**, artist of the World of Art group. One of the originators of the Religious Philosophical Meetings in St Petersburg 1901–1903. Emigrated to Paris 1926.

**Berdiaev, Nikolai Aleksandrovich (1876–1948)**, originally a Marxist philosopher but, with **Sergei Bulgakov**, broke with dialectical materialism to edit the ground-breaking *Problems of Idealism* and the 1905 journal *Questions of Life*. A religious thinker who valorises Personalism and individual freedom, his work is probably more widely translated and read than that of any other luminary of the Russian Religious Renaissance. Exiled with other religious thinkers in 1922. In Paris edited the émigré journal *Put'*.

**Bergson, Henri Louis (1859–1941)**, French philosopher whose opposition to mechanistic reasoning and advocacy of the intuitive approach were influential on European literature, aesthetics and thought throughout the first half of the twentieth century.

**Blok, Aleksandr Aleksandrovich (1880–1921)**, Russian Symbolist poet.

**Bonch-Bruevich, Mikhail Aleksandrovich (1888–1940)**, radio-technician, founder of radio station in Nizhnii Novgorod.

**Bondarenko, Il'ia Evgrafovich (1870–1947)**, architect educated in Moscow and Zurich. Author of several books on church architecture. Chairman of the Commission for the Preservation of Art and Antiquities in the Trinity St Sergius Monastery 1918–1919. Later director of the museum Old Moscow and worked with the management of the Museum of Architecture.

**Boskin, Mikhail Vasil'evich (1875–1930)**, artist. Member of the Commission for the Preservation of Art and Antiquities in the Trinity St Sergius Monastery 1918–1920.

**Bossuet, Jacques Bénigne (1627–1704)**, French theologian famous for the eloquence of his oratory and the hard-line conservatism of his opinions.

**Brianchaninov, Ignatii, Archbishop of the Caucasus and the Black Sea (1807–1867)**, see **Ignatii**.

**Briantsev, Nikolai Ivanovich (18??–1937)**, chemical engineer. Worked with Florensky on Solovki.

**Brikhnichev, Iona Panteleevich (1879–1968)**, classmate of **Iosif Dzugashvili** at a Tiflis seminary. Brikhnichev took holy orders, became a member of the

Christian Brotherhood for Struggle and, defrocked in the aftermath of the 1905 Revolution, became active in sectarian publishing, editor of *Novaia Zemlia* and, after the October Revolution, an anti-religious propagandist.

**Briusov, Valerii Iakovlevich (1876–1924)**, Symbolist poet and novelist. Leader of the Moscow Symbolists and editor of *Vesy* (*The Balance*).

**Bronstein, Lev Davydovich (Leon Trotsky) (1879–1940)**, leading Bolshevik, first Soviet Commisar for Foreign Affairs 1917–1918. Commander-in-Chief of the Red Army from spring 1918. Held that worldwide revolution should precede what Stalin called Socalism in One Country and led the Left opposition in the 1920s. Expelled from the Party and deported in 1929, after which he continued to oppose Stalin in exile until the latter had him assassinated in 1940.

**Büchner, Friedrich Karl Christian Ludwig (1824–1891)**, German materialist philosopher.

**Bugaev, Boris Nikolaevich**, see **Bely**.

**Bugaev, Nikolai Vasil'evich (1837–1903)**, Professor of Mathematics at Moscow University and founder of the Moscow Mathematical Philosophical Society. Florensky attended his lectures 1900–1903 and was profoundly influenced by his ideas on discontinuous functions (arhythmology) and his philosophy, which posited the existence of non-discreet monads capable of merging with one another and, eventually, with the Primal Monad.

**Bulgakov, Sergei Nikolaevich (1871–1944)**, friend and close collaborator of Florensky's, son of a priest of the Russian Orthodox Church, consecrated priest as Father Sergii in 1918, but originally moved with Berdiaev from Marxism to idealism, wrote with special attention to economics in *Problems of Idealism* and in the journal *Questions of Life* and worked as Professor of Economics from 1906 to 1918. Member of State Duma in 1906. Associated with the Christian Brotherhood for Struggle, the Vladimir Solov'ev Society and the Circle of Seekers for Christian Knowledge. After a few years as a priest in the Crimea was exiled with other religious thinkers in November 1922. Via Prague he finally settled in Paris as Professor of the St Sergius Theological Institute. From 1928 was vice-president of the St Alban and St Sergius Society. Although his sophiology aroused controversy, he was a much-loved and respected priest whose books have been published in many languages.

**Burdiukov, Ivan Ivanovich (1905–1937)**, native of Udmurtia of Russian origin, graduate of Azerbaijan Oil Institute, worked with Florensky on Solovki.

**Burliuk, David Davidovich (1882–1967)**, classmate of Florensky's at Tiflis Second Classical Gymnasium. Futurist artist and central figure of the Russian

Futurist movement. Though at first active in Soviet art, Burliuk emigrated to the United States via Japan in 1920 and 1922 respectively where he settled, revisiting Russia in 1956 and 1965.

**Bykov, Nikolai Ivanovich (1855–1939)**, head of the research station in Skovorodino. A kindly, cultivated man, he established friendly relations with the Florensky family and Florensky taught his son **Igor** mathematics while his younger son **Kolia** made friends with Florensky's **Mika**.

**Bykov, Igor and Kolia**, see **Bykov, Nikolai Ivanovich**.

**Cantor, Georg (1845–1918)**, German mathematician whose work on transfinite numbers and set theory exercised considerable influence on Florensky's thought.

**Chainikov, Kuz'ma Pavlovich (real name of Kuzebai Gerd) (1898–1941)**, Udmurt poet and ethnographer. Worked with Florensky on Solovki.

**Chamberlain, Houston Stewart (1855–1927)**, British disciple of Wagner and **Nietzsche** whose 1899 book *The Foundations of the Nineteenth Century* on the superiority of the Germanic peoples influenced the elaboration of National Socialist ideology.

**Chaplygin, Sergei Aleksandrovich (1869–1942)**, expert in mechanics and hydrodynamics, Academician. His name figures together with **Luzin**'s and Florensky's in **Gidiulanov**'s 1932 confession but he was not arrested.

**Chekrygin, Vasilii Nikolaevich (1897–1922)**, Russian artist and follower of **Fedorov**, who compulsively drew and painted the universal Resurrection to be brought about by science and prayer. Member of Makovets.

**Chernyshev, Nikolai Mikhailovich (1885–1973)**, painter. Born Tambov region, educated in Mocow, Paris and St Petersburg. Member of the World of Art and of Makovets group (1922–1926). His work was represented at 'Paris–Moscow' exhibition 1979 and at 'Paintings of the 1920s and 1930s' in St Petersburg 1991.

**Chernyshevsky, Nikolai Gavrilovich (1828–1889)**, Russian novelist and radical publicist. His utilitarian aesthetic, embraced by the Populists and hotly disputed by the Symbolists, were to contribute to the Soviet doctrine of Socialist Realism.

**Chetverikov, Sergei Ioannovich (1867–1947)**, Russian priest educated at the MDA. Emigrated in 1920, founder of the Society in Memory of **Ioann of Cronstadt**, caught in retreat in the Valaam Monastery in Estonia by the Soviet invasion, accepted the Moscow Patriarchate in 1946, became a monk in the monastery of St Job in Ladomirovo and, before his death, took the Great Schema.

**Christ, Jesus**. Logos, Second Person of the Holy Trinity.

**Churchill, Winston (1874–1965)**, politician and writer. Prime minister of Great Britain during the Second World War.

**Čiurlonis, Mikolaius Konstantinas (1875–1911)**, Latvian artist and composer, proponent of synaesthesia.

**Dante, Alighieri (1265–1321)**, Italian poet, author of the *Vita Nuova*, lyrical poems of ideal love linked by a prose commentary, and *The Divine Comedy*, depicting the soul's journey through Hell, Purgatory and Paradise, which greatly influenced the Romantic, pre-Raphaelite and Symbolist movements in European art and literature. Florensky was particularly interested in his handling of spatial concepts.

**David, Archimandrite (Dmitrii Ivanovich Mukhranov) (??–1931)**, monk of the St Andrew Skete on Mount Athos, chosen leader of the *Imiaslavtsy*. Florensky cooperated closely with him in Moscow prior to the planned reconsideration of the dispute by the 1917 Church Council. David, without compromising his position on the veneration of the Name of God, worked for reconciliation with the Church and was personally permitted to continue to act as priest by **Patriarch Tikhon**. He tonsured **Aleksei Fedorovich Losev** as Monk Andronik in 1929.

**Dedekind, Jules Wilhelm Richard (1831–1916)**, German mathematician renowned for his work on irrational numbers and definition of the ideal in algebra.

**Derviz, Baron Vladimir Dmitrievich (1859–1937)**, first director of the Sergiev Art-Historical Museum on the premises of the Trinity St Sergius Monastery created in 1920. Father-in-law of **Vladimir Favorsky**.

**Derzhavin, Gavrilo Romanovich (1743–1816)**, Russian Court poet renowned for his stately odes.

**Diagilev, Sergei Pavlovich (1872–1929)**, founder-editor of *The World of Art*, impressario of Russian art, opera and ballet. Remained abroad after the 1917 Revolution.

**Dobroliubov, Aleksandr Mikhailovich (1876–1944)**, decadent poet who renounced literature to 'go to the people' and found his own sect known as the Dobroliubovtsy.

**Dostoevsky, Fedor Mikhailovich (1821–1881)**, Russian novelist.

**Dubasov, F. V. (1845–1912)**, Admiral of the Fleet and Governor General of Moscow 1905–1906.

**Duns Scotus, John (1266–1308)**, Scottish Franciscan theologian and philosopher. Originator of the form 'haecaity' (thisness) which has been interpreted in the sense of 'particularity'.

**Dursu Uzala,** native Siberian tracker, hero of a book by the Russian explorer V. K. Arsen'ev and an eponymous film by **Kurosawa**.

**Durylin, Sergei Nikolaevich (1877–1954)**, member of the Circle of Seekers after Christian Knowledge and the Commission for the Preservation of Art and Antiquities of the Trinity St Sergius Monastery 1918–1920. Friend of artist **Mikhail Nesterov**. Later took holy orders as Father Sergii.

**Dzugashvili, Iosif Vissarionovich (Stalin) (1870–1953)**, educated at Tiflis Theological Seminary, expelled in 1898 and joined Russian Social Democratic Labour Party. Adhered to Bolshevik faction in 1903, General Secretary of Central Committee from 1922 from which position he gradually eliminated Left and Right opposition under the slogan of 'Socialism in One Country'. His undisputed supremacy in the Soviet Government was finally established by the Great Purge of 1937 and as Generalissimo, Commander-in-Chief of the Armed Forces, he ruled absolutely throughout the Second World War and until his death.

**Efimov, Ivan Semenovich (1878–1959)**, Russian sculptor and graphic artist. Teacher at Vkhutemas and friend of Florensky.

**Efimova, Nina Iakovlevna Simonovich**, see **Simonovich-Efimov**.

**Egorov, Dmitrii Fedorovich (1869–1931)**, lecturer in mathematics at Moscow University. Originator of Egoroff's Theorem.

**Egorov, Father Ioann (Ivan Fedorovich) (1872–1922)**, liberal priest, member of the Circle of 32 and the Union for Church Renewal, cooperated with the Christian Brotherhood for Struggle and founded the Active Church albeit within the confines of the Russian Orthodox Church. After his death, however, his followers failed to obtain the Church's agreement to ordain their chosen candidate to act as his successor and broke away as a movement called Religion in Conjunction with Life which survived until 1927.

**El'chaninov, Aleksandr Viktorovich (Sasha) (1881–1934)**, close friend of Florensky's at the Second Tiflis Classical Gymnasium and, with **Iraklii Tseretelli**, founder of the literary-philosophical circle. Studied at the Historic Philological Faculty of St Petersburg University 1900–1906 then active in various Moscow religious philosophical publishing projects and stayed for some time with Florensky in Sergiev Posad. From 1912 worked as a schoolteacher in Tiflis. Emigrated in 1921 and took holy orders in France, encouraged by **Father Sergii Bulgakov**. Author of the posthumously published *Notebooks*, Paris 1935, a spiritual classic translated into many languages.

**Elizaveta Fedorovna (1862–1918)**, Grand Princess, sister of the Tsarina Aleksandra Fedorovna, founder of the Martha and Mary Convent in Moscow and patroness of the home for retired Red Cross nursing sisters where Florensky served as a priest. A professed nun of the Russian Orthodox Church, she was sympathetic to the imiaslavtsy. Canonised in 1992.

**Ern, Vladimir Franzevich (Volodia) (1882–1917)**, classmate of Florensky's at Second Tiflis Classical Gymnasium and shared a room with him during the first two years of his course at Moscow University, where he studied at the Historic Philological Faculty. With **Sventsitsky**, founder of the Christian Brotherhood for Struggle, 1905–1907. Philosopher and close friend of **Viacheslav Ivanov**.

**Eros**, Greek god of love. The myth of Psyche and Eros lends itself to interpretation as the story of the redemption of the human soul through passionate love. This interpretation, also present in the Gnostic version of the Sophia myth, is dear to the heart of, if not literally accepted by, all neo-Platonics, including Florensky.

**Euclid (third-century BC)**, Greek geometrician. His famous theorems provide an object lesson in sequential reasoning which Florensky, though acutely aware of its limitations, frequently applies to philosophical and theological problems.

**Evdokim, Bishop (Meshchersky) (1869–1935)**, Rector of the MDA from 1903-1909.

**Ezhov, Nikolai Ivanovich (1895–1939)**, Commissar for Internal Affairs, head of the NKVD from 1936 and organiser of the Great Purge, succeeded by Beria in 1938, disappeared in 1939, described in Khrushchev's secret speech of 1956 as a 'degenerate'.

**Faraday, Michael (1791–1897)**, British physicist. Largely self-taught by working as assistant to Sir Humphrey Davy at the Royal Institute, he subsequently made a name for himself in chemistry and electro-magnetics. Florensky was attracted by Faraday's combination of autodidacticism, passion for hands-on experiment and luminous faith. He belonged to a small sect which he served faithfully all his life as a lay preacher.

**Favorsky, Andrei Evgrafovich (1843–1924)**, father of **Vladimir Favorsky**, worked on the Commission for the Preservation of Arts and Antiquities in the Trinity St Sergius Monastery.

**Favorsky, Maria Vladimirovna (1890–1959)**, wife of **Vladimir Favorsky** and daughter of **Baron Derviz**, author of reminiscences about the Florensky family in post-revolutionary Sergiev Posad.

**Favorsky, Nikita Vladimirovich (1915–1941)**, artist, son of **Vladimir Favorsky**, killed in the Second World War, schoolfriend of **Kirill** and **Olga Florensky**.

**Favorsky, Vladimir Andreevich (1884–1964)**, Russian artist, xylographer, theoretician and teacher of art. Resident in Sergiev Posad 1919–1938. Invited Florensky to lecture at Vkhutemas of which he was director 1923–1925. Author of several portraits of Florensky and his children and an ex-libris. Designed covers for *Imaginary Points in Geometry*, 'Number as form' and the journal *Makovets*.

**Fedor, Archimandrite (Aleksei Mikhailovich Bukharev) (1824–1871)**, Russian Orthodox theologian whose Study of the Apocalypse was banned by the Holy Synod in 1862 for what was perceived as an alarmist and disrespectful critique of the state of the Church in Russia, infiltrated, as Bukharev considered, by Protestant rationalism and Roman Catholic authoritarianism through the seminaries and theological academies. Florensky exhumed and published this controversial work in *Bogoslovskii vestnik* 1913–1916.

**Fedor, Bishop (Aleksandr Vasil'evich Pozdeevsky) (1876–1940?)**, Rector of the Moscow Theological Academy 1909–1917, member of the Circle of Seekers after Christian Enlightenment, director of Florensky's Master's thesis and author of a positive review.

**Fedorov, Nikolai Fedorovich (1828–1903)**, maverick religious thinker who believed that mankind would, through scientific and ascetic endeavour, learn to resurrect the dead and direct the Earth through space, so peopling the Universe.

**Fet (Afanasii Afanas'evich Shenshin) (1820–1891)**, Russian lyric poet.

**Fichte, Johann Gottlieb (1762–1814)**, German Romantic philosopher. Substituted the noumenon or ideal projection of reality in the human mind for the concept of Deity. Ardent patriot.

**Filosofov, Dmitrii Vladimirovich (1872–1940)**, journalist and author, cousin of **Diagilev** and co-founder of *The World of Art*. Close friend and collaborator of the **Merezhkovsky**s. Emigrated in 1920.

**Florensky, Aleksandr Aleksandrovich (1888–1938)** Florensky's brother. Geologist, mineralogist, ethnographer and art historian. Died in a concentration camp in the province of Magadan.

**Florensky, Aleksandr Ivanovich (1850–1908),** Pavel Florensky's father. Railway engineer, assistant to the Director-in-Chief of the Caucasian railway network.

**Florensky, Andrei Aleksandrovich (1899–1961),** Florensky's youngest brother. Engineer, specialist on marine and off-shore installations. Stalin Prize winner.

**Florensky, Anna Mikhailovna (Anya)** see **Giatsintov.**

**Florensky, Elizaveta Aleksandrovna (Lily, married name Koneev) (1886–1959),** Florensky's sister. Artist and art teacher.

**Florensky, Iulia Aleksandrovna (Liusia) (1884–1947),** Florensky's eldest sister, a practising psychiatrist. Married Mikhail Mikhailovich Aretiani, one child Aleksandr (1910–1911). Divorced.

**Florensky, Iuliia Ivanovna (Aunt Julia) (1848–1894),** Florensky's much-loved aunt who lived with his parents and cared for him as a small boy.

**Florensky, Ivan Andreevich (1815–1866),** Florensky's grandfather. Educated for the Church until 1836 when he entered the Moscow Medical Surgery Academy. Army doctor.

**Florensky, Kirill Pavlovich (Kira) (1915–1982),** Florensky's son. Geo-chemist, astro-geologist and mineralogist. A crater on the other side of the moon bears his name.

**Florensky, Mariia Pavlovna (Tin-a-Tin or Tika) (b. 1924),** Florensky's youngest daughter. Chemist.

**Florensky, Mikhail Pavlovich (Mika) (1921–1961),** Florensky's youngest son. Geologist, killed in an automobile accident while prospecting in the Far East of the Soviet Union.

**Florensky, Nataliia Ivanovna (née Zarubina) (1909–1996),** wife of **Vasilii,** mother of **Pavel Vasil'evich Florensky.**

**Florensky, Ol'ga Aleksandrovna (Valia) (1892–1914),** Florensky's sister. Artist and poet. Married **Sergei Troitsky,** 1910.

**Florensky, Ol'ga Pavlovna (Olen or Olechka) (1918–1998),** Florensky's daughter. Botanist. Married Sergei Zosimovich Trubachev in 1946, mother of **Igumen Andronik,** and **Maria Sergeevna Trubachev.**

**Florensky, Ol'ga Pavlovna (née Salome Saparova or Saparian) (1859–1951),** mother of Florensky, married **Aleksandr Ivanovich Florensky** 1880. Armenian by birth but raised in Georgia where she lived until 1915, in which year she removed to Moscow with her youngest daughter **Raisa.**

**Florensky, Pavel Vasil'eich (b. 1936)**, grandson of Pavel Florensky. Member of the Academy of Sciences, active in research on Florensky's heritage and an editor of his *Works*.

**Florensky, Raisa Aleksandrovna (Gosia) (1894–1932)**, artist, editor of journal *Makovets*, sister of Pavel Florensky. Lived from 1915 with her mother in Moscow, nursed by **Anna Mikhailovna** before her death from tuberculosis and died at her brother's home in Sergiev Posad.

**Florensky, Vasilii Pavlovich (Vasia) (1911–1956)**, eldest son of Pavel and **Anna Florensky**, Geologist, mineralogist.

**Florovsky, Father Georgii Vasil'evich (1893–1979)**, Russian émigré priest and theologian. Finished Classical Gymnasium in Odessa 1919 and Historic Philological Faculty of Odessa University in 1916 where he continued as *privat-dozent* until emigrating to Bulgaria in 1919 and on to France in 1921. Took holy orders in 1922. Member of Brotherhood of St Sophia from 1924, but opposed **Bulgakov**'s concept of Sophia and was highly critical of Florensky's *Pillar and Ground of Truth*. From 1948, pursued a distinguished career at St Vladimir Theological Academy, Harvard and Princeton. Publications include many works on Patrology, *Puti russkogo bogosloviia*, first published Paris 1937 and *Vera i Kul'tura, izbrannye trudy po bogosloviu i filosofii*, St Petersburg, 2002.

**Franklin, Benjamin (1706–1790)**, polymath American thinker, printer, author, scientist and statesman, compiler of the much-quoted *Richard's Almanac* and author of *The Way to Wealth*. His *Autobiography* 1886 reveals him as 'one of the most versatile geniuses the world has known'.

**Frenikov, Major**, Officer of the MVD responsible for checking Florensky and his fellow-prisoners on their arrival from Solovki into the holding prison from which they were executed.

**Freud, Sigmund (1856–1939)**, Austrian neurologist and psychologist, founder of psychoanalysis.

**Friz, Hugo de (1848–1935)**, Dutch biologist.

**Fudel', Father Iosif (1864–1908)**, member of the Circle of Seekers after Christian Knowledge. His son, Sergei Iosifovich Fudel (1900–1977) is the author of reminiscences of Florensky and of the first book on Florensky's thought, published in Paris in 1972, under the pseudonym F. I. Udelov. **Novoselov** records with pleasure how the younger Fudel' defended Florensky as the gateway from contemporary thought to the Orthodox faith against Novoselov's critique of the piece on **Khomiakov**.

**Gekhtman, Georgii Nikolaevich (1870–1956)**, teacher of literature and classics at the Second Tiflis Classical Gymnasium and founder of the school Philosophical Society. An inspirational teacher, he predicted Florensky would go far in spite of his 'unimpressive appearance' and 'apparent absentmindedness', which, he added, was in fact the hallmark of extreme concentration.

**Gerd, Kuzebai**, see **Chainikov, Kuz'ma Pavlovich**.

**German, Igumen (1844–1923)**, elder of the Russian Orthodox Church, Prior of Zosima Pustyn from 1897, who wielded considerable influence with **Elizaveta Fedorovna**.

**Giatsintov, Anna Mikhailovna (Anya) (1889–1973)**, village schoolteacher from a priest's family. Married Pavel Florensky 1910, mother of five children. Joined her husband in exile in Nizhnii Novgorod 1928 and in Skovorodino, 1934. Preserved his children, memory and home.

**Giatsintov, Father Aleksandr Mikhailovich (1882–1938)**, priest at Kutlovy Borki. Brother of **Vasilii** and **Anna**.

**Giatsintov, Nadezhda Petrovna (1863–1973)**, mother of **Anna Florensky**.

**Giatsintov, Vasilii Mikhailovich (1885–1951)**, engineer. Close friend of Florensky's, from 1910 his brother-in-law.

**Gidiulanov, Pavel Vasil'evich (1874–1937)**, Professor of Canon Law. His fabricated 'confession' was responsible for the arrest of Florensky in 1933. In spite of a promise that the confession would earn him his freedom, he was sentenced to ten years in a labour camp in Kazakhstan, then shot.

**Giotto, Ambrozio di Bondone (?1266–?1336)**, Italian artist and architect. Originally worked in the Roman-Italo-Byzantine style, but his frescoes in Padua are generally considered pioneering works for the introduction of perspective as understood by the High Renaissance.

**Gippius, Zinaida Nikolaevna** see **Hippius**.

**Glagolev, Professor Sergei Sergeevich (1865–1937)**, theologian. Director of studies for Florensky's thesis at the MDA.

**Glinka, Aleksandr Sergeevich (pseudonym A. Volzhsky) (1878–1940)**, friend of **Sergei Bulgakov** active in the 'Christian Brotherhood for Struggle' and various Moscow religious philosophical societies.

**Glubokovsky, Nikolai Nikanorovich (1863–1937)**, theologian, emigrated 1920, moved to Paris at the invitation of Father Sergii Bulgakov, where he taught at the St Sergius Theological Institute from 1925–1931.

**Goethe, Johann Wolfgang von (1749–1832)**, German writer, poet and scientist. Much admired by **Aleksandr Ivanovich Florensky** and by Florensky himself.

**Gorky, Maxim (real name Aleksei Maksimovich Peshkov) (1868–1936)**, renowned Russian writer, autodidact, friend of **Tolstoy** and Chekhov, early associated with the revolutionary movement in Russia. Shocked by the arbitrary nature of Bolshevik power, he left the Soviet Union to live on Capri in 1921, but returned permanently to Russia in 1931. Treated with respect by the Government as a world celebrity, Gorky was in a position to intercede on behalf of members of the intelligentsia who had fallen foul of the authorities, something he was frequently asked to do.

**Gorodensky Mikhail**, Pavel Florensky's physics teacher at Tiflis Classical Gymnasium.

**Grimm**, brothers **Jacob Ludwig (1785–1863)** and **Wilhelm Karl (1786–1813)**, German philologists, collectors of folktales (three volumes 1812–13) which both reflected and nourished the Romantic revival of interest in national roots.

**Gudzovsky, A. V. (18??–?1966)**, half-Georgian scientist from Batumi. Colleague of Florensky's at the permafrost station in Skovorodino and prototype for one of the characters in the narrative poem 'Oro'.

**Hamlet**, Prince of Denmark, archetypal hero of Shakespeare's eponymous play. Subject of an early article by Florensky.

**Hegel, Georg Wilhelm Friedrich (1710–1831)**, German idealist philosopher. His thought on history and religion promotes the idea that 'religion' is the understanding of the way things hang together 'in the broadest possible sense of the term' which, he feels, is finally 'due to us'. He adumbrated the argument of Ivan Karamazov's devil that, should we finally attain to such an understanding, history would be over. The doctrine 'what is actual is rational' was at first embraced then vigorously rejected by Hegel's Russian disciples, but his influence persisted with the doctrine of the dialectic, understood by Strauss, Feuerbach and Marx as essentially sociological. Florensky, disliking the mechanistic terminology of thesis, antithesis and synthesis, opted for the opposing methods of the Ontological School, which perceived Being as primary in relation to human rationality.

**Heine, Heinrich (1797–1856)**, German Romantic poet.

**Heraclitus (540–475)**, Greek philosopher and astronomer from Ephesus. He wept for the follies of humanity and insisted everything is in a state of flux, so that change is the only reality. He also maintained that fire is the origin of all things; nothing is born and nothing dies. The stoics owe much to his opinions.

**Hildebrand, Adolf R. von (1847–1921)**, German sculptor, writer on art. His *Problems of Form in Figurative Art* was translated by **V. A. Favorsky** and **N. B. Rozenfeld** (Moscow, 1914) with a preface by the former. Although the principles of this book are founded on traditional aesthetics and the art of the Renaissance, it registers a lively protest against nineteenth-century Naturalism.

**Hippius, Zinaida Nikolaevna (married name Merezhkovsky) (1869–1945)**, poet, short-story writer and literary critic, the moving spirit of the new religious consciousness. Her views on religion and love influenced Florensky's sister **Ol'ga** who, however, eventually broke with both **Merezhkovsky**s, in part under her brother's influence, in part because she genuinely found them too abstract. Hippius emigrated in 1920 and writes about Florensky (although she confesses that the time is not ripe to do so) in her Memoirs *Zhivye litsa.*

**Hoffmann, Ernst Theodor Amadeus (1776–1822)**, author of the Romantic fantasies *The Tales of Hoffmann.* Worked as Kapellmeister and judge.

**Holoszy, Shimon (1857–1918)**, Hungarian artist and director of private art schools in Munich and Budapest.

**Humboldt, Friedrich Wilhelm Christian Ferdinand Freiher Karl von (1767–1855)**, German scholar and diplomat, regarded by many as the father of comparative linguistics. He maintained that language, as a vital and dynamic organism, is the key to understanding both the operations of the human mind and the distinctive differences of various national cultures.

**Hume, David (1711–1776)**, Scottish philosopher and historian. Author of *History of England 1754–62*, in six volumes, which was read by Florensky in French on Solovki. Florensky had much sympathy with British empiricism and for all his insistence on the reality of Symbol would, albeit from the heart of his own mystic experience, not have quarrelled with Hume's dictum that philosophy 'cannot go beyond experience; and any hypothesis, that pretends to discover the ultimate original qualities of human nature, ought at first to be rejected as presumptuous and chimerical'.

**Iakovenko, Boris Valentinovich (1884–1948)**, Russian neo-Kantian thinker active in Russia in the early twentieth century. One of the editors of the collection *Logos.*

**Iakovlev, Konstantin Sergeevich (1891–1937)**, Udmurt scientist who worked with Florensky on Solovki and, like him, was shot in the late autumn of 1937.

**Ignatii, Archbishop (Dmitrii Aleksandrovich Brianchaninov) (1807–1867),** hierarch of the Russian Orthodox Church and theologian, advocate of the practice of the Jesus prayer, canonised in 1988.

**Ilarion, Father (*c.* 1845–1916),** ex-Athonite schemamonk retired to live as a hermit *In the Caucasian Mountains,* the title of a book advocating his use of the Jesus prayer, first published 1907, which was at the root of the *imiaslavtsy* dispute originating from its use by monks of the St Andrew Skete on Mount Athos as a devotional aid. The book was pronounced unorthodox by the Athonite author-ities and again by the organ of the Russian Holy Synod *Tserkovnyi vestnik,* but was defended in an apologiia by **A. K. Bulatovich,** published by **Novoselov** with an anonymous preface by Florensky and supported behind the scenes by Ilarion's friend **Igumen German** of Zosima Pustyn and by members of the royal family, notably **Elizaveta Fedorovna.**

**Il'in, Vladimir Nikolaevich (1891–1974),** educated in the Mathematical, Philosophical and Historic Philological Faculties of Kiev University and at the Kiev Conservatoire (course in composition 1908), emigrated to Constantinople 1919 and arrived in Paris via Berlin in 1925 where he became a *dotsent* at the Sergius Theological Institute (1925–1941) from which he was excluded for transferring allegiance to the Moscow Patriarchate. Wrote on a variety of subjects for émigré journals and continued to compose music.

**Il'insky, Vladimir A. (18??–1917),** student friend of Florensky's at MDA who helped him and **Troitsky** compile *chastushki.*

**Ioann of Cronstadt (1829–1908),** renowned preacher and pastor at the Russian naval base of Cronstadt. Author of the anonymous *Way of the Pilgrim,* first published in English as by a monk of the Eastern Church, a book advocating the Jesus prayer, which subsequently enjoyed great popularity in Russia. Canonised in 1964 by the Russian Church in exile, in 1990 by the Russian Orthodox Church.

**Ipollitov, Pavel Afanas'evich (1889–1947),** choir conductor and composer. Musical director of the Malyi Theatre. Co-author with Florensky of a musical annotation on the bells of the Trinity St Sergius Monastery to complement **Mikhail Shik**'s contribution to the report of the Commission for the Preservation of Art and Antiquities.

**Isidor, Father (Ivan Andreevich Kozin-Gruzinsky)(1814/37–1908),** an elder of the Gethsemane Skete attached to the Trinity St Sergius Monastery and Florensky's spiritual father during his student years. Subject of a memorial tribute 'Salt of the earth' by his 'unworthy spiritual son'.

**Iushchensky, Andrei (1898–1911)**, Russian boy said to have been ritually murdered by Beilis.

**Ivanov, Dmitrii Iosifovich (1880–1938)**, artist, fellow-prisoner of Florensky's on Solovki.

**Ivanov, Viacheslav Ivanovich (1868–1947)**, Russian poet and philosopher with a particular interest in Ancient Greek religion as a pagan Old Testament. Emigrated to Rome in 1924 where he joined the Greek Catholic or Uniate Church.

**Ivensen P A**, Swedish aircraft designer. Imprisoned on Solovki.

**Izvolsky, Petr Petrovich (1866?–1928)**, conservative statesman. Procurator of the Holy Synod from 1906–1909. Emigrated to France in 1920 and took holy orders in the emigration in 1922.

**James, William (1842–1910)**, American psychologist, much translated into Russian, whose *Varieties of Religious Experience* and other works had considerable influence on Russian psychology and religious thought in the early twentieth century.

**Jason**, mythical Greek hero, captain of the Argonauts on their expedition to find the Golden Fleece.

**Job**, Old Testament protagonist of the Book of Job, the Servant of the Lord, who God permitted to be tempted to rebel against the divine Providence; a figure for affliction in all Bible-reading countries.

**Jung, Carl Gustav (1875–1961)**, Swiss psychologist and founder of analytical psychology, influenced by neo-Platonists, **Schopenhauer**, **Nietzsche** and **James**, **Jung** differed from **Freud** largely in his emphasis on the collective unconscious and on archetypes.

**Kamenev, Lev**, see **Rozenfeld**.

**Kant, Immanuel (1724–1804)**, German philosopher, much criticised by Florensky's generation for positing the impossibility of knowing the ideal or 'noumen' while building a whole ethos on faith in its existence, advocating the belief that we can only approach the Absolute through abiding by 'the moral law within' and contemplating 'the starry sky above'. However, though Florensky as a Symbolist and Ontologist disputed this acceptance of unknowing and disliked the valorising of morality, he revered Kant as a 'Copernicus among philosophers' for introducing the term 'antonym' to philosophical usage and devoted much study to this concept in his work.

**Kapp, Gisbert Ernest (1852–1922)**, Austrian electrical engineer, secretary to the German Association of Electrical Engineers 1894–1904 and Professor of Electrical Engineering in Birmingham till 1918, where he was awarded the Telford Medal. His *Principles of Electric Engineering*, 1916, and other books on technology show interest in the philosophical implications of his specialism.

**Kapterev, Pavel Nikolaevich (1889–1955)**, member of the Commission for the Preservation of Art and Antiquities at the Trinity St Sergius Monastery 1918–1920. Scientist, Florensky's companion in Svobodny and Skovorodino. Author, with **N. I. Bykov**, of a book on permafrost.

**Kartashev, Anton Vladimirovich (1875–1960)**, lecturer at the St Petersburg Theological Academy who, in the course of the Religious Philosophical Meetings of 1901–1903, became close to the **Merezhkovskys**' inner circle and, dismissed from the Academy, worked as lecturer on the Bestuzhev Courses for Women. Later, reconciled to the Church, he acted as last Ober-Procurator to the Holy Synod and Minister for Religious Confessions to the Provisional Government in 1917 which led to his arrest after the Bolshevik Coup. In 1919 he escaped via Finland and founded and chaired the Russian National Committee in Paris at the St Sergius Institute where he acted as lay member of the Diocesan Council 1924–1936 and 1946–1960 and published a massive *History of the Russian Church*, 1959.

**Kaufmann (Nicholas Mercator) (1622–1687)**, seventeenth-century mathematician from the Netherlands who was active in Copenhagen, Leiden, Paris and London. Author of treatise *Logarithmo technico*.

**Keats, John (1795–1821)**, English Romantic poet.

**Khlebnikov, Velimir (1885–1922)**, Russian Futurist poet whose mathematical and linguistic ideas greatly interested Florensky.

**Khomiakov, Aleksei Stepanovich (1804–1860)**, Slavophile writer and theologian. Advocate of a *rapprochement* between the Eastern Orthodox and the Anglican Church and the first to use the term *sobornost* (collegiality, co-inherence) to define the special quality of Russian Orthodoxy.

**Khvolson (or Chvolson), Daniil Abramovich (1819–1911)**, Orientalist of international repute who defended Jews from the insidious charge that they were capable of practising human sacrifice, maintaining that even the Ancients had not done so since the ram was substituted for Isaac.

**Kiseleva, Natalia Aleksandrovna (1859–1919)**, directress of the home for retired nursing sisters of the Red Cross in whose House Church Florensky served. A firm friend, instrumental in the acquisition of the family's last, beloved home on Dvorianskaia ulitsa.

**Kozbinsky, Ivan (1861–1900)**, Russian botanist and geographer.

**Kolechits, Avel' Andreevich (1887–19??)**, agronomist. Arrested in 1930 and sentenced to ten years of hard labour, he cooperated with the OGPU interrogators to secure Gidiulanov's 'confession' and was rewarded in 1932 by premature release into exile in the Urals.

**Komarovsky, Vladimir Alekseevich (1833–1937)**, Russian artist, author of the portrait of Florensky on Solovki. Shot in 1937.

**Kornilov, Aleksandr Aleksandrovich (1862–1925)**, a graduate of St Petersburg University, Kornilov authored a book *Among the Starving Peasantry* and was exiled to Saratov for protesting against police brutality in the quelling of student disorders in 1901. On his return became a founder member of the Constitutional Democrat Party and a member of the Circle of Seekers after Christian Knowledge.

**Kotliarevsky, Grigorii Porfirovich (1887–1937)**, Ukrainian philologist. Fellow-prisoner of Florensky's on Solovki.

**Kotliarevsky, Sergei Andreevich (1873–1939)**, historian. Chairman of the History of Religion branch of the University Student Society attended by Florensky, **Bely**, **Ern** and **Sventsitsky** in 1903–1904.

**Kozhevnikov, Valentin Alekseevich (1852–1917)**, Russian historian of culture. Member of the Circle of Seekers after Christian Knowledge, disciple of **N. F. Fedorov**.

**Kuprianova, Aleksandra Nikolaevna**, niece of **Archbishop Ignatii (Brianchaninov)**. Contributor to *Bogoslovkii vestnik*.

**Kurosawa, Akira (1910–1998)**, Japanese film director.

**Kuznetsov, Nikolai Dmitrievich (1850–1929)**, Russian artist, member of the Ambulant Society and of the Circle of Seekers after Christian Knowledge.

**Lakhtin, Leonid Kuz'mich (1863–1927)**, lecturer in mathematics at Moscow University and Rector from 1904–1905.

**Laplace, Pierre Simon, Marquis de (1749–1827)**, French analyst, probability theorist and physicist, an exponent of celestial mechanics, he offered proof that planetary perturbations do not disturb but maintain the stability of the solar system.

**Leibniz, Gottfried Wilhelm (1646–1716)**, German rationalist, philosopher and polymath. His perception of the universe as consisting of monads as discreet units created and set in motion by a Primal Monad, God, and thereafter subject to causality except for rare interventions in the order of things by miraculous or Divine Causality, was questioned by **Nikolai Bugaev**.

**Lemprière, Dr John (*c.* 1765–1824)**, British author of a famous eighteenth-century *Classical Dictionary of Proper Names Mentioned in Ancient Authors*.

**Lermontov, Mikhail Iurevich (1814–1841)**, Russian Romantic poet.

**Lileevs**, a family of singers and musicians engaged in light opera with whose children Florensky was friendly in Batumi, possibly related to Emilia Avgustovna Lileeva (1823–1893), a well-known soprano.

**Lindsay, Lord Alexander Dunlop (1879–1952)**, British philosopher.

**Litvinov, Roman Nikolaevich (1890–1937)**, Professor of Chemical Technology from Nizhnyi Novgorod. Friend of Florensky's on Solovki.

**Lopatin, Lev Mikhailovich (1855–1920)**, lecturer in psychology at Moscow University whose course of lectures Florensky attended on an extra-curricular basis while studying mathematics. Chairman of Moscow Psychological Society 1899–1917.

**Losev, Aleksei Fedorovich (1893–1988)**, Russian religious thinker and specialist on Classical Mythology and Aesthetics who took the part of the *imiaslavtsy* in 1917. Considered by many to be a follower of Florensky. He took secret monastic vows and was received under the name of Andronik in 1929 and, in 1930, was arrested and condemned to ten years of hard labour for 'militant idealism'. Losev lost his sight in the camps but was subsequently freed thanks to the intervention of M. I. Ulianova and **E. P. Peshkova** (Lenin's widow and **Maxim Gorky**'s first wife) and, although forbidden to publish on philosophy, managed to continue a scholarly and pedagogical career, first in the provinces, then in Moscow.

**Lossky, Vladimir Nikolaevich (1903–1948)**, Russian theologian. Exiled from the USSR in 1922, he lived and worked in Prague and Paris where he published many books on Russian Orthodox thought and practice.

**Luzin, Nikolai Nikolaevich (1883–1950)**, mathematician, one year junior to Florensky at Moscow University who took over from him as secretary to the Moscow Mathematical-Philosophical Society. Later worked in France with **Poincaré** and maintained contact with foreign scholars into the Soviet period, for which he was cast as 'in charge of foreign links' as a member of **Gidiulanov**'s imaginary counter-revolutionary society. A lifelong friend, who treasured Florensky's *Pillar and Ground of Truth*.

**L'vov, Vladimir Nikolaevich (1872–1934)**, Procurator of the Holy Synod under the Provisional Government in 1917.

**Machiavelli, Niccolo (1469–1527)**, Italian political thinker, author of *Il Principe* (*The Prince*).

**Mamonov, Nikolai Nikolaevich (18??–19??)**, Doctor, later Professor of Medicine, who looked after the dying Chekhov and was asked to report on the alleged poisoning of Lenin in 1918. Member of the Circle of Seekers after Christian Knowledge.

**Mamontov Aleksandra Savvichna (1878–1952)**, daughter of **Savva Mamontov** and administrator of the Abramtsevo estate after his death, first curator of the museum after nationalisation.

**Mamontov, Savva Il'ich (1841–1918)**, proprietor of the estate Abramtsevo where he founded an artist's colony and a private opera. Mamontov was bankrupted in 1901, but the estate continued as an artists' colony and is today a museum.

**Mansurov, Pavel Borisovich (1860–1932)**, civil servant, director of the Foreign Ministry Archive. Member of the Circle of Seekers after Christian Knowledge.

**Mansurov, Sergei Pavlovich (1890–1929)**, Church historian. Member of the Circle of Seekers after Christian Knowledge and of the Commission for the Preservation of Art and Antiquities of the Trinity St Sergius Monastery 1918–1920. Left Sergiev Posad in 1925 and became a priest of the Orthodox Church in 1926. Died of tuberculosis.

**Martens, Ludvig Karlovich (1875–1948)**, member of the Communist Party. Editor of the First Soviet *Technical Encyclopedia*.

**Masaryk, Thomas (1850–1937)**, President of Czechoslovakia 1920–1935.

**Mashkin, Vladimir Mikhailovich (Archimandrite Serapion) (1854–1905)**, mathematician who spent four years on Mount Athos before taking monastic vows. Corresponded with Florensky from the Optyno-Pustyn Monastery and hoped for a meeting to discuss the significance of higher mathematics for religious faith adumbrated in an unfinished work which Florensky undertook to edit after his death pre-empted the plan to meet. A meeting of minds certainly took place while Florensky was struggling with this task, which proved beyond his powers to complete. Mashkin undoubtedly confirmed Florensky in his own ideas and possibly influenced their further development, though the imputation of plagiarism made by **Archimandrite Nikanor** is unlikely to be substantiated, even if a scholar is found capable of deciphering and making sense of the over 2,000 pages of manuscript which defeated Florensky.

**Medea**, legendary Queen of Colchis, depicted in Euripedes' tragedy as having poisoned her own children and as lover of **Jason**, whose Argonauts she protected on their flight from her country.

**Medtner, Emilii Karlovich (pseudonym Wolfling) (1872–1936)**, author of book on **Goethe**, music critic and translator of **Jung**, director of the Moscow publishing house Musagetes, brother of the composer Nikolai Medtner. At one time worked closely with **Bely** but broke with him in 1918.

**Melik-Begliarov, David Sergeevich (Datiko) (1875–1913)**, agronomist, Florensky's first cousin.

**Melik-Begliarov, Elizaveta Pavlovna (Aunt Liza, née Saparian/Saparov) (1854–1919)**, Florensky's maternal aunt, mother of **Datiko** and **Margarita**.

**Melik-Begliarov, Margerita Sergeevna (Margot) (1872–19??)**, Florensky's first cousin, married Kh. A. Otanian in 1906.

**Melik-Begliarov, Sergei Teimurazovich (18??–1905)**, Elizaveta Pavlovna's husband.

**Mendeleev, Dmitrii Ivanovich (1834–1907)**, chemist, originator of the periodical system.

**Mendeleev, Liubov' Dmitrievna (1881–1939)**, daughter of **Dmitrii Mendeleev**, wife of the poet **Blok**, at one time idolised by **Blok** and his close friends **Bely** and **Sergei Solov'ev** as a figure for the Divine **Sophia**.

**Mephistopheles**, clownish folklore devil. In **Goethe**'s Faust, he negotiates the purchase of Faust's soul and binds himself to his service until the moment when Faust himself will call on time to stop.

**Merezhkovsky, Dmitrii Sergeevich (1865–1961)**, literary critic, novelist, poet and thinker, initiator, with his wife **Zinaida Hippius**, of the Religious Philosophical Meetings in St Petersburg 1901–1903. Emigrated in 1920.

**Mikhail, Bishop (Semenov) (1874–1916)**, close at one time to the Brotherhood for Christian Struggle and Union for Church Renewal, Father Mikhail subsequently broke with the Russian Orthodox Church to found the Golgotha Church as Bishop Mikhail.

**Mlodzeevsky, Boleslav Kornelievich (1858–1923)**, lecturer in mathematics at Moscow University when Florensky was studying there.

**Morozova, Margarita Kirillovna (1873–1958)**, beautiful wife of the wealthy merchant Morozov and patron of the religious philosophical circle grouped around her publishing house Put', which brought out Florensky's *Pillar and Ground of Truth*.

**Mozart, Wolfgang Amadeus (1756–1791)**, Austrian composer, particularly beloved of Florensky.

**Mukhranov, Dmitrii Ivanovich** see **David, Archimandrite**.

**Muratov, Pavel Pavlovich (1881–1950)**, traveller and aesthete. Worked in 1919 in the Byzantine Section of the Moscow Institute of Historico-Artistic Research and Museum Study, where he invited Florensky to read his paper on 'Reverse perspective'. Emigrated to Rome in 1922.

**Myers, Frederick William Henry (1843–1901)**, British psychologist interested in religious experience.

**Nesterov, Mikhail Vasil'evich (1862–1942)**, Russian painter associated with the Abramtsevo Moscow School and also with the World of Art Society. Author of the dual portrait of Florensky and **Bulgakov** 'The Philosophers' painted in 1917.

**Nietzsche, Friedrich (1844–1900)**, German philosopher and poet whose writings had great influence on Silver Age Russia. His conviction that 'man is something that must be overcome', his anti-Christian morality and the Dionysian inspiration of his *Birth of Tragedy from the Spirit of Music* influenced Orthodox and Marxist thinkers alike and coloured the theory and practice of Russian Symbolism.

**Nikanor, Arkhimandrite (Nikolai Pavlovich Kudriavstsev) (1884–1923)**, theologian who accused Florensky, his senior by one year at the MDA, of heresy and plagiarism in a vituperative critique of *The Pillar and Ground of Truth*. Nikanor became a monk in 1911 and rose rapidly from Archimandrite to Igumen to Bishop of Bogorodsk. He died of tuberculosis.

**Nikitenko, Aleksandr Vasil'evich (1803–1877)**, author of famous literary reminiscences and Professor of Literature at St Petersburg University, fellow of the Russian Academy of Sciences.

**Nikon Archbishop (Rozhdestvensky) (1851–1918)**, chairman of the Publishers Advisory Board to the Holy Synod. Sent to try to establish order among the Russian monks during the Athonite Rebellion – supported by 5 officers and 118 soldiers. Later opposed the *imiaslavtsy* in print.

**Novoselov, Mikhail Aleksandrovich (Abba Mikhail) (1864–1938)**, once a disciple of **Tolstoy**, Novoselov founded the Circle of Seekers after Christian Knowledge and published a series of topical and often controversial books in his Religious Philosophical Library series, 1902–1917. From 1918 a member of the Underground Church in which he is believed to have taken monastic vows under the name of Mark and become an archbishop. Imprisoned in 1928 and died in solitary confinement. Canonised.

**Obolensky, Prince Aleksei (1856–1933)**, liberal statesman. Briefly Procurator of the Holy Synod 1905–1906.

**Odysseus**, legendary hero of Homer's *Odyssey* and important character in the *Iliad*, distinguished among other heroes for his prudence and sagacity. The Latin form of his name is Ulysses.

**Ognev, Ivan Florovich (1855–1928)**, Professor of the Histological Institute at Moscow University. Neighbour of Florensky's in Sergiev Posad. They collaborated on a design for an ultra-microscope in 1920.

**Ognev, Sofia Ivanovna (1846–1940)**, wife of **Professor Ognev** who helped Florensky by taking dictation, notably of the book *For My Children* and the essay 'Iconostasis'.

**Olsuf'ev, Count Iurii Aleksandrovich (1879–1939)**, member and, from September 1919, Chairman of the Commission for the Preservation of Art and Antiquities at the Trinity St Sergius Monastery 1918–1920. After the Revolution he lived in Sergiev Posad where he organised a kind of private collective farm to nourish other members of the Commission, their families and ex-servants of the monastery. In 1928 published together with Florensky *Amvrosii, Fifteenth-century Wood-carver of the Trinity St Sergius Monastery*, which figured prominently in the campaign launched against the Commission in that year. To escape arrest he removed to Novgorod. Worked in the Central State Restoration Studios 1928–1932 and from 1934 at the Tret'iakov Gallery, taking part in numerous expeditions to study icons and frescoes in the Novgorod region. Arrested 24 January 1938 and shot on 14 March the same year, accused of 'spreading anti-Soviet rumours'.

**Origen (185–252 AD)**, Christian theologian of the Alexandrine Church, influenced by Middle Platonism. Advocated a doctrine of universal salvation, perceiving hell as a temporary purgatory for the preparation of impure souls for heaven, and maintained the eventual repentance and salvation of the Devil.

**Pakshin, Petr Nikolaevich (1893–1937)**, artist, fellow-prisoner of Florensky's on Solovki.

**Pascal, Blaise (1623–1662)**, French religious philosopher, mathematician and physicist with whom Florensky is sometimes compared.

**Pavlinov, Pavel Iakovlevich (1881–1966)**, artist, member of Makovets.

**Pavlov, Ivan Fedorovich (1849–1936)**, Russian physiologist, educated at theological seminary, St Petersburg University and the Military Medical Academy, where he subsequently taught. Nobel Prize for Medicine in 1904, Copley Medal of Royal Society in 1915. His teaching of conditioned reflexes was held to confirm materialist ideology and he was honoured by the Soviet State but remained a firm churchman and was openly critical of anti-religious policies.

**Pekok, Gotlieb Fedorovich** and **Aleksandra Vladimorovna (née Ushakov) (c. 1850–1901)**, relations by marriage of Florensky's (Aleksandra Fedorovna was the sister of his grandfather's stepmother). Gotlieb Fedorovich taught singing and their daughter Aleksandra sang at the Scala in Milan under the name of Alina Marini.

**Pelagius (c. 354–425 AD)**, lay theologian from Ireland. Questioned Augustine's doctrine of Original Sin but his more optimistic view of human nature was condemned as heresy in 418.

**Perrault, Charles (1628–1703)**, French poet and writer of the classic collection of fairytales *Contes de ma mère Loye*, 1697.

**Persephone**, daughter of Jupiter and Ceres, also called Proserpine. Abducted by Pluto King of the Infernal Regions, when gathering flowers on the plains of Sicily, but allowed to return to Earth to spend spring and summer with her mother.

**Peshkova, Ekaterina Pavlovna (1887–1965)**, first, divorced wife of **Gorky** who, as head of the International Red Cross in Russia, was known for the compassionated energy with which she interceded for political prisoners.

**Petrov, Father Grigorii (1868–1925)**, liberal priest involved in the Circle of 32, the Union of Church Renewal and the Christian Brotherhood for Struggle.

**Petrovskaia, Nina Ivanovna (1884–1928)**, wife of Sergei Aleksandrovich Sokolov (pseudonym Krechetov) (1879–1936), the proprietor of Grif publishing house, Nina Ivanovna was beloved of **Briusov** and **Bely** and was the prototype for Briusov's heroine Renata in *The Fiery Angel*. She is the subject of a sympathetic memoir by Khodasevich and died in the emigration.

**Petrovsky, Aleksei Sergeevich (1881–1958)**, senior by one year to Florensky at the MDA. Close friend of **Bely**.

**Picasso, Pablo (1881–1973)**, Spanish artist resident in France. Founder of Cubism.

**Pivovarchuk, Mikhail Kosmich (18??–19??)**, student of the MDA arrested together with Florensky for the unauthorised publication of the latter's sermon 'The cry of blood'.

**Plato (427–347 BC)**, Greek philosopher, a pupil of Socrates and preserver of his oral teaching, he was a primal influence on Florensky's thought, teaching methods and inclination towards the dialogical form of expression. The idea of pre-existent forms, the incarnation of which is for Florensky the highest aspiration of the wise, is of vital importance to him, as are the concepts of **Eros** and anamnesis and the conception of the body as a 'republic' governed by the head, motivated from the heart and ensured of vital continuity by the lower organs.

**Pobedonostsev, Konstantin Petrovich (1827–1907)**, Procurator of the Holy Synod at the time of the Religious Philosophical Meetings. An intelligent man, but afraid of change and widely regarded as a pillar of reaction.

**Poincaré, Jules Henri (1854–1912)**, French mathematician and physicist, professor of the Université de Paris and President of the French Academy of Sciences.

**Popov, Aleksandr Stepanovich (1859–1905)**, Russian physicist and electro-technician who independently, before Marconi, invented radio-telegraphy, demonstrated a receiver in 1895 and a successful transmission in March 1896. **Luzin**'s claim that Florensky had grasped the principle of the invention 'before Popov' (i.e. at the age of 15 or 16) probably means 'independently from'.

**Popov, Ivan Vasil'evich (1867–1938)**, theologian. Editor of *Bogoslovkii vestnik* when Florensky was a student at the MDA.

**Potapov** see **Anatolii**.

**Popova, Liubov' Sergeevna (1889–1924)**, Russian Cubist painter.

**Potebnia, Aleksandr Afanas'evich (1835–1891)**, Ukrainian philologist, very influential in Symbolist circles, founder of the Psychological School in Russian linguistics.

**Prometheus**, mythical hero who stole the fire from the chariot of the Sun, made the first man and woman from clay and animated them with the flame, thereby so exasperating the gods that he was condemned to be bound to a rock on Mount Caucasus where, for 30,000 years, an eagle (or vulture) was to tear away at his never diminished liver. Within a mere 30 years, however, he was freed by Hercules. An altar was erected to Prometheus in the groves of Academe and games held half-yearly in his honour. He is also credited with teaching men the use of plants, medicine and how to train animals.

**Protasov, Nikolai Dmitrievich (1885–1940)**, member of the Commission for the Preservation of Art and Antiquities in the Trinity St Sergius Monastery and of the Moscow Department for Museum Affairs.

**Pushkin, Aleksandr Sergeevich (1799–1837)**, Russian poet and prose writer.

**Pythagorus (c. 580–c. 490 BC)**, Ionian Greek mathematician, founder of the religious movement Pythagoreanism.

**Rachinsky, Grigorii Alekseevich (1853–1939)**, well-connected founder and chairman of the Vladimir Solov'ev Society.

**Radzilovsky, Georgii Ivanovich**, head of the political department of OGPU during Florensky's 1933 interrogation.

**Rasputin, Grigorii Efimovich (1872–1916)**, the scandalous 'Elder' from the Khlysty sect who wielded untold influence over the Tsarina and her family thanks to his ability to 'talk down' the flow of blood from the haemophilic Crown Prince Aleksii. He had, to begin with, influential backers but also, and increasingly, bitter opponents in the Russian Orthodox Church.

**Remizov, Aleksei Mikhailovich (1877–1957)**, Russian writer who first came to prominence in the Silver Age. Emigrated 1919. Although associated with Symbolism, Remizov was particularly interested in the revival of elliptical Russian syntax, Europeanised since the early nineteenth century, both to retell old tales and to produce graphic stories of the contemporary world. In this, he influenced the early Zamiatin and the neo-Realists.

**Robinson Crusoe**, fictional hero of the eponymous book, 1719, by Daniel Defoe, based on Alexander Selkirk, a sailor stranded for several years on a desert island.

**Rousseau, Jean Jacques (1712–1778)**, Swiss philosopher of the Enlightenment. Composer. Rousseau was influential on the Romantic cult of the Noble Savage. His book *Emil or on Education* (1762) was publicly burnt but left a lasting impression on the hearts and minds of liberal Europe, including Russia.

**Rowland, Henry Augustus (1848–1901)**, American physicist, eminent in spectroscopy.

**Rozanov Tatiana Vasil'evna (1895–1975)**, daughter of **Vasilii Rozanov**. Secretary to the Commission for the Preservation of Art and Antiquities in the Trinity St Sergius Monastery, 1918–1921.

**Rozanov, Vasilii Vasil'evich (1856–1919)**, thinker and writer, contributor to Symbolist journals and popular newspapers. Friend of Florensky.

**Rozenfeld, Lev Borisovich (Kamenev) (1883–1936)**, classmate of Florensky's at Second Tiflis Classical Gymnasium. Later leading Bolshevik who, however, opposed Lenin's coup in 1917 in favour of a broad Socialist coalition. Nevertheless, after October Revolution he became chairman of the Central Executive Committee of Soviets and later deputy Chairman of the Council of People's Commissars. Ambassador to Italy 1923–1927. Sided with **Stalin** against **Trotsky** after Lenin's death but later, with **Trotsky** and Zinoviev, headed Left Opposition to **Stalin**. Arrested 1935, executed 1936.

**Rublev, Andrei (?1360–?1430)**, Russian icon painter, renowned especially for his depiction of the Holy Trinity for the Trinity St Sergius Monastery. Canonised in 1989.

**Rudin**, type of the Romantic dreamer in **Turgenev**'s eponymous novel.

**Rühmkorff, Heinrich Daniel (1803–1877)**, German physicist. Inventor in 1851 of an early version of the induction coil.

**Sacharov, Andrei Dmitrievich (1921–1989)**, Soviet physicist, one of the creators of the hydrogen bomb. Academician, outspoken human rights activist, awarded Nobel Prize for Peace in 1975. In 1980 exiled to Gorky (formerly Nizhnii Novgorod) but recalled in 1985 by Gorbachev and became an architect of *glasnost*.

**St Andrew of Crete (660–740)**, preacher and poet. Bishop of Gortyna in Crete. Author of much liturgical poetry, notably of the penitential Great Canon still sung in Orthodox churches in Lent.

**St Athanasius the Great (*c.* 296–373)**, Bishop of Alexandria. Opponent of the Arian heresy. The authorship of the Nicene Creed is attributed to him, but this is disputed.

**St Augustine (354–430)**, Bishop and Doctor of the Church. Author of the famous *Confessions*.

**St David Mtatsmisnky (seventh century)**, Georgian saint and martyr, patron of church in Tiflis where Florensky was christened.

**St Feofan the Recluse (1815–1894)**, Bishop Theophanus or Feofan was a renowned nineteenth-century writer on spiritual matters, canonised by the Russian Orthodox Church.

**St Francis of Assissi (*c.* 1181–1228)**, founder of the Friars Minor, ascetic and poet, beloved of all Christian confessions for his active charity and love of the natural world. St Francis was declared patron saint of ecologists by Pope John Paul II in 1979.

**St German (fifteenth century)**, saint of Solovki. He accompanied **St Savattii** to the island in 1429, then, after his death, brought in **St Zosima** who was responsible for the founding of the monastery.

**St Gregory the Theologian or the Great (540–604)**, Pope of Rome and Doctor of the Church. From 579–585 was papal agent at Constantinople and as Pope was able to strengthen the authority of Rome in the East as well as in the West. Famously described his office as that of 'the servant of the servants of God'. It was Pope Gregory who despatched St Augustine of Canterbury to convert the English.

**St Isaac Sirin or Isaac the Great (*c.* 347–438)**, Bishop of the Armenian Church, translator of the Bible, one of the founders of Armenian literature.

**St John Chrysostom (347–407)**, Bishop and Doctor of the Church, trained as a lawyer, John was famous for his eloquence, hence the title Chrysostom, 'of the golden lips'. From 398–403 he was Archbishop of Constantinople but owing to outspoken criticism of abuses was permanently banished from his see in 404, first to Armenia and, in the year of his death, to the more secure and distant Iberia.

**St Mary Magdalene (first century)**, one of the women who followed and ministered to Christ in Galilee and, according to St John, the first person to whom the Risen Christ appeared, entrusting her with a message for His disciples. Florensky served as priest in the Mary Magdalene House Church for retired Red Cross nursing sister in Sergiev Posad from 1912 until it was closed down in 1921.

**St Maximus the Confessor (580–662)**, Abbot, born at Constantinople and died a martyr's death near Batumi. Supported Pope Martin I in his opposition to the doctrine of Monotheism and thus fell foul of the Emperor Constans II. Famous for the beauty and elegance of his mystical and ascetic writings.

**St Paul (born Saul of Tarsus) (d. 67 AD)**, the Apostle to the Gentiles, author of the Epistles, beheaded in Rome. For Florensky, who bore his name, Paul was a special authority, an 'erotic' in thought, capable of embracing and trenchantly expressing antonymic ideas.

**St Phillip (Fedor Stepanovich Kolychev) (1507–1569)**, Abbot of Solovki, Metropolitan of Moscow from 1566, martyr.

**St Savatii (fourteenth–fifteenth century)**, Hermit Saint of Solovki, who came to the island in 1429 after leading an ascetic life in the Kirillo-Belozersky and Valaam Monasteries from which he fled to withdraw further from the world and escape his own fame.

**St Seraphim of Sarov (1759–1833)**, canonised in 1903, St Seraphim, like **St Sergius**, spent many years as a hermit in the Russian forest and was granted visions of the Theotokos. He was a gifted spiritual counsellor and revered as one at times transfigured by the Divine Light. The canonisation of this comparatively modern saint – of whom it was said that he was a contemporary of **Pushkin's** though neither knew of the other's existence, just a year before Florensky and **Bely** asked **Bishop Antonii's** blessing to become monks – provided a strong impetus for reconciliation between the intelligentsia and the Church.

**St Sergius of Radonezh (c. 1314–1392)**, Abbot and founder of the Trinity St Sergius Monastery. An exceptionally harmonious figure, remembered as a peacemaker but also for blessing the forces of Prince Dmitrii of the Don before the Battle of Kulikovo Field, which halted Tatar encroachment. In his life, Sergius was a nature lover who advocated humility and simplicity, but also a visionary with a special devotion to the Virgin Mary. In his time, the monastery engendered other missionary foundations and proved a generous patron to writers and artists, notably the icon-painter **Rublev**. It is of the ethos of Sergius' monastery that Florensky was thinking when he described himself as a Romantic with a medieval (fourteenth-century) turn of mind.

**St Vladimir (995–1015)**, Grand Prince of Kiev who married Ann, sister of the Byzantine Emperor, and was responsible for the Baptism of Rus into the Greek Orthodox Faith. St Vladimir is the title of a lyric poem by Florensky, eschatological rather than historical in character, the content of which suggests that he was thinking of **Vladimir Solov'ev** rather than the Vladimir whom the Russian Church acknowledges as 'Equal to the apostles'.

**St Zosima (fifteenth century, d. 1478)**, **St Savatii's** successor on Solovki in 1436 and founder of the monastery there.

**Samarin, Fedor Dmitrievich (1858–1916)**, Slavophile politician. With **Novoselov** founder member of the Circle of Seekers after Christian Knowledge.

**Saparian, Arzhak (Saparov, Arkadii Pavlovich) (1854–1921)**, Florensky's uncle.

**Saparian, Elizaveta Pavlovna**, see **Melik-Begliarov**.

**Saparian, Ol'ga Pavlovna**, see **Florensky**.

**Saparian, Pavel Gerasimovich (Saparov) (1818–1878)**, Florensky's grandfather, Armenian merchant trader in luxury goods from France and the Orient.

**Saparian, Repsimia Pavlovna (Remso, also known in Russian as Raisa) (1865–early 1930s)**, Florensky's aunt. Second marriage to Leonid Grigor'evich Konovalov, d. 1920.

**Saparov** see **Saparian**.

**Schelling, Friedrich Wilhelm Joseph von (1775–1854)**, German Romantic philosopher. Advocated doctrine of identities or correspondences (the identity of the Real and the Ideal, of Being and Thought). Sometimes known as *Naturphilosophie*, this doctrine was embraced in its aesthetic implication by French, German and Russian Symbolism.

**Scherbov, Ivan Pavlovich (1875–1925)**, lecturer in theology at the St Petersburg Theological Academy who attempted to broker a reconciliation between **Bulatovich** and his opponent the *imiaborets* **Professor Troitsky**.

**Scherner, Karl Albert (1825–1829)**, Professor of Philosophy in Breslau, precursor of **Freud**'s dream symbolism in his 1861 book *Das Leben des Traumen*.

**Schopenhauer, Arthur (1788–1860)**, German philosopher whose works, translated by Ananassii Fet, were seminal for Russian thought and literature in the late nineteenth / early twentieth centuries. Symbolists (notably Bely) sought escape from what they saw as his life-denying pessimism, which was labelled Buddhist, through Nietzsche or in a return to Christianity, but his *The World as Will and Idea* exerted a lasting fascination.

**Schubert, Franz Peter (1797–1828)**, Austrian composer. Florensky's mother sang his lieder and Florensky liked to play his music for piano.

**Schumann, Robert Alexander (1810–1856)**, German pianist and composer. From 1844, his unstable mental condition caused problems in his career though it did not immediately affect his work as composer. From 1854 confined to an asylum.

**Scriabin, Aleksandr Nikolaevich (1877–1915)**, Russian composer who believed in the possibility of writing a symphony the performance of which, under the right conditions, would change the world. Florensky considered he was misled by this 'magic' ambition, which drove him to neglect the laws of music in search of synaesthesia and the 'mystic chord'.

**Semennikov, Varvara Nikolaevna**, mother of Nikolai Semennikov, a schoolfriend of Florensky's, who helped Florensky and **Ern** at the outset of their university career.

**Semenov, Tian-Shansky, Leonid Dmitrievich (1880–1917)**, poet who, after Bloody Sunday in January 1905, joined the revolutionary underground.

**Serapion, Arkhimandrite**, see **Mashkin, Vladimir Mikhailovich**.

**Sergii, Patriarch (Ivan Nikolaevich Starogorodsky) (1867–1944)**, Orientalist, theologian and hiero-monk, Rector of the St Petersburg Theological Academy and chairman of the Religious Philosophical Meetings in St Petersburg 1901–1903. After the death of **Patriarch Tikhon**, Sergii became Locum Tenens to a vacant patriarchal throne and preserved the Russian Orthodox Church as a legal presence in the Soviet Union by a policy of loyalty to the Government, a policy which eventually led to the collapse of the more pro-Soviet Living Church faction but which, at the time, was much criticised. Florensky, as ever non-factional, accepted that he was doing his best in an extraordinarily difficult situation. After the Second World War, Sergii became Patriarch.

**Shaginian, Marietta Sergeevna (1888–1982)**, Russian writer and memoirist of Armenian descent, at one time strongly influenced by **Zinaida Hippius** and **Bishop Mikhail**'s Golgotha Church. Later espoused Communism, became a Party member in 1942 and received the Lenin Prize for a cycle of works on Lenin in 1972. Her memoirs *Chelovek i vremia* are the source for an altercation with Florensky, who apparently spelt out why his friends from the **Novoselov** group were trying to wean her from the influence of **Hippius**, whom they suspected of homosexual tendencies. 'So now we know what these ecclesiastics think about when they're alone', **Hippius** commented.

**Shakespeare, William (1564?–1616)**, English playwright.

**Shchukin, Sergei Ivanovich (1852–1936)**, great Russian art collector. Emigrated in 1919, leaving his collection, which included **Picasso** and Matisse, to a nephew Dmitry Ivanovich Schukin who continued to curate it after nationalisation in the Pushkin Museum until he lost his sight and died in 1932.

**Shentalinsky, Vitaly**, chairman of Commission for the Literary Legacy of Writer-Victims of Repression. Investigative journalist, author of *The KGB's Literary Archive*, translated from the Russian by John Crowfoot, London 1995. For Florensky see 'A Russian Leonardo da Vinci', pp. 101–123.

**Shik, Mikhail Vladimirovich (1887–1938)**, member of the Commission for the Preservation of Art and Antiquities in the Trinity St Sergius Monastery 1918–1920. Subsequently became a priest of the Orthodox Church.

**Shirinsky-Shikhmatov, Prince Aleksei Aleksandrovich (1862–1930)**, conservative statesman, Procurator of the Holy Synod in 1906.

**Shmidt, Anna Nikolaevna (1851–1905)**, an eccentric admirer of **Vladimir Solov'ev** who believed herself to be an incarnation of the Divine Sophia.

**Shmidt, Lieutenant P. P. (1887–1906)**, Russian naval officer of Jewish extraction executed in 1906 for supporting mutinous sailors. The execution prompted Florensky's sermon 'The cry of blood', for which he was later arrested and briefly imprisoned.

**Shupeiko, (d. 1939)**, investigator responsible for compiling case against Florensky in 1933. Later executed for misconduct during interrogations.

**Simonovich-Efimov, Nina Iakovlevna (1877–1948)**, artist who created and worked singularly beautiful carved puppets. Wife of **Efimov**. Author of reminiscences about Florensky and several portraits.

**Skvortsov, Vasilii Mikhailovich (1859–1932)**, editor of *The Missionary Review (Missionerskoe obozrenie)* 1896–1917 and chargé d'affaires to **Konstantin Pobedonostsev**, Procurator of the Holy Synod at the time of the Religious Philosophical Meetings in St Petersburg. Emigrated to Serbia in 1920 and took part in the first Council of the Russian Church Abroad at Karlsbad in 1921, after which he eschewed ecclesiastical politics and occupied a comparatively humble teaching post in a Serbian Orthodox Theological seminary.

**Socrates (449–399 BC)**, Greek philosopher who wrote nothing but many of whose sayings were recorded by **Plato** and, differently, by **Xenophon**. His teaching method was to ask questions and promote argument. Since he left no written record, it is difficult to determine to what degree the figure bearing his name in **Plato**'s later dialogues is in fact voicing his thoughts.

**Sohm, Rudolf (1841–1917)**, German theologian. Florensky's translation from his *Kirchenrecht Band 1, Die geschichtlichen Grundlagen*, Leipzig, 1892 was published Moscow, 1906.

**Solov'ev, Sergei Mikhailovich (1885–1945)**, nephew of **Vladimir Solov'ev** and close friend of **Blok** and **Bely**. Author of the book of poems *Crucifragium* and active in Symbolist and religious philosophical circles. After the October Revolution became a priest of the Uniate Church, thus by his acceptance of the supremacy of the Pope of Rome following in the footsteps of his revered uncle, whose *Collected Works* he edited.

**Solov'ev, Vladimir Sergeevich (1853–1900)**, Russian Christian thinker and literary critic. His cult of Sophia, a figure for Divine Wisdom, and his apologia for a Christianity compatible with and relevant to the modern world had a profound influence on Florensky's thought. Solov'ev was a poet and eschatological visionary, the author of the influential novel *Antichrist* and was devoted to the idea of Christian Unity. Like **Viacheslav Ivanov** and his nephew **Sergei**, Solov'ev went through a ceremony of conversion to the Greek Catholic Rite.

**Solzhenitsyn, Aleksandr Isaevich (1918–2008)**, Russian author famous for unvarnished depiction of life in labour camps (the GULAG) in the Soviet period. Nobel Prize winner in 1970. Exiled from USSR in 1974, returned to Russian Federation in 1995.

**Sophia**, the Greek word for 'wisdom', conceived by Florensky and after him by **Bulgakov** as the personification of the Old Testament Wisdom and a figure for the interpenetration of Spirit and matter and thus for the incarnation of **Christ**, the God-bearing humanity of the Virgin Mary and the Community of the Church inspired by the Holy Spirit. Russia, particularly, is rich in churches dedicated to and icons, albeit of comparatively late provenance, depicting Sophia as the Holy Wisdom in feminine form. In Gnostic mythology, however, Sophia is perceived as a separate Being, an Aeon, present like **Christ** at the creation of the world but entrammelled in compassion for the fallen world and thus entrapped in matter. Rather in the fashion of the Sleeping Beauty, She is destined to be rescued by **Christ**, Her Divine Bridegroom. This essentially erotic version of the Sophia myth undoubtedly inspired **Vladimir Solov'ev** and much of the poetry of the Silver Age and is hard to separate from Florensky's and **Bulgakov**'s liturgical and iconographic meditations on the theme, which eventually led to accusations of Gnosticism and heresy.

**Spencer, Herbert (1820–1903)**, English positivist philosopher who takes an optimistic view of the perfectibility of the human condition based on Utilitarian ethics and social evolution.

**Speransky, Count Mikhail Mikhailovich (1772–1839)**, Russian mystic, thinker and liberal statesman, advocate of reform from above. Subject of an essay by **El'chaninov** with an introduction by Florensky.

**Stalin** see **Dzhugashvili**.

**Stein, Ludvig**, fictional name of phantom German Jesuit engineer supposed to have served as liaison between Florensky's alleged conspiracy, the Third Reich and the Vatican.

**Steiner, Rudolf (1861–1925)**, Austrian founder of the Anthroposophical Society in 1912.

**Stolypin, Petr Arkad'evich (1862–1911)**, statesman and Prime Minister of Russia from 1906 until his assassination at the Kiev Opera in 1911. Regarded as a safe pair of hands to restore order in Russia and stamp out terrorism in the aftermath of the 1905 Revolution while at the same time instituting a programme of economic reform, which laid the foundation for a remarkable pre-war upsurge in prosperity.

**Sumarokov, Aleksandr Petrovich (1717–1777)**, eighteenth-century Russian author and *kultur-träger* who became a byword for his failure to harmonise old and new in the written language. Director of the Russian Theatre 1756–1761.

**Suslova, Apollinaria Prokof'evna (1839–1918)**, Dostoevsky's mistress and prototype of many of his 'demonic' women. Rozanov's first wife.

**Sventsitsky, Valentin Pavlovich (1879–1931)**, friend of **Ern** and co-founder of the Christian Brotherhood for Struggle. Author of a novel, *Antichrist*, 1908, which brought the movement into disrepute. Took holy orders after October Revolution.

**Tareev, Mikhail Mikhailovich (1867–1934)**, theologian, Professor of MDA. Editor of *Bogoslovskii vestnik* after Florensky in 1917.

**Tatlin, Vladimir (1885–1953)**, Russian constructivist painter and designer, identified also with Cubism and Futurism. A leading figure in post-revolutionary art, he taught at Vkhutemas 1918–1920 before removing to Leningrad.

**Taumann, Gustave (1861–1938)**, German physio-chemist.

**Tavgeridze, Shalva (18??–1910)**, Georgian student who on 2 November 1910 murdered Florensky's friend and brother-in-law **Sergei Troitsky**. In spite of the family's intercession, he was executed.

**Teilhard de Chardin, Pierre (1881–1955)**, French monk and theologian who sought to reconcile science, particularly the theory of evolution, with religious revelation as aspects of the same Truth. Like **Vernadsky** and Florensky, he uses the terms 'biosphere' and 'noosphere', although the meaning with which he invests them is not wholly identical.

**Ternavtsev, Valentin Aleksandrovich (1866–1940)**, official of the Holy Synod instrumental in setting up the Religious Philosophic Meetings in St Petersburg 1901–1903. Friend of the **Merezhkovsky**s and of **Novoselov**.

**Tikhomirov, Lev Aleksandrovich (1852–1923)**, politician and publicist. Originally a member of the executive committee of the revolutionary group Narodnaia Volia, he edited their journal from abroad 1883–1888 but renounced his revolutionary views and returned to Russia where he continued to publish, but in right-wing journals, and wrote a book on the theory of absolute monarchy. Member of the Circle of Seekers after Christian Knowledge, he corresponded with Florensky about the Hebrew scriptures in 1914.

**Tikhon, Patriarch (Vasilii Ivanovich Belavin) (1865–1925)**, after his enthronement as Patriarch of all Russia in 1917, Tikhon spoke out vigorously against the confiscation of Church property by the State and suffered arrest. There was a threat that he might be replaced by one of the more cooperative leaders of the Living Church, but he was later released and allowed to continue as Patriarch, albeit of a much-weakened Church, until his death in 1925.

**Tiutchev, Fedor Ivanovich (1803–1873)**, Russian poet and diplomat.

**Tolstoy, Lev Nikolaevich (1828–1910)**, Russian novelist. His *Confession*, 1884, and his teaching of the simple life were a profound influence on Florensky, especially in the late 1890s at the time of his first spiritual crisis.

**Troitsky, Sergei Semenovich (1881–1912)**, addressee of 'Letters' in *The Pillar and Ground of Truth*. Close friend of Florensky's, one year senior to him at the MDA. Married his sister Ol'ga in 1909, assassinated 1910.

**Troitsky, Sergei Viktorovich (1878–1972)**, theologian, professor, specialist in Canon Law, opponent of the *imiaslavtsy*. 1920 emigrated to Yugoslavia.

**Trotsky, Leon** see **Bronstein, Lev Davydovich**.

**Trubachev, Deacon Sergii (Sergei Zosimovich) (1919–1925)**, conductor and Deacon. Son of a pupil of Florensky's, who had officiated at his wedding in 1918. Married **Ol'ga Pavlovna Florensky** in 1946. Author of valuable reminiscences and articles on Florensky, music and life in Sergiev Posad.

**Trubachev, Igumen Andronik**, see **Andronik**.

**Trubachev, Mariia Sergeevna (b. 1951)**, Florensky's granddaughter. Active in curating and publishing his archive.

**Trubetskoi, Prince Evgenii Nikolaevich (1863–1920)**, religious thinker. Pillar of the Vladimir Solov'ev Religious Philosophical Society and the publishing house Put'.

**Trubetskoi, Prince Sergei Nikolaevich (1862–1905)**, lecturer in philosophy at Moscow University. Florensky attended his seminar while studying mathematics.

**Tseretelli, Iraklii Georgevich (1881–1959)**, classmate of Florensky's at the Second Tiflis Classical Gymnasium and fellow-founder of their schoolboy literary philosophical society. Member of the Menshevik Party. Minister for Post and Communication during the Provisional Government.

**Tsvetkov, Sergei Alekseevich (1880–1964)**, member of the Circle of Seekers after Christian Knowledge. Friend of Rozanov's. Worked for Put' publishers.

**Tuberovsky, A. M. (1881–1939)**, author of Master's thesis for the MDA on 'On the Resurrection of Christ' discussed by Florensky as official opponent on 2 May 1916. After the October Revolution he retired to his father's country parish where he served as a priest.

**Turgenev, Ivan Sergeevich (1818–1883)**, Russian novelist.

**Vadkovsky**, see **Antonii, Metropolitan**.

**Vernadsky, Vladimir Ivanovich (1867–1945)**, academician, Russian mineralogist, bio- and geo-chemist and philosopher who used the terms biosphere and noosphere. Human society, he considered, has a part to play in the biosphere (knowable not only through logic but through philosophy and religion). On the basis of human effort to perfect social organisation of the biosphere, humanity can form a noosphere. The same applies to cooperation between man and his cosmic environment. It is necessary that humanity become a channel for (or learns to channel) cosmic energy in order to withstand the enthropic tendencies of the biosphere.

**Vernes, Jules (1828–1905)**, French writer of science fiction.

**Vitruvius, Marcus Vitruvius Pole (first-century BC)**, Roman author of a book on architecture and construction. An official under the Emperor Augustus.

**Volkert**, an early critic of **Freud**'s dream theory in 1875.

**Voll, Karl (1867–1917)**, writer on art. His *Experiment on the Comparative Study of Pictures* translated by **Favorsky** and **N. B. Rozenfeld** in 1916.

**Voloshin, Maximilian Aleksandrovich (Max) (1877–1913)**, late Symbolist poet, artist and publicist.

**Volzhsky, A.**, see **Glinka**.

**Vvedensky, Aleksei Ivanovich (1861–1913)**, professor, theologian, authority on Kant. One of Florensky's teachers and well-wishers at the MDA. Founder of the Ontological School of Theology pre-dominant in *Bogoslovkii vestnik*.

**Vvedensky, Dmitrii Ivanovich (1873–1954?)**, theologian, 1919–24 taught in the town gymnasium at Sergiev Posad. Roomed with Florensky in exile in Nizhnii Novgorod in 1928.

**Vvedensky, Ivan Alekseevich (18??–19??)**, graduate of the MDA. Cooperated with Florensky on the latter's reports for the Commission for the Preservation of Art and Antiquities in the Trinity St Sergius Monastery, 1918–1920. **Maria Sergeevna Trubacheva** mentions Vvedensky as having been introduced to the Commission by Florensky.

**Weierstrass, Carl Theodor Wilhelm (1815–1897)**, German mathematician and analyst, described continuous but nowhere differential functions in such a way as to undermine the intuitive approach to these concepts.

**Witte, Sergei Iulevich (1849–1915)**, liberal statesman. Prime minister of Russia from 1903–1906.

**Wulff, Oskar Konstantin (1864–1946)**, German art critic and historian, originator of the term 'reverse perspective' ('die umgekehrte Perspektive').

**Wundt, Wilhelm Maximilian (1832–1920)**, German psychologist and philosopher who established the first recognised psychology laboratory at the University of Leipzig.

**Xenophon (430–350 BC)**, Greek patron of the arts, historian, author of several Socratic dialogues, which complement and in some ways contradict Plato's, and of works on other subjects such as history education and political theory.

**Yudina, Maria Veniaminovna (1899–1970)**, concert pianist. Close friend and admirer of Florensky.

**Zarubina, Nataliia**, see **Florensky**.

**Zavitnevich, Vladimir Zinov'evich (1853–1927)**, professor, author of two-volume monograph on **Khomiakov** controversially reviewed by Florensky in 1916.

**Zhegin, Lev Fedorovich (1892–1969)**, artist and memorist.

**Zhukovsky, Nikolai Egorovich (1847–1921)**, Professor of Mathematics at Moscow University. Chairman of the undergraduate section of the Moscow School of Mathematical Philosophy.

**Zinov'eva-Annibal, Lidiia Dmitrievna (1866–1907)**, short-story writer. Wife of the poet Viacheslav Ivanov, but continued to write under her maiden name.

# Appendix 1

In *Pro et Contra* the section 'Vokrug Knigi "Stolp i utverzhdeniia istiny"'
(pp. 211–366) reprints, with notes, the following contemporary reviews.

Bishop Fedor (A. V. Pozdeevsky 1876–1943), rector of the MDA from
1909–1917, in a review of the version presented for Florensky's Candidate's
Degree '*O dukhovnoi istine*', 1912, first published in *Bogoslovskii vestnik*, May,
1914, while emphasising the author's claim that the book is for the catachumen
rather than for the converted, comes out strongly in support of its scholarly
merit and religious orthodoxy; S. S. Glagolev, Florensky's official 'opponent',
and a professor of the MDA, gives a still more enthusiastic endorsement of the
originality, style and content of a book he declares to be far beyond the compass
of the ordinary academic dissertation in the official *Zhurnal sobranii Soveta
Imperatorskoi Moskovskoi Dukhovnoi Akademii za 1914 god*, Sergiev Posad,
1916. Archimandrite Nikanor (Florenksy's junior by one year at the MDA, a
rapidly rising ecclesiatic soon to become an austere and severe abbot and later
Bishop of Bogorodsk), in the journal *Missionerskoe obozrenie*, Nos 1–2, 1916,
disagrees vituperantly with his theological colleagues, implying that Florensky's
efforts in *O dukhovnoi istine* and *Stolp i utverzhdenie istiny* are a chaotic travesty
unworthy of the award of a higher degree, 'a bouquet of mutually exclusive
heresies' plagiarised from the still unpublished candidate's dissertation of
A. Mashkin. This blistering attack had been turned down by Antonii Khrapovitsky
(a conservative cleric who, in public at least, preferred to distance himself from
the unconventional Florensky but who had approved his thesis for the degree
of Master of Theology) for his journal *Vera i razum*, and when it did come out,
prompted Florensky not to self-defence but to clearly Isidor-inspired gratitude
for the humiliation inflicted after too much praise. From without the Church
*Stolp i utverzhdenie istiny* was predictably excoriated by Boris Iakovenko in
*Severnyi vestnik*, March 1914, as 'the philosophy of despair', a quixotic, escapist
attack on rationalism by a repellent, though impressively learned, hysteric
who has found, like others of the new religious movement among the intelligentsia, that he is miserable without faith, a 'standart work' [in English sic]
for this absurd movement. From within the religious-philosophical movement,
Florensky also found himself under fire – for his commitment to the Orthodox
Church and renunciation of the intelligentsia, especially its values of tolerance

and freedom of thought, its concern with man in history and man in society. Nikolai Berdiaev, in a highly qualified and telling critique (which has since engendered a whole sub-bibliography of its own) accused Florensky in *Russkaia mysl'*, 1914 of 'stilizovannoe pravoslavie' (stylised Orthodoxy). Like Iakovenko, he sees 'despair' as the point of departure for Florensky's conversion (comparing him to Pascal and Kant), but, in the spirit of the Merezhkovskys' critique of 'historical Christianity', accuses him of wishing to return to the Childhood of the Church, of having stifled the mathematician in himself and of attempting to stifle stillborn the teeming 'heresies' to which any exercise of free thought in Orthodox Theology will inevitably give rise. This leads – says Berdiaev – to an unpleasant 'semitic' fanaticism particularly in the digs at the Roman Catholic Church and the apology for 'jealousy' in the last chapter, whereas Florensky's true nature is that of 'an original, at times verging on eccentric. That is what is interesting about him, sometimes attractive, sometimes repulsive.' His book is the confession of a soul in full flight from its true self, clutching at the stability of custom in the stuffy daily life of the Russian Orthodox Church. Prince Evgenii Trubetskoi, spoke about *The Pillar and Ground of Truth* at a meeting of the Religious-Philosophical Society in February 1914 in a paper published as 'Svet favorskii i preobrazhenie uma' in *Russkaia mysl'*, May 1914, subjecting the work to a careful philosophical critique on the basis of an attentive, benevolent but not uncritical reading. Taking as his text the famous dichotomy of the transfiguration of Christ on Mount Tabor and His disciples' failure to heal the idiot boy at the foot of the mountain, Trubetskoi gives Florensky credit for continuing the work of Vladimir Solov'ev in attempting to include both events in a holistic vision and singles out as Florensky's special contribution his highlighting of artistic and liturgical insights hitherto neglected in Orthodox theology and the powerful Augustinian surge from the darkness of Sin and Hell towards Truth and Light. The chief defect of the book, however, is Florensky's failure to distinguish between irreconcilable antonyms ('*tertium non datur*') and the reconciliation of opposites (*coincidentia oppositorum*) in Church and liturgical texts, which leads to the suggestion that the Truth itself is antonymic in essence, which leads in turn to denial of reason; but the mind, as was shown by the incarnation of Christ, should be transfigured, not denied. Florensky's alogism results from insufficient attention to the Person of Christ and from the author's struggle against his own 'internal foe' – the 'intelligent' in himself.

The émigré criticism anthologised in the *Pro et Contra* series resulted from the reissue of Florensky's *Pillar and Foundation of Truth* in Paris, 1930 and includes reviews by Vladimir Il'in and Georgii Florovsky, both as republished in later works. Il'in's, first published in *Put'*, Feb. No. 28, pp. 116–119, situates the book in the neo-gnosticism of the Silver Age, but has little new to say of its content. Florovsky's, as published in *Puti russkogo bogosloviia*, 1937, reissued in 1981, contains, on the contrary, a fundamental critique of the book, which has (belatedly) coloured contemporary Russian perceptions of Florensky as a 'Christian without Christ', as a Westerniser 'dreamily and aesthetically seeking salvation in the East', whose Orthodoxy is tainted by the 'ambiguity and instability of the religious-philosophical movement' in pre-war Russia and clouded by 'the sediment of erotic *prelest*' [false revelation]. The true subject of the book, Florensky's conversion, notes Florovsky, springs from the apocalyptic unease of the turn of the century which haunts his and Bely's poetry and looks not so much towards the Second Coming of Christ as to the Coming of the Holy Spirit. Chapters on Florensky in various Histories of Russian Thought published in the emigration – Zenkovsky, Losskii and Zernov – take due account of Berdiaev, Trubetskoi and Florovsky, while emphasising the encyclopaedic breadth of Florensky's learning, the consensus being that *The Pillar and Ground of Truth* is an extraordinary, highly subjective work which, in spite of the overtones of Pascal and St Augustine, belongs very much to its own time, to 'the religious Renaissance' in early twentieth-century Russia.

# Appendix 2

The great Byzantine cathedral of St Sophia in Constantinople was dedicated to the Holy Wisdom of God, the 'pre-existent Word', thought of not so much as a distinct Feminine Being as an attribute of the Second Person of the Holy Trinity, but the idea of 'Sophia' as a separate entity was already in the air. There are Western allegorical pictures of Wisdom as a Woman Crowned and, in Russia, a tradition came into being of icons depicting the Holy Sophia crowned and enthroned, attended by the Mother of God on one side and John the Baptist on the other and watched over from above by the Holy Trinity – or, in another form, as the Bride of Christ, the Response of the World to God incarnate, the Church. It was this absorption of Sophia as a distinct and separate being into the iconography and also, under the guise of the Old Testament Wisdom, into the liturgical practice of the Church which made it possible for Vladimir Solev'ev to assume and for Florensky to demonstrate (at least to the best of his concentrated understanding) Sophia as an inspiring figure, symbolic rather than allegorical, at once cosmic in Her Old Testament association with the creation of the world and human in Her closeness to Christ, His Church and the imponderable assent of the Mother of God to become the instrument of incarnation. She is, Florensky reasoned, present in all these, but identical with none. In this, he is close to some of the earliest Fathers who identified the concept of Sophia with the Holy Spirit, but Florensky makes no such identification, establishing the Holy Trinity firmly as sufficient unto Itself, but maintaining the concept of Sophia as acceptable within the thinking of the Church: a figure for Humanity and Nature, beloved of the Creator and inspiring for the created, a place of encounter between them. She manifests Herself, Florensky considered, where the material is transparent to the spiritual, for instance in the azure which cloaks the blackness of space on a cloudless day, in the finest particles of atmospheric dust which, lit by the rising or setting sun (a figure for the Divine Light) colour the sky, in the very dust from which God created man. Uncertain how Florensky's poetic flights would be received by the Holy Synod, Bishop Fedor (Pozdeevsky) warned that the inclusion of the chapter on Sophia (as well as those depicting his admired and trusted pupil's highly idiosyncratic concepts of Gehenna, Friendship and Jealousy) would force his resignation as examiner. His report on the thesis without these chapters emphasises the writer's Orthodoxy and there was no attempt to discipline Florensky for including them in *The Pillar and Ground of Truth*. It was the reflection of Florensky's (and, of course, Solov'ev's) ideas in the sophiology of his good friend Sergei Bulgakov which later, in the emigration at a time when Florensky was sidelined from theological controversy on Solovki, led to a charge of heresy, never substantiated against Bulgakov personally and tainted, to some extent, by Church politics, and to a serious controversy in which the cult of Sophia, in the thinking of Solov'ev, Florensky and Bulgakov, was opposed as insufficiently Christocentric, spiritually obscure and contaminated by erotic mysticism – not only by Bulgakov's enemies but by his dearly loved and loving spiritual child Georgii Florovsky. In 1935, Bulgakov was accused of heresy by the Synod of Karlsbad and his bishop, Evlogii, ordered the calling of a Commission to investigate the charge. The Russian Orthodox Church condemned sophiology *per se* in the same year, but was not in a position to pursue the matter in Paris. Evlogii's stance was complicated by the fact that, disliking the monarchism and political conservatism of the so-called *Karlovchane*, the faction of the émigré Church that rejected the *locum tenens* in Moscow as a Communist stooge, he had remained loyal to Moscow only to seek a third spiritual head outside Russia altogether in the Patriarch of Constantinople when, in 1935, he felt unable to confirm Metropolitan Aleksii's assertion, clearly made under duress, that there was no persecution of Christians in the USSR. He was thus, to a certain degree, independent of both Russian authorities but could not afford to ignore the clamour raised. After a two-year debate, in 1937, Bulgakov was personally exonerated from heresy and the charges against him by his fellow-émigrés Vladimir Lossky, Georgii Florovsky and Sergei Chetverikov, were not unanimously upheld. The defence was based on the unimpeachable character of Father Sergii, whose sophianic writings, it was suggested, could be considered *theologoumena*, expressions of private opinion not binding as doctrine. The opposition, based on the feeling that Bulgakov's sophiology came near to suggesting a Fourth Person of the Trinity (an idea which he, like Florensky, specifically disowned) and on concern for sound doctrine and the possible confusion Bulgakov's ideas might cause in the minds of the uninstructed, nevertheless pronounced both the Karlovchane and the Russian Orthodox Church to have been 'premature and harsh' in their accusations. The majority of the Bishop's Council affirmed that the questions raised by Bulgakov, if not the conclusions arrived at, were 'legitimate and no heresy' and his writings on the subject, though still considered perilous for 'simple souls' by the Orthodox Church, were widely translated (e.g. S. Bulgakov, *The Wisdom of God: A Brief Summary of Sophiology*, Oxford, 1937) and influential far beyond its bounds. Excellent accounts of the controversy and its ramification in English are to be found in the special Sergius Bulgakov number of *St Vladimir's Theological Quarterly*, Vol. 49, Nos 1–2, 2005 and, in Russian, in the Russian Christian Humanist Institute's *Sergei Bulgakov: Pro et Contra.* 'Lichnost' i tvorchestvo v otsenke russkikh myslitelei i issledovatelei: antologiia: Vol. I compiled, introduced and annotated by I. I. Evlampiev, responsible editor D. K. Burlak, St Petersburg, Izd-vo Russkogo Khristianskogo Gumanitarnogo Instituta, 2003; Vol. 2 forthcoming. For a measured discussion of the degree to which Florensky's sophiology can be said to differ from both Solov'ev's and Bulgakov's, see Robert Slesinski, *Pavel Florensky: A Metaphysics of Love,* Westwood, New York, 1984, Chapter VII 'Sophiology: an exigence of human thought and experience' and more particularly the sub-section 'Positions anterior and posterior to Florensky', pp. 194–196.

# Notes

## Notes on Foreword

1    Loren Graham and Jean-Michel Kantor, *Naming Infinity: A True Story of Religious Mysticism and Mathematical Creativity*, Belknap Press of Harvard University Press, Cambridge, MA, 2009, Chapter 4, especially pp. 86–90.

2    A. N. Parshin, 'Nauka i religiia vo vzgliadakh P.A. Florenskogo', *Vestnik russkogo khristianskogo dvizheniia*, No. 160, 113.

3    Pavel Florensky, *The Pillar and Ground of Truth: An Essay in Orthodox theodicity in Twelve Letters*, translated by Boris Jakim, Princeton University Press, Princeton, 1997, 50.

4    Niklas Luhmann, *Trust and Power*, Wiley, Chichester, 1979, p. 20.

5    Russell Hardin, *Trust and Trustworthiness*, Russell Sage, New York, 2002, p. 131.

6    Guido Möllinger, *Trust: Reason, Routine, Reflexivity*, Elsevier, Amsterdam, 2006, pp. 111–115.

7    Father Pavel Florenskii, 'Troitse-Sergieva Lavra i Rossiia', *Vestnik russkogo khristianskogo dvizheniia*, No. 117, 6, 14, 18.

## Notes on Chapter 1: Childhood

1    *Carl Jung: Memories, Dreams, Reflections*, recorded and edited by Ariela Jaffe, translated from German by Richard and Clare Winston, Collins, London. First published in Fontana Library of Theology and Philosophy, 1967, 2nd impression 1969, p. 86.

2    According to one account in the sixteenth, to another in the eighteenth century.

3    According to family recollection, this was the Austrian geologist Academician Abick who frequented the Saparov's house (according to one source he stayed with them as the guest of Pavel Saparov) when working in Tiflis. His 'letters' *Aus Kaukäsischen Länden Reisebriefe* I and II were published in Vienna in 1895. See Florensky, *Detiam moim*, compiled by Igumen Andronik (Trubachev), M. S. Trubachev, T. V. Florenkaia, P. V. Florenskii, "Moskovskii rabochii", Moscow, 1992, (*For My Children*), p. 375.

4    *For My Children*, p. 133.

5    *For My Children*, pp. 70–71.

6    *For My Children*, p. 255.

7    Florensky used the Russian word *mazushchemusia* which could be translated as 'using make-up (or grease-paint)'. I thought of using 'smeared' but the word carries moral overtones which have no place in this context and loses the sense, very present in the

Russian verb *mazat'sia*, of deliberately applied make-up. P. Florensky, *For My Children*, p. 142.

8    *For My Children*, p. 142.

9    *For My Children*, p. 90.

10   *Sboku* – lit. from the side. *For My Children*, p. 99.

11   Ibid.

12   *For My Children*, p. 158.

13   *For My Children*, 152–153.

14   *For My Children*, p. 153.

15   *For My Children*, p. 154.

16   *For My Children*, p. 259 and p. 123.

17   The Russian journal *Priroda* and Gaston Tissandier's *La Nature*.

18   Lemprière's *Classical Dictionary of Proper Names Mentioned in Ancient Authors*, a new edition by F. A. Wright MA, Routledge & Kegan Paul Ltd, London, 1963 (first published 1788).

## Notes on Chapter 2: School

1    Cf. Igumen Andronik (A. S. Trubachev), 'P. A. Florenskii. Zhiznennyi put'', in the collection *P. A. Florenskij e la cultura della sua epokha*, Atti del Convegno Internazionale, Università degli studi di Bergamo, a cura di Michael Hagemeister e Nina Kauchtschischvili, Blaue Hörner Verlag, Marburg, 1995, p. 2. Further *P. A. Florenskij*, Bergamo.

2    M. Hagemeister, Introduction to P. A. Florensky's 'Imaginary points in geometry', *Nachala*, No. 4, 1993, p. 13. The translation from the German, here and elsewhere unless otherwise stated, is my own.

3    Aunt Julia had prepared Florensky for the obligatory first confession and communion before entering school but appears to have made little or no impression at the time.

4    See V. I. Keidan, *Vzyskuiushchie grada (They Who Seek for a City)*, Iazyki russkoi kultury, Moscow, 1997, p. 53. Further *Vzyskuiushchie grada*.

5    V. F. Ern to E. D. Ern, letter of 11 April 1910, *Vzyskuiushchie grada*, p. 262, letter 183.

6    P. A. Florenskii, 'Pamiati Vladimira Frantsevicha Erna', in Sviashchennik Pavel Florenskii, *Sochineniia v chetyrekh tomakh*, Vol. 2, in the series Filosofskoe nasledie, tom 124, Izd-vo Mysl', Moscow, 1996, p. 346. Further references to Florenskii's *Works* in four volumes will be given as S for *Sochineniia*.

7    V. F. Ern to E. D. Ern, letter of 25 November 1910, *Vzyskuiushchie grada*, p. 266, letter 230.

8    Private collection. Reproduced in Pavel Florensky, *Beyond Vision: Essays on the Reception of Art*, compiled and edited by Nicoletta Meisler, translated by Wendy Salmond, Reaktion Books, London, 2002, p. 17.

9    *For My Children*, p. 63.

10   *For My Children*, pp. 71–72.

11   Sviash. A. V. El'chaninov, 'Iz vstrech s P. A. Florenskim 1909–1910', first published *Vestnik RKhD*, Paris, 1984, No. 142, (iii), pp. 68–77. Quoted here from the anthology *P. A. Florenskii. Pro et Contra. Lichnost' i tvorchestvo Pavla Florenskogo v otsenke russkikh*

*myslitelei i issledovatelei*, ed. K. G. Isupov in the series Russkii put', Izd-vo R.KhGI, Saint Petersburg, 1996, p. 37. Further *Pro et Contra*. The memoir is also quoted inserted in chronological snippets among letters by Ern, Bulgakov, Trubetskoi, Florensky *et al.* in *Vzyskuiushchie grada.*

12    *For My Children*, pp. 204, 203.

13    *For My Children*, pp. 201–202.

14    El'chaninov, having taken a degree in history and philology at St Petersburg University, followed Florensky into the Theological Academy but never completed the course, preferring a free form of service as secretary to the Moscow Religious Philosophical Society in memory of Vladimir Solov'ev and editor of various religious publications. In 1912 he returned to Tiflis as a schoolmaster, describing himself in a letter to Ern as an 'adulterer' (no doubt also not in the coarse sense of the word) in his relationship with the 200–300 children he taught 'and loved within certain bounds' (see 'Dva pis'ma k V. F. Ernu (1912))', *Vestnik RKhD*, Paris, No. 142(iii), 1984, pp. 78–79. He married Tatiana Vladimirovna Levandovskaya in 1918 and emigrated in 1921. He became a priest in 1925 under the influence of Father Sergii Bulgakov, and was much loved, especially by his younger parishioners. His *Notebooks*, originally *Sviashchennik A El'chaninov*, Zapisi, Paris, 1935 have become a classic of spiritual literature translated into many languages.

15    Although Florensky takes the break with El'chaninov on himself, the latter wrote of him in 1910: 'I never knew him to be the first to grow cold towards anyone, to get tired of the other person, to seek freedom, a change', A. V. El'chaninov, *Pro et Contra*, p. 87.

16    Russian variations of proper names are legion. Pavlik is the normal diminutive of Pavel (Paul). 'Pavlusha' used by his father and friends is more affectionate. 'Pavlia' appears to hav been pecular to his mother and her family.

17    According to Fritz and Sieglinda Mierau in their introduction to 'Letters from the journey to Germany' *Pavel Florenskij – Tradititon und Moderne*, Beiträge zum Internationalen Symposium an der Universität Potsdam, 5–9 April 2000, eds Norbert Franz, Michael Hagemeister and Franz Haney, Peter Lang, Frankfurt am Main, 2001 (further *Pavel Florenskij* (Potsdam, 2000), pp. 431–463. This was the so-called Rühmkorff's coil, the first version of the induction coil.

18    The account of the trip to Germany and extracts from family letters are taken from *Die Korrespondenz der Deutschlandsreise*, a publication introduced and translated into German by Fritz and Sieglinde Mierau, op. cit. The letters were prepared for publication by members of Florensky's family and A. A. Sauches. For more about the Melik-Begliarovs see *For My Children*, pp. 472–477.

19    A. I. Florensky to P. A. Florensky, 27 July/8 August 1897, Pavel Florenskij (Potsdam, 2000), p. 458.

20    The chronology of Florensky's schooldays is not clear from his memoirs and the author stands open to correction.

21    *For My Children*, pp. 190–191.

22    *For My Children*, p. 194.

23    See *For My Children*, note 20, p. 505 for Florensky's own account of his disillusion and for statements to this effect by Max Plank's tutor Professor Jolly and J. J. Tomson, president

of the Royal Society, both of whom appeared to think that all the cardinal questions had been solved and it remained only to tidy up a few details.

24   *For My Children*, p. 197.

25   *For My Children*, p. 193.

26   *For My Children*, p. 206.

27   Cf. P. A. Florenskii, 'Pavel', *S* III(2), pp. 306–323.

28   *For My Children*, p. 264. At a lecture on Tolstoy and Florensky delivered at the Moscow conference of 3 October 2007, Pavel Florensky remarked that this letter had not been found in Tolstoy's archive and may never have been sent.

29   Carl Jung, *Memories, Dreams, Reflections*, recorded and edited by Aniela Jaffe, translated from the German by Richard and Clara Winston, Collins, London, first published in Fontana Library of Theology and Philosophy, 1967, second impression 1969, p. 119 *et seq.* Jung became interested in spiritism during his second year at medical school.

30   See V. Rozanov, 'Pamiati Vl. Solov'eva', *Mir iskusstva*, No. 15–16, 1900, pp. 33–36.


*Notes on Chapter 3: From the Physico-Mathematical Faculty at Moscow University to the New Religious Consciousness*

1   Final remarks at a discussion between 'the two cultures' organised by the International Balzan Foundation at the Royal Society, London, 13–14 May 2002. *Meeting the Challenges of the Future*, ed. Walter Rüegg, Leo S. Olschki Editore, 2003, p. 196.

2   *For My Children*, p. 164.

3   S. S. Demidov, in the article 'O matematike v tvorchestve P. A. Florenskogo' (On mathematics in the work of P. A. Florensky) writes that 'without understanding of the significance of mathematics in his method of understanding the world, outside the frame of his opinions on the place of mathematics in the Universe it is impossible adequately to evaluate either his method or his philosophical views'. P. A. Florenskij (Bergamo, 1995), p. 171. S. M. Polovinkin considers that the Moscow School of Philosophy and Mathematics provides, if not the key to Florensky's encyclopaedic thought, then at least the one fundamental formative influence of which it is possible to speak with any certainty. See S. M. Polovinkin, 'P. A. Florenskii: Logos protiv khaosa', *Pro et contra*, p. 625. This article is a fragment (Chapter 2) of Polovinkin's eponymous book, Znanie, Moscow, 1989.

4   P. A. Florenskii, 'Pis'ma 1900 goda' (Pervyi semestr pervogo kursa universiteta) Letters of 1900 (First semester of the first course at university) pub. by Pavel V Florenskii, *Novyi zhurnal*, 1999, Vol. 515, pp. 227–238. Further 'Letters of 1900'. P. A. Florenskii, letter of 15 October 1900 to O. P. Florenskaia, p. 229.

5   'Letters of 1900', Letter of P. A. Florenskii, 17 October to A. I. Florenskii, p. 231.

6   'Letters of 1900', Letter of P. A. Florenskii 25 October 1900 to A. I. Florenskii, p. 233.

7   Ibid., p. 232.

8   S. M. Polovinkin, 'O studencheskom matematicheskom kruzhke pri Moskovskom matematicheskom obshchestve v 1902–1903 gg' (On the students' mathematical circle attached to the Moscow Mathematical Society in the years 1902–1903). *Istoriko-matematicheskie issledovaniia*, Issue 30, Nauka, Moscow, 1986, pp. 148–158.

9   S. M. Polovinkin, 'P. A. Florenskii: Logos protiv khaosa', *Pro et Contra*, p. 624.

10  According to Plato, the memory of Truth with which a child is born into the world that has to be rediscovered at the cost of mature intellectual effort and concentrated recall.

11  S. I. Demidov (op. cit. cf. n. 2) makes the point that Bugaev had not taken on board the work of Borel, Lebesgue and Baire – French mathematicians who throughout the 1890s had been working on the theory of real-valued functions, taking as their point of departure G. Cantor's set theory – and that, for this reason, Florensky's university years were in fact a time of some confusion and intensive searching for new ways in the School as a whole.

12  'Letters of 1900', P. A. Florenskii, Letter to A. I. Florenskii from P. A. Florenskii, 27 September 1900, p. 222.

13  For Florenskii and Luzin, destined to become an internationally respected Academician who almost lost his place at the Academy of Sciences in 1936 because of his closeness to Florenskii and his ideas, see Demidov, op. cit., pp. 176–177; Polovinkin, as in n. 8; and their correspondence published by Demidov, Polovinkin, A. N. Parshin and P. V. Florenskii in *Istoriko-matematicheshie issledovania*, Issue 31, Nauka, Moscow, pp. 125–190.

14  See letter of 24 August 1900 from P. A. Florenskii to O. P. Florenskaia in Pavel Florenskii. 'Pis'ma 1900 goda', pp. 211–215 and notes. Florenskii refers to Aleksandra Vladimirovna as 'grandmother' and recalls stories of her kindness to his beloved Aunt Julia, *For My Children*, p. 325.

15  The details of Ern's and Florensky's life at the hostel we owe to his letters home and to a classmate from the Tiflis Gymnasium, E. Arkhipov. See *Vzyskuiushchie grada*, pp. 58–59.

16  P. A. Florenskii, 'Kant E. Fizicheskaia monodalogiia. Ot perevodchika' (Kant E. Physical monodology. Translator's foreword), *Bogoslovskii vestnik*, No. 9, pp. 95–99. S I, pp. 682–686.

17  Cf. Wolfgang Uhlman, 'Florenskijs Beiträge zu einer Logik des Diskontinuität', *Pavel Florenkij – Potsdam*, 2000, DP 151–159.

18  N. V. Bugaev, *Matematika kak orudie nauchnoe i pedagogicheskoe* (*Mathematics as a Scientific and Pedagogic Tool*), Moscow, 2nd edition 1875, p. 28.

19  See N. V. Bugaev, 'Osnovnye zadachi evoliutsionnoi monodalogii' ('Fundamental problems of evolutionary monadology'), *Voprosy Filosofii i Psikhologii*, Kn. 2(17), 1893, pp. 31, 34, 35. Here and throughout, the account of Bugaev's monadology is based on my understanding of the extensive and admirably lucid account given by S. M. Polovinkin in 'P. A. Florenskii: Logos protiv khaosa', *Za i protiv*. Any inaccuracies, however, are my own.

20  Florensky is here distinguishing between the abstract axiomatic concepts of points, straight lines and surfaces and natural space (translator).

21  P. A. Florenskii, Letter to A. I. Florensky of 23 September 1900, 'Pis'ma 1900 goda', p. 224.

22  P. A. Florenskii. 'Ob odnoi predposylke mirovozreniia' (On one premise towards a world view), first published in *Vesy*, No. 9, 1904, pp. 24–35, here quoted from *Sochineniia* I, p. 70. The article is a variant of Florensky's introduction to his candidate's dissertation. Aleksandr Ivanovich, having followed the development of his son's thought through his letters, had perceived the possibility of a reconciliation of his own scientific world-view

with Pavel's mystic intuitions, and very much wanted him to write a book on the subject, but the dissertation and the fuller version of its introduction in fact remained unpublished until 1986 (see *S* I, p. 707). The fact that, while at university, Florensky published his thoughts on mathematics exclusively in the 'decadent', Symbolist press is proof of how receptive they were to the thrust of his thinking (see note 25).

23    See letter of 12 November 1901 from Vasilii Skvortsov to D. S. Merezhkovsky, RGALI, F. 419, opis' 1, ed. khr. 2.

24    See letters 6 and 7, V. F. Ern to A. V. El'chaninov 9.10.1903 and El'chaninov to Ern 14.10.1903, *Vzyskuiushchie grada*, pp. 60-63. El'chaninov's letters to Florenskii remain unpublished in the Florenskii family archive, but see T. A. Shutova, 'Florenskii i El'chaninov: Iz Atin k Ierusalimu nebesnomu', *Le Messager*, 190, 11-2005, 1-2006, pp. 200-201.

25    Florenskii's contributions to these journals were as follows: 'O sueverii', (On superstition, *Novyi put'*, No. 3, 1903, pp. 91-121 (see also *S* I as 'O sueverii i chude', pp. 44-69, written January 1902); 'Ob odnoi predposylke mirovozreniia' (On one premise towards a world view), *Vesy*, No. 9, 1904, pp. 24-35 (see also *S* I, pp. 70-78, written towards the end of 1905 as the introduction to the philosophical preface to his candidate's dissertation entitled 'Ideia nepreryvnosti kak element mirosozertsaniia' (The idea of discontinuity as an element of a world view); 'O simvolakh beskonechnosti (ocherk idei G.Kantora)' ('On symbols of infinity (an account of the ideas of G. Cantor)'), *Novyi put'*, No. 9, 1904, pp. 173-235 (see also *S* I, pp. 79-128), the first extensive exposition of Cantor's theory of transfinite sets in Russian and among the earliest examples of interest in set theory on the part of mathematicians at Moscow University; 'Spiritizm kak antikhristianstvo' (Spiritism as anti-Christianity) *Novyi put'*; No. 3, 1904, pp. 149-167. (See also *S* I, pp. 129-145 (originally entitled a review of 'Two narrative poems' which treated A L Mirospol'sky's 'Lestvitsa', 1902 and Andrei Bely's 'Severnaia simfoniia I'aia, geroicheskaia', 1903). Florensky objected to the 'pretentious' title wished onto the article by the editors of *Novyi put'* who had, he complained, severely distorted the text to the disadvantage of Miropol'sky (A. L. Lang, a friend of Valerii Briusov's and contributor to the earliest 'Russian Symbolists' volumes). It was Florenskii's 'mathematical world view' that particularly intrigued Briusov, always interested in a synthesis of art and science, who records discussing mathematical infinity with the multilingual mathematician and publisher Poliakov as early as 1901. For the Merezhkovskys, Florensky was an intriguing example of a new type: the educated layman who sets out to defend the possibility of acausal phenomena, believes in God and wishes to embrace Christianity while not forgetting the 'things of this earth' – such as beauty, culture and social equity. They did not, however, approve of his increasing self-identification with the Russian Orthodox Church. Other works of Florenskii's written under the influence of the Symbolists, more particularly under the influence of Andrei Bely, were his own book of poems *V vechnoi lazure* (*In the eternal azure*) privately published in Sergiev Posad, 1907, a poetic piece in the style of Bely's Symphonies 'Eskhatologicheskaia mozaika' (An eschatological mosaic) and a review of Bely's first collection of verse *Zoloto v lazure* (*Gold in Azure*), neither of which last were published in his lifetime, but see *Kontekst, Literaturno-teoreticheskie issledovaniia*, Nauka, Moscow, 1991, pp. 62-92 where they are published with a commentary

by E. V. Ivanova and L. A. Iliunina from texts prepared by Igumen Andronik, O. S. Nikitina, S. Z. Trubachev and P. V. Florenskii. For a fuller publication of the eschatological mosaic as part of the longer poem 'Saint Vladimir' see *Pavel Florenskii i simvolisty. Opyty literaturnye. Stat'i. Perepiska*, compiled and ed. E. V. Ivanova, Yazyki Slavianskoi Kul'tury, Moscow, 2004, pp. 213–322 (further: Ivanova, Florenskii i Simvolisty).

26  Leaving aside for the moment the divergent opinions of Florensky's contemporaries, the most important critique of Florensky's Orthodoxy was made by Archpriest Georgii Florovsky in *Puti russkogo bogosloviia* (*The Ways of Russian Theology*), originally Paris 1939, (here quoted from the second indexed edition published by YMCA-Press, Paris, 1981), who perceives his *magnum opus The Pillar and Ground of Truth* (1914) as 'the most characteristic monument of the pre-war era' and typical of all the faults of the religious philosophical movement, though he rightly identifies Florenskii with Moscow rather than St Petersburg societies and publishing houses. N. M. Zernov includes Florenskii in his generally positive assessment of *The Russian Religious Renaissance* as does N. O. Losskii, both in his *History of Russian Philosophy*, London, 1952, and in the article 'The successors of Vladimir Solov'ev', *Slavonic Review*, June 1924, pp. 92–109. Losskii sees both Florenskii and the movement of which he was a part as an essential bridge between the Church and secular society and Florenskii's thought as an important factor for his own conversion. V. V. Zenkovskii in his *Istoriia russkoi filosofii* (History of Russian Philosophy) Vol. 2, 2nd edition, Paris, 1989, pp. 413–430 is more ambiguous; stressing the inconsistency of Florensky's own attitude to the new religious consciousness, maintaining now that it is based on 'a true idea' (*Pillar*, p. 129) and, in the next breath, disassociating himself from it, he concludes: 'Florensky is in many ways alien to 'the new religious consciousness', alien to the neo-romanticism which we have seen, for instance, in Berdiaev, but invisible threads of some kind attach him to both' (*Pro et Contra*, p. 428). N. K. Bonetskaia in 'P. A. Florenskii i 'novoe religioznoe soznanie'' (originally in *Vestnik RKhD*, Np. 160, 1998, pp. 90–112 but quoted here from *Za i Protiv* pp. 649–667) goes so far as to say it is wrong to consider Florensky as an Orthodox writer at all and that 'Together with Berdiaev, Rozanov and Merezhkovsky Florensky personifies the profound and fundamental crisis of Orthodoxy in the XX century' – a curious judgement on three very different thinkers one of whom (Florenskii) dedicated his life to the service of the Church. The collection *P. A. Florenskij e la cultura della sua epoca* (Marburg, 1995) contains a number of articles on Florensky and individual representatives of the Russian religious renaissance, including Bernice Glatzer-Rosenthal's 'Pavel Florensky as "God-seeker"', pp. 67–82, which gives a factual account of Florenskii's relations with representatives of the Russian religious renaissance and concludes sensibly that his later work, after he found 'a spiritual home' in the Orthodox Church, represents a continued dialogue with them' (p. 78). In the same collection, theologians such as Bishop Anatolii (Kuznetsov) and Priest-monk Inokentii (Pavlov) place Florensky in the tradition of the 'ontological' school of the Moscow Theological Academy, which maintained that God could be approached not only through revelation but also through knowledge, and emphasise his talent for exegesis of Holy Writ through Hebrew, Greek and Latin and his knowledge of the Fathers of the Church; it is, they consider, only natural that he also responds to contemporary thoughts. In this, the men of the Church are closer to the original reviewer of Florensky's *Pillar and Ground of*

*Truth* Bishop Fedor (A V Pozdeevskii) in *Bogoslovskii vestnik*, May 1984, reprinted in *Za i protiv*, pp. 211–243, who declares firmly that, although Florenskii's work will be of most importance to people still outside of but approaching the Church, it is truly Orthodox in its basic orientation.

A spirited rebuttal of all such critiques of Florensky's Orthodoxy is provided by E. V. Ivanova, 'Nasledie o: Pavla Florenskogo: a sud'i kto?' *Pro et Contra*, pp. 609–624. A further reaction is the way in which the uniquely authorative grandson and keeper of Florenskii's archive Igumen Andronik presents the new religious consciousness as an unremittingly anti-Orthodox movement and exaggerates Florensky's alienation from them (as, indeed, from all secular culture) in later life. See Igumen Andronik (Trubachev), *Obo mne ne pechal'tes'* ... *Zhizeopisanie sviashchennika Pavla Florenkogo*, izd-vo Izdatel'skii Sovet Russkoi Pravoslavnoi Tserkvi, Moscow, 2007, pp. 30–31.

27   Ternavtsev had warned at the first meeting that the Church should not look on the meetings as 'a mission to the Intelligentsia' but Merezhkovsky, carried away by his love of formulaic utterances, had described himself as 'a catechumen', 'in the ranks of those who wish to learn and demand teachers', so that representatives of the Teaching Church were never altogether sure what was required of them. Bishop Sergii, the chairman, on his summing up at the end of the first season's talks in 1902, had been sufficiently impressed by the sincerity and urgency of the debate, particularly as regarding the Church's teaching on marriage and on the use of force, to find a happy mean between the uncompromising tone of his opening statement at the First Meeting and a more emollient approach by defining the aim of the discussions as being to

> clarify Christian truth and on that basis to be reconciled with one another. That is our aim and we will endeavour to attain it and not to lose heart if our views so far do not altogether correspond. God grant these differences will disappear and we will achieve reconciliation.
>
> (*Zapiski religiozno-filosofskikh sobranii (Verbatim Reports of the Religious Philosophical Meetings)*, St Petersburg, 1906 (further *ZRFS*), p. 248)

However, it became increasingly clear over the 1902–1903 season that the intelligentsia, whilst avid for spiritual experience which would resolve their doubts, found the men of the Church dull and slow. In the debate on the 'holy flesh' at the 11th session, Merezhkovsky had exclaimed that none of their answers had satisfied him because his questions could not be answered by the mind alone, only by 'reality', to which one of the churchmen had replied earnestly that the answer was indeed given 'in reality' in the sacrament of Holy Communion (*ZRFS*, p. 241). Merezhkovsky and his party, to whom he referred ever more frequently as 'we' but which did not comprise all representatives of the Intelligentsia all of the time, showed no desire to seek the living truth in sacrament, unlike the practising Ternavtsev, the ritual-friendly Rozanov whose grudge was that he could not practise because divorced and 'living in sin', and the ultra-Orthodox Mikhail Novoselov, later a firm friend of Florenskii, who also, like him, had gone through a period of admiration for Tolstoy, having actually tried (and failed) to found an agricultural colony. Yet, said Merezhkovsky at the nineteenth Meeting, when he listened to Rozanov or Ternavtsev, their words sounded to him like a call to prayer, 'but the voices of the clergy are as it were foreign to us, as though they were not religious, there is nothing in them to ignite the heart'. Again he was met with the invitation: 'You are welcome to come to Church!' (*ZRFS*, p. 497). The words were a heartfelt exclamation from Father Innokentii, a usually rather quiet priest, but at the next session Novoselov took up the cudgels for the Church in favour of 'repentance-good works-sacraments' (*ZRFS*, p. 529), provoking Merezhkovsky, who considered him a sermonising bore, to reply hotly in terms of 'our side' and 'your side'. Both he and Filosofov declared there was nothing to be hoped for from the 'Historical Church', by which they meant the Protestant, Roman Catholic and Eastern Orthodox (*ZRFS*, p. 136) and Dmitrii Sergeevich completely alienated the clergy by comparing these to 'the Church of Peter' which, in denial of Christ, was due to be struck with thunderbolts by the 'Coming Church of John', when and only when it would again repent, weeping. Nevertheless, it was neither the Church not the intelligentsia that wished to break off the debate but the secular power, and the ferment it produced in men's minds lingered on. Whether or not Florenskii was actually present at any of the meetings seems doubtful, but he would certainly have read the debates published in *The New Way*, and discussed the questions they raised within the framework of the Student Society for discussion of the history of religion.

28    P. A. Florenskii, *Bogoslovskie trudy*, Sbornik 23, Moscow, 1982, p. 267.

29    *Verst* – a pre-revolutionary Russian distance measurement, rather less than a kilometre.

30    'Metropole house' – now the Metropole Hotel with art-nouveau mosaics by Mikhail Vrubel. The first editorial office of *The Balance* was in a narrow passageway hard up against this building.

31    Andrei Belyi, *Nachalo veka* (*The Beginning of the Century*) Seriia literaturnykh memuarov, ed. A. V. Lavrov, Khudozhestvennaia literatura, Mowcow, 1990, pp. 301–302. Further A. Belyi, *Nachalo veka*.

32    Letter from P. A. Florenskii to O. P. Florenskaia of 24 January 1904. Quoted by E. V. Ivanova in 'Kistoriia otnoshenii s Andreem Belym' (see n. 33) from the family archive. The occasion mentioned was a Christmas reception at Bely's own home at which Bal'mont recited and most of the Symbolist literati were present.

33    For a detailed account of the relationship between Bely and Florensky see E. V. Ivanova 'K istorii otnoshenii s Andreem Belym' ('To the history of relations with Andrey Belyi') in *Kontekst*, Literaturno-teoreticheskie issledovaniia 1991 ANSSSR, Nauka, Moscow, 1991, pp. 3–22. The article, which complements and corrects Bely's own account, posits a much closer friendship than the poet admits to in his memoirs and this is borne out by the publication of the correspondence (pp. 23–61), of Florensky's unpublished review of Bely's first book of poetry *Gold in Azure* (*Zoloto v lazure*, 1904), of his own attempt at a Symbolist poem 'The Eschatological Mosaic' ('Eskatologicheskaia mozaika'), Part II, pp. 68–92 and of extracts from his 1935–1936 letters from the Solovki Prison Camp to his daughter, who was interested in Russian Symbolism in general and in Andrei Bely in particular. The correspondence between Bely and Florensky was also published in German in *Pavel Florenskij, Leben und Denken* Bd. 1 by Fritz and Sieglinde Mierau, Ostfelden, Ed Tertium, 1995 and engendered a number of reviews detailed in Hagemeister's bibliography of German sources in Pavel Florenskij (Potsdam, 2000). See

also Vladimir M Piskunov, 'Pavel Florenskii i Andrei Belyi (k postanovke voprosa)' (Pavel Florensky and Andrei Bely (to set the problem)), A. P. Florenskij (Bergamo, 1995), pp. 89–100. See also Ivanova, *Pavel Florenskii i simvolisty.*

34     A. P. Florenskii, letter of 3 March 1904 to O. P. Florenskaia, letter 9. *Vzyskuiushchie grada*, p. 64, first published in the *Journal of the Moscow Patriarchate*, 1985, No. 3. The journal is translated into English but I have here used my own translation from the Russian.

35     Letter from Andrei Belyi to A. P. Florenskii of 28 June 1904. *Kontekst*, p. 31. 'I find Antonii overwhelming. I revere him more than anyone, am aware of the immeasurableness of the power within him, but ... there are people of the steppes and open spaces, who admit the striking effect of mountain scenery, but nonetheless ... are drawn to the wide-open spaces of the Steppe.'

36     The most detailed account of Florensky's relationship with his spiritual director is Igumen Andronik. 'Episkop Antonii (Florentsov) – dukhovnik sviashchennika Pavla Florenskogo', *Zhurnal moskovskoi patriarkhii*, 1981, No. 8–9 (available in Eng. translation). See also A. El'chaninov, 'Episkop-starets', *Put'*, 1926, No. 4, pp. 157–170.

## Notes on Chapter 4: The Melting Pot. Autumn 1904–Autumn 1908

1     From P. A. Florenskii's article 'O sueverii i chude' (On superstition and miracle), first published under the title 'O sueverii' (On superstition), *Novyi put'*, 1903, No. 8, pp. 91–121, written in Moscow, January 1902, but quoted here from Florenskii, *S* I, pp. 54–55.

2     Florenskii's famous paper on 'Imaginary points in geometry' (O mnimost'iakh v geometrii), first published Moscow 1922 with supplements on Vladimir Favorsky's cover design and on Dante's depiction of space in the *Divine Comedy*, was originally a university essay written under the direction of Professor Leonid Lakhtin in 1902. In the 1920s, the mathematical thought was still sufficiently fresh for Florensky to read a revised version of the paper at a conference of the Russian Association of Engineers in 1921. See Milan Zust, *A la recherche de la Vérité vivante. L'Expérience réligieuse de Pavel A Florensky (1882–1937)*, Lipa Edizione, Rome, 2002, p. 76 (further Milan Juste, 'À la recherche de la vérité vivante') and the introduction to Michael Hagemeister's ground-breaking republication of the entire 1922 text in P. Florenskii, *Minimosti v geometrii*, Specimenae philologicae Slavicae, supplement band 14, Verlag – Otto Sagner, Munich, 1985.

3     One of Florenskii's poems, written July 1903, is dedicated to L. M. Lopatin. He attributes the term 'sub-liminal' to Dr Meier, i.e. to F. W. H. Myers. See E. V. Ivanova, *Pavel Florenskii i simvolisty*, p. 134 for poem and note on p. 185. It is quite possible that he was also familiar with the use of the term by William James (1842–1910), either from Lopatin's lectures (see L. M. Lopatin 'Bessoznatel'naia dushevnaia zhizn''), Kurs psikhologii (Lektsii 1901/1902 akademicheskogo goda) Moscow. 1903 or through James's *Textbook of Psychology* which was translated into Russian in 1896. James was elected an honorary member of the Moscow Psychological Society in 1901. See Randall A. Poole, 'William James in the Moscow Psychological Society: Pragmatism, Pluralism, Personalism' and

Aleksandr Etkind, 'James and Konovalov's The Varieties of Religious Experience and Russian Theology between Revolutions', in *William James in Russian Culture*, eds Joan Delaney Grossman and Ruth Rishkin, Lexington Books, Lanham, MD, 2003, pp. 131–158 and 169–188.

4    For a summary of various versions of the accusation that Florenskii's theology shows him to have been a 'Christian without Christ', an expression he himself anticipated in a footnote to *The Pillar and Ground of Truth* (n. 66, p. 638) in which he declared his intention to add a chapter which would refute any such accusation – see the Conclusion of Milan Zust's *A la recherche de la Vérité vivante*, pp. 305–312. Zust makes an excellent case for the defence, based on the importance of Orthodox Christology *implicit* in Florenskii's texts (including *The Pillar and Ground of Truth*) and on the commitment to Christ expressed through his daily life, his understanding of culture as cult, his attitude to scholarship and teaching as a shared exploration of a world redeemed and, finally, by the witness of a long martyrdom. Where there is such experience of existential commitment, Zust implies, there is no need to seek precise formulations. As an example of the opposing point of view, he quotes the verdict of one of Florensky's sternest and certainly most authoritative Orthodox critics, Father Georges Florovsky, which, republished in revised form in the book *Puti russkogo bogosloviia* (YMCA-Press, Paris, 1981, pp. 493–498), stated that 'in Florensky's "Theodicy" there is, strangely, no Saviour … he somehow misses out on the incarnation and passes straight on from the Trinity to the Doctrine of the Holy Spirit. In Florensky's book there are simply no Christological chapters' (quoted from *Pro et Contra*, an excellent source for the whole dispute, pp. 361, 362). Florovsky could not have seen the Christological passages from 'The empirical and the empyrean', first published in 1986, nor could Berdiaev or F. Marxer, also cited by Zust as deploring the absence of specific discussion of Christ in Florensky's *Works*. What is more remarkable is that they appear to have escaped the attention of Zust himself and not to have rated special studies in the many symposiums devoted to Florensky since the republication of the piece in Volume I of the *Collected Works* – together with an extended essay on 'The Church in holy writ', also relevant to the question of Florensky's Christology and also, having been undertaken as course work for the Academy in 1906, unpublished during the author's lifetime and for many years thereafter. Florensky's recently published notebook for 1904–1905 is also Christocentric, as is his poetry. See *Ivanova, Florenskii i simvolisty*, pp. 24–42.

5    P. A. Florenskii, 'Empireia i empiriia', *Bogoslovskie trudy*, Sbornik 27, Moscow, 1986, pp. 298–322. Florensky, for whom publication was a secondary consideration to the actual process of sorting out his thoughts for himself in writing, did, some time after graduating from the Academy, reread the dialogue and find that, although the content had withstood the test of time, 'the form required attention'. He made a number of alterations and added footnotes, including an explanation of the word 'Empireia' (Empyrean) as 'heaven, the place of light, the higher part of the world'. On 2 January 1916 he recorded typing out a third and final version of the article on his Remington and giving it to read to either M. A. Novoselov or a fellow-priest. The borrower entrusted the typescript to a janitor, who lost it. Part of this third version, however, survived, and the editors, having determined that the revision of the second version, found intact in Florensky's archive,

was minimal and stylistic in character, based the published text on the second version with a few amendments from the available part of the third. This text was reprinted in *S* I, pp. 146–178, from which all quotations are taken. The above summary of the fate of the dialogue is based on the excellent note to this edition, pp. 716–717.

6    *Starets* lit. 'elder'. A spiritual director who, having passed through a long period of training in obedience and self-abnegation, had acquired considerable freedom 'in the Holy Spirit' and the charismatic gifts of advising, comforting and inspiring others.

7    P. A. Florenskii, 'Sol' zemli' (The salt of the earth), subtitled as 'The story of the life of the Elder of the Gethsemane Skete Priestmonk Father Isidor, collected in order and expounded by his unworthy spiritual son Pavel Florensky originally published in *Khristianin*, Nos 10–11, 1908 and Nos 1–5, 1909. Also *S* I, pp. 571–637.

8    Two years later, in an extended third-year essay for the Academy on 'The concept of the Church in Holy Writ', Florenskii was to write:

> It is noteworthy that the first teachers of the Slavs St Methodius and St Cyril translated as *sobornaia*, of course understanding *sobornost* not in the sense of a count of votes [or quantity of different voices], but in the sense of the inclusiveness (*vseobshnost'*) of being, of purpose and of all spiritual life which gathers all people to itself irrespective of their local, ethnographic, historic or whatever particularities. The Church is called catholic [here Florenskii is quoting St Cyrill of Jerusalem, Homile XVIII, n. 23, where the saint maintains the Church is called Catholic. He uses *sobornaia*] because 'it is present in all the Universe from the ends of the Earth to the [furthest] ends, because everywhere and in all fullness it teaches one and the same doctrine which it is needful for people to know, the doctrine of things visible and invisible, heavenly and earthly, which brings all the family of mankind to the true faith, rulers and subjects, learned and simple folk, and which everywhere physics and heals all kinds of sins, committed in body and in mind, and which comprises all perfection manifested through deeds, words and all spiritual gifts'. (Quoted from 'Poniatie Tserkvi v sviashchennom pisanii', *S* I, p. 403)

9    Cf. T. A. Shutova, 'Florenskii i El'chaninov', *Le Messager*, No. 190, pp. 192–208. El'chaninov was called up to serve in the army shortly after enrolling in the Theological Academy and chose not to return because, at the time, he found the courses insufficiently relevant to modern life. Instead he became involved in work for Moscow religious publishing houses then, later, took up teaching in his native Tiflis until eventually, under the influence of Father Sergii Bulgakov, he entered the priesthood in the emigration, where he served in Nice and Paris. While his letters to Florenskii are preserved in the family archive, Florenskii's to him are presumed lost, having been 'hidden' from police searches with various friends and relatives during the time El'chaninov was active in the Christian Brotherhood for Struggle.

10   'In his book Florenskii has astoundingly little to say about the sacraments', writes Florovsky (op. cit., p. 361). In 'Empireia and empiriia' he writes of them, somewhat anecdotally, it is true, but extensively and returns to the subject in a Rozanov-style call for letters detailing actual experience published in the journal *Khristianin*, 1907, Vol. I, No. 1, pp. 2005–210; Vol. 2, No. 6, pp. 35–65; and Vol. 3, No. 10, pp. 436–439, under the title 'Questions of religious self-knowledge' (Voprosy religioznogo samopoznaniia), all in *S* I, pp. 528–549. The importance he attached to the existential approach

mooted here is shown by his undertaking a separate publication in booklet form that same year (Sergiev Posad, 1907). In this publication, the 26-year-old student of the theological academy defines the sacraments as follows: 'Sacraments, as an idea, are the first shoots of the divinisation of the creature, hearths which exude God's warmth. They are those points through which, before all others, a new, particular creative energy penetrates and transforms humanity and, through humanity, the whole of being' (S I, p. 529). Later, of course, Florenskii was to experience sacrament through priesthood.

11     Pavel Florenskii, 'Empireia i empiriia', S I, pp. 153, 156–7, 166, 164, 178.

12     Gavril Romanovich Derzhavin (1743–1816), 'Khristos'. *Sochineniia Derzhavina c ob'iasnitel'nymi primechaniami la Grota*. T3, 1866: 'O Syi, Kotorogo perom, / Ni brennym zreniem, ni slukhom / Nizhe vitiistva iazykom / Ne mozhno opisat', a dukhom / I veroi plamennoi molit''.

13     Quoted by A. S. Trubachev in 'Introduction' to the first publication of Florensky's memoirs in *Literaturnaia ucheba*, 2, March/April, 1988, p. 146. See also *For My Children*, p. 246.

14     Such was, indeed, the view from without. From the point of view of insiders within the Church the Moscow Theological Academy was comparatively liberal and the journal *Bogoslovskii vestnik*, which had become the organ of the Academy under the rectorship of Antonii Khrapovitskii in 1891 and of which Florensky himself was to edit the Philosophical Section from 1912 to 1917, 'served as the vanguard of Church reform' and led the coverage of the burning issues it was hoped and, from 1901 to 1906, believed would be addressed at a Church Council or *Sobor*. Even after the immediate expectation of the convening of such a Council began to fade, the journal maintained an enlightened attitude. See James W. Cunningham's *A Vanquished Hope: The Movement for Church Reform in Russia 1905–1906*, St Vladimir's Seminary Press, New York, 1981, pp. 63, 70–71.

15     Later Florensky came to regard his years at Moscow University as a period of 'catharsis' or purgation which prepared him to accept the antinomies of Christian thought. The years as pupil and lecturer at the Moscow Theological Academy were years of 'apprenticeship' and only after ordination did he enter into the 'practice' of Christian life.

16     Florenskii collaborated with Bishop Antonii on a conservation project (which some consider to have been a formative influence on his later attitudes to the preservation of the Trinity St Sergius Monastery as a living museum) and on the organisation of various missionary and educational iniatives among young people disaffected from the Orthodox Church and inclined towards experiments in the occult.

17     Optyno-Pustyn was a monastery famed for its *Startsy* situated to the south of Moscow and revered beyond the bounds of the Orthodox Church, thanks to a connection with Vladimir Solov'ev, Dostoevsky and Slavophile writers such as Samarin, Khomiakov and the brothers Aksakov. It was rumoured that Tolstoy, on his deathbed flight from home, had been on his way to Optyno-Pustyn.

18     A. P. Florenskii, 'Sol' zemli', S I, pp. 571–657. Florensky wrote this stylised account of his

'Elder's' life 'for the people' after his death in 1908. He says he wept as he wrote, but it is impossible to read this most affectionate memoir without a smile.

19    Abramtsevo, a country estate originally belonging to the Aksakov family, acquired by the merchant *mycaenas* Savva Mamontov in the late 1860s. Abramtsevo was the nucleus of the Moscow School of artists, home to Mamontov's private opera and a centre for folk culture and thus the cross-pollination of high art with traditional Russian forms and skills.

20    Mikhail Nesterov was an Abramtsevo artist of the Moscow School whose work featured on the pages of Diaghilev's *The World of Art* and who attained international renown as a leader of the 'new, mystical school' in exhibitions arranged by him at various venues in Europe. His pictures border on the sentimental but at their best, as in 'The vision accorded to the youth Bartholemew', a depiction of the young St Sergius, standing with a dark monk in the translucent countryside at Radonezh near Mamontovo where the saint had lived with his parents, his depictions of monks against a background of delicate birch trees and grey river, and his 1917 dual portrait of Florensky walking with Bulgakov, attain a contemplative transparency suggestive of paradise shining through the natural world.

21    A famous example of the binding nature of this unwritten code was the unexpected discovery by the right-wing newspaper tycoon Suvorin that he was in complete agreement with Dostoevsky, author of that most devastating critique of revolutionary terrorism *The Possessed*, that, should they stumble across a plot to commit a terrorist act against the State, neither would inform the police. Florenskii observed this code all his life. In his 1904 poem 'St Vladimir' (published by E. V. Ivanova in *Pavel Florenskii i simvolisty*, pp. 213–273), he envisages a situation in which passengers evicted from one train on their flight to the mountains are ordered to 'clear the platform', where they are awaiting the next in comparative comfort, and to drag their luggage into the rain-lashed forest. The three 'brothers' who have led them into this pass could have spared themselves all this, if they had told the stationmaster who they were:

> He would have been honoured to do them all kinds of favours, because the three of them were well connected; they came from high-ranking families. But the three did not want to be distinguished from their brothers – from the other passengers, poor things. And so they kept quiet, said nothing. They were glad to suffer for Christ's sake. And all night they prayed, rejoicing, although it was cold and they were soaking wet. It was a little bit comic – a little bit, but then of course they were little children – children. (Ibid., p. 301)

When in 1935 Florensky refused the Czech Government's offer of asylum should he be released from the camps, the situation was no longer comic and he was no longer a little child, but in 1904 he could not think of himself as worthy to 'suffer for Christ's sake' without irony, especially as he was well aware that he and his friends were inspired as much by schoolboy solidarity as by the courage of martyrs. For a detailed account of Florensky's relationship with the Christian Brotherhood for Struggle see E. V. Ivanova, 'Florenskii i "Khristianskoe bratstvo bor'by"', *Voprosy filosofii*, No. 6, 1993.

22    A. P. Florenskii, letter of 18 July 1904 from Tiflis to Andrey Bely, ibid., pp. 463–464.

23   A. Belyi to A. P. Florenskii, letter of 12 August from *Serebrianyi Kolodez,* ibid., pp. 465 and 466.

24   S. N. Bulgakov, *Ot marksizma k idealizmu. Sbornik statei 1896–1903,* St Petersburg, 1903. In his autobiography, Bulgakov recalls that he himself had helped pave the way for the Revolution of 1905 but came to be shocked by the 'spiritual essence' of the Revolution:

> From that time on I put what distance I could between myself and Revolution and sought to fence myself off from it with the utopian and naïve idea of creating a *Christian* liberation party, for which it was necessary to found a 'Union of Christian politics' (an early prototype of the Living Church). (Bulgakov, *Avtobiograficheskie zametki* (Posmertnoe izdanie), YMCA-Press, Paris, 1946.)

The Union as such did not take off and Bulgakov confined his energies to support for the Christian Brotherhood for Struggle.

25   A well-annotated selection of letters in V Keidan, *Vzyskuiushchie grada* (letters 17–61, pp. 73–129) give an insider's view of the struggles of Ageev, with the somewhat ambivalent help of Petrov who sought a starring role and an independent organ for himself, and other progressive priests to cooperate with Bulgakov, Ern and Sventsitsky in various publishing projects until Sventsitsky's lecture on 'Terror and immortality' on 5 December 1906 led to the closing down of the Moscow Religious Philosophical Society in memory of Vladimir Solov'ev and, towards the end of November 1906, the Synod began to take active measures against priests and theologians who were also members of left-wing political parties. There followed a serious government clampdown on the Brotherhood and the beginning of its ideological disintegration. Florensky's name occurs only as that of a desirable contributor to various putative journals, in connection with his arrest after the sermon 'The cry of blood' and as the author of a postcard to Bulgakov dated 18 March 1906, letter 32, pp. 94–98, expressing readiness to put the latter in touch with possible sympathisers amongst the clergy and to distribute pamphlets.

26   Compare *Vzyskuiushchie grada,* letter 20, pp. 82–83 for Kartashev's dismissive description of Ageev's circle to the Merezhkovskys, as 'mere priests ... busy about their own little affairs and fondly imagining that their domestic squabbles add up to an all-Russian rebellion'. Anton Kartashev, at that time a lecturer at the St Petersburg Theological Academy and a member of the Merezhkovskys' inner circle, later acted as last Ober-Procurator of the Holy Synod and Minister for Religious Confessions to the Provisional Government.

27   P. A. Florenskii, letter to Andrei Belyi of 15 July 1905, E. V. Ivanova, *Florenskii i simvolisty,* pp. 470–471.

28   Ibid. In fact, Florensky never returned to the review, but for his lasting admiration for and interest in Bely's work see his letters to his family from Solovki, published in *S* 4.

29   E. V. Ivanova, op. cit., pp. 53–54.

30   The text of the letter is available as part of Ivanova's publication on Florenskii and Bely, *Florenskii i simvolisty,* pp. 518–534.

31   The society later became known as the Moscow Religious-Philosophical Society in memory of Vladimir Solov'ev.

32    P. A. Florenskii, letter to Andrei Belyi of 31 January 1906, from Sergiev Posad, E. V. Ivanova, *Florenskii i simvolisty*, pp. 474–476.

33    P. A. Florenskii, letter to Andrei Belyi of 14–18 November 1910 from Sergiev Posad, ibid. pp. 476–477.

34    The Society was founded and chaired by Grigorii Rachinsky (1859–1939) on the initiative of Sergei Bulgakov. Other founder members besides Andrei Belyi and Florensky were Viacheslav Ivanov, Nikolai Berdiaev, Ern, Sventsitsky and Prince E. N. Trubetskoi.

35    P. A. Florenskii to S Bulgakov, letter of 18 March 1906, *Vsyskuiushchie grada*, letter 32, pp. 94–95.

36    Quoted by C A Volkov in 'P. A. Florenskii', *Pro et Contra*, p. 155. The text of 'Vopl' krovi', published in Sergiev Posad in the 1906 pamphlet, has yet to be reprinted in *Sochineniia*, but see the full account of Florensky's sermon, arrest and the subsequent intervention of the Rector of the Academy containing the text of the students' appeal to the Church authorities and of Bishop Evdokim's letters in support of Florenskii and Pivovarchuk to F. V. Dubasov, Governor of Moscow, in Pavel Florenskii: 'Cherez podvig i krest', published in *Novii zhurnal*, No. 243, 2006. See also Igumen Andronik. 'Gomileticheskoe nasledie sviashchennika Pavla Florenskogo; *Nyne i prisna*, No. 23–24, 2006, pp. 153–184.

37    Boris Pasternak's epic narrative poem 'Lieutenant Shmidt' was written in the mid-1920s, one of several evocations of the pathos of 1905 and the victims of reaction in a search for revolutionary subjects which still held an emotional appeal at the time of the poet's growing revulsion for the Bolshevic 'surgery' which he had once admired.

38    V. F. Ern to A. V. El'chaninov, *Vzyskuiushchie grada*, letter 34, p. 95.

39    Bulgakov to A. S. Glinka, letter of 17 May 1906, *Vzyskuiushchie grada*, letter 36, p. 98.

40    Pavel Florenskii, *V vechnoi lazure*. The brochure was made up from offprints of a publication in the journal *Khristianin*, 1907 No. 4. See E. V. Ivanova 'O literaturnykh opytakh Florenskogo', *Pavel Florenskii i simvolisty*, p. 21. One poem, 'In pace' was published 9 April 1906 in Bulgakov's short-lived Kievan newspaper *Narod*.

41    P. A. Florenskii, 'Immanuil Kant. Fizicheskaia monodalogiia', *Bogoslovskii vestnik*, No. 9, 1905, pp. 95–127.

42    See E. V. Ivanova. 'San Sergie e la formazione interiore de Pavel A. Florenskii', in N. Kautchtschivchwili, A. Mamaid (ed.) *San Sergio e el suo tempo*, Magnano, 1996, pp. 246–247. Also Ch. 3, n. 23.

43    Inevitably, perhaps, there were accusations of plagiarism. See M. Zust, n. 2. For a detailed account of these, initiated by Archimandrite Nikanor's (N. P. Kudriavtsev) review of *The Pillar and Ground of Truth* in *Missionerskoe obozrenie*, I and II, 1916, and revived by R. A. Gal'tseva and A. M. Pentkovsky in separate studies published 1988 and 1990. The speculation is based on the fact that Mashkin's major opus did indeed remain unpublished and, as Zust rightly points out, could only be substantiated by a detailed study of the text. In the course of 1906 Florensky published 'Pis'ma i nabroski arkhimandrita Serapiona Mashkina' (Letters and rough notes of Archimandrite Serapion Mashkin) in *Voprosy religii*, I, 1906, pp. 174–183 and, in the same number of this journal, 'K pochesti vyshnago znaniia. Cherty kharaktera Arkhimandrita Serapiona' ('In honour of higher knowledge. Traits of Archimandrite Serapion's character'), where he comments on his hero's undeserved obscurity and unmarked grave and exclaims with some pathos: 'Where

shall I find a publisher for these 2250 pages? Where shall I find a reader for you?' (p. 217). As the 1906 letter to Bely shows, he was hard put at that time to find a reader for himself. Indeed, he and Vvedensky were among Mashkin's very few potential readers. Florensky did, however, return to work on the archive with a publication of letters from V. N. Amfiteatrov to Archimandrite Serapion in *Bogoslovskii vestnik*, No. 6, 1911, pp. 327–350 and No. 2, 1914, pp. 508–534 and with data 'towards a life': 'Dannye k zhizne-opisaniiu arkh. Serapiona Mashkina', *Bogoslovskii vestnik*, No. 2–3, 1917, pp. 317–354. All the above were republished in *S* 1.

44    *S* 1, p. 211.

45    Among Florensky's translations over this period are: R. Zom 'Tserkovnyi stroi v pervye veka khristianstva' (translation from the German of R. Sohm's *Kirchenrect. Band I. Die geschichtlichen Grundlagen*, Leipzig, 1892), published in book form, Moscow, 1906; 'Molitva Simeona Novogo Bogoslova' (A prayer of St Simeon the New Theologian), *Khristianin*, No. 1, 1907, pp. 245–247 and 'Plach' Bogomateri: predislovie k kanonu' ('The lament of the Mother of God: preface to the canon'), *Khristianin*, 3, 1907, pp. 601–606.

46    This essay was first published in 1974 under the title of 'Ekklesiologicheskie materialy. Poniatie tserkvi v sv. pisanii', *Bogoslovskie trudy*, 12, 1994, pp. 73–183 and subsequently in *S* I, pp. 318–488.

47    In the Merezhkovskys' journal *Novyi put'* Rozanov had had his 'own corner' in which he often published readers' letters on intimate subjects relevant to ecclesiastical regulations on the remarriage of widowed priests, divorce, etc. – with his own commentary and introduction.

48    P. A. Florenskii, 'Voprosy religioznogo samopoznaniia' (Questions of religious self-knowledge), *Khristianin* I, 1, 1907, pp. 205–216; II, 3, 1907, pp. 365–453; III, 10, 1907, pp. 436–439 and, in book form under the same title, Segiev Posad, 1907.

49    A. P. Florenskii, 'Predislovie k stat'e A El'chaninova "Mistitsizm MM Speranskogo"', (Introduction to an article by A. El'chaninov 'The Mysticism of M. M. Speransky' *Bogoslovskii vestnik*, No. 1, 1906, pp. 90–93; A. P. Florenskii, 'Antonii romana i Antonii predaniia' (The Anthony of the novel and the Anthony of tradition), *Bogoslovskii vestnik*, No. 1, 1907, pp. 119–159.

50    P. A. Florenskii,' O tipakh vozrastaniia' (On types of growth), *Bogoslovskii vestnik*, No. 7, 1906, pp. 530–568. Also in *S* 1, pp. 281–318. Notes, pp. 725–728.

51    *Stolp i utverzhdenie istiny*, Put', Moscow, 1914. Begun as a candidate's dissertation during his four years as a student, presented for a Master's degree under the title 'O religioznoi istine' (Of religious truth) and so published in Sergiev Posad. The fuller version contained chapters which Florenskii's well-wishers felt would be unacceptable to the Synod, which had to approve the degree.

52    From the introduction to *Stolp*.

53    P. A. Florenskii, *Sobranie chastushek Kostromskoi gubernii Nerekhtovskogo uezda*, izd. Kostromskoi gubernskoi uchenoi arkhivnoi komissii, Kostroma, 1909 (1910 on the cover).

54    Viacheslav Ivanov, 'O russkoi idee', *SS*, Vol. III, pp. 321–338.

55    Pavel Florenskii, 'Kostromskaia storona', *Pavel Florenskii i simvolisty*, p. 187. The poem was written on 5 August 1905, on his first visit to Tolpygino.

56   P. A. Florenskii, letter to Andrei Bely of 15 July 1905, E. V. Ivanova, *Pavel Florenskii i simvolisty*, p.38. In this letter Florensky writes of his article 'On types of growth' as 'a mathematical-psychological approach to the question of 'those who are under the direct protection of Sophia', p. 37.

57   P. A. Florenskii, 'O tipakh vozrastaniia', *S* I, pp. 316–317.

58   Ibid., p. 312.

59   Acronym for Moskovskaia dukhovnaia Akademia, the Moscow Theological Academy.

60   P. A. Florenskii, 'Dogmatizm i dogmatika', *S* I, 550–570 and notes, which give a verbatim report of discussion of the paper, pp. 740–751.

61   Ibid., p. 745.

62   Ibid., p. 748.

63   Florenskii's attitude to the Merezhkovskys, later to harden into ideological hostility, was long ambivalent. In the 15 July 1905 letter to Bely he sends them greetings and describes, with perception and sympathy, a recent meeting in which he felt Hippius's affected manner to be rather a

> manifestation of an inner fear of striking a false note. It's odd and I can't really explain to you what exactly I'm trying to say, but I know very well that there are such people who, fearing insincerity, put on a mask of insincerity, the kind of insincerity that does not distort the genuine nature of their personality. (E V Ivanova, p. 39)

Hippius, he continued, had favoured him with a most unflattering, indeed offensive analysis of his own character – which he very much feared might be all too accurate: 'She voiced a suspicion that tormented me and torments me all the time, but which I'm not prepared to discuss with anyone else' (ibid.). However, he had perceived so much 'hidden pain and delicacy' that he had felt very close to her and her husband, although aware that both, particularly Merezhkovsky, were 'miffed with me' for adherence to the Church. Hippius's later misdescription of Florensky as *zhestokovyinnyi* (harsh and rigid) and a 'fanatic' probably stems from his successful efforts to free one of his younger sisters from the influence of her inner circle, which his friend Bulgakov had, after their return from Paris in 1908, regarded as sectarian on the basis of rumours of the celebration of some kind of Holy Communion without a priest. For the truth about these rumours, see Z. N. Hippius, 'O byvshem', pub. by Temira Pachmuss in *Vozrozhdenie* (La Renaissance), Paris, 1970, pp. 218, 219, 220 and 221. Florensky's letters to the sister in question (Ol'ga known to the family as Val'ia) have been published in the journal *Nashe nasledie*, Nos 79–80 and the following number for 2006. In 1906 he refers to the Merezhkovskys as 'just a little (*chutochku*) un-Orthodox', though he may subsequently have felt some responsibility for supplying her with their address.

64   A. P. Florenskii, 'Gamlet', *S* I, p. 269.

65   A. P. Florenskii, *S* I, p. 675.

66   P. A. Florenskij, *Mnimosti v geometrii*, M 1922, Nachdruck nebst einer einführenden Studie vom Michail Hagemeister, Specimina Philogiae Slavicae, herausgegeben von Olexa Horbatsch and Gerd Freidhof, Verlag Otto Sagners, Munich, 1985.

67    P. Florenskii 'Elegiia na otupenie P Florenskogo', Tolpygina, *E. V. Ivanova, Florenskii i simvolisty*, pp. 169-170.

68    *Batiushka* – literally, 'Little father'; affectionate appellation for a priest equivalent to 'Father', 'mon père'.

69    P. A. Florenskii, 'Sol' zemli', *S* I, pp. 571-637, first published in *Khristianin*, 1908, Nos 10-11 and 1909, Nos 1 and 5, and as separate title, Trinity St Sergius Monastery, 1909.

70    Valentin Sventsitsky, *Antikhrist (The Antichrist)*, Moscow, 1907.

71    P. A. Florenskii, 'Kosmologicheskie antinomii Immanuila Kanta' *S* II, pp. 3-33 first published *Bogoslovskii vestnik*, No. 4, 1909, pp. 597-625 and as a separate brochure, Sergiev Posad, 1909. 'Obshchechelovecheskie korni idealizma', *S* III (2), pp. 145-168, first published in *Bogoslovskii vestnik*, No. 2, 1909, pp. 284-297 and No. 3, pp. 409-423.

## Notes on Chapter 5: The Quiet Mutiny

1    Pavel Florenskii, 'Amor fati', in E. V. Ivanova, *Pavel Florenskii i simvolisty*, p. 59.

2    V. R. Ern, letter to E. D. Ern of 12 September 1908, Moscow-Tiflis, *Vzyskuiushchie grada*, pp. 174-175.

3    P. A. Florenskii, *Stolp i utverzhdenie istiny. Opyt pravoslavnoi feoditsii v dvenadtsati pis'makh (The Pillar and Ground of Truth: An Attempt at Orthodox Theodicy in Twelve Letters)*, Moscow, 1914, reprinted Gregg International Publishers Ltd, England, 1970 (further *Pillar and Ground*), Letter 10: Sophia, p. 819.

4    Nina Zurubova, 'Mysli i vpechatleniia odnoi materi', *Sbornik pamiati Sergeia Semenovicha Troitskogo (Symposium in Memory of Sergei Semenovich Troitskii)*, Tiflis, 1912, p. 8.

5    S. S. Troitskii, 'Iz perepiski s druziami', from *Pamiati S S Troitskogo*, p. 38, letter of 23 July 1907 to his friend F. A. Bolshakov, whom he had been instrumental in converting from the Old Ritualists. In writing of Sergei Semenovich Troitskii, I have made uncritical use of this collection of articles compiled and published in memoriam by Troitsky's family and friends, unaware of the fact that they published the extract from Florensky's article 'O tipakh vozrastaniia' ('On types of growth'), containing what I describe in Chapter 4 as the first literary love letter to Troitsky, without his, the author's, permission. In a letter to Sergei Aleksandrovich Tsvetkov of 5 April 1912 published by Pavel Vasilievich Florenskii in *Novyi zhurnal (The New Review)*, Book 234, 2009, pp. 149-150, Father Pavel makes it quite clear that he now considers the figure of the Friend as an idealised composite portrait inspired not only by Troitsky but also by Bely and Ern. Tsvetkov, who has met Troitsky once and seen him entirely in the light of this idealised portrait, should not, Florensky tells him, be misled. Troitsky was an aesthete whose conversation, work and death were superficially rather than inwardly beautiful ('krasivo no ne prekrasno'). 'As far as S[ergei] S[emonovich] is concerned', he writes, 'at the present I feel no particular love for him, but neither do I bear him ill will. One should pray for him, but exaggerated praise, being untrue in essence, will hardly delight him now … The compilers of the Collection are at odds with me, and I with them' (p. 150). It seems to me that this continued denial of the friend he once loved so dearly reflects Florensky's feelings in 1912, not when their closeness was at its height, and should be considered together with

the fact that, as priest, he continued to remember Sergei at the alter when he celebrated the liturgy, but I also feel the letter to Tsvetkov should be recorded in his biography at the first mention of the memorial Collection.

6   Ibid., letter of 16 August 1907, p. 39.

7   Cf. P. A. Florenskii, letter to his mother of 21 January 1906, quoted by Ierodiakon Andronikov in 'Osnovnye cherty lichnosti, zhizn' i tvorchestvo sviashchennika Pavla Florenskogo', *Pro et Contra*, p. 496.

8   Ol'ga, while still a schoolgirl, became so interested in Merezhkovsky's ideas that she obtained his address from her elder brother and wrote him a fan letter. For the romance by correspondence which followed see 'Tri tysiachi verst i chetvert' veka prolegli mezhdu nami', publication by P. V. Florenskii and Tatiana Shutova, *Nashe nasledie*, No. 79–80, 2006, pp. 14–135 and No. 82, 2007, pp. 26–47, which also contains publications of her correspondence with Troitsky and many drawings.

9   Z. N. Gippius, *Dnevniki*, NPK Intelvak, Moscow, 1999, p. 145.

10  S. S. Troitskii, cf. letter dated 24 December 1907, 'Iz perepiski s druz'iami', published in *Pamiati S S Troitskogo*, p. 42.

11  A. V. El'chaninov, diary entry for 4 March 1909, *Vzyskuiushchie grada*, pp. 189–190.

12  V. F. Ern, letter to E. D. Ern, of 4 December 1909, *Vzyskuiushchie grada*, p. 216.

13  A. V. El'chaninov, diary entry for 24 September 1909 in which he recalls a conversation with Florenskii in the spring of 1908, *Vzyskuiushchie grada*, p. 209.

14  Ibid., diary entry for 18 October 1909, p. 212.

15  Ibid., diary entry for 10 October 1909, p. 213.

16  A. V. El'chaninov, op. cit., diary entry for 7 July 1909, pp. 201–2.

17  Keidan suggests Vasilii was the addressee of the letters, but Igumen Andronik, the keeper of Florenskii's archive, ascribes the book without hesitation to the period when the influence of Troitsky and Father Isidor were in the ascendant.

Further Florenskii's working notebook for 1904–1905, recently published by E. V. Ivanova in *Florenskii i simvolisty*, pp. 323–413, shows him to have been absorbed in work towards the book from an early stage of his studies at the Theological Academy. The chapter on Friendship was completed in 1908, the chapter on Jealousy added in 1909.

18  See Appendix 1.

19  For those who read Russian, by far the most convenient place to go for an anthology of the Russian reception of *The Pillar and Ground of Truth* is the second section of *P A Florenskii: Pro et Contra. Lichnost' i tvorchestvo Pavla Florenskogo v otsenke russikh myslitelei i issledovatelei. Antologiia*, Izd-vo RkhGI, St Petersburg, 1996, prepared for publication and edited by K. G. Iusupov, see Appendix 1.

20  *Pillar and Ground*, p. 2. In this account of the genesis of the two main versions of *The Pillar and Ground of Truth* I have simplified the history of various stages of publications of and from the text given by R. Slesinski in *Pavel Florensky: A Metaphysics of Love*, St Vladimir's Press, New York, 1984, pp. 40–42 and in Ieromonakh Andronik (Trubachev), *Teoditseia I antropoditseia v tvorchestve sviashchennika Pavla Florenskogo*, Vodolei, Tomsk, 1998, p. 11, both of which recount in detail the differences between Florenskii's Master's thesis *O dukhovnoi istine* and his book *Stolp i utverzhdenie istony*, Put', Moscow, 1914.

21    *Pillar and Ground*, p. 5.
22    *Pillar and Ground*, p. 64.
23    Trubetskoi objected to this, pointing out Christ's gentleness with his disciples; Thomas was allowed to put his hand in the wound. The mind, Trubetskoi argues, was redeemed with the rest of man and *can* expand to comprehend the mystery of being.
24    *Pillar and Ground*, p. 70.
25    *Pillar and Ground*, p. 71.
26    *Pillar and Ground*, p. 73.
27    *Pillar and Ground*, p. 76.
28    *Pillar and Ground*, pp. 93–94.
29    *Pillar and Ground*, p. 108.
30    *Pillar and Ground*, p. 129.
31    *Pillar and Ground*, p. 128.
32    *Pillar and Ground*, pp. 140–142.
33    *Pillar and Ground*, p. 147. Trubetskoi suggests Florenskii should have used here the term he does use elsewhere in the book, 'the reconciliation of opposites', rather than suggest that antonyms remain unresolved even in Ultimate Truth.
34    Florensky specifically mentions Vailati's publications in *Rivista filosophica*, 1903, and *Revue de Met*, November 1904.
35    *Pillar and Ground*, p. 157.
36    *Pillar and Ground*, p. 158.
37    *Pillar and Ground*, p. 160.
38    *Pillar and Ground*, p. 161.
39    *Pillar and Ground*, p. 164.
40    *Pillar and Ground*, p. 168.
41    *Pillar and Ground*, p. 128. Florensky maintains that the search for Harmony in Nature, science as we know it, is a product of monotheism and the Testament of the Son, the Logos, and ventures the supposition that recent discoveries about discontinuity may be a sign of the coming of the End.
42    In this context we are given a glimpse of a very different, positive and self-confident Florensky at work in the Glavelektro Institute, where for some years after the Revolution he was employed as a consultant and laboratory director. Installed in a glass cubicle in the corridor of the Institute he was at the mercy of all and sundry who required his advice. L. F. Zhegin ('Vospominaniia o Florenskom', *Pro et Contra*, p. 163) recalls how a young man, a student or employee of the Institute, came up to him and began to hold forth on his solution to some problem Florensky had set him. 'That's not the way of it', said Florenskii. The other insisted, not very politely, interrupting and waxing indignant. Again, in the same calm, unflustered tone: 'Do it your own way, but it won't work!' Further evidence of Florensky's practical grasp of applied science is provided by the premiums and patents granted him during his work on obtaining iodine from seaweed on Solovki and by his account of his early experiments in physics in *For My Children* (see Chapter 2).
43    Florensky formulated this very clearly in his lecture on the 'Limits of gnosis', part of his 1908 course on the history of philosophy, revised 1909 and published in *Bogoslovskii vestnik*, No. 1, 1913, where he concludes:

To understand that, given the finite potential of a consciousness conditioned by the epoch, the moment in history and in one's own life, it is granted us to be filled with infinite content, and for this very reason to curb our lust to *explore and reveal* this content, to refrain from always chasing after the future means to live in the present but at the same time to acquire wisdom, because for such people it is not the evil of the day that eclipses eternity, but eternity that gazes from the depths of the evil of the day. (*S* I, p. 59)

44    *Pillar and Ground*, p. 174.

45    Florenskii, and other Russian writers, differentiate between *rassudok* (ratio, the ability to calculate and reason) and *razum* (intellect, the gift of logical, creative thought).

46    *Pillar and Ground*, p. 231.

47    Florenskii posited a bodily hierarchy: the head as seat of reason, the chest as centre of life (breath) and the lower body as the subconscious foundation, the impersonal principle of genesis. He distinguished between the types of mysticism linked to the head, the chest and the belly, favouring Eastern Orthodox ascetism 'of the chest' as the most balanced and vital.

48    *Pillar and Ground*, p. 278.

49    *Pillar and Ground*, p. 279.

50    *Pillar and Ground*, pp. 289–290.

51    Florenskii here specifically mentions a sexual link and the epithet 'winged' belongs, of course, to Eros. This attitude to mysticism even more perhaps than the following chapter on Sophia which posits the *eidos* of Creation as a Female Being, not necessarily an erotic concept in itself, is presumably at the root of many doubts as to the unalloyed purity of his inspiration. It is, however, hard to deny the ontological reality of sex or the part of sublimated sexual impulse not only in the wholeness of creation, but in all creative activity. That Florenskii made no such denial is not proof of moral turpitude.

52    See *O dukhovnoi istine. Opyt pravoslavnoi teoditsii*, Moscow, 1913, pp. 576 and LXIII. The oral examination or 'Defence' of the dissertation took place on 19 May 1914. In a letter of 20 October 1917 to the theologian N. N. Glubokovskii Florenskii wrote:

About my dissertation 'On Spiritual Truth' all I really want to say is that neither there, nor anywhere else, did I ever write as much as a single comma to curry favour with anybody whatsoever. But [illegible] what matters is [illegible] I had to sacrifice my book not because I was afraid of the Holy Synod but because I was not morally justified in demanding the Synod's sanction for those parts of my book which seemed to my examiner unworthy of such sanction, and this I write with a clear conscience: I would not allow anyone to constrain my conscience and my thought, but for that very reason I had no wish to put pressure on anybody else's conscience or understanding, even if it concerned me [illegible] so, what was missed out in 'On Spiritual Truth' as compared with 'The Pillar and Ground of Truth'? In the first place, the lyrical passages. To the best of my understanding, those passages were not an ornament [illegible] to the book, but were methodological prologues [illegible] to the chapters. How successful they were is not for me to judge. But I wanted precisely this kind of prologue, which would prepare the reader's understanding of the dogmatic and philosophic constructions. Further, several chapters/letters were omitted which seemed to me to represent the philosophico-theological [goal] of the book. And that was not done without pain. As for the footnotes, they were abbreviated for purely financial reasons …

He would, he concludes, prefer Glubokovsky to judge his work by *The Pillar and Ground of Truth*, but he himself has not a single copy left and doesn't know where to lay hands on one. See A. Kiparisov, 'Dva pis'ma sviashch. Pavla Florenskogo N. N. Glubokovskomu', *Vestnik R KhD 159-11-1990*, pp. 177–178.

53  See Appendix 2.

54  *Pillar and Ground*, p. 391.

55  *Pillar and Ground*, p. 392.

56  *Pillar and Ground*, p. 396.

57  *Pillar and Ground*, p. 434.

58  *Pillar and Ground*, p. 438.

59  *Pillar and Ground*, pp. 445, 446.

60  *Pillar and Ground*, p. 459.

61  *Pillar and Ground*, pp. 462–463.

62  *Pillar and Ground*, p. 482.

63  *Pillar and Ground*, p. 483.

64  *Pillar and Ground*, p. 488.

65  S. N. Bulgakov, '*Sviashchennik o Pavel Florenskii*', quoted from *Pro et Contra*, p. 396, first published in *Vestnik R KhD*, Nos 101–102, 1971, pp. 126–136.

66  N. Berdiaev, *Samopoznanie (opyt filosofskoi avtobiografii)*, *Sobranie Sochinenii* I, YMCA-Press, Paris, 1983 (2nd edition), p. 215.

## Notes on Chapter 6: The Four-leafed Clover

1  St Andrew of Crete. *The Great Canon. St Mary of Egypt. The Life*, eds and trs Sister Katherine and Sister Thekla, Library of Orthodox Thinking, published by the Greek Orthodox Monastery of the Assumption, Mulgrave, Newport Pagnell, 1980, p. 42.

2  Quoted by Ierodiakon Andronik, 'Osnovnye cherty lichnosti, zhizni i tvorchestva Sviashchennika Pavla Florenskogo', *Pro et Contra*, p. 500 and in the Introduction to his monograph *Teoditsia i antropoditsia v tvorchestve Pavla Florenskogo*, Vodolei, Tomsk, 1998, p. 10.

3  Igumen Andronik (Trubachev), 'Zhizn' i sud'ba', *S* I, p. 17.

4  Letter from V. C. Ern to E. D. Ern of 2 September 1910, *Vzyskuiushchie grada*, pp. 277–278. For a panegyric to Anna Mikhailovna as a model of Orthodox womanhood see Igumen Andronik, op. cit, p. 18 and the same author's 'Golubka moia bednaia', *Literaturnyi Irktusk*, 1989, October, pp. 14–15.

5  S. N. Bulgakov, 'Sviashchennik o Pavel Florenskii (1943)' first published *Vestnik R KhD*, 1971, No. 101–102, pp. 126–135, and also in *Florenskii. Pro et Contra*, pp. 396–397.

6  Pavel Florenskii, letter to A. M. Florenskaia of 27 July–August 1928, published by V. P., P. V. and Iu. O. Florenskiye, 'Florenskii v nizhnem' in *Nizhegorodskii kupets, Cherno-belyi al'manakh filosofii i literatury*, No. 1, 1999, p. 74.

7  Cf. M. Polovinkin, 'Revnostnaia druzhba'. Quotes from Bulgakov's *Yalta Diary* in *Tradition und Moderne*, Peter Lang Gambel, Frankfurt-am-Main, 2001, pp. 48–50.

Bulgakov's reflexions on Florenskii in the troubled diary of May 1922 are the other side of the reverential hero worship expressed in the better known obituary (see n. 5) and are perhaps most closely paralleled by Cassius's jealous comment on Brutus: 'But under him my genius is rebuked / As, it is said, Mark Antony's was by Caesar's', or, as Irina B. Rodzianskaia points out in her article S. N. Bulgakov i P. A. Florenskii', *Florenskij, Bergamo*, 1995, pp. 114–127, by the relationship of Salieri to Mozart. Bonetskaia, dismissive of either thinker's claim to be truly Orthodox, likens them to Faust and Wagner, N. K. Bonetskaia, 'Russkii Faust i russkii Vagner', *S. N. Bulgakov. Pro et Contra*, I, Russian Christian Humanitarian Institute, St Petersburg, 2003, pp. 854–884. Further *Bulgakov. Pro et Contra*.

8   See, for instance E. K. Apushkina's account of the Florensky household as quoted by Igumen Andronik, 'Zhizn' i sud'ba', P. A. Florenskii *S* I, p. 18.

9   P. A. Florenskii, 'Imena', *S* III(2), p. 238.

10   Ibid., p. 315.

11   Ibid., pp. 246–248.

12   P. A. Florenskii, letter 29 of 5–6 September 1935 to his son Vasilii, on the occasion of his marriage to Nataliia Zarubina in August 1935, *S* IV, p. 289.

13   P. A. Florenskii, letter 25 of 24–25 July 1935, *S* IV, pp. 268–70.

14   Now Ulitsa Adademika Favorskogo.

15   P. A. Florenskii, letter of 24 March 1912 to S. N. Bulgakov, Arkhiv sviashchennika Pavla Florenskogo, Issue 4, *Perepiska so sviashchennikom Sergiem Bulgakovym*, ed. Igumen Andronik, Introduction by S. M. Polovinkin, Vodolei, Tomsk, 2001, p. 47. Further *Perepiska s Bulgakovym*.

16   P. A. Florenskii, letter of 11 May 1911 to Vasilii Rozanov, quoted by Igumen Andronik, op. cit, *S* I, p. 19.

17   Cf. S. N. Bulgakov, 'Sviashchennik o Pavel Florenskii', *Pro et Contra*, p. 396.

18   P. A. Florenskii, letters to V. P. Florenskii of 12 April 1935, *S* IV, pp. 204–206 and letter of 5–6 September 1935, *S* IV, p. 289.

19   Sergei Bulgakov, in the *Yalta Diary* May 1922, quoted by M. Polovinkin, *Tradition und Moderne*, p. 49. More fully in *Bulgakov. Pro et Contra*, pp. 112–143.

20   Cf. P. A. Florenskii, letter to V. A. Kozhevnikov of 2 March 1912, quoted by Ierodiakon Andronik (Trubachev), 'Osnovnye cherty lichnosti, zhizn' i tvorchestvo sviashchennika, Pavla Florenskogo', *Zhurnal Moskovskoi Patriarkhii*, 1983, No. 4, p. 15. When the OGPU searched Florensky's service flat in Moscow after his 1933 arrest, they reported they had found no copies of *The Pillar and Ground of Truth* 'or other books on mysticism or pornography' (V. Shantalinsky, *The KGB's Literary Archive*, tr. John Crowfoot, The Hawai Press, London, 1995, p. 115).

21   A case in point is the series of reports on Orthodox life in Paris from Aleksandra Nikolaevna Kuprianova, the niece of Bishop Ignatii (Brianchaninov) which appeared in *Bogoslovskii vestnik* between 1914 and 1916 as 'Letters from France'. Sviashchennik Pavel Florenskii. *Perepiska s M. A. Novoselovym*, Arkhiv Sviasch P Florenskogo, Issue 2, Izd-vo Vodolei, Tomsk, 1998 (further *Perepiska s Novoselovym*), note 2, pp. 123–124.

22   P. A. Florenskii, 'Predely gnoseologii', *Bogoslovskii vestnik*, No. 1, 1913.

23　See 'Ostaius' vash dobrozhelatel' i bogomolets'. K istorii vzaimootnosnenii sviashchennika Pavla Florenskogo i mitropolita Antoniia (Khrapovitskogo), pub. P. V. Florenskii and S. B. Sholomov, *Zhurnal Moskovskoi Patrarkhii*, No. 6, 1998, pp. 67-80.

24　See Igumen Andronik (Trubachev), 'Sviashchennik Pavel Florenskii – Professor MDA', *Bogoslovskie trudy*, Sbornik MDA-300 let (1685-1985), Moscow, 1986, pp. 226-232.

25　See notes to P. A. Florenskii, 'Pervye shagi filosofii', *S* II, pp. 738-741.

26　P. A. Florenskii, 'Lektsia in lectio', *Bogoslovskii vestnik*, No. 4, 1909.

27　C. A. Volkov, 'P. A. Florenskii', *Pro et Contra*, pp. 145-148.

28　See S. I. Fudel', 'Ob o Pavle Florenskom', *Pro et Contra*, p. 52.

29　See P. A. Florenskii, 'Otzyv ekstraordinarnogo professora Imperatorskoi Moskovskoi Dukhovnoi Akademii sviashchennika Pavla Florenskogo o sochinenii dotsenta toi zhe Akademii A. Tuberovskogo 'Voskresenie Khristovo'' ...', *S* II, pp. 192-271 and notes pp. 750-755.

30　For the impact of James on Russian theology see Joan Grosman and Ruth Rishchin (eds), *William James in Russian Culture*, Lexington Books, Boulder, 2003, particularly articles by Ranall A. Poole and Alexander Etkind. Florensky suggests that Tuberovsky's enthusiasm for James' book on 'religious experience' is misplaced, because James neither lays claim to any such experience for himself nor has anything to say on such subjects as martyrdom, Eastern mysticism or the mysticism of the Orthodox Church, which Florensky considered 'the only normal and healthy mysticism' (P. A. Florenskii, op. cit., p. 261).

31　P. A. Florenskii, op. cit., *S* II, p. 270.

32　Ibid., p. 277.

33　Ibid., p. 235.

34　P. A. Florenskii, 'Imiaslavie kak filosofskaia predposylka', dictated to S. I. Ognev from materials prepared between 1 October and 4 November 1922, *S* III(1), pp. 254-255.

35　P. A. Florenskii, 'Privetsvennania rech' na iubileinom chestvovanii A. I. Vvedenskogo', first published *Bogoslovskii vestnik*, 1912, No. 2, *S* II, p. 190.

36　Adherents of the Ontological School in the Moscow Theological Academy were, according to Igumen Andronik (Trubachev), Protopriest Fedor Golubinsky, V. D. Kudriavtsev-Platonov, Serapion Mashkin and, of course, A. I. Vvedensky and Florenskii himself. 'Zhizn' i sud'ba', *S* I, p. 14.

37　P. A. Florenskii, 'Privetstvennaia rech' na iubileinom chestvovanii A. I. Vvedenskogo', *S* II, p. 191.

38　Vl. Ern, letter to E. Ern of 21 May 1914, *Vzyskuiushchie grada*, p. 579.

39　Cf. P. A. Florenskii, 'Ne voskhishchenie nepsheva', first published *Bogoslovskii vestnik*, No. 7, pp. 512-562 and, with 'Smysl' idealizma', as a separate brochure in Sergiev Posad, 1915, also *S* II, pp. 145-188 and notes, pp. 745-749. For Florensky and Ivanov, see Andrei Shishkin, *Realizm Viacheslava Ivanova i o Pavla Florenskogo', Florensky, (Florenskij*, Bergamo, 1995), pp. 101-114 and Robert Bird, 'Catharsis-Mathesis-Praxis. The mystic triad in the aesthetics of Viacheslav Ivanov', *VII Internazionale Vjaceslav Ivanov: poesia e sacra scrittura*, a cura di Andrej Chishkin, I, Europa Orientalis, Rome, 2002, pp. 289-302.

40    Zinaida Hippius, 'Zadumchivyi strannik', *Zhivye litsa*, Zabytaia Kniga, Moscow, Khudozhestvennaia literatura, 1991, p. 356. See, however, Merezhkovsky's letter to Ol'ga in which he quotes her brother's mild warning that he 'is just a little bit (*chutochku*) un-Orthodox' in *Nashe nasledie*, No. 79–80, 2006, p. 125, letters of October 1907 and April 1908 and the conclusion of the publication in No. 81 of the same journal.

41    Marietta Shaginian, *Chelovek i vremie*, Moscow, 1980, pp. 252, 286.

42    Cf. N. Berdiaev, *Russkaia ideia*, YMCA-Press, Paris, 1946, pp. 238, 239 and *Samopoznanie*, YMCA-Press, Paris, 1949–1983, pp. 164–166 as well as his reviews of *Stolp i utverzhdenie istiny* and 'Vokrug Khomiakova' in *Pro et Contra*, pp. 266–284 and 380–381.

43    Sergei Bulgakov, letter of 7 August 1922 to P. A. Florenskii, published in *Perepiska s Bulgakovym*, p. 161.

44    Sergei Bulgakov, letter of 7 July 1908 to P. A. Florenskii, op. cit., p. 27.

45    See Sergei Bulgakov, letter of 1 July 1912 to P. A. Florenskii, op. cit. p. 53.

46    See Sergei Bulgakov, letter of 16 October 1911 to P. A. Florenskii on how to contact Bukharev's widow, op. cit., p. 46. The book on the Apocalypse was also published in a separate edition, Sergiev Posad, 1916.

47    See Sergei Bulgakov, letter to P. A. Florenskii of 9 December 1916 re discussions with L. M. Lopatin, editor of the journal *Voprosy filosofii i psikkologii*, op. cit, p. 135.

48    See Sergei Bulgakov, letter to P. A. Florenskii of 15 February 1914, op. cit, p. 78.

49    See Sergei Bulgakov, letters to P. A. Florenskii of 4 April and 29 June 1914, op. cit, pp. 87–89.

50    The meetings of the Society sometimes attracted as many as 60 participants. Founder members were: M. A. Novoselov, V. A. Kozhevnikov, F. D. Samarin, N. N. Mamonov, P. B. Mansurov. Closely associated with the work of the circle, besides Bulgakov and Florensky, were Fedor (Pozdeevskii), Bishop of Volokolamsk and Rector of the MDA, A. A. Kornilov, A. I. Novgorodtsev, the brothers Trubetskoi, Father Iosif Fudel, V. F. Ern, V. P. Sventsitskii and A. V. El'chaninov, L. A. Tikhomirov, Father Evgenii Sinadskii, S. P. Mansurov, A. S. Glinka-Volzhskii, S. N. Durylin, N. S. Arsen'ev, N. O. Kuznetsov, S. A. Tsvetkov and Florensky's pupil Fedor Andreev.

51    Quoted in N. B. Nikitin's and S. M. Polovinkin's introduction to *Perepiska s Novoselovym*, 1998, p. 120. Further for Novoselov (and his relationship with Florensky), see E. S. Polishchuk's 'Mikhail Aleksandrovich Novoselov I ego 'Pis'ma k druz'iam' in M. A. Novoselov, *Pis'ma k druziam*, izd-vo Pravoslanogo Bogoroditskogo Sviato-Tikhonovskogo Instituta, Moscow, 1994, pp. v–lii.

52    *Imiaslavtsy* – lit. those who glorify the Name, were practitioners of the Jesus prayer, who believed that God was actually present in His Name, that to invoke the Name was to put oneself in the Presence.

53    See note 10 (*S* III(1), p. 569) to 'Predislovie sviashchennika Pavla Florenskogo k knige ieroskhimonakha Antoniia (Bulatovich) *Apologiia very vo Imia Bozhie i vo Imia Iisusa Khrista*, first published Religiozno Filosofskaia Biblioteka, Moscow, 1913.

54    *Khlysty* – members of an orgiastic sect which believed in possible reincarnations of Christ through a chosen female 'God-bearer'.

55    'Zamechania sviashchennika Pavla Florenskogo na knigu ieromanakha Antoniia (Bulatovicha)', *Apologiia very vo Imia Bozhie i vo Imia Iisusa Khrista*, *S* III(1), p. 296.

56    See "'Ostaius' Vash dobrozhelatel' i bogomolets" – k istorii vzaimootnoshenii sviash-chennika Pavla Florenskogo i mitropolita Antoniia (Khrapovitskogo)', published by P. V. Florenskii and S. V. Sholomov, *Zhurnal Moskovskoi Patriarchii*, 6–1998, letter of 14 November 1916 from the Metropolitan to Florenskii, p. 74.

57    It was Ioann of Cronstadt's sayings about the Jesus prayer that had been published in English and enjoyed great popularity both in English-speaking religious circles and, when translated back into Russian, in his native land.

58    'Pis'mo sviashchennika Pavla Florenskogo Ivanu Pavlovichu Shcherbovu', 13 March 1913, Sergiev Posad S III(1), pp. 296–297.

59    The theses with Florenskii's acerbic annotations can be read in S III(1), pp. 298–350 as can his considered 1922 'Imiaslavie kak filosofskaia predposylka', S III (1) pp. 252–287. *Imiabortsy* – those who opposed the *imiaslavtsy's* doctrine of the Name.

60    Novoselov, who became a monk after the October Revolution and whose name is among those of the 'new martyrs' for the energetic part he played in the Catacomb Church, was always happy to admit the *imiaslavtsy* as true Orthodox, but the attitude of the residual Official Church was ambivalent, and the intransigent communities which had foregathered around the disgraced monks, some in remote valleys of the Caucasus, were subjected to particularly virulent persecution by the Soviet authorities and, by the beginning of the Second World War, had been virtually wiped out. For a detailed and impartial recent study by a bishop of the Orthodox Church see Episkop Ilarion (Alfeev), *Sviashchennaia taina tserkvi, Vvedenie v istoriiu i problematiku imiaslavskikh sporov*, Vols 1 and 2, Aleteia, Saint Petersburg, 2002.

61    P. A. Florenskii, letter of 29 December 1915 to Archbishop Antonii (Khrapovitskii), partially published in S III(1), p. 351 and, in the context of the ongoing relationship between the two prelates, in *Zhurnal Moskovskoi Patriarkhii*, 6–1988, pp. 76–78.

62    P. A. Florenskii, 'Okolo Khomiakova', S II, pp. 278–236. Published as a separate brochure in Sergiev Posad, 1916.

63    P. A. Florenskii, op. cit, p. 313.

64    Ibid., p. 314.

65    Ibid., p. 326.

66    Ibid., p. 336.

67    The 'Letter from the Caucasus' was in fact dated Sergiev Posad: 28 September 1913.

68    See V. V. Rozanov, 'Oboniatel'noe i osiazatel'noe otnoshenie k krovi u Evreev', *Sakharna, Sobranie sochinennii*, ed. A. N. Nikoliukin, Respublika, Moscow, 2001, pp. 311–317 and S II pp. 705–707 and notes p. 808.

69    'Blood – that is a very special sap'.

70    Z. N. Gippius, *Zhivye litsa*, p. 351.

71    Florenskii's authorship of these letters was established comparatively recently and elicited an impassioned attack by the greatest Western Florensky-specialist, Michael Hagemeister 'Wiederverzauberung der Welt: Pavel Florenskijs Neues Mittelalter' in *Pavel Florenkij – Tradition und Moderne*, pp. 212–42.

72    Letter of 26 November 1913, quoted in notes to V. V. Rozanov, *Sakharna*, p. 436.

73    Letter of P. A. Florenskii to V. V. Rozanov of 12 October 1913, quoted in *Sakharna*, p. 438.

74    Oral information from Dina Magomedova, who had the task of re-editing Simonovich-

Efimova's notes, partially published by her son, for an as yet unrealised Italian publication.

75    See letter of 29 July to 15/17 August 1918 to Sergei Bulgakov, *Perepiska s Bulgakovym*, pp. 130–132.

76    P. A. Florenskii, 1909 letter to V. V. Rozanov.

77    Cf. Sergei Chesnokov, 'Tema evreiskoi pis'mennosti v perepiske L. A. Tikhomirova i P. A. Florenskogo', Russkaia Liniia, Biblioteka periodicheskoi pechati, 21 March 2006, http// www.Hist.ra/st.php?idar=103273, p. 3.

78    P. A. Florenskii, 'Predislovie k sborniku "Izrail v proshlom, nastoiashchem i budushchem"', Moscow, 1915, *S* II, p. 707.

79    It was a major theme of his polemics with the Church that they could not be legally married because Rozanov could not obtain a divorce from his first wife Apollinaria Suslova, who had been Dostoevsky's mistress and the model for many of his tormenting, demonic women, whereas Rozanov and his Varvara Dmitrievna had a large family and lived as husband and wife.

80    V. V. Rozanov, *O sebe i o zhizni svoei*, Moscow, 1990, p. 189.

81    P. A. Florenskii, letter to M. V. Nesterov of 1 June 1922, quoted by P. V. Palievskii, 'Rozanov i Florenskii', *Pro et Contra*, pp. 488–489.

82    Now Pionerskaia ulitsa and still preserved as the family home of his descendants.

83    Now Ulitsa Burdenko 16/12, Apt. 51 and functioning as a museum to Florensky's memory.

84    See Petrovskii, 'Vospominaniia o Velimire Khlebnikove', *Lef*, 1923, No. 1, p. 146 and M. V. Iudina, *Stat'i. Vospominaniia. Materialy*, Moscow, 1975, p. 272.

85    Cf. P. A. Florenskii, letter to his daughter Ol'ga of 10/11 March 1936, *S* IV, pp. 406–407.

86    P. A. Florenskii, 'Tochka', in 'Symbolarium (Slovar' simvolov)', *S* II, 574–590.

87    See Igumen Andronik (Trubachev), *Teoditsia i antropoditsia v tvochestve sviashchennika Pavla Florenskogo*, Vodolei, Tomsk, 1998.

88    See Diakon S. Trubachev *Izbrannoe. Stat'i i issledovaniia*, 'Progress-Pleiada', Moscow, 2005, p. 303, citing P. A. Florenskii, 'Troitse-Sergieva Lavra i Rossiia', *S* II, p. 352 and 'Puti i sredotochiia (vmesto predisloviia). Iz neokonchennogo truda *U vodorazdelov mysly – Esteticheskie tsennosti v sisteme kul'tury. Sbornik nauchnykh statei*', Moscow, 1986. For Florenskii and music see Part 2, pp. 139–218 of *Pamiati Pavla Florenskogo. Fifosofiia. Muzyka*. Sbornik statei k 120-letiu so dnia rozhdeniia O. Pavla (1882–2002). Sankt-Peterburgskaia gosudurstvennaia Konservatoriia imeni N A Rimskogo-Korsakova. Tvorcheskii tsentr imeni Pavla Florenskogo, St Petersburg, 2002.

89    P. A. Florenskii, letter to mother of 28/29 July 1936, *S* IV, pp. 525–526.

## *Notes on Chapter 7: Catastrophe 1917–1926*

1    P. A. Florenskii, 'Predvaritel'nye plany i zametki k lektsiiam', 1921, *S* III(2), p. 367.

2    Revelation 15.1–3. These verses, at the suggestion of Florensky, were inscribed on the grave of his friend Vasilii Rozanov, author of *The Apocalypse of our Time*.

3    V. V. Rozanov, letter of 11 April to M. Spasovsky, quoted by Igumen Andronik,

'Moskovskii kruzhok. Publikatsii iz semeinogo arkhiva Florenskikh', *Literaturnyi Irktusk*, December 1988, p. 8, but cited here from Evg. Ivanova, 'V. V. Rozanov, Pis'ma 1917–1919 godov', note 4 to 'O poslednikh dniakh i konchine V. V. Rozanova', *Literateraturnaia ucheba*, Jan.–Feb. 1990, Book I, p. 75.

4     Florenskii uses the unattractive word *knout* as a figure for pain imposed by authority which has to be endured in silence as a form of asceticism, but which strengthens and hardens the inner man, making him more fit for service. It was a pain he suffered during his *mathesis* but Rozanov, whose genius flowered from one long whinge against the Church's hard line on marriage and divorce, was shocked when his friend used the image – not in judgement, but in a bracing call to put up with unavoidable suffering in silence.

5     P. A. Florenskii, letter to S. Bulgakov of 29 July (15/17 August) 1917, *Perepiska s Bulgakovym*, pp. 137–139.

6     P A Florenskii, 'Pamiati Vladimira Franzevicha Erna', *S* II, pp. 346–351.

7     *Ham* in Russian is a synonym for the unmannerly insubordination of the biblical prototype who 'uncovered his father's nakedness' and Florensky here coins a word, substituting 'hamo' for 'auto' (or possibly 'demo') in the relevant 'cracies'.

8     P. A. Florenskii, 'Puti sredotochiia (vmeste predisloviia)', *S* III(1), p. 39.

9     P. A. Florenskii, 'Dialektika', *S* III(1), p. 122.

10    P. A. Florenskii, 'Antinomiia iazyka', *S* III(1), p. 153.

11    P. A. Florenskii, 'Organoproektsiia', *S* III(2), p. 403.

12    P. A. Florenskii, 'Khoziaistvo', *S* III(2), p. 439.

13    Ibid., p. 441.

14    Ibid., p. 442.

15    P. A. Florenskii, letter to V. A. Vvedensky of 21 September 1929, *S* III(2), pp. 451–452.

16    P. A. Florenskii, 'Zolotoe secheniie', *S* III(2), p. 462.

17    Ibid.

18    P. A. Florenskii, notes for a new course of lectures to students of the Moscow Theological Academy in the Petrov Monastery, *S* III(2), p. 367.

19    P. A. Florenskii, ibid., *S* III(2), p. 380.

20    My free translation (A. P.). In Russian: O, veshchaia dusha moia, / O, serdtse polnoe trevogi, / O, kak ty b'eshsia na poroge / Kak by dvoinogo bytiia.

21    P. A. Florenskii, second lecture in the series on the cultural-historical place of the Christian world view, *S* III(2), p. 391. (The emphasis is mine, A. P.)

22    P. A. Florenskii, tenth lecture in the series on 'The place of Christianity in the modern world', *S* III(2), p. 434.

23    P. A. Florenskii, twelfth lecture, op. cit., *S* III(2), p. 443.

24    Ibid., p. 444.

25    Ibid., p. 448.

26    P. A. Florenskii, Appendix to thirteenth lecture in the series on 'The place of Christianity in the modern world', *S* III(2), p. 454.

27    Ibid., p. 455.

28    Cf. Ieromonakh Andronik (Trubachev), *Teoditseia i antropoditsia v tvorchestve sviash-chennika Pavla Florenskogo*, Arkhiv sviashchennika Florenskogo, Issue 3, Vodolei,

Tomsk, 1998, p. 58. The article from which the sentence he quotes is taken was published by Florensky in the journal *Vozrozhdenie*, Moscow, 1916, No. 6.

29    P. A. Florenskii, 'Otzyvy P. A. Florenskogo o rabotakh studentov', *Russkaia literatura*, No. 1, 1991, pp. 137–138.

30    In Russian, Vol'naia akademiia dukhovnoi kul'tury.

31    The Russian acronym was Vkhutemas.

32    P. A. Florenskii, *Mnimosti v geometrii*, Pomorie, Moscow, 1922. Republished with notes and commentary in German by Michael Hagemeister, in the series Specimina Philologicae Slavicae, Supplement 14, Verlag Otto Sagner, Munich, 1985.

33    P. A. Florenskii, 'Imiaslavie kak filosofskaia predposylka', *S* III(2), pp. 252–286.

34    See Florensky's letter to Patriarch Tikhon on the tasks of the Commission, *Zhurnal Moskovskoi Patriarkhii*, 10, 1990, p. 23 and T. V. Rozanova, 'Vospominaniia', *Voprosy literatury*, October 1990, pp. 212–215.

35    The 'second', but in actual fact 'first' edition of the report was published in an edition of 1,000 copies as *Troitse-Sergieva Lavra*, Indrik, Moscow, 2007.

36    For English renderings, see Donald Sheehan and Olga Andreev's translation of the 'Iconostasis', St Vladimir's Seminary Press, Crestwood, New York, 1996, and Wendy Salmand's renderings of a selection of articles on art, introduced and edited by Nicolletta Misler, in *Pavel Florensky, Beyond Vision: Essays on the Perception of Art*, Reaktion Books, London, 2002. Florenskii's articles on art compose the first and only volume of YMCA-Press's *Collected Works* (*Sobranie sochinenii*, I, YMCA-Press, Paris, 1985) and are concentrated in Volume II of the Moscow *Sochineniia*. 'The Trinity St Sergius Lavra and Russia' has also been translated by Robert Bird, Variable Press, New Haven, CT, 1995. Misler's commentary to the versions of Florenskii's articles in *Beyond Vision* are particularly useful for the correction of minor errors which inevitably arose from the extraordinary conditions under which Florenskii wrote – or, more often, dictated – his post-revolutionary works.

37    *Panaghia* – medallion of round, square or oval form depicting the Theotokos (or more rarely the Holy Trinity, the Crucifixion or the Ascension) worn by hierarchs of the Orthodox Church.

38    See Misler in *Pavel Florensky: Beyond Vision*, p. 199.

39    Cf. for instance, Michael Hagemeister, 'Wiederverzauberung der Welt; Pavel Florenkijs Neues Mittelalter' in *Pavel Florenskij, Tradition und Moderne*, pp. 27–28.

40    The text of 'Iconostasis' in *S* II, pp. 419–526 was carefully prepared from typescript and from the previous publication in book form by Iskusstvo, Moscow, 1994 with a commentary by A. G. Dunaev. The first, incomplete publication appeared in the theological journal *Bogoslovskie trudy*, Sbornik 17, Moscow, 1977 and, in a translation by the author of this book, as an appendix to John Stuart's *Ikons*, London, 1975. A full English translation by Donald Sheeham and Olga Andreev was published by St Vladimir's Seminary Press, Crestwood, New York, 1996 (see note 31).

41    For the lasting importance of *The Pillar and Ground of Truth* see the letter from N. N. Luzin, Florenskii's university friend, then an internationally respected doctor of mathematics at Moscow University, written 5 May 1919 to request a spare copy which he needs to have by him 'not just to read through but to read', 'The Correspondence of N. N. Luzin

and P. A. Florensky', published by S. S. Demidev, A. N. Porshina, S. M. Polovinkin and P. V. Florenskii in *Istoriko-Matematicheskie Issledovaniia*, No. XXXI, Nauka, Moscow, 1989, p. 188.

42  For Florenskii's remarkable strength and stamina see S. Bulgakov's obituary article: 'Sviashchennik o Pavel Florenskii', *Pro et Contra*, pp. 394–395.

43  *Gesamtkunstwerk* – a Wagnerian term for a synaesthetic work of (performance) art which would appeal to all the sense.

44  *Lampadki* – small oil-lamps hung before icons.

45  P. A. Florenskii, 'Khramovoe deistvo kak sintez iskusstv', *S* II, pp. 373–376. The article, read before the Commission in an attempt to define its aims on 27 October/9 November 1918, was published in *Makovets*, No. 1, 1922, pp. 28–32.

46  Cf., for instance, Florenskii's legally published *Opis' panagii Troitse-Sergievskoi Lavry XII–XIX VV*, Sergiev Posad, 1923.

47  From the diary entry on the Exhibition of Ancient Icons in the Historical Museum, Moscow, 1923, quoted by Sergei Trubachev in *Izbrannoe*, Progress-Pleiada, Moscow, 2003, p. 432.

48  Cf. *Muzeia*, 1988, No. 157, pp. 78–79, published by S. Trubachev, also in *Izbrannoe*, p. 460.

49  P. A. Florenskii, letter to A. S. Mamontova of 30 July 1917, *S* I, p. 247.


## Notes on Chapter 8: Diversification – Art, Music and Science 1919–1933

1  P. A. Florenskii, letter of 13 March 1936 to his daughter Ol'ga, *S* IV, p. 407. For Florensky's work in applied science see Igumen Andronrik (Trubachev), 'Nauchno-teknicheskhaia izobretatel'naia i obshchestvennaia deiatel'nost' P. A. Florenskogo v 1920–1933', a paper read on 27 April 1988 at the Round Table discussion of 'Florensky on science' at the Institute of the History of Natural History and Technical Studies of the Academy of Sciences, published in *Voprosy istorii estestvoznaniia i tekhniki*, pp. 211–227.

2  P. A. Florenskii, letter of 19–20 March 1921, Saturday to Sunday night at V. I. Lisen's to 'my dear children', sviashchennik Pavel Florenskii *Vse dumy – o vas. Pis'ma sem'e iz lagerei i tiurem 1933–1937*, ed. and compiled by P. V. Florenskii and N. A. Zhivolup, 'Satis' Derzhava, St Petersburg, 2004, p. 29.

3  See P. A. Florenskii, *Analiz prostranstva i vremeni v khudozhestvenno-izobrazitel'nykh proizvedeniiakh*, eds Pavel Florenskii, Maria Trubacheva and Oleg Gennisaretskii, Progress, Moscow, 1993 and extracts in the YMCA *Sobranie sochinennii*, T I, pp. 217–354 under the same title, from the journal *Dekorativnoe iskusstvo SSSR*, No. 1, 1982.

4  Florensky founded this particular part of his lectures for Vkhutemas on a passing reference to 'the Fathers of the Church' who taught that 'non-existence was absence of energy' and to a book by P. V. Preobrazhensky published by the Department of Physical Sciences of the Society of Amateurs of Natural Science, *Nekotorye zakony illiuzii*, T. VII, Issue 2, 1905. He also illustrated illusory effects with a series of geometrical diagrams, giving simple, visual conviction to complex theory.

5  For Favorsky's teaching in English, see *Vladimir Favorsky*, compiled and edited by Yuri Molok, intro. Mikhail Alpatov, tr. Avril Pyman, Progress Publishers, Moscow, 1967. For

an English rendering of Florensky's 'Explanation of the cover' see Kirill Sokolov and Avril Pyman, 'Father Pavel Florensky and Vladimir Favorsky: mutual insights into the perception of space', *Leonardo*, Vol. 22, No. 2, 1989, pp. 237–244.

6    See P. A. Florenskii, 'Privedenie chisel (K matematicheskomu obosnovaniiu chislovoi simvoliki)', *Bogoslovskii vestnik*, 1916, Vol. 2, No. 6, pp. 292–321 and 'Pifagorevye chisla', completed 28 October 1922 but first published in *Trudy po znakovym sistemam*, 5, Tartu, 1971, then in *S* II, pp. 632–648. A further two chapters in Florensky's archive remain to be published at this time, *S* II, p. 800.

7    Florenskii's article 'On realism' was written for *Makovets*, 3, 1923, which did not appear in print, but see note 8.

8    P. A. Florenskii, 'O realizme', *S* 2, p. 527. For more on Florensky's association with *Makovets* see O. N. Gennisaretskii, 'P. A. Florenskii vo Vkhutemase' in the catalogue to his sister Raisa's 1986 exhibition in Moscow and, in English, John Bowlt, 'Pavel Florensky and the *Makovets* group', *P. A. Florenskij* (Bergamo, 1995), pp. 131–148.

9    P. A. Florenskii, 'V dostokhval'nyi Makovets' (Pis'mo N. N. Baritinu, 28 March/16 April, 1925), *S* II, p. 628.

10   P. A. Florenskii, 'Predislovie k knige N Ia. Simonovich-Efimovoi', *Zapiski Petrushnika* (GIZ, Moscow, 1925), *S* II, p. 535. The Introduction, written in 1925, was in fact first published in Ivan Efimov's *Ob iskusstve i khudozhnikakh* (Moscow, 1972), pp. 170–172.

11   Father Fedor is, in my opinion, a far more likely candidate than Father Pavel for the authorship of the disputed article 'On Blok', which first appeared as by an unnamed but recently deceased 'Petrograd Priest' in Berdiaev's *Put'* (Paris, 1931) and, for the second time, printed from a different but almost identical typescript which had belatedly reached Paris via Harbin, under the name of P. A. Florenskii, in *Vestnik RSKhD* (Paris, 1974). The attribution, written in an unknown hand on this typescript, possibly derives from the fact that the article quotes Florensky at length and derives much from his ideas, but the judgemental approach and the lack of interest in what E. Etkind calls 'The material of verse', as well as the original attribution in *Put'* and the absence of work towards an article on Blok in Florensky's archive, put it among the most dubious of *dubia*. See, however, the ongoing discussion between E. V. Ivanova and V. A. Fateev on this subject in, respectively, 'Ob atributsii doklada o Bloke' in E. V. Ivanova, *Florenskii i simvolisty*, pp. 633–661 (which refers back to Ivanova's first article on the subject *Literaturnaia ucheba*, Book 6, November/December, 1990, pp. 106–114), Fateev's 'P. Florenskii ili F Andreev?', *Trudy gosudarstvennogo muzeia istorii Sankt-Peterburga*, Issue 4, St Petersburg, 1999, pp. 269–287 and Avril Pyman, 'Aleksandr Blok i o. Pavel Florenskii', *Shakhmatovskii vestnik*, Issue 9, Nauka, Moscow, 2008, pp. 152–165.

12   M. Iudina, 'Liudi bozhestvennoi liubvi', p. 156, quoted by Sergei Trubachev, *Izbrannoe*, p. 379.

13   Quoted by Sergei Trubachev, *Izbrannoe*, pp. 386–387.

14   Ibid., p. 389.

15   Both letters are quoted from the family archive by S. Trubachev in *Izbrannoe*, pp. 416, 417.

16   *Panikhida* – a service of intercession for the salvation of the departed often arranged by relatives and friends on anniversaries of birth or death.

17    Cf. P. V. Florenskii, 'Sviashchenstvo Pavla Florenskogo', *Vestnik RKhD*, No. 160, 1990, pp. 84–88.

18    For Florenskii's original article dated 4 June 1923 see 'Zapiska o khristianstve i kul'ture', *S* II, pp. 547–560 and notes pp. 788–794. The abbreviated English version came out in *Pilgrim*, July 1924, No. 4, pp. 53–57. For the very moderate and non-Slavophile 'Zapiska o pravoslavii' see *S* II, pp. 537–546 and notes p. 788. This was not published in English translation and Florensky does not appear to have been kept informed of the fate of his works.

19    See Florensky's strongly worded letter of March 1929 to Mark L'vovich Tsitron, refusing to undertake the editing of Rozanov's *Complete Works* (which he had begun under contract to Z. I. Grzhebin after the author's death and before that publisher removed to Berlin) for a Russian publication outside the Soviet Union. For the first time in full: P. V. Palievskii, 'Rozanov i Florenskii', *Pro et Contra*, pp. 479–481.

20    L. F. Zhegin, 'Vospominaniia o P. A. Florenskom', *Pro et Contra*, p. 103.

21    P. A. Florenskii, *Dialektriki i ikh tekhnicheskoe primeneniie*, Moscow, 1924.

22    Igumen Andronik quotes from Florensky's diary for 23 September (OS) 1921 a passage recounting his prayerful preparation for such lectures which he saw in parallel to his entering the Theological Academy as a representative of lay society wishing to be received by the Church, as a deliberate effort as representative of the Church to be acceptable to lay society. *Obo mne ne pechal'tes'*, pp. 74–75.

23    The section on Science was written between 25 November and 26 December 1923.

24    Recounted by Igumen Andronik, 'Nauchno-tekhnicheskaia izobretatel'naia deiatel'nost P A Florenskogo 1920–1933', *Obo mne ne pechal'tes'*, p. 214.

25    For a detailed and lively account of the affair, see D. Iu. Vasil'ev, *P A Florenskii. Arest i Gibel'*, Grado-ufimskaia Bogoroditskaia Tserkov', Ufa, 1997.

26    'Florenskii v Nizhnem', publication by V. P., P. V. and Iu. O. Florenskie, *Nizhegorodskii Kupets*, No. 1, Nizhnii Novgorod, 1999, pp. 62–80.

27    The word 'manure' (*navozom* in the instrumental case) is printed with two question marks. It may be a misreading for *nagruzkoi* (a burden) but possibly it has some private, half-jokey connotation. Olsuf'ev figures in reminiscences of the period as driving cartloads of manure for his 'collective farm', which fed his friends and on which Anna, in contrast to some of the more bookish priests, was extremely helpful, through the streets of Zagorsk. She may, in her great modesty, have told her husband that, unlike the talented and creative people by whom she was surrounded, her calling was merely to warm and fertilise like manure, not to play an active part. Though curious in context, the word has no abusive connotations.

28    Ibid., letter of 28 July/8 August 1928, p. 74.

29    Ibid., p. 76.

30    Ibid., pp. 75–76.

31    F. A. Florenskii, 'Raboty po grafiti vo VEI', *Gornyi zhurnal*, No. 10/11, 1930. For a full list of Florensky's publications on applied science see *Pavel Florenskii* in the series *Vozvrashchenie zabytykh imen*, *Nashe nasledie*, Moscow, 1989, published works, Nos 1–69, pp. 31–32.

32    From a letter to N. Ia. Simonovich-Efimova quoted by S. Trubachev, *Izbrannoe*, pp. 384–385.

33 P. A. Florenskii, 'Fizika na sluzhbe matematiki' and 'Sotsialisticheskaia rekonstruktsia i nauka', *Voprosy elektromaterialovedeniia v VEI*, 1932, Vols 4 and 8.

34 *Sharashka* – special prison for those capable of scientific work useful to the State. Prisoners' slang.

35 According to their friend, the artist Mikhail Vasilievich Nesterov, Anna Mikhailovna's whole soul was in her smile. 'Everything. The attitude to her children as well, of which I was a chance observer, confirmed that the whole of her was in her smile', quoted from notes made by a friend in 1912 by S. Trubachev, *Izbrannoe*, p. 356.

36 See P. Florenskii, *S* III(1), pp. 28–35, 504–507. Quoted by S. Trubachev, *Izbrannoe*, pp. 286–287.

## Notes on Chapter 9: Permafrost

1 P. A. Florenskii, 'Na Makovtse', *S* III(1), p. 33.

2 The conversation was recorded by Mariia Fedorovna Andreeva, one of Andreev's twin daughters, and published by Diakon Sergei Trubachev, Ol'ga Florenskaia's husband in 'Vospominaniia o Marii Veniaminovne Iudine', op. cit., pp. 649–670.

3 P. A. Florenskii, 'Zaveshchanie', in the book *Vse dumy o vas. Pis'ma sem'e iz lagerei i tiurem 1933–1937*, Satis' Derzhava, St Petersburg, 2004, pp. 27–28.

4 M. Am-lii, *Rabochaia Moskva*, 17 May 1928.

5 Ibid. These extracts are cited by Vitaly Shentalinsky in *The KGB's Literary Archive*, translated by John Crawford, The Harvill Press, London, 1995 and are quoted, as are all extracts from this book, in Crawford's translation, p. 103.

6 For details see the section 'Ot otzyvov k donosam', in *P. A. Florenskii – Pro et Contra*, RkhGI, St Petersburg, pp. 457–469 and the relevant notes.

7 Shentalinsky, op. cit., p. 110.

8 Shentalinsky, op. cit., pp. 111, 116.

9 Shentalinsky, op. cit., p. 112.

10 See, for example, Nadezhda Mandel'stam, *Vospominamiia*, Izdatel'stvo imeni Chekhova, New York, 1970, p. 105 and L. K. Chukovskaia, *Zapisi ob Anne Akhmatovoi. 1952–1962*, Vol. 2, Moscow, 1997, p. 422.

11 Shentalinsky, op. cit., p. 114.

12 Shentalinsky, p. 113.

13 Ibid.

14 See P. A. Florenskii, 'Predpologaemoe gosudarstvennoe ustroistvo v budushchem' *S* II, pp. 647–681 and notes pp. 803–865.

15 See, for instance, Igumen Andronik's note to the publication, *S* II, p. 804.

16 Shentalinsky, op. cit., p. 115.

17 P. A. Florenskii, letter 31 to Kirill of 24–25 November 1935, *S* IV, p. 340.

18 Pavel Florenskii, *Oro, liricheskaia poema, Solovki 1934–1937. Zabaikal'e 1934–*, Moscow, 1995. Introduction, pp. 31–35.

19 Florenskii was allowed to write to his wife and receive parcels in prison once the interrogations were concluded. A letter of 23 May asks for a sheet, a handkerchief, just one for

he had some with him and, if it was permitted, a few onions as the food in the Lubyanka was filling but short on vegetables. A later letter of 11 July assures her that he has all he needs and begs her to stop sending things.

20 Anna Mikhailovna's and Iulia's letters are quoted from pp. 726–727 of the notes to *S* IV.

21 P. A. Florenskii, letter of 12 November 1933 to Ol'ga Pavlovna, *S* IV, p. 39.

22 P. A. Florenskii, *S* IV, p. 176 autoquote in letter no. 93, 22 February 1937 to his family. Florenskii was a competent rather than a great poet and it was, to him, a matter of principle to hew precise, bracing form from the inchoate chaos of camp life: hence the four-footed, iambic metre and the masculine rhymes, which he found difficult to maintain but considered essential to lend 'Oro' that quality of wide-awake vigour (*bodrost'*), with which he aimed to imbue the poem, the poet and the reader.

23 P. A. Florenskii, letter of 28 November 1933, *S* IV, p. 47.

24 P. A. Florenskii, letter of 17 January 1934, *S* IV, p. 66.

25 *Dacha* – a small holiday house, hired for the season or constituting a second home.

26 P. A. Florenskii, letter of 18 February 1934, *S* IV, p. 80.

27 Cf. Shentalinsky, op. cit., p. 114. The raiding party took many things belonging to Vasilii and Kirill, right down to kitchenware, and forbade the janitor to show Anna Mikhailovna the list of confiscated books, which were, in fact, simply stolen.

28 P. A. Florenskii, letter of end February 1934, *S* IV, pp. 81–82.

29 P. A. Florenskii, letter from A. M. Florenskaia of 4 March 1934, *S* IV, notes p. 731.

30 P. A. Florenskii, letter to Vasilii of 8 April 1934, *S* IV, p. 109.

31 *Kisel'* – a Russian drink made of juice from fruit or berries, cooked with sugar and thickened with cornflower or potato starch.

32 P. A. Florenskii, letter of 23 July 1934 from Anna Mikhailovna to Ol'ga Pavlovna Florenskaia, quoted in notes, *S* IV, p. 736.

33 *S* IV, p. 737.

34 Quoted from a letter to B. I. Vernadsky of 2 December 1934, *S* IV, p. 738.

35 P. A. Florenskii, letter to Anne Mikhailovna of 13 October 1934, *S* IV, pp. 139–146.

36 P. A. Florenskii, letter 1 of 24 October 1934 to his family, *S* IV, p. 40–41.

37 A beautiful book in English on the natural and cultural history of the Solovetskie Islands is Roy R. Robson's *Solovki: The Story of Russia Told through its most Remarkable Islands*, Yale University Press, New Haven, 2006.

38 Cf. *S* IV, p. 143.

39 P. A. Florenskii, letter 2 of 5 November 1934 to Anna Mikhailovna, *S* IV, pp. 141–143.

40 P. A. Florenskii, letter of 7 October 1934 to Vasilii Pavlovich, *S* IV, p. 146.

41 *Urki* – prisoners' slang for hangers-on of the hard-core criminal fraternity.

42 P. A. Florenskii, letter of 3 December 1934 to Anna Mikhailovna, *S* IV, pp. 148–149.

43 P. A. Florenskii, letter 5 to Ol'ga of 16 December 1934, *S* IV, p. 158–160.

44 P. A. Florenskii, letter 8 of 8 February 1935 to his family, *S* IV, p. 177.

45 Ibid., p. 172.

46 P. A. Florenskii, letter 88 of 8 February 1935 to Anna Mikhailovna, *S* IV, p. 179.

47 P. A. Florenskii, letter 8B of 11 August 1935 to Ol'ga Pavlovna, *S* IV, p. 181. Cf. also letter 6 of 1 February 1935, pp. 163–166.

48 Cf. letter from R. I. Litvinov to his family of 23 March 1935, *S* IV, notes p. 742.

49   P. A. Florenskii, Letter 11 to Ol'ga Pavlovna, *S* IV, pp. 196–197.

50   See *S* IV, p. 742, notes. Florenskii had published an article on the possibilities of obtaining energy from wind and sun in the journal *Eletrifikatsiia*, No. 1, 1925, pp. 10–16.

51   P. A. Florenskii, letter 17 to Ol'ga Pavlovna of 26 April 1935, *S* IV, p. 220.

52   P. A. Florenskii, letter 24 of 12 July 1935 to his family, *S* IV, p. 260.

53   P. A. Florenskii, letter 59 of 27–28 April 1936 to his family, *S* IV, p. 445.

54   P. A. Florenskii, letter 29 of 5–6 September 1935 to his family, *S* IV, pp. 287–288.

55   P. A. Florenskii, letter 30 of 16 September 1935 to his family, *S* IV, pp. 290–300.

56   P. A. Florenskii, *S* IV, p. 296.

57   P. A. Florenskii, letter 30 of 10 September 1935 to Ol'ga Pavlovna, *S* IV, pp. 294–295.

58   P. A. Florenskii, letter 40 of 7 December 1935, *S* IV, p. 340.

59   P. A. Florenskii, letter 48 of 7 February 1936, *S* IV, p. 387.

60   P. A. Florenskii, letter 51 of 29 February – 1 March 1936 to Anna Mikhailovna, *S* IV, p. 398.

61   Letter 51 and notes, *S* IV, p. 751, for quotation from Ia. I. Chichikov's reminiscences of Solovki: *A bylo vse tak*, Moscow, 1991, p. 401.

62   Letter 52 of 10–11 March 1936, *S* IV, p. 404.

63   Ibid.

64   P. A. Florenskii, letter 52 of 10–11 March to Ol'ga Pavlovna, *S* IV, p. 406.

65   P. A. Florenskii, letter of 3 April to Vladimir Ivanovich Vernadskii.

66   See *S* IV, p. 436.

67   P. A. Florenskii, letter 57, enclosure for M. V. Yudina, 19–20 April 1936, *S* IV, p. 443.

68   P. A. Florenskii, letter 68 of 20–21 July 1936 to Anna Mikhailovna, *S* IV, p. 515.

69   P. A. Florenskii, letter 72 of 18–19 August 1936, *S* IV, p. 539.

70   P. A. Florenskii, letter 87 of 7 January 1937, *S* IV, p. 639.

71   P. A. Florenskii, letter 70 of 28–29 July 1936 to Ol'ga Pavlovna, *S* IV, pp. 525–526.

72   See *S* IV, notes p. 778. The memorist was R. V. Chirkov.

73   P. A. Florenskii, letter 82 of 23–27 November 1936, *S* IV, p. 610.

74   P. A. Florenskii, letter 83 of 10 December 1936, *S* IV, p. 611.

75   P. A. Florenskii, letter 97 of 4 April 1937, *S* IV, p. 690.

76   See *S* IV, p. 692.

77   P. A. Florenskii, letter 99 of 11 May 1937 to his family, *S* IV, p. 701.

78   Ibid., *S* IV, p. 702.

79   P. A. Florenskii, letter 101 of 4 June 1937 to his family, *S* IV, p. 706.

# Index